Motivational Styles
in Everyday Life

Motivational Styles in Everyday Life

A Guide to Reversal Theory

Michael J. Apter, Editor

American Psychological Association
Washington, DC

Published by
American Psychological Association
750 First Street, NE
Washington, DC 20002

Copies may be ordered from
APA Order Department
P.O. Box 92984
Washington, DC 20090-2984

In the U.K., Europe, Africa, and the
   Middle East, copies may be ordered from
American Psychological Association
3 Henrietta Street
Covent Garden, London
WC2E 8LU England

Typeset in Goudy by World Composition Services, Inc., Sterling, VA

Printer: United Book Press, Inc., Baltimore, MD
Cover Designer: NiDesign, Baltimore, MD
Technical/Production Editor: Emily I. Welsh

The opinions and statements published are the responsibility of the authors, and such opinions and statements do not necessarily represent the policies of the APA.

Library of Congress Cataloging-in-Publication Data

Motivational styles in everyday life: A guide to reversal theory / edited by Michael J. Apter.—1st ed.
   p. cm.
   Includes bibliographical references and indexes.
   ISBN 1-55798-739-4 (alk. paper)
   1. Reversal theory (Psychology)   I. Apter, Michael J.
BF503.M695 2001
153.8—dc21   00-067409

British Library Cataloguing-in-Publication Data
A CIP record is available from the British Library.

Printed in the United States of America
First Edition

To the memory of Dr. K. C. P. Smith, 1910–1999

CONTENTS

Contributors

Michael J. Apter, PhD, Georgetown University, Washington, DC, and Apter International, Uppingham, England

R. Iain F. Brown, MEd, University of Glasgow, Glasgow, Scotland

Stephen Carter, MsC, Apter International, Uppingham, England

Mary R. Cook, PhD, Midwest Research Institute, Kansas City, MO

Andrew S. Coulson, PhD, Imperial Cancer Research Fund, London

Mitzi Desselles, PhD, Apter International, Uppingham, England

David Fontana, MEd, PhD, Cardiff University, Cardiff, Wales, and John Moores University, Liverpool, England

Mary M. Gerkovich, PhD, Midwest Research Institute, Kansas City, MO

Ken Heskin, PhD, Swinburne Sarawak Institute of Technology, Kuching, Sarawak, Malaysia

John H. Kerr, PhD, University of Tsukuba, Tsukuba, Japan

Kathryn D. Lafreniere, PhD, University of Windsor, Windsor, Ontario, Canada

David M. Ledgerwood, MA, University of Windsor, Windsor, Ontario, Canada

Gareth Lewis, MsC, Nottingham, England

Rod A. Martin, PhD, University of Western Ontario, London, Ontario, Canada

Mark R. McDermott, PhD, University of East London, London

Stephen J. Murgatroyd, PhD, Chief Executive, Lifeskills International Ltd., Yorkshire, England

Kathleen A. O'Connell, PhD, RN, Teachers College, Columbia University, New York

Sven Svebak, PhD, Norwegian University of Science and Technology, Trondheim

PREFACE

The concept of motivational style is a new one in psychology, although the phenomenon to which it refers is evident in everyday life. By *motivational style* is meant a distinctive orientation to the world based on a fundamental psychological value—such as achievement, love, or freedom. Different styles are often described in everyday speech in such ways as "serious" or "affectionate" or "challenging" and are more like changing moods than fixed traits. The contention of the present book is that an understanding of such motivational styles, their relationship to each other, and the manner in which they are induced and expressed, are indispensable to a full account of human experience and behavior. Furthermore, these styles should be more than just taken into account—they should be given a central place in our attempt to make sense of the everyday world of human activity. This is because they are more than mere peripheral aspects of mental life but can be seen rather as pivotal organizing processes. This means, among other things, that their recognition provides opportunities for integrating different areas of psychology and different approaches and levels of analysis. Such at least is the premise, and perhaps the promise, of reversal theory.

Reversal theory has now been in existence for some 25 years, during which time—while receiving little attention from mainstream psychology—it has quietly and surely developed into a broad psychological theory with grounding in both empirical research and in clinical and other types of practice. Indeed, by present-day standards it can claim to be an unusually general and integrative theory. Many of those working within this conceptual framework, including myself, felt that the time had come to draw descriptions of these different lines of research and practice into a single volume and to provide in this way a systematic overall review of the theory and a perspective on its present status.

Reversal theory had its origins, in the early 1970s, in the child guidance clinics in the west of England directed by Dr. K. C. P. Smith. The key observation, which was the starting point for the development of the theory, was that the very same presenting problem could arise in opposite ways and could represent very different kinds of meaning for different children. For example, one child could be truant because he or she was afraid of school, whereas another child could be truant because he or she found school to be boring. One child could steal out of genuine distress, whereas another child could steal for the pure fun of it. It was clearly necessary to go beyond the overt problem behavior to an understanding of the subjective experience of the child, if one was, as a therapist, going to intervene in a way that would be productive. For instance, it would probably be unhelpful to try to persuade a child who was bored with school that there was nothing to fear in the classroom. In a range of cases such as these, Dr. Smith noted that the same behavioral problem could be associated either with the nervous, sensitive, shy child or with the child who was boisterous, difficult, and easily bored. In one case the child was troubled, in the other case troublesome. He coined the term *telic* for the first type of child and *paratelic* for the second.

I was fortunate to be able to work with Dr. Smith during this period, and a further basic observation emerged from this collaboration. This was that the same child could change from being telic to being paratelic under different circumstances. For example, a child who is afraid of school might enjoy the dangerous challenge of learning to swim, whereas a child who is bored with school might be frightened of dogs. In other words, it became apparent that telic and paratelic were more like changeable states or styles than like fixed traits. The same child could be nervous at some times and boisterously confident at others. It followed that it was necessary to understand which state was associated with the problem behavior of a child rather than assuming that the child was always in the same state.

Following a period of careful self-observation, we found that we could identify both of these states in ourselves and that therefore they were not confined to children or to the generation of disturbed behavior patterns. In talking to other adults, including the parents of the children who came to the clinic, as well as colleagues and friends, we found that they were also able to discern both of these states under different circumstances. Early on we could see that these states were not emotions as such but rather were styles characterized by vulnerability toward particular emotions such as anxiety or boredom and deriving in each case from a certain kind of posture toward the world.

From these simple beginnings, and helped by a background in cybernetics (Apter, 1966, 1971), I developed a dynamic system that was based on the concept of *reversal*—the switch between opposite states such as the telic and paratelic states. Because the concept of reversal played such a central part in the explanations of the system, it was soon decided to name it *reversal theory*. Over subsequent years, this theory was added to and elaborated until it became the full-scale system that is presented here. Among valued collaborators in this theoretical work have been Sven Svebak, Stephen J. Murgatroyd, Kathleen A. O'Connell, and Stephen Carter.

The theory was first made public (albeit in a rudimentary form) at a one-day conference devoted to it in Bristol, England, in 1975 (Smith & Apter, 1975). Following the conference a reversal theory study group was set up in the United Kingdom, and this group met regularly for nearly 10 years, being eventually superseded by the international Reversal Theory Society that was set up in 1983. In that year, the first international conference on reversal theory took place in Wales, and this has been followed by other biennial international conferences organized by the society in Canada, The Netherlands, the United States, Norway, Australia, and England. Papers from these conferences have been published in a number of volumes (Apter, Fontana, & Murgatroyd, 1985; Apter, Kerr, & Cowles, 1988; Kerr, Murgatroyd, & Apter, 1993). An international sport and reversal theory group has also been set up by John Kerr and has held conferences in Japan, Hong Kong, and Australia. This has become, under Dr. Kerr's guidance and inspiration, a strong network of researchers. Other more local conferences have been organized over the years, including the Ken Smith Memorial Conference, which took place in Bristol, England, in March 2000. In 1999, Stephen Carter, Marie Shelton, and I created Apter International to market reversal theory products and services, including profiling instruments, surveys, workbooks, workshops, and other consultancy services, to professionals.

On the publishing side, the first journal paper was a modest note that I wrote (Apter, 1976) on the experience of arousal, and the first book providing a complete and detailed account of the theory itself (as it stood at that time) was my (1982a) *The Experience of Motivation: The Theory of Psychological Reversals*. In 1989, *Reversal Theory: Motivation, Emotion, and Personality* (Apter, 1989b) was published. This work described the complete theory—now extended beyond what had been presented in the earlier book—and also reviewed the research and applications that had subsequently been generated by the theory. Other books have related the theory to different particular areas: Apter (1992) to excitement-seeking, Kerr (1994) to soccer hooliganism, Kerr (1997a, 1999, 2001) to sports, Kerr and Apter (1991) to adult play, and Svebak and Apter (1997) to stress and health.

A note about terminology would not be out of place here. Although the term *motivational style* has been used in the title of this book, this is a fairly recent addition to the vocabulary of reversal theory. In most of the book the term *metamotivational state* is used because this is the term that has actually been used in the literature under review to refer to the opposing orientations that have been identified and investigated in the theory.

ACKNOWLEDGMENTS

This preface gives me the opportunity to recognize again the importance of the work of Kenneth C. P. Smith. It is with deep appreciation that I dedicate this volume to him.

The preface also allows me recognize and thank some of those who, as primarily practitioners, teachers, or administrators rather than researchers, are represented by relatively few citations in the text but have contributed in many essential ways to the development and use of the theory and have been stalwarts in the "reversal theory community." These include Carolyn Apter-Rapport, Sarajane Aris, Marlene Atleo, Emma Bellew, Leslie Bradford, Kate Broom, Mary Ann Cejka, Mitzi Desselles, Michael Ford, Anita Jaffe-Dick, Andrew Kerry, Denny Mallows, John Mathews, Mieke Mitchell, Lynn Pedigo, Sylvia Rhys, Cyril Rushton, Juan Carlos Palavecino, Doug Sawyer, Marie Shelton, Paul Slattery, Albert Kai Toh, Ans ter Woerds, and Jean Walters.

My sincere thanks are due to the following people for their thorough and insightful advice concerning early drafts of chapters: Rick Ansoff, Mitzi Desselles, Lee Branum-Martin, Kate Broom, Mary M. Gerkovich, John H. Kerr, Jay Lee, Gareth Lewis, Alan Lipman, Eric Loonis, Richard Mallows, Kathleen A. O'Connell, and George Wilson. On matters to do with reversal theory terminology throughout the book, the advice of John H. Kerr has been invaluable.

I would also like to thank Henri Sztulman for his invitation to be a member of the Centre d'Etudes et de Recherches en Psychopathologie (CERPP) at the University of Toulouse Le Mirail for a period during the editing of this book.

It is my special pleasure to be able to record my sincere appreciation to Susan Reynolds, acquisitions editor at APA Books, for her support of this project and her always helpful and understanding advice; to Linda McCarter, development editor at APA Books, for bringing a keen eye and a firm guiding hand to the project; and to Chris Davis, supervisor, technical editing and design at APA Books, and Emily Welsh, technical/production editor at APA Books, for their painstaking editorial work.

Finally, I particularly thank my wife Mitzi Desselles for her wholehearted support during the writing and editing of this book and for her many kinds of invaluable help—technical, professional, practical, conceptual, and not least, emotional.

I

INTRODUCING THE
BASIC CONCEPTS

1

AN INTRODUCTION
TO REVERSAL THEORY

MICHAEL J. APTER

Why do we sometimes enjoy and sometimes detest the very same things, for example listening to loud music, eating fast food, being around babies, shopping for clothes, driving to work? Why do we spend so much time doing things that serve no obvious biological purpose such as swapping jokes, listening to our favorite music, watching a football game, visiting an art gallery? Why, in fact, do some of us voluntarily do things that appear to work against our biological needs by placing us in real danger such as bungee jumping, rock climbing, and white-water rafting? Why do most of us occasionally enjoy doing what we are not supposed to do—breaking the speed limit, telling secrets, starting arguments, sharing dirty jokes, drinking too much? Why do we sometimes avoid doing things that we know we need to do: filling out tax forms, answering the mail, taking the car for servicing? Why is it that sometimes we get more enjoyment from anticipating some activity than from actually doing it, and why is it that real joy often comes at unexpected moments and in unexpected ways? Why do we sometimes deliberately hurt the ones we love? Real life is rich in such paradoxes and puzzles, and the attempt to make sense of them lies at the heart of reversal theory.

More specifically, *reversal theory* is often defined as a structural–phenomenological theory of motivation, emotion, and personality. *Structural–phenomenological* (Apter, 1981c, 1982a) means that the theory is about the structure of conscious experience, and the definition also implies something of the integral role that motivation and emotion are seen to play in this structure.

Useful as it is, this definition does not bring out the full richness and generality of the theory. For one thing, reversal theory can and has been presented in a number of theoretical perspectives. In particular, it has been presented as an action theory (Apter, 1979), a form of systems theory or

3

control theory (Apter, 1981b; Hyland, Sherry, & Thacker, 1988; Lee & Branum-Martin, 1999), a phenomenological theory (Apter, 1981c, 1993), a humanistic theory (Murgatroyd & Apter, 1981b), a biological theory (Apter, 1982a, chap. 13; Apter & Svebak, 1992), an adjunct to learning theory (Anderson & Brown, 1987; Cowles & Davis, 1985), an evolutionary theory (Apter, 1992, chap. 12; Van der Molen, 1984, 1986a), and as a form of chaos theory (Murgatroyd, 1993b).

Additionally, the theory has also been presented in ways that focus on and make central different general content areas including motivation (Apter, 1982a), personality (Apter, 1984a), arousal (Apter, 1981d; Svebak & Stoyva, 1980), emotions (Apter, 1988b, 1991a), stress (Apter 1991c; Svebak & Apter, 1997), counseling (Murgatroyd, 1981b) and addiction (Brown, 1988; Loonis, 1999b; Miller, 1985).

Furthermore, even though the topics just listed are, in different ways, central to the theory, the theory has also been used to examine in a systematic way a wide variety of particular types of behavior and experience. Thus reversal theory has been applied to such diverse and varied phenomena as art therapy (Broom, 2000), religious states of mind (Apter, 1985), suggestibility and hypnosis (Apter, 1991d), family communication patterns (Apter & Smith, 1979a, Wilson & Wilson, 1996), military combat (Apter, 1992, chap. 11; Foster, 1993), crime and imprisonment (Apter & Smith, 1987), romantic problems (Lafreniere, 1997), myth and ritual (Apter, 1982a, chap. 12), educational philosophies (Apter, 1982d), antique collecting (Smith & Apter, 1977), blood donation (Apter & Spirn, 1997), rape (Apter, 1992, chap. 10), Zen Buddhism (Fontana, 1981b; Hyers, 1985), and national development (Moghaddam, Bianchi, Daniels, Apter, & Harré, 1999)— among many others, including those to be dealt with in later chapters.

In all these cases, the same basic structure and mechanisms can be discerned, and in this way reversal theory demonstrates certain powers of integration. It is also integrative in that it can be equally related to the social sciences in one direction (e.g., Foster, 1988) and the biological sciences in the other (e.g., Apter & Svebak, 1992). Furthermore, it deals with both normal and pathological phenomena, and it has both pure and applied aspects. Hetherington (1983) has also argued that in general it helps to integrate the study of human behavior with the study of human experience. In other words, in all these ways, apparently dissimilar phenomena and different areas of psychological discourse can be related through the conceptual structure provided by reversal theory.

It is, incidentally, notable that reversal theory has also had some influence outside the realm of professional researchers and practitioners. Sports writer David Foot has used the theory in his biographies of two great cricketers, Harold Gimblett (Foot, 1982) and Wally Hammond (Foot, 1996). Writer and sailor Derek Lundy (1998) has likewise used the theory in his book on the Vendée Globe around-the-world yacht race in 1996–1997. The British composer Sir Michael Tippett (1987) declared the influence of reversal theory in his oratorio *The Mask of Time*, which even has a section entitled "Reversal."

SOME GENERAL CHARACTERISTICS

It may be helpful at the outset to emphasize some general characteristics of the theory:

1. As already indicated, the theory is about the structure of experience (hence structural phenomenology). This does not mean that it is restricted to subjective phenomena but rather that it seeks to understand behavior in terms of phenomenal structures. In this respect the approach is an "inside-out" approach: whatever the topic, it starts from subjective meaning and works outward into behavior, physiology, performance, and relationships.
2. The theory emphasizes the way in which motivation is fundamental to and pervasive in experience. That is, motivation enters into and provides a continuing internal context for all of our perceptions, thoughts, and actions. It underlies the very structure of experience that is the focus of the theory, giving each kind of experience a distinctive meaning. And this meaning is therefore pre-linguistic in the sense that it is immediately intuited without the need for linguistic formulation.
3. Personality is seen by the theory as understandable in terms of *intra*-individual change rather than *inter*-individual differences. People are seen as being characterized as patterns over time (what we might call *self-patterns*) rather than as sets of fixed traits. At the heart of the theory therefore is a focus on *the individual over time*, the emphasis on the time dimension bringing out people's essential changeability. For this reason it has been called a "state theory of personality" (Fontana, 1983) and contrasted in this respect with more traditional trait theories.
4. The theory recognizes the necessary self-contradictions of human nature. People want different, even opposite, things at different times, even in the same situation at different times. This helps explain irrational behavior (O'Connell, 1991) and also *paradoxical behavior* (Apter, 1982a), defined as behavior that seems not to aid survival (e.g., aesthetic and religious

behavior) and that may even appear to militate against it (e.g., dangerous sports).

THE FOUR DOMAINS OF EXPERIENCE

There are many ways into the theory, as has been demonstrated by the various contrasting general introductory accounts that may be found in the literature (e.g. Apter, 1987, 1989a, 1997b; Apter & Fontana, 1985; Frey, 1997a; Kerr, 1987d; Khomyk, 1998; Lachenicht, 1985b, 1987, 1988; Lafreniere, 1993; Murgatroyd, 1985a; O'Connell, 1991, 1993b; Potocky & Murgatroyd, 1993; Scott, 1986).

A good starting point is this: If we examine subjective experience carefully, we find that, at a certain level of analysis, it has a number of characteristics that are universal and essential to the very nature of experience itself. These are an unavoidable part of everyone's subjective experience at all times. It is possible to identify four such domains (see Figure 1.1).

The first is the way that mental life is always structured in terms of *means-and-ends*. That is, one is always aware of a certain directionality, however minimal, and of the routes that are implied by this directionality. There is always, at some level of awareness, a sense of where one is going and what one is doing to get there—of purpose and of action.

The second is the way that experience is structured in terms of *rules* governing how one should behave. For the purposes of this discussion, the word *rules* means any kind of pressure experienced by the individual, includ-

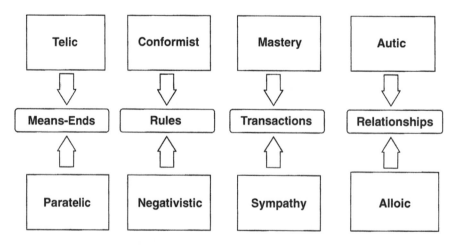

Figure 1.1. The motivational matrix that lies at the heart of reversal theory.
Note. From *Manual for the Apter Motivational Style Profile (AMSP)* (p. 6), by Apter International, 1999(e), Rutland, England: Author. Copyright 1999 by Apter International. Reprinted with permission.

ing explicit laws or orders, expressed expectations, customary ways of doing things, implicit conventions, habitual routines, and so on. Much of life is governed in ways of which we are not aware by the habits that correspond to such expectations and routines, but there is a sense in which we are always aware, however minimally, of their presence. When we stop at a traffic light, we are aware of the need to do so. Sometimes, of course, this awareness becomes focal—for example, if the light is changing. (Note that the sociological issue of what the rules "really" are in a situation is not relevant here; we are talking about the rules as they happen to be understood by a given person at a given time.)

The third domain is that of our experience of *transactions*. That is, we are always aware of interacting with something or another, be it a person, a machine, a situation, a part of our own body, or an image or idea, and we are aware of the transactions that may be involved in such interactions: the passing back and forth of words, money, attention, gestures, and so forth.

The fourth domain is that of our experience of *relationships*. Whenever we interact with something or someone (or some group or situation), we are aware not only of what passes between us, but also of a more direct relationship that may be open or closed, intimate or formal, and so on. Central here is whether or not we identify with the object of our attention or feel separate from it.

REVERSAL AND THE EIGHT STATES

Now we come to an extraordinary observation, and one that lies at the heart of reversal theory. This is that for each of these four domains of experience, there are two *opposite* ways of experiencing them. This means that domains cannot be experienced in both ways at the same time, although they may be experienced one way or the other at different times and must be experienced as one or the other at any given time. In short, the members of each pair are mutually exclusive and exhaustive, and switches can occur backward and forward between them. Let us look at each domain in turn.

Starting with means-and-ends, we can notice two alternatives. The first is that everything centers on the end or goal, and the means are simply chosen in the attempt to reach this goal, having little importance beyond that. We might be driving in order to get to work, studying calculus to pass an examination, or gardening to have a presentable garden that will not upset our neighbors. The whole psychology of motivation is based on the assumption that this is the only way of experiencing means and ends: the end comes first, and the means follow. The rat's activity in a maze is assumed to be about reaching the goal box, and if one route does not work, then another will be chosen. The human participant is presented with some task to perform in the laboratory, and it is assumed that his or her varied actions are directed specifically and constantly to this overriding end. Behaviors and actions are performed solely to reach goals.

However, if we inspect our own experience we find that this is not always the way in which we see things. Sometimes there is a sense in which the means come first, and the end follows. In other words, what we want to do is to enjoy the ongoing activity, whatever the outcome, and the end is simply there, but of no great importance. I may be driving at a particular time because I enjoy driving, and if I have a goal it is only because I cannot physically drive nowhere. I may be studying calculus because I enjoy it, and if it helps me to pass an examination, so much the better. I may be gardening because I enjoy the act of gardening in and of itself. This does not mean that the goal plays no part, but rather that it is there as an excuse, a *raison d'etre*, a way of organizing the activity, or a way of enhancing it. Having a destination and a deadline might make driving fast more interesting. Having a plan for the garden might make gardening more interesting. Yet in both of these examples, there is a paradoxical sense in which the ends are the means and the means are the ends. That is, the goal has the function of making the activity more fun—the goal serves the activity, rather than vice-versa.

This does not mean that at a given moment one cannot be aware of both the value of the goal and the value of the activity; but one of these will be in the foreground and the other in the background. One of them will be the primary reason for the activity and the other a bonus. In the course of the activity, one may switch from experiencing it in one way to experiencing it the other way, and perhaps back again. This is rather like the way in which a figure-ground reversal figure is perceived (like the drawing that can be seen either as a black vase on a white background or two white faces on a black background). While studying calculus for a test, one may at a certain point forget the test and enjoy what one is learning, only to switch back again later to being aware that the test is the important thing.

We have words in everyday language to describe these two states of mind or motivational styles: We call them *serious* and *playful*. However, in everyday language these words are sometimes used in a sense that goes against the phenomenological distinction that has been made here. For instance, we may say that we are doing something seriously when we mean "determined to succeed," even if we realize that it is trivial. On the other hand, a professional sportsman is said to play the game, even though success or failure may have the most significant consequences for him, his team, his family, and his career. For this reason, reversal theory introduces two technical terms. It calls the serious-minded state the *telic state* (from the Greek *telos* meaning a goal) and the playful state the *paratelic state* (adding the Greek *para* meaning alongside).

Now let us consider the second domain, that of rules in the widest sense. Again, we can discern two opposite ways of experiencing these, which we can think of as opposite motivational styles or states. First, rules are welcomed: They provide structure and meaning in a situation and help guide action. With rules, one knows what one is supposed to do, and by obeying them, one adapts, belongs, and fits in. By doing what seems to be the "right thing" one can feel good about oneself, and by knowing what the right thing is in the first place one can sometimes rejoice in a certain *savoir faire*. Although it is unfashionable to use these terms, in other societies and at other times people would be happy to characterize the desirable state here as *dutiful* and *virtuous*. Furthermore, behavior can be more efficient and effective when routines are followed that have established themselves over time. Again, in psychology the assumption seems to be that this is the only way of feeling about things. Much of social psychology, for example, is about conformity and obedience and the development of group norms.

On the other hand, it is also possible to switch out of this adapting, fitting-in state to experience rules in an opposite way. Now rules come to be felt as restrictions and confinements. One feels the need to break free, break out, or even break something. So, for example, one smokes behind the bicycle shed, walks on the grass, parks in the wrong place, wears inappropriate clothes, swears, is rude, or approaches a task in an unorthodox way. In all such ways, one feels a certain kind of personal freedom as a result. Anger is an emotional expression of this: When one is angry one wants to do what one should not do (e.g., hit somebody), and in fact momentary satisfaction can come from such action. Another expression of this is mischievousness or, in children, naughtiness. This desire for disruption and disobedience, this spirit of rebelliousness, may not be as frequent as the orthodox conforming state, but it is one that we will all recognize in our lives.

In reversal theory, the two states are called the *conformist state* and *negativistic state*. The term *negativism* is drawn from the clinical literature where it is used to apply to the extreme contrary behavior that can occur in catatonic schizophrenia and from the developmental literature where it refers to the childhood behavior of the "terrible twos."

The next domain of experience is that of *transactions*. Suppose that someone gives you something. There are two ways in which you could experience this. One way is that you were able to take it as a consequence of your personal power and control over the situation. The other way is that it was freely given you because you are amiable and attractive. Likewise, suppose that you give something to someone else. Again, you could experience this in the same two ways. On the one hand you could experience it in terms of power—in this case as a lack of power or control, a weakness that led you to give up something that you would rather have kept. On the other hand it could be experienced in terms of likability. In this case you would see yourself as willingly giving something to someone that you care about and were fond of. It can be seen from this that the very same transactions can be experienced in markedly different ways. These ways are opposite because in one case one is seeing the world as a form of contest and in the other as a form of cooperation. In one case, toughness and strength are "what it is all about," whereas in the other case what counts is sensitivity and tenderness. From one perspective what is seen as brutalism is seen from the other as hardiness. From one perspective what is seen as wimpiness is seen from the other as gentleness and graciousness. Having a disagreement with a loved one and then making up might involve switching from one view of the world to the other.

In reversal theory, the first perspective is called the *mastery state* (because the term *mastery* is general enough to be able to refer without awkwardness to mastery over people, situations, objects, machines, or tasks). The second perspective is called the *sympathy state*, for obvious reasons, although it should not be taken to imply that the person being interacted with is necessarily in need of comfort or help.

Finally, there are two opposite ways of experiencing one's relationship to another person, situation, group, or object. In the first, one feels oneself to be separate from the "other," and it is what happens to oneself that counts. One wants the other to give to, or yield to, oneself. One might want to feel superior and in control. In the second case, it is the other who takes precedence in one's feelings. Now one wants to give or yield to the other. Perhaps it is one's child, a colleague one is mentoring, a student one is coaching, or a team that one is part of. In these cases one may genuinely have greater concern, at the moment in question, for their welfare or success than for one's own.

In reversal theory, the self-oriented state is called the *autic state* (from the Greek *auto* meaning self), and the other-oriented state is called the *alloic state* (from the Greek *allos* or other). As with the other pairs of states, it is possible to switch between them, even in the course of the same activity. For example, one may reprimand a child and then identify with the child and feel something of the child's anguish. One may go out of one's way to please a friend and then suddenly find oneself feeling resentful that all the pleasing seems to go in one direction. One may be supporting a football team, but the team is playing so badly that at a certain point one finds oneself no longer caring but looking at one's watch and wondering whether one should head on home.

In fact, to add just a touch more complexity here, there are two versions of the autic and the alloic states (discussed more fully in Apter, 1988a). In the autic state, in which one is concerned primarily with oneself, the first version involves an interaction with some "other" in which case it is called the *autocentric* version. Thus, one might be negotiating with someone or

repairing a car. In the second version, the interaction is with oneself alon as in cutting one's toenails or looking in the mirror. This is called the *intro* *autic* version of the state. Turning to the alloic case, the first version, calle the *allocentric* version, involves interacting with another with whom on identifies, such as a child one is feeding. The second case involves identifyin with another that one is not in fact directly interacting with, e.g., a heroin on the movie screen. The latter is the *pro-autic* version of the alloic stat (which implies that the other "stands for" oneself, being a kind of "surrogat self"). In other words, within both the autic and the alloic states there ar (a) a version in which one experiences oneself to be interacting directl with the other (the autocentric and the allocentric cases) and (b) a versio in which one's phenomenological field is almost entirely taken up with single entity. In the latter version, the single identity is either onese (in the intra-autic case) or an identified-with surrogate self (in the pro autic case).

It will be realized that the autic and alloic states may each be associate with either the mastery or sympathy states. Thus, in the autic–master combination one will be concerned with personal power, whereas in th alloic–mastery combination one will be focused on vicarious power. In th autic–sympathy combination one will be concerned with being sympathize with, whereas in the alloic–sympathy combination one will be looking t sympathize with someone or something else.

So far the word *switching* has been used to denote the sudden jum from one perspective to the other, but the term used in reversal theory o course is that of *reversal*, which emphasizes the way in which the switch i not just a change but also a switch between opposites. Because this proces plays such a central part in the explanations that the theory provides, thi is reflected in the name of the theory itself. Reversal theory claims that unless this process is taken into account in psychological explanations, i will be impossible to get a full understanding of many mental and behaviora phenomena and that one's view of human psychology will be seriousl restricted as a result.

As we shall see in the next and later chapters, the theory goes beyond this basic structure in a number of ways and becomes necessarily more complex. But if this basic structure is grasped, then this will provide a framework for understanding the rest of the theory. The structure is shown in Figure 1.1 that represents each of the four domains and the opposite ways of experiencing within each domain. This figure may be usefully used as a reference throughout the book. We may think of this figure as representing a "motivational matrix" and this motivational matrix as being pivotal to the rest of the theory. The various characteristics of the four pairs of contrasting states or motivational styles, as they have been described here, are summa-rized in Exhibit 1.1.

Exhibit 1.1.
Characteristics of the Contrasting Metamotivational States (Styles)

Telic
Serious; goal oriented; future oriented; looking for progress and achievement; sensible and cautious; planning ahead and focused; anxiety-avoiding; valuing tranquillity and calmness

Paratelic
Playful; activity oriented; present oriented; looking for fun and immediate enjoyment; adventurous and thrill seeking; spontaneous and open; excitement seeking; valuing stimulation and intensity

Conformist
Conforming and conventional; compliant and accepting; looking for structure through rules, customs, and routines; trying to fit in; adaptable; valuing tradition; agreeable, dutiful and obedient

Negativistic
Challenging and unconventional; defiant and rejecting; looking to break free of rules and restrictions; mischievous; hostile; valuing freedom; critical, dissident, and rebellious

Mastery
Competitive; confrontational; concerned with power, strength, and control; valuing toughness, hardiness, and emotional control; seeing life as a contest and struggle; wanting admiration and status

Sympathy
Affectionate; friendly; concerned with intimacy, kindness, and care; valuing tenderness, sensitivity, and compassion; seeing life as harmonious and cooperative; wanting to be liked and loved

Autic
Concerned primarily with self; trying not to identify with others; taking personal responsibility; valuing individuality

Alloic
Concerned primarily with others; looking to identify with others; unselfish; valuing transcendence beyond oneself

MOTIVATIONAL STATES

Let us look a little more closely at these states. It will be realized that the term *state* is not being used here in the way in which it is sometimes used in psychology to depict a particular emotion or mood. Rather, the states that have been introduced here are of a higher order that represent a range of possible specific emotions, and a class of things, which come to the foreground of attention and can provide pleasure or pain.

At base, these states can each be seen as representing a fundamental psychological motive that has been assimilated into the whole structure of experience and that underlies a set of particular needs and goals. For example, the telic state underlies such specific needs in society as earning a living, advancing one's career, owning and improving one's house, having health insurance, and investing for retirement. Calling the fundamental motives *psychological* reminds us that we are dealing here with motives that are

primarily about one's own personality and feelings of selfhood and identity rather than about one's body. In other words, the motives are indeed psychological in this sense rather than biological. But biological motives become assimilated to these psychological motives. Thus, one can eat in a way in which one is aware of eating the right things for one's health (i.e., in the telic state) or to enjoy the taste (in the paratelic state), or because it is expected (conformist state) or because you want to break away from what is expected (negativistic state), or because someone has given it to you (autic–sympathy state), and so on.

Because these psychological motives come in opposites, they cannot all be satisfied at the same time. But they can all be satisfied over time, and in a sense this can be seen as the reason for the reversal process—that is, it is "nature's" way of ensuring, in the normal way of things, that the individual has the possibility of every type of psychological satisfaction. The downside of this is that when one does reach a state of satisfaction, it is not likely to last for long. Every satisfaction turns sooner or later, through reversal, into a kind of dissatisfaction. This is perhaps the source of that "Divine Discontent" which seems to be such a central characteristic of human nature.

Looking at the states more systematically, they may each be seen as being made up of four components: (a) a fundamental core motive or value, (b) a desired feeling, (c) a distinct way of experiencing, or style of interacting with, the world, and (d) (in combination with other states) a particular range of possible emotions. It is also possible to discern different phenomenological "frames" as being present or absent for the different states, but this will not be pursued further here—for more on this, see Apter, 1993, and also chapter 11. It will therefore be realized that these states are complex and multifaceted.

In Table 1.1 we see each state defined in all of these ways, except for the different ranges of emotion, which only emerge in relation to state combinations (this topic will be taken up below). In many ways, the key

Table 1.1.
Defining Characteristics of the Eight Metamotivational States (Styles)

States	Core Value	Desired Feeling	Way of Experiencing
Telic	Achievement	High significance	Serious
Paratelic	Fun	Low significance	Playful
Conformist	Fitting in	Low negativism	Conforming
Negativistic	Freedom	High negativism	Challenging
Mastery	Power	High toughness	Competitive
Sympathy	Love	Low toughness	Affectionate
Autic	Individuation	Low identification	Self-oriented
Alloic	Transcendence	High identification	Other-oriented

term is that of *core motivational value*. The other descriptors in the table are ways of formalizing this concept in relation to each state and putting it in more exact and testable forms.

Thus, the core motivational value of the telic state is that of achievement. In this case, satisfaction comes from achievement itself or the feeling of movement and progress toward achievement. The desired feeling is that of *high significance*. In this state one wants what one is doing to be important in ways that go well beyond the immediate action itself. The general style or orientation is a serious one: One eschews triviality and time wasting. In contrast, the core motivational value of the paratelic state is that of fun, of "enjoyment now." Satisfaction here comes from immediate gratification. The associated feeling that is desired is that of *low significance*. When one is looking to have fun one wants to be cut off from the important and serious things of life and just do things for their own sake.

In the conformist state, the core value is that of fitting in, or adaptation to the situation in which one finds oneself. The desired feeling here is that of *low felt negativism*, which means a self-perception that one is not violating or has not violated some rule or another (this descriptor could equally have been inverted and labeled high *felt conformity*). Thus, when meeting someone important one probably wants to "do the right thing." At work, one may want to fit into the routines and cause as little disruption to others as possible. In making a decision one may want to be reasonable and sensible. In contrast, in the negativistic state, the core value is that of freedom, and now felt negativism is valued highly: the best way of feeling free is to break free of rules because these are now experienced as restricting. The general orientation is what one might call a challenging one, where *challenging* is to be understood as a resistance to rules and ways of doing things rather than to competition with individuals (which is what the mastery state is often about). This is what children feel when they enjoy being "naughty" and mischievous and what adults feel when they are being difficult or provocative.

In the mastery state the fundamental value is that of power or control, the relevant desired feeling being that of *high toughness*: one wants to feel tough and hardy and resilient. We can call the general orientation here a *competitive* one. In the sympathy state, the key value is that of love (or, to put it more mildly, kindness or caring). Now the desired feeling is that of *low toughness*. In other words, sensitivity and tenderness are desired, and these are felt to be the opposite of toughness. This is how a parent often likes to feel with a child or a child with a pet (O'Connell, 1991; O'Connell & Apter, 1993). As with the other feeling dimensions discussed here, the dimension could be inverted and described as something like *felt tenderness*.

Finally, in the autic state individuation is the core value—that of being an individual. The feeling desired here is that of *low identification* (i.e., remaining separate and independent). The general style is a self-oriented one: It is what happens to oneself that matters most. In the alloic state, *transcendence* is the core value—that of going beyond oneself, of being assimilated by, and merging into something larger, greater, and all-encompassing. The desired feeling, which in an extreme form has been called the *oceanic state*, is that of *high identification*. The style in the alloic state is one that is other-oriented, and in this case it is what happens to the "other" that is, at that moment, experienced as the most important thing. In other words, this state represents a genuinely unselfish altruism, albeit one that derives from feeling part of, or identifying with, the other.

There are a number of things to note about this analysis:

1. None of these eight states is intrinsically good or bad. Each has its own possible satisfactions and dissatisfactions, its pleasures and displeasures, and its contributions or detriments to the lives of others (Apter International, 1999b; Wilson & Wilson, 1997). In this respect, it is healthy to be an "all-rounder," able to experience all the states with facility. Different states may, however, be more or less appropriate in different situations, because different situations may provide the possibility of satisfying one value to a greater extent than another. Thus, it is probably more appropriate to be at a party in the paratelic than the telic state but to be in a courtroom in the telic rather than the paratelic state. Likewise it is probably more appropriate to be in the mastery than the sympathy state while competing in a sport but to be in the sympathy rather than the mastery state when putting a child to bed. Many institutions and their associated architecture are set up with the intention of inducing one state rather than another. Thus, sports stadiums tend to induce the mastery state, theaters and cinemas the paratelic state, official buildings the telic state, and so on. Generally speaking, and other things being equal, it is probably most adaptive to be in the state that these environmental contexts imply, because they also usually provide ways of satisfying the particular states in question.

2. Because states are multifaceted, it is possible to have internal conflicts within a state. For example, the telic need for low arousal (see below) can conflict with the need for high significance—because the more significant an activity is experienced as being, the more likely it is to raise arousal levels. Thus, an executive might take on a project with the full realization that she is going to feel anxious because of the risk involved but is willing to tolerate the anxiety to achieve what she considers to be a significant purpose. A nurse, in the sympathy

state, may have to "be cruel to be kind" in giving an injection and be willing to tolerate the feelings of toughness that this evinces in her to feel that she is caring fully for the patient. This means that conflicts within states can arise as an intrinsic part of the nature of the states themselves. Conflict in this sense is built into the very structure of motivational experience.

3. At a given time, according to the general analysis that has been given here, and as represented in Figure 1.1, four motivational states will be active—one from each pair—making up an array of states. However, typically only one or two of these states will be at the foreground of attention. For example, in playing cards, the paratelic and mastery states may be at the focus of attention, in breast feeding a baby it might be the sympathy and alloic, in telling a risqué joke it might be the paratelic and negativistic. Table 1.2 provides some other examples of the states and focuses that might occur in some different everyday situations in the course of getting up and going to work.

4. We cannot necessarily tell from the outside—from a person's behavior or performance or interactions—which state some-

Table 1.2.
A Hypothetical Chronological Sequence of Arrays
of Metamotivational States

Situation	Array of States (Motivational Styles)	Emotions
1. Enjoying a hearty breakfast	*Paratelic,* conformist, sympathy, autic	Mild excitement
2. Washing up, so that spouse will not have to do it	*Paratelic,* conformist, sympathy, *alloic*	Mild boredom, strong virtue
3. Getting dressed: choosing the right clothes for a meeting	Telic, *conformist, mastery,* autic	Mild anxiety, mild pride
4. Organizing papers to take to work	*Telic,* conformist, *mastery,* autic	Mild anxiety, mild pride
5. Kissing spouse good-bye	Telic, conformist, *sympathy, autic*	Strong gratitude
6. Driving to work: listening to the radio	*Paratelic,* conformist, mastery, autic	Mild excitement
7. Driving to work: being cut off by another driver	*Telic, negativistic,* mastery, autic	Strong anger
8. Arrival at work	*Telic,* conformist, mastery, autic	No noticeable emotion

Note. Focal states are in italics.

16   *AN INTRODUCTION TO REVERSAL THEORY*

one is in. Just by observing someone from the outside working on a computer we cannot tell if that person is trying to enjoy himself or to achieve some important purpose. And we may easily be fooled. We may think that a young person is behaving in a negativistic way by wearing what for some people (perhaps the majority) would be outlandish dress or by adopting some offensive manner, but they may actually experience such actions at a particular time as conforming to a group of friends. We may think that someone is looking after someone else (alloic sympathy), but they might be cynically manipulating the situation to their own personal advantage (autic mastery). Thus, we cannot equate states with activities in any simple and unchanging way. Different people may experience the same activity in quite different ways. And, more to the point, the very same person may experience the same activity in different ways at different times, even during the course of the activity itself. This principle, which we may think of as the principle of behavioral indeterminacy, emphasizes again that the states are defined phenomenologically, not behaviorally.

5. Many complex social activities involve people being in different states, often at the same time, so that a whole kaleidoscope of changing combinations may occur. For example, Kerr (1994) in his book on soccer hooliganism showed how a number of the states enter into and contribute in their own ways to this social problem. In particular, he showed how the paratelic, negativistic, and mastery states all play an important part. Thus, descriptions by hooligans themselves (and the book is full of fascinating quotations from those involved) show that the activity is a form of game in its own rights and one that is frequently highly exciting. It also provides a way of breaking out of the normal constraints of society, and it provides the possibility for confrontation and control. Kerr showed how misunderstandings about what is happening, especially by the police and by other authorities that typically fail to discern the paratelic gamelike nature of the activity, can in itself lead to serious violence.

6. Developmentally, motivational states may derive from simpler *protofunctions* (Apter, 1999a). For example, the telic and paratelic states may derive from the protofunctions in the infant of anticipation and focus, respectively, the conformist and negativistic states from acquiescence and resistance (e.g., accepting and rejecting the nipple), the mastery and sympathy

states from manipulation and expression (e.g., reaching for something or crying for it), and the autic and alloic states from separation and attachment. This developmental aspect of the theory will need to be elaborated in future publications. One interesting possibility is that psychosis may arise from the incomplete development of one or more meta-motivational states from its underlying protofunction.

EMOTION AND AROUSAL

Reversal theory postulates two basic emotional variables, both of which are phenomenological. The first is that of *felt arousal*, by which is meant the degree of feeling of being worked up, emotionally involved, intense, and the like that the individual experiences. The second is *felt transactional outcome*, by which is meant the degree to which one experiences oneself to be gaining or losing in ongoing transactions (e.g., the degree to which one gains or loses such things as points in a game, money in a negotiation, or prestige in a conversation). Particular emotions arise from the conjunction of particular values of the relevant emotion variable (felt arousal or felt transactional outcome) with a particular combination of motivational states.

In these terms, a pattern can be discerned which involves the combination of (a) the telic–paratelic pair with the conformist–negativistic pair, both these pairs, in their various combinations of states, operating on felt arousal; and (b) the mastery–sympathy pair with the autic–alloic pair, both these pairs, in their different state combinations, operating on felt transactional outcome. When we look at the particular combinations within each of these two sets, together with different values of the two emotion variables, a set of 16 basic emotions emerges.

Let us enter into this area by examining arousal. Now the standard theory in this area for nearly half a century has been optimal arousal theory as developed originally by Donald Hebb (1955), the Canadian neurologist. Hebb noticed, in his studies of people during sensory deprivation, that low sensation and resulting low arousal could have an adverse effect. This meant that what we might term *minimal arousal theory* (a kind of commonsense theory that is consistent with the drive reduction idea in learning theory) would not work, because it implies that low arousal would be pleasant. In minimal arousal theory, the supposition is that the lower the arousal the better, high arousal being felt as anxiety and low arousal as relaxation. Hebb suggested that an inverted U-curve should be substituted, in which the best arousal level is moderate, high hedonic tone giving way to lower hedonic tone as arousal levels moved either higher or lower than this optimum level. (He also saw this level as optimal for performance as well as hedonic tone.)

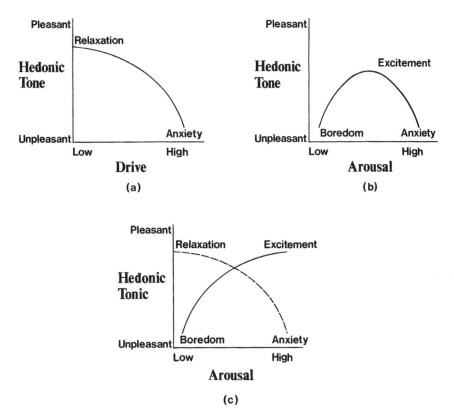

Figure 1.2. Hypothetical graphs representing the theories of relationship between basic motivational variables and hedonic tone.
Note. (a) Drive reduction and similar theories; (b) optimal arousal theory; (c) reversal theory.
From *Reversal Theory: Motivation, Emotion and Personality* (p. 181), by M. J. Apter, 1989, London: Routledge. Copyright 1996 by M. J. Apter. Reprinted with permission of the author.

Minimal arousal theory and optimal arousal theory are shown at (a) and (b) in Figure 1.2.

This was a definite improvement, because it allowed boredom (unpleasant low arousal) to enter the picture and explained why sometimes people do things to raise their levels of arousal (such as play sport or watch thriller films) as well as to lower their arousal. It can also be seen that this is an essentially homeostatic theory (using the term *homeostasis* in its widest possible systems-theory sense to imply a system that is constructed such that, when disturbed, it tends to return, like a heating system with a thermostat, to a single preferred level of some variable).

However, it does not take much reflection to realize that optimal arousal theory also will not work, and given this, the amazing thing is that it has survived for as long as it has. Let us briefly list some of the problems:

1. High and low arousal are not necessarily unpleasant, as must be the case in terms of the inverted U-curve. Indeed, high and low arousal can be particularly pleasant, and we have words to describe the emotions that we feel in such cases: *excitement* and *relaxation*. One only has to think of the intensely pleasant arousal of sexual excitement (not to mention of seeing the soccer team one supports scoring a goal, a gunfight in a thriller movie, or the fascination of a revolutionary new idea or technique) to realize that something important is going on in the upper right quadrant of the graph—something that is entirely missed in the optimal arousal model (Apter, 1979; Svebak & Stoyva, 1980). Likewise, it is possible for the relief and relaxation after some job has been accomplished to be sensuously pleasurable in its own way—something can happen in the upper left quadrant, too, and this also has been missed by Hebb and those who have followed him and who see these two upper quadrants of the graph as being essentially empty.

2. Hebb realized that relaxation and excitement must be fitted into his scheme somewhere, and so he suggested that excitement might go to the upper side of the optimal point of the curve (as shown in Figure 1.2[b]) and relaxation to the symmetrically opposite lower side of the optimal point. But this is problematic, both because it necessitates that the arousal levels are very similar for these two contrasting emotions and also because it means that there cannot be mild boredom or mild anxiety. There cannot be mild boredom or mild anxiety because mild boredom would necessarily become relaxation as arousal increased from low to moderate, and mild anxiety would necessarily become excitement as arousal decreased to moderate levels from high.

3. As arousal increases and decreases the same emotions will necessarily always be felt in the same sequence. In other words, as arousal goes up and down, we would have to feel the emotions in the order boredom–relaxation–excitement–anxiety–excitement–relaxation–boredom. This might occur once in a while but seems unlikely as a general rule. (For example, do you feel excitement on the way to, and coming away from, a medical examination? Do you feel excitement before and after the peak moment of arousal while listening to a Beethoven symphony, but anxiety at the peak itself?)

All these problems are overcome at one stroke if we substitute for a single curve the two curves shown at (c) in Figure 1.2. This is the reversal theory solution, the two curves (sometimes described in reversal theory, for obvious reasons, as the butterfly curves) representing the telic and paratelic states, respectively (or rather arousal-seeking and arousal-avoidance, which are associated with these two states). This substitution of an X for the inverted U overcomes all the problems listed and would appear to be the most parsimonious way of doing so:

1. We can now get into the top left and right quadrants of the arousal–hedonic tone space and account for very high arousal, which is very pleasant, and very low arousal, which is very pleasant, as well as the very unpleasant versions of these two arousal levels already accounted for in optimal arousal theory. This means that excitement can now be as intense as anxiety and relaxation as low in intensity as boredom.

2. We can now have strong and mild forms of all four emotions: relaxation, boredom, excitement, and anxiety. That is, each of these emotions is mild at moderate levels of felt arousal and becomes increasingly strong as felt arousal moves away from the level of moderate arousal toward high arousal in the case of anxiety and excitement and low arousal in the case of boredom or relaxation. It should be noted that, in the case of boredom and relaxation, the strength of the emotion is inversely related to intensity in the sense of felt arousal: There is no contradiction in having a strong emotion related to low arousal.

3. Given that we can jump from a point on one curve to the point immediately above or below it (this is a reversal), as well as moving continuously in either direction along the curves themselves, it is possible to experience any of these four emotions in any chronological sequence. Thus, one might, for example, in sequence, (a) start in a state of boredom, (b) find something stimulating to do and become excited, (c) then realize that there is danger in what one has done and reverse to anxiety, (d) overcome the danger and become relaxed, and (e) reverse into a state of boredom. It will be appreciated that the changes listed here as (b) and (d) involve continuous change up or down one of the curves in Figure 1.2(c), while the changes listed as (c) and (e) involve discontinuous switches from one curve to the other. The more extreme that felt arousal is, the more dramatic the effects of a reversal; reversals that occur in roughly the middle of the felt arousal dimension, however, may be hardly noticeable.

4. It will be appreciated that, if the curves meet in the way shown in the figure at (c), then moderate arousal can still be

moderately pleasing, so that this useful aspect of the optimal arousal model is retained.

Further advantages of this two-curve model also accrue. In particular, it becomes possible to begin to understand some of the discontinuities of the experience of arousal and some of the paradoxical and pathological behaviors associated with this. For instance, we can now see that people engage in risky sports and are willing to experience anxiety because each time they overcome a danger they reverse into the paratelic state and enjoy the arousal that has been caused by the danger. That is, they experience what had been anxiety before the reversal as excitement afterward. In this way a bungee jumper turns "bad arousal" instantaneously into "good arousal," and the greater the anxiety before the reversal, the greater the excitement immediately afterward (Apter, 1992). As Svebak puts it in the title of one of his papers (Svebak 1991a): "One state's agony, the other's delight."

Of course it is possible for things to work the other way around and for excitement to become anxiety. While experiencing sexual excitement, for instance, something may be experienced that is taken to be threatening (for example, reminding the person of an earlier episode of impotence), causing a reversal into the telic state and subsequent anxiety and dysfunction. Note here that it is not that the feeling of anxiety has inhibited the sexual excitement—the way that matters are typically put in the literature of sexual therapy. It is that the anxiety *is* the sexual excitement experienced in the "wrong" state. Among other things, this means that, paradoxically, the stronger the sexual excitement before the reversal, the greater the anxiety afterward. The implication for treatment here, as in so many types of anxiety disorder, is not that the arousal should be reduced on such occasions of dysfunction (through drugs, relaxation training, desensitization, etc.). Rather it is that the way the arousal is experienced should be changed, so that a paratelic-to-telic reversal can be resisted or the paratelic state quickly reinstated after such a reversal.

At first sight it might seem that the claim that high arousal is always pleasant in the paratelic state flies in the face of common sense. After all, this would mean that all strong emotions would have to be pleasant, including bad emotions like horror, anger, and grief. In fact, however, a moment's self-reflection shows that far from being a weakness of the theory, this is one of its strengths. After all, we do enjoy all these emotions provided that we experience them in a playful context (i.e., a context that is removed from "real" life). So when we go to the theater we can enjoy a tragedy, when we go to the movies we can enjoy a horror film, and when we read a thriller book we can enjoy the anxiety, and the greater the tragedy, horror, or anxiety the better. Enjoying such "bad" emotions is an everyday part of most people's lives, and something not convincingly explained in other theories of emotion. In order to distinguish between the serious unpleasant forms of such emotions and the disengaged enjoyable paratelic forms, reversal theory uses the terms *parapathic emotions* to refer to the latter and puts the particular parapathic emotion in quotation marks: "horror," "disgust," and so forth. (The term *parapathic* comes from the ancient Greek *para* meaning alongside and *pathos* meaning emotion.) Incidentally, one is tempted to speculate that if there are indeed *defense* mechanisms, as Freud suggested, which allow us to repress unpleasant emotions, perhaps there are also what one might term *offense* mechanisms that are used by the paratelic state to facilitate ideas that will stimulate emotions, including parapathic emotions (Apter, 1982a).

It is also possible, in these terms, to begin to see why we love to expose ourselves to what in the telic state we perceive as incongruities, dissonances, ambiguities, stupidities, and illogicalities. In the telic state, these are an annoyance that offends our rationality and that may even make us anxious if they obstruct our serious purposes. But in the paratelic state, the arousal that they produce can be so enjoyable that we seek out and construct them, especially in a form identified in reversal theory as *cognitive synergies* (the term *synergy* coming from the ancient Greek *ergos* meaning work and *syn* meaning together). These involve an identity that can be two mutually exclusive things at the same time and thus escape from the laws of logic. We can in fact see these as underlying such playful cognitive processes as make-believe, pretense, metaphor, humor, and art. Thus, in looking at a painting we know that it is a two-dimensional painted canvas hanging on the wall, but we also see it is, say, a three-dimensional landscape. When we enjoy slapstick we see people as both people and objects. This is a complex topic that is pursued further later in the book (see chapter 12).

It is possible that, if the felt arousal dimension were to be extended to even higher and lower arousal, the two curves depicted in Figure 1.2(c) would reach a peak and then descend again toward the unpleasant arousal range. In other words, it is possible that one could reach a point that is too low to be pleasurable, even in the telic state. This might correspond to what one would want to call *apathy*, and it is also possible that one might reach a point that is too high to be pleasurable in the paratelic state. This would perhaps correspond to *mania*. In this case we would have two inverted U-curves instead of the single inverted U-curve of optimal arousal theory. This point will be taken up again in chapter 14 in connection with the topic of depression.

EMOTIONS: SOMATIC AND TRANSACTIONAL

So far we have been dealing with a basic set of emotions: anxiety, relaxation, excitement, and boredom. But clearly a comprehensive theory needs to include other important emotions in this structure. Where, for example, does anger come from—an emotion that is entirely omitted from the optimal arousal model? The reversal theory explanation is that this is an emotion that arises when the negativistic state is active, and when this is the case anxiety is converted to anger. In this respect, we must assume that the set of emotions that we have previously discussed are essentially conformist emotions (in which conformity is a kind of default state), and when there is a reversal to the negativistic state then, although the basic arousal–hedonic structure remains the same, the actual emotions will be different. If anger is the unpleasant negativistic form of anxiety, then something like mischievousness will be the pleasant negativistic form of excitement. We might then see relaxation being converted to placidity (which is pleasantly tranquil while hinting at the possibility of aggression) and boredom to sullenness (an unpleasant but low arousal, brooding form of the negativistic state). This is all represented in Figure 2.2, which is in the next chapter.

The telic–paratelic and the conformist–negativistic states therefore, in different combinations and in conjunction with different levels of arousal, generate eight possible basic emotions. All these emotions relate to felt arousal, and thus we can refer to them as the set of *somatic emotions*, and we can refer to the two pairs of states as the *somatic states*. Many emotions, however, involve interactions between self and other, and these arise out of different combinations of the other two pairs of states, the mastery–sympathy and the autic–alloic pair (Apter & Smith, 1985). We can think of these, by contrast, as *transactional emotions*, and they derive not from felt arousal but from felt transactional outcome, which means the degree to which one feels that one is gaining or losing from some interaction. In this case we can refer to the two pairs of states as the *transactional states*. The pattern of butterfly curves remains the same, and we finish up with a complementary set of eight emotions, but these emotions are now derived from felt transactional outcome rather than arousal.

Because both arousal and felt transactional outcome are always part of experience, then we will always feel, to some degree or another, a somatic emotion *and* a transactional emotion, for example, pride and excitement, resentment and anger, virtue and anxiety. Remember, though, that if either felt arousal or felt transactional outcome is experienced at, or toward, the midpoint, then little or no emotion will be felt at all on the dimension concerned.

The transactional emotions and their relationships are shown in the butterfly curves of Figure 2.2 in the next chapter. These curves are hypothetical, as are those for the somatic emotions shown in the same figure, and the particular shapes may vary in different people and at different times, while following the same general crossover pattern (Apter, 1982a, chap. 10; Thomas-Peter, 1996).

In the mastery state, gaining will be felt as either pride or shame (depending on whether the autic or alloic state is concurrently active). That is, one perceives oneself to be pleased, even triumphant, at winning or gaining. But when one is putting the other person first, one will feel ashamed at having taken something away from the other. Also in the mastery state, losing is felt as either humiliation or modesty (again depending on which state, autic or alloic, is co-active). So being controlled and dominated is unpleasant if one is thinking of oneself, but if one is thinking of the other first, one can be pleased at having let that person gain. In the sympathy state, gaining will be experienced as either gratitude (autic) or guilt (alloic). That is, if you are thinking of yourself first it is nice to be given, whereas if you are thinking of the other person first the same thing can feel uncomfortable, especially if what you gain is substantial. Losing in the sympathy state will be experienced as resentment (autic) or virtue (alloic). Thus, if you are not given what you expected, and you are thinking of yourself, this is unpleasant, whereas not gaining from or even giving to the other can be pleasant if one is putting the other first. In all of these cases, reversal can occur so that what was previously pleasant can instantaneously become unpleasant and vice versa. You can feel grateful that someone has just bought you lunch but then can suddenly feel guilty about it (autic to alloic reversal in combination with the sympathy state). You can be pleased with yourself and proud for showing off successfully in a conversation and then realize that you have humiliated the other person and feel ashamed (autic to alloic reversal in combination with the mastery state).

In total, then, there are 16 basic emotions, half of them pleasant and half of them unpleasant. These form what one might think of as the deep structure of emotional experience.

A final point to note in relation to this analysis is that each of the emotion terms that have been used here really represents a set of related emotions. Thus, excitement represents also such terms as thrill, ecstasy, euphoria, and the like; anger represents irritation, annoyance, fury, and so forth. These different terms for emotions highlight differences in strength, temporal components, and other aspects of the affect concerned. But the basic deep structure as described here remains the same.

METAMOTIVATION, MOTIVATIONAL STYLE, AND MULTISTABILITY

It is possible to think of the different states as "*motivational* states." However, it would be more precise to refer to them as *metamotivational* states, and this is the way that they have usually been referred to in the theory. This is because these states are *about* motivation; they are different ways of interpreting aspects of experience that are to do with motivation. In other words, they are about different ways of experiencing arousal, toughness, significance, and so forth. If the latter may be seen as motivational, then these interpretations are at the higher metamotivational level. So a basic thesis of reversal theory is that, although motivational variables involve continuous dimensions (e.g., low to high arousal), interpretations at the metamotivational level come in pairs of opposites and therefore involve discontinuity.

While on terminology, it should be noted that these states are also sometimes referred to in the reversal theory literature as metamotivational *modes*. This term has the advantage of implying that they are dynamic and active and that each may encompass a range of possible forms (whereas the term *state*, in contrast, has static, passive, and limiting overtones). A further term that is being used increasingly, and which is used in the title of this book, is motivational *style* (e.g., Apter International, 1999a; Apter, Mallows, & Williams, 1998). The term "style" also implies a certain dynamic aspect together with the idea that the very same style can confront and handle a range of different possibilities. These states, modes, or styles have also been referred to as *selves* or *subselves* (e.g., Wilson & Wilson, 1996). Whatever term is used, it should be realized that these pairs are like pairs of computer programs that can operate in alternative ways on the same data sets.

It will be realized from all this that, unlike other theories of motivation, reversal theory understands the necessity of referring to two levels of analysis: the motivational and the metamotivational. Change can occur at either level, but the upper, metamotivational level involves transitions that are abrupt and discontinuous (constituting reversals). In this respect psychological life is seen as displaying regular transformations and human nature as essentially changeable, inconsistent, and even self-contradictory over time. Nor is this bad, because it allows people to pursue all of the different satisfactions that are available to human experience by spreading them out temporally in the course of daily life (Lachenicht, 1988). In this way the individual can achieve a kind of "psychodiversity" which, like "biodiversity" (which suggested the term "psychodiversity") is a healthy way to exist. In this respect, the healthy person is necessarily unstable rather than stable.

Putting this in another way, human motivation from the reversal theory perspective is not homeostatic. All other major theories of motivation in psychology imply that there is some single preferred level of some stipulated motivational variable—low drive, zero tension, moderate arousal, and so forth. Reversal theory argues that for the important motivational variables, there is in each case two preferred levels, so that the system as a whole displays *bistability* rather than *homeostasis* (Apter, 1981b). When we add different bistable states to each other, we finish up with a form of *multistable* system. For those not clear on these concepts, some examples might help.

A thermostatically controlled room has already been given to illustrate homeostasis. A further example of a homeostatic system would be a car on cruise control, since it has a single preferred state in terms of the variable of speed. An example of a bistable system would be a sport in which the teams change around at half time so that the direction of play for each team is inverted: For a given team the preferred state changes from one end of the field to the other. Another example would be a light switch, because these switches are built in such a way that if they are pushed they either switch over completely to the opposite position, or if the push is not sufficient, fall back to the original position. An example of a multistable system would be a row of light switches.

A multistable system of the kind postulated in reversal theory generates sequences of state combinations over time, and together with the different emotions, feelings, and behaviors that arise as the person interacts with his or her environment, great complexity can emerge. It is this kind of complexity that we all experience in the course of our everyday lives. It has been illustrated in reversal theory terms by means of some brief narratives or metamotivational diaries that have documented such moment-to-moment change (e.g., Murgatroyd, 1985a; Potocky & Murgatroyd, 1993). Particularly helpful in their micro-level detail are the narrative accounts of Frey (1999) and Males (1999). A hypothetical example of what a sequence of metamotivational states might look like is shown in Table 1.2. It is to be understood that different people may experience the different kinds of conventional activity depicted in this table in association with different metamotivational states than those shown here and might experience different levels of and types of emotions. The table is merely illustrative of the idea that state combinations change fairly frequently during the course of everyday life activities.

CAUSES OF REVERSAL

What brings about a reversal? Reversal theory suggests that the reversal process itself is involuntary and is provoked (or inhibited) by three categories of interacting factors. When the strength of the factors for change, taken together, is strong enough to override the factors working against change, then a reversal will occur.

The largest and most diverse factor is that of environmental situations or events. For example, a threatening event (or, more precisely, an event that is experienced by the individual as threatening) will induce the telic state, an unfair event the negativistic state, an overwhelming event the alloic state, and so on. The resulting reversals are called *contingent reversals* in the theory. They involve not only events but also settings. For example, a church is likely to induce or maintain the conformist state, a football stadium the paratelic state, and a police station the telic state. Cultural rituals can also induce different states (Foster, 1993). For example, Christmas tends to induce the paratelic and sympathy states. It is also possible for individuals themselves to induce or maintain different states in each other through appropriate gestures, posture, and emotional expression. A smile, for example, may tend to induce the sympathy state and a frown the telic state.

The second factor is that of frustration, a complicated phenomenon that can have many different effects. But if the individual is frustrated in attaining the satisfaction that is sought in the ongoing state (e.g., achievement, significance, or low arousal in the telic state), then this will eventually, other things being equal, induce the opposite state in which one fantasizes achievement, makes jokes about one's situation, or looks for distractions. If a person does not get the feeling of control (mastery state) that he or she wants in trying to use a computer, at a certain point he or she will reverse to the sympathy state, wanting reassurance and emotional support and commiseration. If a group that one is identifying with (alloic state) rejects the person, then he or she is likely to stop identifying with the group (autic state). Frustration obviously takes a while to take effect, otherwise we would never pursue goals in the face of obstacles for very long without changing our goals.

The third cause of reversal is what one might call *satiation*, the idea that some force for reversal builds up over time, irrespective of changing circumstances and frustration, so that a reversal becomes easier to induce as time goes on and eventually will occur in the absence of anything other than this force for change in itself. At this point a reversal occurs spontaneously and subjectively for no special reason and can even take the individual by surprise. Once the reversal has occurred, satiation will then start to build up, making the individual increasingly vulnerable to change in the opposite direction. The resulting cyclical pattern is rather like that involved in the sleeping–waking cycle. After one has been asleep for long enough one will wake up, even though nothing has occurred to wake one; and after one has been awake for long enough, one will in the normal way of things go to sleep, even though nothing particular has happened to make one sleepy. This implies that there is an internal rhythm for metamotivational change— a rhythm that may become overlaid by circumstances and events but that ensures that, even under unchanging conditions, reversals will continue to occur from time to time. We are reminded here of perceptual reversal figures like the Necker cube (see Figure 12.1, chapter 12), the old-woman–young-woman figure, and so forth that seem to spontaneously reverse when we look at them. It will be a matter for the future to discover whether these different types of spontaneous reversal, metamotivational and perceptual, involve similar neuronal mechanisms.

This idea of satiation sets reversal theory apart from learning theories and role theories that, like reversal theory, emphasize states rather than traits. Unlike such "situational" theories, reversal theory argues that it is possible to be in different states, because of the point on the satiation cycle, at different times even in the same situation. This is a much more radical form of antitrait position: People can be different from themselves not only under different conditions but even under the same conditions. A mother taking her son to soccer may feel alloic sympathy on one day and autic mastery on another. Going for a run one day may be experienced as telic and on another as paratelic.

One final point to notice about the reversal process is that it is involuntary. That is, one cannot simply decide to reverse in the same direct way that one can decide to lift one's arm. But this does not mean that one cannot induce a reversal indirectly and thus bring reversals in some measure under (indirect) control. Thus, one can put oneself in a situation that is likely to induce a particular state, for example, sit at one's desk to induce the telic state, go to a bar to induce the paratelic state. It may even be possible to induce a different state by means of thoughts or images (Apter, 1982a, chap. 14), for example, the way in which some athletes "self-talk" (Purcell, 1999a, 1999b). This obviously has important implications for therapy, counseling, and coaching.

The reversal process, then, plays a central part in human emotional–motivational processes. That is, reversal processes are involved in determining which set of metamotivational states is active at a given time. This array of states then determines the feelings and emotions that are possible at that time and leads into the behaviors that the individual will perform to maximize hedonic tone in terms of this array.

DOMINANCE, LABILITY, AND SALIENCE

When we come to looking at how people differ from each other it is clear that, in terms of the concepts that have been developed here, we cannot assign people to fixed positions on trait dimensions. This is because fixed positions of this kind imply that people do not change or fluctuate in relation to these dimensions in the course of their everyday lives. But this does not mean that certain personal characteristics cannot be aggregated over time in such a way as to provide some kind of picture of that person's self-pattern. For example, we could estimate the actual amount of time that someone spends in one motivational state rather than the other, in a pair of states. This would provide us with a *state balance* for that pair of states. Furthermore, we could infer from this that, other things being equal, there is an innate bias underlying the tendency to spend more time in one state than the other. We could refer to this innate bias as *dominance*. Thus, one person might have an inbuilt tendency to be more often in the sympathy state and another to be more often in the mastery state. We could refer to the former person as sympathy dominant and to the latter as mastery dominant. And it is possible for people to be sympathy or mastery dominant to different degrees. We may suppose that dominance affects the frequency of different states largely through the speed with which satiation builds up in one direction or the other in each pair of states.

Dominance described in this way sounds like a trait, and in a certain sense it is. But it is very different from the typical mainstream trait concept because, for example, someone can be extremely telic dominant but still spend time in the paratelic state and be as paratelic in that state as someone who is paratelic dominant. Again, we see the necessity to think in terms of at least two levels: (a) that of how someone is at a given time (state) and (b) that of how they tend to be over time (state balance influenced by dominance).

Another important way in which people can differ is in terms of *lability*—how easily and readily they reverse. Thus, some people are more labile, or reversible, than others, meaning that they reverse more frequently. This is independent of dominance. Thus, someone might spend one-fifth of their time in the negativistic state and four-fifths in the conformist state but switch between them frequently, whereas someone else may experience the same proportions over a period of time but switch much less frequently.

There are a number of other ways in which people can differ. One more should be mentioned here. Different pairs of states (i.e., different domains) may be more or less important in people's lives in the sense that they tend to be more or less frequently at the center of awareness, more or less frequently focal. Thus, one person may tend to be highly aware of the means–ends domain and another of the relationship domain. These differences are referred to in the theory as differences of *salience*.

THE SYSTEM AS A WHOLE

Let us put these concepts together to show how the system works as a whole. This is represented in the flow diagram in Figure 1.3 in which, to keep things manageable, only two of the four pairs of metamotivational states are shown. These may be taken to be either the somatic or the transactional pair. (Also the diagram does not cover every aspect of the process, but it does map out the main features.)

At the heart of the diagram we see these two pairs of states represented in oval boxes. Leading into these boxes are the factors that determine which state in each pair is actually active, and leading away from the boxes are

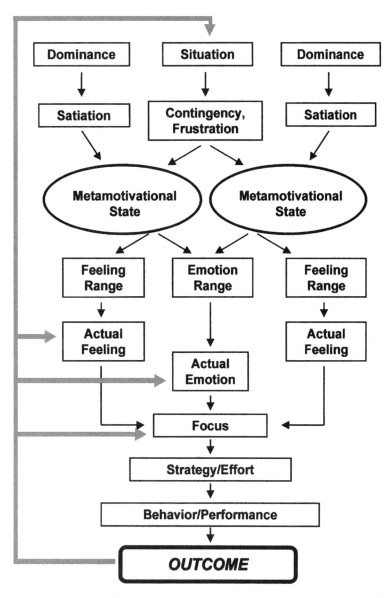

Figure 1.3. The pattern of influences underlying experience and behavior, according to reversal theory.

the effects of this state combination. On the input side we see the three types of factor that influence whether a reversal will occur, two of these (contingency and frustration) deriving from the environmental situation and the third from the level of satiation at the time in question, which is influenced by dominance. On the output side we see that the ongoing metamotivational states determine the two feeling ranges that will be experienced, and—in combination—the emotion range. From these ranges, two particular feelings and one emotion will be experienced. These feelings and emotions will lead into behavior, the particular behavior chosen depending among other things on which of the two metamotivational states is most focal (remembering that they may occasionally be equally focal). It will also depend on the person's favorite strategies in the kind of situation prevailing and on the amount of time and effort that he or she is willing to commit to the performance.

The actual outcome of this performance will determine which emotions and feelings will immediately ensue and which state will be the most focal. These feedback loops are shown in the flow diagram with a gray line. The consequent outcome will represent a new situation that in turn influences which metamotivational states are active next, through playing a part (along with level of satiation of the ongoing states) in inducing or inhibiting reversals. This feedback loop is also shown with a gray line. In this way a new cycle of states, feelings, and behaviors will be initiated.

If we put all four pairs of states together (i.e., going beyond the diagram as it stands), the story remains essentially the same. The difference is that on the output side the choice of action will depend on the emotions and feelings from four states instead of two and in particular the emotions and feelings that are associated with the most focal state or states from across these four.

Let us look at a hypothetical illustration. I have just finished my morning's work in an office and am starting on my lunch break. My telic state is satiated after several hours of serious work, and I have now reversed into the paratelic state. My alloic state is also satiated—I have been working with a team for much of the morning—and I am now in the autic state, even though I am still talking to members of the team as we all make our way out of the office. Because the talk is now about personal matters, however, this has been a strong enough influence to induce in me the sympathy state. Meanwhile the conformist state remains in operation. Of these four states, the paratelic, conformist, sympathy, and autic, it is the paratelic and the autic that are the most focal as I walk toward my car. (At this point we have reached the level in the flow diagram represented by the oval boxes containing the term "*metamotivational state*".)

I decide that I will enjoy myself and to hell with everyone else and that I will do this by driving to a music store not far away and buying myself a compact disc. This is a relatively low-effort strategy that I adopt from time to time. The outcome (the last line in the flow diagram) is that in a short time I am in the store at a local mall, looking through the discs. As a result, my actual feeling in relation to the paratelic (and conformist) states is one of mild excitement and in relation to the autic state (and the sympathy state, which continues to be active) is one of gratitude that I have a job that allows me these little luxuries. My feelings are ones of low felt significance and low identification. The low felt significance is good in the paratelic state, because it means that I recognize that what I am doing is for its own sake. The low identification is also pleasant because it means that I experience my actions as independent and individual, and this is what I want in the autic state. These particular emotions and feelings arise in the flow diagram through the feedback loops, and this completes one cycle through the flow chart.

At the next cycle all kinds of things could happen. Perhaps on the way out of the shop I am reminded by something I see that I have to get a key cut, and this switches me into the telic state. Or perhaps I see a group of schoolchildren soliciting contributions for a good cause, and this induces the alloic state. Or perhaps the conformist state satiates and the resulting negativistic state becomes salient, and all of a sudden I find myself wanting to do something I should not do, like smoking, which is prohibited in the mall. Whichever of these happens, what I actually do will depend again on which states are active and the most focal, how much effort I want to invest in the activity, and so on. Once more the outcome will determine my subsequent feelings and emotions. If my negativistic state is more focal than my alloic and sympathy states, then I may deliberately refrain from giving money to the charity. This may immediately give me a feeling of high felt negativism, and the freedom that goes with this, and also the emotion of mischievousness, but at the same time I will also experience the bad feeling of guilt that goes with gain in the alloic–sympathy state combination. And perhaps in the next cycle the alloic and sympathy states become more focal and the guilt accordingly becomes more central in my experience, so that I decide to go back and give some money after all.

This narrative brings out the way in which everyday life, as it is experienced, is a tangled web of changing desires, perceptions, feelings, and emotions that flitter in and out of awareness in a perpetual swirl. But at the same time, underlying this complex conscious flow, with its tides and crosscurrents, there is structure. There is the synchronic structure of the eight pairs of states, as represented in Figure 1.1, and there is the diachronic structure represented in the flow diagram in Figure 1.3.

STRUCTURE OF THIS BOOK

The aim of *Motivational Styles in Everyday Life: A Guide to Reversal Theory* is to provide a definitive statement of reversal theory and to document the publications that it has generated. It is hoped that those coming to the theory for the first time will, as a result, be able to grasp and evaluate the theory as a whole, as well as be guided in further specialist reading in their particular areas of interest. For those already working with the theory, the book should constitute a useful reference text and a marker for the future.

This introduction has illustrated the main concepts of the theory. In chapter 2, I describe the theory more formally and fully in terms of a set of propositions that are organized hierarchically into different levels of abstraction. This chapter therefore provides a basic structure for integrating all the material in the rest of the book. Chapter 3, by Mitzi Desselles and myself, documents the various types of psychometric measures, including both state and dominance measures, which have been developed over the years to test or apply the theory. It also discusses some of the psychometric problems that are highlighted from the reversal theory perspective. Chapter 4, by Ken Heskin and myself, delves into some of the basic research that has been carried out on the central concepts of the theory, especially in relation to the reversal phenomenon itself. In particular, it describes research showing that reversals occur on a continuing basis over time, that they can be induced by a number of factors, that state at a given time may be different from dominance over time, and that arousal systems are bistable rather than homeostatic. Chapter 5, by Gareth Lewis and Sven Svebak, provides further empirical grounding for the theory by reporting on psychophysiological research dealing with such concepts as reversal and the difference between state and dominance. One of the main findings to emerge from this chapter is that the telic–paratelic dichotomy, although originally identified phenomenologically, has an objective physiological reality.

The next seven chapters explore reversal theory research in a number of major topic areas within psychology. Chapter 6, by Rod A. Martin and Sven Svebak, deals with stress and develops the reversal theory distinction between effort-stress and tension-stress. One of the most interesting things to emerge from this research is the way in which stress is not only coped with but even actually desired in the paratelic state. In fact, in the paratelic state it appears that, up to a certain point, it is the absence of stress that is stressful. Chapter 7, by Kathleen A. O'Connell and Mary R. Cook, reports on the work that has been carried out on smoking and smoking cessation and in particular the finding that lapses by people trying to give up smoking are more likely to occur in some metamotivational states than in others. Given the relative lack of success in predicting lapsing by trait theories, this represents a definite advance and also has practical implications. Important psychophysiological research is also reported in this chapter. Chapter 8, by R. Iain F. Brown, deals with addiction in general rather than just smoking and is centered on a new general theory of addiction that is based in part on reversal theory. The topic dealt with in chapter 9, by Mark R. McDermott, is that of rebelliousness, which is associated with the reversal theory concept of negativism. This chapter summarizes reversal theory research extending beyond antisocial behavior to many other phenomena. In chapter 10 by

John H. Kerr, the theme is that of sport and exercise. This is one of the best-researched areas in reversal theory, and the chapter reviews the main findings from work on a diversity of different activities from many parts of the world involving a variety of people, from casual amateurs to elite athletes. Chapter 11, by Mary M. Gerkovich, describes work in reversal theory applied to risk-taking and includes a discussion of the concept of protective frames. Although cognitive synergy has not been a major topic thus far in reversal theory research, chapter 12, by Andrew S. Coulson, examines the concept, especially in relation to such phenomena as aesthetics and humor, and reports on the research that has been generated.

The following three chapters look at areas of practical application. The first of this set, chapter 13 by Stephen Carter and myself, deals with management and organizations, which is a recent but rapidly expanding area of application. The chapter discusses the insights and practical applications of the theory in the workplace and also describes some psychometric instruments developed for use in organizations. Chapter 14, by Kathryn D. Lafreniere, David M. Ledgerwood, and Stephen J. Murgatroyd, deals with the area from which reversal theory originally arose, namely psychiatry and clinical psychology. This chapter looks at issues concerning both diagnosis and treatment, noting how the theory provides a new taxonomy for psychopathology and a systematic approach to eclectic therapy. The chapter also contains some brief case histories. The next chapter, chapter 15 by David Fontana, takes a thoughtful look at a number of topics that have traditionally been the province of humanistic psychology, such as self-awareness, personal change, adult play, creativity, and spirituality. In fact this chapter goes beyond practical application to raise some fundamental issues concerning human nature. In chapter 16, the final chapter of the book, I point us in future directions and bring matters to a conclusion by suggesting what reversal theory might have to offer to psychology as a whole, emphasizing eight major benefits that the theory may be said to represent.

2

REVERSAL THEORY AS A SET
OF PROPOSITIONS

MICHAEL J. APTER

In this chapter, reversal theory, as a whole, is described in a more formal way than in the introductory chapter; it is presented as a set of propositions making up a hypothetico–deductive system. (An earlier set of propositions was put forward, when the theory was at a much earlier stage of development, by Apter, 1981a.) The intention in this chapter is to make the theory as clear and complete as possible, the aim being to state rather than to justify, explain, or illustrate. In this respect, this chapter is therefore more of a reference document than a reading text. We may of course expect that the theory will continue to evolve in the future, just as it has done in the past, in the light of new evidence and new needs (both practical and conceptual). But it is useful to have a description of the theory as it stands now in terms that are, as far as possible, definitive and unambiguous.

The propositions in the chapter are arranged hierarchically into various levels of abstraction and generality. They start at level 1 with some statements that represent the general approach that has been adopted, the underlying assumptions that undergird the theory and that start to mark it off as a distinctive paradigm. Of these assumptions, the first one is really the most basic, specifying the approach as structural–phenomenological. At level 2 are some very general statements that start to put the underlying assumptions in the form of a system. These propositions state that there are metamotivational states that come in opposites, that people reverse between these, and so on. Level 3 starts to expand upon all of this in terms of specific states that relate to specific aspects of experience. This comes in two parts. The first is the core structure of the theory, and it is this structure that was the main focus of the introduction. All the parts of this hang together as a pattern, and this pattern can be represented in diagrammatic form. The second part deals with a set of spin-off concepts and propositions that elaborate on this central core.

At level 4 are a set of statements that are inferences derived from the more abstract propositions for particular areas of psychology, including particular topics and problems. They are typically tied in with other ideas and information from the fields concerned. Finally, at level 5 is a conceptual framework that simply guides the way in which research questions can be asked in different areas and how they can be asked in a systematic and comprehensive manner. Some of the propositions go beyond what has been discussed in the introduction, and these propositions are, for the most part, elaborated further in later chapters.

LEVEL 1: BASIC ASSUMPTIONS

There are four basic assumptions in reversal theory:

1. *Structural–phenomenological:* Conscious experience has structure.
2. *Motivational:* This structure derives from motivation.
3. *Temporal:* This structure changes in systematic ways over time.
4. *Universality:* Certain fundamental aspects of this structure apply to all human beings.

LEVEL 2: BASIC PROPOSITIONS

There are 10 basic propositions in reversal theory:

1. *Motivational Experience:* There is a set of continuous subjective motivational variables (e.g., felt arousal, as defined below) such that any given value of each variable can be experienced in different ways at different times, giving rise to different emotions or feelings and different levels of positive or negative hedonic tone. Let us refer to these "ways" as *metamotivational states*. When a particular state is playing a part in determining experience, we can say that it is *active* (we can also use the terms *metamotivational mode* and *motivational style* to refer to these states).
2. *Motivational Oppositionality:* Metamotivational states come in pairs of opposites, each state representing a preferred level (in the cybernetic sense) of a subjective motivational variable. These states are opposite in the sense that the preferred levels represented by each state are at or toward opposite ends of the dimensions concerned. In this respect a pair of states is

mutually exclusive, because only one or the other in a pair can be active at a given time.

3. *Bistability*: Under a variety of circumstances, discontinuous switches between the metamotivational states constituting a pair will occur, meaning that the position of the preferred level of the variable concerned will jump to an opposite position. This has the effect of inverting the dimension concerned in relation to hedonic tone. Let us refer to such a discontinuous change or switch as a *reversal*. The whole system comprised of such bistable subsystems can be regarded as *multistable*.

4. *Exhaustiveness*: For a given pair of metamotivational states, one or the other will be active during the whole of waking life. The set of states that is active at a given time may be referred to as the state *array*.

5. *Focality*: Not all metamotivational states that are active at a given time will be equally central in experience (even though they all make a contribution), and typically only one or two in the array will be particularly focal in awareness at that time. States move in and out of focal awareness over time, so that which active states are focal is continually subject to change. The *focality* of a state at a given time is its relative degree of importance, in comparison with the other coactive states, in the individual's phenomenological field at that time.

6. *Hedonic Tone*: Movement toward the preferred level of a motivational variable will be accompanied by increasingly pleasant emotions or feelings, and increasingly positive hedonic tone, these reaching their optimal levels at the preferred level itself. The opposite is the case when there is movement away from the preferred level.

7. *Behavioral Indeterminacy*: There is no simple one-to-one relationship between types of overt behavior and metamotivational states, and therefore we cannot always accurately infer the latter from the former alone.

8. *Dominance*: Each individual person has some degree of internal bias toward one or the other metamotivational state within each pair of metamotivational states. The degree of bias that an individual displays toward one rather than the other member of a pair of metamotivational states is known as the degree of *dominance* of that state.

9. *Salience*: Each individual person tends to be more aware, over time, of some pairs rather than of other pairs. This means that the members of some pairs tend more often to be more focal than those of other pairs. The *salience* of a pair of metamotiva-

tional states is the degree to which, for an individual, the pair as a whole tends to be central or peripheral in awareness, irrespective of which member of the pair is dominant.

10. *Completeness:* No metamotivational state is inherently superior to its opposite, and every state has something valuable to contribute to the life of the individual and to the individual's family, work group, and community. *Motivationally rich* environments tend to evoke and support all of the different states and to provide for their satisfaction.

LEVEL 3: CORE STRUCTURE AND ASSOCIATED CONCEPTS

Core Structure

The different parts of this core structure are spelled out in the following set of propositions concerning aspects of the metamotivational state pairs (namely, ways of experiencing, feelings, emotions, and motivations), reversals, and individual differences.

Ways of Experiencing

There are four pairs of opposite metamotivational states, each pair dealing with one *domain* of experience (i.e., with one basic and ever-present aspect of the structure of mental life):

1. The telic–paratelic pair deals with the experience of *goals-and-means*. In the *telic state*, the goal is of overriding importance, with the means being chosen in the attempt to achieve the goal. In the *paratelic state*, the ongoing behavior and experience are of paramount importance, with any goals being seen as ways of facilitating or enhancing the behavior or experience. This pair is also known as the *serious* (telic) and *playful* (paratelic) pair. The telic state tends to be associated with planning ahead and the paratelic state with spontaneity.

2. The conformist–negativistic pair deals with the experience of *rules and constraints* (including conventions, expectations, and routines). The *conformist state* sees rules as useful ways of structuring behavior, and the *negativistic state* sees them as essentially restrictive. The negativistic state is also known as the *challenging state*.

3. The mastery–sympathy pair deals with the experience of *transactions* or exchanges with other people, things, or situations. The *mastery state* sees transactions as being about taking or

yielding up, and the *sympathy state* sees them as being about giving or being given.

4. The autic–alloic pair deals with the experience of *relationships* with other people, things, or situations. The *autic state* tends to see the other as separate and unrelated, and the *alloic state* tends to identify with the other. The other in the alloic state is experienced either as an *extended self* (e.g., the individual experiences being part of a team) or as a *surrogate self* (e.g., the individual experiences the other as an identified-with hero). This pair is also known as the *self-oriented* (autic) and *other-oriented* (alloic) pair.

Feelings

The variables dealt with by each pair, are the following:

1. The telic–paratelic pair deals with felt significance (the telic state preferring high felt significance and the paratelic preferring low). *Felt significance* is the degree to which the individual experiences himself or herself to be pursuing goals that are important beyond the current ongoing situation (high felt significance) or is doing things for the sake of those things themselves in the present moment (low felt significance).

2. The conformist–negativistic pair deals with felt negativism (the conformist state preferring low felt negativism, and the negativistic state preferring high). *Felt negativism* is the degree to which the individual experiences himself or herself to be violating perceived rules, customs, or expectations (high felt negativism) or conforming to them (low felt negativism). This variable can also be referred to as *expressed negativism*.

3. The mastery–sympathy pair deals with felt toughness (the mastery state preferring high felt toughness, and the sympathy state preferring low). *Felt toughness* is the degree to which the individual experiences himself or herself to be behaving in a way that is tough and hardy (high felt toughness) or that is sensitive and soft (low felt toughness).

4. The autic–alloic pair deals with felt identification (the autic state preferring low felt identification, and the alloic preferring high). *Felt identification* is the degree to which the individual experiences himself or herself to be associated with or part of some other person or identity (high felt identification) or to be independent of others (low felt identification).

All the relationships described here are represented in terms of the set of hypothetical graphs shown in Figure 2.1.

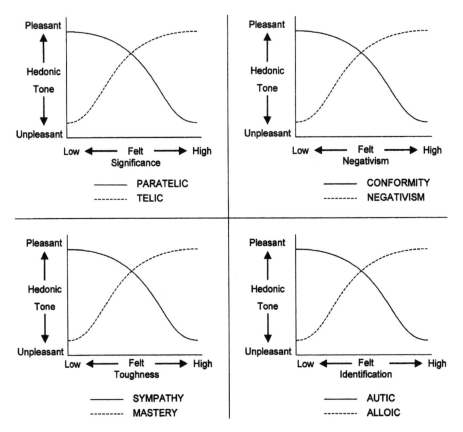

Figure 2.1. Hypothetical curves representing the contrasting ways in which feelings are experienced in different metamotivational states.

Emotions

The following propositions apply to emotions:

1. The telic–paratelic pair and the conformist–negativistic pair also in their various combinations deal with felt arousal. Let us refer to these two pairs as the *somatic pairs*. *Felt arousal* is the degree to which the individual feels himself or herself to be worked up, emotionally involved, and intense.

2. The mastery–sympathy pair and the autic–alloic pair also in their various combinations deal with felt transactional outcome. Let us refer to these two pairs as the *transactional pairs*. *Felt transactional outcome* is the degree to which the individual feels himself or herself to be gaining or losing in a transaction.

3. Depending on the level of the felt arousal variable and which two of the two pairs of somatic metamotivational states are

active, different emotions will result. The emotional ranges are as follows (from low to high arousal):

- Telic, conformist: Relaxation to anxiety
- Paratelic, conformist: Boredom to excitement
- Telic, negativistic: Placidity to anger
- Paratelic, negativistic: Sullenness to mischievousness.

4. Depending on the level of the felt transactional outcome variable and which two of the two pairs of transactional metamotivational states are active, different emotions will result. The emotional ranges are as follows (from felt transactional loss to felt transactional gain):

- Mastery, autic: Humiliation to pride
- Mastery, alloic: Modesty to shame
- Sympathy, autic: Resentment to gratitude
- Sympathy, alloic: Virtue to guilt.

5. All the relationships described here are represented in terms of the set of hypothetical graphs shown in Figure 2.2. Please note the following:

- The emotional terms used here are to be taken in each case as being representative of a related set of terms, such as "thrill" or "euphoria" for "excitement"; "calmness" or "tranquillity" for "relaxation"; and so on.
- The precise shape and position of the curves shown in Figure 2.2 may shift under different circumstances.
- For both felt arousal and felt transactional outcome, emotions derive from the experience of matching or mismatching the preferred and actual levels of these variables.

6. It follows that at any given time the individual may be aware of two types of emotion: a somatic emotion and a transactional emotion.

7. Hedonic tone in the case of the somatic emotions is experienced as some degree of pleasure or displeasure. Hedonic tone in the case of the transactional emotions is experienced as some degree of happiness or unhappiness.

8. In the paratelic state, other pleasurable intense forms of experience can substitute for high felt arousal. These include cognitive fascination and sensual pleasures.

9. *Envy* and *jealousy* are emotion terms that represent the desire to have something that someone else has, but the former is a mastery term and the latter a sympathy term.

10. There is a possibility for conflict between feelings and emotions in the sense that a particular action may increase the hedonic tone with respect to one while reducing it with

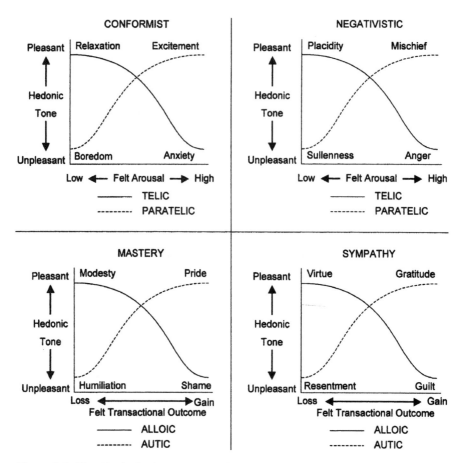

Figure 2.2. Hypothetical curves representing the contrasting ways in which emotions are experienced in different combinations of metamotivational state.
Note. From *Reversal Theory: Motivation, Emotion, and Personality* (pp. 18, 102, 113, 116), by M. J. Apter, 1989, London: Routledge. Copyright 1996 by M. J. Apter. Reprinted with permission of the author.

respect to the other. (For example, in the telic state, a particular action may increase both felt significance, which is pleasant in this state, and felt arousal, which is unpleasant.)

11. There is a higher-level evaluative process that estimates the subjective likelihood of pleasure or happiness at a given time. This may be thought of as involving the moods of optimism and pessimism and the related emotions of hope and despair.

Motivation and Values

The following propositions apply to motivation and values:

1. Each metamotivational state is based on a *core value*, that is a psychological (rather than biological) need. Specifically,

- Telic: Achievement
- Paratelic: Fun
- Conformist: Fitting in
- Negativistic: Freedom
- Mastery: Power
- Sympathy: Love
- Autic: Individuation
- Alloic: Transcendence.

Each of these value terms represents a set of more or less synonymous or related words, for example, "progress" for "achievement," "enjoyment" for "fun," "adaptability" for "fitting in," "release" for "freedom," "strength" and "control" for "power," "affection" and "care" for "love," "assertiveness" for "individuation," and "altruism" for "transcendence."

2. Each value provides a *meaning* to action and feelings of self-worth when achieved.

3. The attainment of each of these values requires, as a prerequisite, the achievement of the relevant feeling. Thus,
   - Achievement cannot be experienced without high felt significance.
   - Fun cannot be experienced without low felt significance.
   - Fitting in cannot be experienced without low felt negativism.
   - Freedom cannot be experienced without high felt negativism.
   - Power cannot be experienced without high felt toughness.
   - Love cannot be experienced without low felt toughness.
   - Individuation cannot be experienced without low felt identification.
   - Transcendence cannot be experienced without high felt identification.

4. Any biological motive (e.g., hunger or thirst) can be experienced in combination with any metamotivational state. (Note that biological motives do not go in pairs of opposites in the way that the motives or values associated with metamotivational states do.)

Reversal

The following propositions apply to reversals:

1. The circumstances that bring about, or tend to bring about, a reversal include
   - certain environmental events and situations (as experienced by the individual)

- frustration in achieving the preferred levels of the relevant variables
- processes of satiation.

Note that environmental states and situations can also serve to maintain current states by tending to inhibit change rather than by tending to induce change. A reversal brought about by an environmental event or situation is known as a *contingent reversal. Satiation* is an internal change over time that makes the individual increasingly susceptible to reversal and that eventually induces a reversal on its own account in the absence of other factors.

2. A reversal occurs when the combined forces for such reversal are greater than those resisting reversal.
3. The processes involved here may work, in detail, in different ways in relation to each pair of states.
4. Reversals of all these types are involuntary. They may, however, be brought to some degree under indirect voluntary control (e.g., by the individual changing his or her setting).
5. On occasion the forces for and against reversal may be so finely balanced that the individual experiences *shimmering,* a rapid oscillation between opposite states.
6. Judging other people as if they were always in the metamotivational state that they were in on one occasion or on a small number of occasions is a mistake known as *chronotyping.*

Individual Differences

Individuals differ, among other things, in respect to

1. Their current dominance (see below) in relation to each pair of metamotivational states. The profile of such dominances over all pairs of metamotivational states is known as the individual's *self-pattern.*
2. Their *lability,* or ease with which reversal occurs, either overall or for each specific pair.
3. The relative *salience* that they tend to experience for each pair of metamotivational states (i.e., the relative importance of each domain of experience in their lives).
4. Their *key states*—the states that tend to occur frequently in their experience and to be focal when they do occur.
5. The way in which coactive states in an array tend to articulate with each other.
6. The kinds of events or situations that tend to induce different metamotivational states.

7. The precise shape and position of the curves that represent for that individual, at that time, the relationship between felt arousal and felt transactional outcome on the one hand and hedonic tone on the other, as shown in Figure 2.2. Likewise for the curves shown in Figure 2.1.
8. The specific strategies they tend to adopt and levels of effort they typically invest in the pursuit of high positive hedonic tone in relation to each metamotivational state when it is active.
9. The life skills and competencies that they bring to bear in each metamotivational state.
10. Their general arousability (see below).
11. Their tendency in general, or with respect to specific states, to evaluate outcomes in an optimistic or pessimistic way.
12. Their general level of awareness of their emotions and feelings. This is a kind of generalized salience.

Associated Concepts

A number of further basic propositions are needed to complete the theory as it stands. These deal with further aspects of the emotions and with stress, relationships, personality, certain aspects of cognition and with clinical problems.

Emotions

There are several further emotion propositions associated with reversal theory:

1. *Arousability*, which is the ease with which an individual is aroused, is different from, and orthogonal to, preference for high or low levels of felt arousal.
2. When one experiences the world as being ultimately safe, even if danger is present, then one experiences the world through a *protective frame*. The protective frame is associated with the paratelic state. There are three main types of protective frame:
   - The confidence frame provides feelings of safety in the face of risk through confidence in one's skills and those of others, the dependability of equipment, and so forth.
   - The safety-zone frame provides feelings of safety through the perception that in fact there is no source of threat.
   - The detachment frame provides feelings of safety through the fact that one is merely an observer.

3. Emotions that are normally unpleasant can be experienced as pleasant in the paratelic state (because they involve high arousal). Such emotions are, under these conditions, known as *parapathic emotions*. The emotions can be represented by placing quotation marks around the name of the emotion (e.g., "anger").

4. Certain beliefs that are widespread in a culture may help produce pleasant emotions, even though they are not veridical. Such beliefs are known as *functional fictions*.

Stress

There are three propositions that relate specifically to stress:

1. If there is a discrepancy between the preferred level of a variable that is related to a metamotivational state and the actual level of that variable, giving rise to an unpleasant emotion or feeling, this will be experienced as a form of *tension* whose strength will be proportional to the degree of the discrepancy. Such tension constitutes *tension-stress* and is inversely related to hedonic tone.

2. Tensions from different discrepancies involving different motivational variables may combine to produce an overall level of tension-stress at a given time.

3. The individual may respond to tension-stress with some degree or another of effortful striving. This is known as *effort-stress*.

Self and Other

The autic and alloic states each come in two forms that have their own names:

1. The autic state consists of (a) the *autocentric state*, in which the individual perceives himself or herself to be interacting with another person, thing, or situation, and (b) the *intra-autic state*, in which the individual is aware only of himself or herself (i.e., there is no significant awareness of "other").

2. The alloic state consists of (a) the *allocentric state*, in which the individual perceives himself or herself to be interacting with another person, thing, or situation, and (b) the *pro-autic state*, in which the individual either perceives himself or herself to be part of some larger identity (e.g., a group) or is so identified with another that there is no significant awareness of self. Note that in the pro-autic state, the emotion ranges

become the same as those for the autocentric state since the "other" is now a surrogate self.

Dominance and State Balance

There are five levels of analysis with respect to the relationship between the states in a pair of states:

1. *Constitutional dominance:* the innate bias that the individual is born with, with respect to a pair of metamotivational states.
2. *Current dominance:* the underlying bias that currently characterizes the individual with respect to a pair of metamotivational states.
3. *State balance:* the actual amount of time that the individual spends in one metamotivational state rather than its opposite over some defined period.
4. *Situational state balance:* the actual amount of time that the individual spends in one state rather than its opposite in some defined type of situation over iterations of that situation.
5. *Event state balance:* the actual amount of time that the individual spends in one state rather than its opposite on a particular defined occasion.

Cognitive Synergy

1. It is possible, even if this defies the laws of logic, to experience an identity as possessing mutually exclusive characteristics. This kind of experience is known as *cognitive synergy* and comes in two forms: (a) *identity synergy,* in which the mutually exclusive characteristics are perceived simultaneously (by involving different levels of interpretation), and (b) *reversal synergy,* in which the mutually exclusive characteristics are perceived in such quick succession that the feeling of identity "carries over" momentarily.
2. Cognitive synergies are enjoyed when the paratelic state is active and disliked when the telic state is active.
3. There are various categories of cognitive synergy, for example real–apparent (in which one characteristic is veridical and the other is only an appearance).

Clinical Problems

Clinical problems can arise in at least three ways:

1. Through abnormally inhibited reversal, such that the individual spends most time with one metamotivational state active rather than the other member of the pair.

2. Through reversal being either overlabile, or occurring at inappropriate moments.
3. Through inappropriate strategies being pursued in relation to a given state. These can be
   - functionally inappropriate (they do not lead toward satisfaction of the core value involved)
   - temporally inappropriate (they cause problems at a later time)
   - socially inappropriate (they cause problems for other people).

LEVEL 4: DERIVED HYPOTHESES

A limitless set of hypotheses concerning different areas of behavior and experience can be deduced from the concepts and definitions stated in levels 1–3, in combination with independent observations and reference to previous research in the area of psychology concerned. To give just a small number of examples of such hypotheses:

1. Stress can be enjoyed in the paratelic state.
2. People experiencing chronic anxiety are likely to be telic dominant and highly arousable.
3. Creativity is more likely when the paratelic and negativistic states are active.
4. Humor involves cognitive synergy experienced in the paratelic state.
5. Telic-dominant people tend to pursue careers that have clear career structures.
6. People are more likely to succumb to the temptation to smoke when they are in the paratelic and negativistic states than when they are in the telic and conformist states.
7. Electromyographic gradients in task-irrelevant musculature are steeper in the telic than the paratelic state for a given task.
8. Personal misunderstanding and arguments between people in everyday life are more likely when the people involved have different active metamotivational states at the time concerned.
9. Different organizational and national cultures may encourage and facilitate different metamotivational states.

LEVEL 5: CONCEPTUAL FRAMEWORK

The concepts of reversal theory provide a structure for asking questions in a systematic way about some particular field of study, especially as these questions relate to motivation, emotion, or personality. Here are some examples. To what metamotivational states does a particular advertising campaign direct itself? What metamotivational states are satisfied by blood donation? What metamotivational state changes are to be found in the experience of parachuting? What combinations of metamotivational states are associated with soccer hooliganism? What different types of dominance are represented among the employees in a given business organization?

*   *   *

Taken together, these propositions constitute reversal theory as it stands at the present time. The ways that these propositions have been used to frame and elucidate certain problems and puzzles in psychology, the evidence of various kinds that bears on the propositions, and the manner in which they have been applied to a range of practical problems, will be the subject of the rest of this book.

II

EMPIRICAL SUPPORT

3

REVERSAL THEORY MEASURES

MICHAEL J. APTER AND MITZI DESSELLES

Before it is possible to test any of the propositions outlined in the previous chapter, it is necessary to have appropriate ways of measuring the states and processes identified. Over the years, researchers who have used and tested reversal theory have developed a number of instruments and techniques, and the aim of this chapter is to review these measures.

Because the starting point in all reversal theory research is subjective experience, tools are needed that will address themselves to mental life. Although attempting to measure experiential phenomena presents certain methodological problems, these are problems that psychologists have been thoroughly familiar with since the origins of the subject. In fact psychologists, especially psychometricians but also social psychologists, those working in psychophysics and, more recently, cognitive psychologists, have over many years developed a variety of techniques for measuring feelings, emotions, perceptions, judgments, self-evaluations, attitudes, opinions, and other essentially mental phenomena. It is this tradition of testing that reversal theory particularly calls on. In doing so, however, it emphasizes two difficulties in applying these kinds of psychometric methodologies:

1. Subjective meanings can have subtleties and nuances and therefore are difficult to "pin down," and yet these subtleties can be profound in their effects.
2. Subjective meanings are changing and unstable and therefore need to be monitored over time, even short periods.

The two main types of test that have been developed so far are those that can be labeled *state measures* and those that can be labeled *dominance measures*. In what follows, we examine each class of measure separately.

STATE MEASURES

There are basically three ways to assess state in psychology, and reversal theory research has made use of all of them in attempting to identify which metamotivational states are operative at a given time in a person's experience. We describe each of these approaches briefly here. (More detail on reversal theory state measures will be found in Cook, Gerkovich, Potocky, & O'Connell, 1993; their use in sport research has been reviewed in detail by Kerr, 1997a, and by Apter, 1999b; problems that arise in developing state measures have been discussed by O'Connell, 1995.)

Self-Report Questionnaires

The earliest and most frequently used of these self-report scales has been the Telic State Measure (TSM; Svebak, Storfjell, & Dalen, 1982; Svebak & Murgatroyd, 1985; Svebak, 1985a). The TSM consists of five 6-point rating scales on which respondents are asked to assess themselves in terms of how they feel either at the time of responding or at some specified recent time (e.g., at a particular moment in a sporting contest in which they have just been engaged). The first three of these scales are used to measure three facets of the telic–paratelic dimension: seriousness versus playfulness, planning versus spontaneity, and low-preferred arousal versus high-preferred arousal. The fourth scale is used to determine the experienced level of arousal at the time in question, and the fifth scale measures the degree of effortfulness. An arousal discrepancy or tension scale (the discrepancy between the actual experienced level of arousal and the preferred level of arousal) may also be derived from this measure. Note that in these terms, someone can be low in arousal but high in tension (where the preferred arousal level is high). It can be seen that, in a sense, the scale provides six single-item subscales. Examples of the use of this instrument in different contexts include Barr, McDermott, and Evans (1993); Svebak and Grossman (1985); Kerr and Vlaswinkel (1993); O'Connor (1992); Svebak (1986a); Martin-Miller and Martin (1988); Cox and Kerr (1989); and Puntoni (1999). In fact, Svebak used the TSM in many of his studies (to be described further in chapter 5 of this volume). The TSM was also used in many of the studies by Kerr and others (to be described further in chapter 10 of this volume); the scale can be found in Kerr (1997a, Appendix F).

Another state measure that has been developed is the Somatic State Questionnaire (SSQ; Cook et al., 1993), consisting of three 4-item subscales (Serious/Playful, Arousal-avoidance/Arousal-seeking, and Negativistic/Conformist). On the basis of pilot studies, the authors decided to use a bipolar rating scale for each item. The respondent was asked to self-rate in terms of a 6-point scale. Typical items are

Feeling cautious 1 2 3 4 5 6 Feeling adventurous
Feeling compliant 1 2 3 4 5 6 Feeling defiant

The subscales have been found to have good internal consistency. Lafreniere (1997); Cook, Gerkovich, and O'Connell (1997); and Cook et al. (1995) have used the SSQ successfully in their research. Items from it have also been used by O'Connell and Brooks (1997). The scale can be found in Kerr (1999a, Appendix A).

A derivative of the SSQ is the Telic/Paratelic State Instrument (T/PSI; Calhoun, 1995) consisting of a 7-item Serious/Playful subscale and a 5-item Arousal-avoidance/Arousal-seeking subscale. This again has bipolar items that give rise to subscales with excellent internal reliability. Items were selected from a larger pool of items on the basis of how well they discriminated between telic and paratelic states, especially with respect to responses to a series of scenarios representing telic and paratelic situations. The situations depicted also varied in terms of low, medium, and high arousal. The subscales can be added to give an overall telic/paratelic score. In their study on risk taking in sports, Cogan and Brown (1999) used the T/PSI scale, and the complete scale, together with scoring instructions, can be found in Kerr (1999a, Appendix B).

Two more state measures deserve mention here. The first is O'Connor's (1992) Negativism State Measure (described further in chapter 9). The second is the Autic Mastery–Sympathy State Measure (O'Connell & Brooks, 1997). This instrument classifies respondents into one of four groups— mastery-gaining, mastery-losing, sympathy-gaining, and sympathy-losing— but is to be used only for situations in which the individual is in the autic rather than the alloic state (gaining and losing is whether the individual is succeeding or not in gaining sympathy or power, see Figure 2.2, chapter 2, in this volume). The items, derived from an initial list of 81 items by means of three discriminant functions analyses of participants' responses to scenarios, are simple self-descriptors like "appreciated," "affectionate," or "incompetent." The resulting scale was used by the authors in their investigation of people's abilities to change their health behaviors either by giving up bad habits or by adopting good habits.

Some state measures have been tailor-made for use only in certain kinds of situations. An example here is the State of Mind Indicator for Athletes (SOMIFA; Kerr & Apter, 1999), which identifies active metamotivational states, over all the pairs, in sporting contests (the scale can be found in Kerr, 1999a, Appendix C). Weinberg (1998) is among others who have used this tool in their research.

Reversal theory state measures tend to have been used in a way in which they are administered at a small number of significant moments, such as at the beginning and the end of a sporting encounter. However, they can also be used for Ecological Momentary Assessment (EMA) or *experience sampling*—for obtaining ratings on a fairly regular basis during the course of everyday life. O'Connell and Cook in chapter 7 describe this type of self-report measure. In their research on smoking cessation, they asked each participant to carry around a hand-held computer. From time to time, during the course of everyday life, the computer prompted the participants to make a series of ratings on up to 28 items concerning the metamotivational states they were currently experiencing. Participants also initiated response to these items when they felt an urge to smoke or when they actually did smoke.

Looking at these scales, on the one hand there are instruments with multiple-item subscales, like the SSQ and the T/PSI, and on the other there are instruments like the TSM and the SOMIFA, with only single items to represent each subscale. The advantage of the former is that the scales can be developed on the basis of statistical procedures, such as item analysis and factor analysis, and therefore have demonstrable psychometric superiority. Multiple items also offer one the chance to overcome the different interpretations given by the respondents on a single item. The advantage of scales with single items to measure each variable is that they take comparatively little time for the respondents to complete and therefore cause less of an interruption to an activity that is in progress. Potential users will have to decide which of these considerations is more important. In the future, when state tests are developed to measure all the states together, the balance of advantage may well shift to the latter kind of test. This is because multiple-item subscales would require the respondent to stop whatever he or she is doing and attend to the test for a significant amount of time.

Verbal Self-Descriptions

Verbal accounts have been obtained and analyzed in three main ways in reversal theory research: interviews, interviews with coding, and think-aloud monologues.

Interviews

One way to obtain information about a metamotivational state is for a researcher to interview each participant directly about the state of mind that he or she had been in at the time of interest. Thus, in one study, participants were interviewed as part of an experiment on muscle tension that took place in a psychophysiology laboratory. The interviewer, who was blind to each participant's scores in the experiment, discussed with them what their metamotivational state had been during the experimental task (Apter & Svebak, 1986). The interview was structured in terms of a basic set of questions, but the interviewer was permitted follow-up questions that could be used to clarify ambiguous or problematic responses. A good interviewer will of course avoid putting words into participants' mouths, or implying which responses are acceptable or unacceptable.

Yet if an interview takes place long after the event, there may be memory problems. Participants' memories may be helped, however, by using prompts from recordings of the activity itself. For instance, McLennan and Omodei (1995), in their study of the experience of orienteering, cleverly had their participants wear helmets with mini-video recorders that recorded their field of action during a run. Later these recordings were used to discuss the participants' metamotivational states at each point in their runs. We must recognize the possibility, however, that the metamotivational state at the time of the interview may bias recall. For instance, a participant who is interviewed in the sympathy state may be more likely to report the sympathy state as having obtained during the period being discussed, either through selective memory or through imposing a sympathy interpretation on the actions that are remembered. This is a methodological problem that will need to be considered carefully in the future.

Interviews and Coding

Making decisions about state of mind does not have to happen during the interview itself. An alternative is to record the interview in some way, such as an audiotape or videotape, for more careful consideration at a later time. Transcripts may also, of course, be used. Either way, judges may code the material into reversal theory categories. The Metamotivational State Coding Schedule has been developed for this purpose (MSCS; Potocky, Cook, & O'Connell, 1993), partly based on O'Connell (1993a). O'Connell, Potocky, Cook, and Gerkovich (1991) have drawn up a detailed manual for the use of the MSCS.

The procedure is for the material to be divided into coding units, each unit representing a single state and a single situation; if either of these change, a new unit is formed. (The necessity for dividing up the material in this way arose because it quickly became apparent that reversals were taking place during the situations being studied.) For each coding unit, the judges decide which states are active. This is done on the basis of a set of assessments, including assessments of the way in which the situation appears to be viewed by the interviewee, and all the emotions and feelings being reported. A lexicon is available, as part of the manual, of the contrasting descriptors likely to be used by respondents in the different states. The recommended procedure is for judges to make their determinations independently and then to come together to discuss disagreements and reach consensus. Cook and colleagues (1993) reported that interjudge agreement is high.

This impressively thorough method has been used systematically in a series of studies on smoking cessation (e.g., Cook, Gerkovich, O'Connell, & Potocky, 1995) that is reviewed in chapter 7 of this volume. It has also been used in sports research (Males, 1999; Males & Kerr, 1996; Males, Kerr, & Gerkovich, 1998), which is described further in chapter 10. It is currently being used by Khomyk to study the effect of the Chernobyl accident on children's patterns of violence (Khomyk, 1998; Khomyk & Burmaka, 1999). It is notable that this technique has been used to measure all of the different metamotivational states rather than just the telic–paratelic pair.

Think-Aloud Monologues

Another approach is for participants to think out loud in real time while they are doing something; their verbalizations are then recorded for later analysis. The resulting verbal material can again be coded in terms of metamotivational states. Purcell (1999a, 1999b) has used this technique in his study of the experience of playing golf. Golfers, during play, were asked to speak their thoughts aloud into a tape recorder attached to their belts. (Retrospective interviews were also conducted.) This could in principle be a powerful technique for tracking people's states over time. O'Connell and Cook used a related technique in their smoking research in which their participants not only responded to a hand-held computer, but also carried a small tape recorder into which they could describe the situation they found themselves in at the time of responding to the computer.

Objective Indices

A third way to approach state identification is to use some easily measurable overt response that can be measured objectively and conveniently and that can be taken to represent one or another state. To be able to do this, one must be able to assume a relationship between the objective measure and the state in question—ideally through having actually demonstrated such a relationship in previous research. Knowledge of this association can then be used to indicate the presence or absence of that state during some activity of interest to the researcher, for example during recreation, at work, or in some area of life that is problematic for the person concerned.

A good example of this technique is the use of color preference as an indicator of telic and paratelic states, basing this technique on previous research showing that hot colors are preferred when the individual wants to increase arousal and cool colors when he or she wants to lower arousal.

This has been used to track telic and paratelic states in office workers (Walters, Apter, & Svebak, 1982). It has also been used to study this pair of states in runners during runs, the athletes simply indicating color preference as they passed a given point (Kerr & Vlaswinkel, 1993). A different example is the use of the participant's choice of materials to work with (computer video games or a computer statistics teaching program) as an index of telic or paratelic state (Lafreniere, Cowles, & Apter, 1988).

In principle, the fact that there are psychophysiological concomitants of metamotivational states (or at least the telic and paratelic states) means that psychophysiological measures may also be used as indices. A documentation of such concomitants, as explored by Svebak and his colleagues, will be found in chapter 5. Combined with telemetric monitoring, this could be a powerful procedure in the future, especially if physiological concomitants can be found for states over and above the telic and paratelic pair.

The advantage of using objective indices is that they can be simpler to use than scales, interviews, and other such techniques and can often be used in ways that do not disrupt ongoing activities. The fact that they are objective rather than subjective, however, is not the advantage that it might appear to be at first sight. This is because such techniques need to be validated to check that the indices are associated with states in the way that is being assumed. But this means that they need to be validated by means of essentially subjective methods, such as interview and self-report, and so subjectivity is not avoided.

DIFFICULTIES IN IDENTIFYING METAMOTIVATIONAL STATE

Identifying and measuring subjective states, such as metamotivational states, is not easy. In particular, problems of language are likely to arise, and there are also issues with validation. Let us look at these two problem areas in turn, especially as they relate to the development of reversal theory instruments.

Linguistic Problems

The problem of language is that many everyday words have different meanings and therefore, when any such words are used in a psychometric measure, one cannot necessarily be sure which meaning is being responded to. An example would be the word *serious*, which we have seen is used as part of the definition of the telic state and is also used in many psychometric instruments like the TSM. It seems that the word can mean *determined*, as in "I was serious about winning," but this is not necessarily telic. It can also mean *focused*, and it can mean *effortful*. One way to deal with this is to

explain to participants the way that the words in a test are intended. Thus, participants should have a list of definitions available to them when they take the TSM, and researchers using this instrument should ensure that participants have read, understood, and remembered these definitions.

The possibility that an emotion is being experienced in parapathic form is also a complication, because a participant may endorse a telic emotion word while actually being in the paratelic state. This appears to be particularly likely with the word *anxiety*, which someone may easily use to describe a pleasant form of parapathic anxiety, such as watching a tense sporting encounter or a thriller film.

A way around all this might seem to be to ask the participants to rate themselves on the underlying dimensions, like the arousal and arousal-preference dimensions (as in the TSM), and then for the researcher to infer the emotion. But here there are similar difficulties. After all, if an abstract word like *arousal* is used, then participants may not understand what one is talking about; arousal is really a psychologist's and psychophysiologist's word. When we carried out an informal study in which we asked nonpsychologists what the word meant, we found that most of them thought, like the word *excitement*, that it referred specifically to sexual arousal.

A radical way to deal with many of these problems would be to train participants in reversal theory or at least to teach them to use words consistently with the way in which they are used in the theory. For example, one could train participants in studies to use the word *excited* to mean pleasant high arousal or to recognize the parapathic forms of emotions. Such training would involve challenging one of the widely accepted rules of modern experimental psychology, which is that participants should be naive. But there are valid reasons to recommend it, and it is already being used in some so-far unpublished lines of reversal theory research on smoking. The team of Cook, O'Connell, and Gerkovich has, as part of their studies of smoking cessation (see chapter 7 in this volume) devised a technique in which participants are taught to recognize the telic and paratelic states for themselves (Kakolewski, Goings, O'Connell, Gerkovich, & Cook, 1996). A further interesting innovation here is that each state is represented, during the testing period, by a *bundle* of words and phrases rather than a single descriptor, the participants choosing the bundle which, taken together, best represents his or her state of mind.

Validation Problems

Test–retest reliability in its traditional psychometric sense is obviously not appropriate for state measures, because these are supposed to track the way in which people change over time. But validity remains an important requirement. The following are some techniques that have been used to assess the validity of metamotivational state measures.

Consensus of Judges

Most of those researchers who have developed reversal theory scales have checked items at an initial stage with a panel of judges familiar with the theory. This provides at least face validity for the items concerned.

Experimental Manipulation

Experimental conditions can be set up that are strong enough to allow the reasonable assumption that they will induce one or another metamotivational state in most participants, which can then be tested for. For example, Svebak and his colleagues have used this approach with the TSM, using such manipulations as the threat of electric shock or watching a comedy film (e.g., Svebak & Apter, 1987).

Testing in Real-Life Situations

This most "ecologically sound" approach involves testing people in strong real-life situations in which it is reasonable to assume that they will be experiencing particular metamotivational states. Thus, Cook and colleagues (1993), in developing the SSQ, compared participants who were leaving on a ski vacation with those who were waiting to see the dentist. Wendel (1999), in developing the Tension Stress Scale (see below), compared participants in three situations: at a social gathering, at college enrollment, and before taking a major examination. Tacon and Kerr (1999), and Kerr and Tacon (1999) used the TSM to compare students in a library, lecture theatre, sports center, and at a party.

Imagined Situations

In this case, respondents rate how they would feel in certain defined situations, so-called "scenarios," that they are asked to remember or to imagine, and which one would expect to be associated with a given state. Calhoun (1995), for example, used this method in developing the T/PSI, and O'Connell and Brooks (1997) used this method in developing mastery and sympathy items for their study of the way people change their health habits. Tacon and Kerr (1999) used the technique with the TSM.

DOMINANCE MEASURES

It will be recalled from the two earlier chapters that *dominance* is the degree of bias that an individual shows between the two members of a pair of states. In other words, it is about an important aspect of an individual's pattern of states over time: If an individual is dominated by a given state then, other things being equal, the individual will spend more time in that state than in its opposite.

Measures of dominance emerged earlier than state measures, probably because they could be treated as measuring traitlike qualities and so incorporated relatively easily into more traditional research designs. (For another review of dominance measures, see Apter & Apter-Desselles, 1993; Kerr, 1997a, chap. 3, documents the use of dominance measures in sports research.)

The Telic Dominance Scale

The earliest instrument to be developed was the Telic Dominance Scale (TDS; Murgatroyd, Rushton, Apter, & Ray, 1978, 1988), and this became one of the mainstays of reversal theory research for many years, although it appears that it is now being superseded. The scale consists of 42 forced-choice items, each item consisting of two possible choices and a "not sure" option. The respondent is asked to answer in terms of which of the two "you would usually prefer." An example of an item would be

> Eating special things because you enjoy them
> Eating special things because they are good for your health
> Not sure

There are three subscales, each of which deals with a different although related facet of telic dominance: Serious-mindedness, Planning-orientation, and Arousal-avoidance. In Aero and Weiner (1981); Apter (1982a, Appendix C); Apter, Kerr, and Cowles (1988, Appendix B); Kerr (1997a, Appendix D); as well as in the original paper by Murgatroyd et al. (1978), one may find the items and scoring keys. Loonis, Bernoussi, Brandibas, and Sztulman (2000) have developed a French version of the scale. Murgatroyd (1985b) gave an early review of research using the scale that provided some norms, including occupational and cross-cultural norms. Loonis (1999c) and Tacon and Abner (1993) have provided norms broken down in a number of ways, those of Tacon and Abner being based on large samples.

Test–retest reliability studies are reported in Murgatroyd et al. (1978) and elsewhere (Cook & Gerkovich, 1993; Kerr, 1997a, Appendix D). It should be noted that, although reliability is not an appropriate criterion of state tests, it is more appropriate for dominance tests, because in these tests people are being asked to rate how they usually are over periods of time (Apter, 1998) although even here we should remember that a person's dominance can change. Incidentally, Tacon and Kerr (1999), using the TSM, showed that people are able to realistically judge their telic and paratelic states at a time different from the time of judgment, which supports the idea that people can make accurate assessments of these states over time.

Initial validation studies are reported in Murgatroyd et al. (1978). Exhibit 3.1 summarizes some examples of the kind of findings that have been obtained using the TDS over the years since Murgatroyd's report, and these are generally consistent with reversal theory. Apart from being of

Exhibit 3.1.
Some Correlations With the Telic Dominance Scale

Note. These significant correlations are all expressed in terms of increasing telic dominance. They could equally have been expressed in terms of increasing paratelic dominance and the relationship would then be inverted.

- A less casual and more organized lifestyle (Svebak & Murgatroyd, 1985)
- Greater care and accuracy in making descriptions (Svebak & Murgatroyd, 1985)
- A lowered sensitivity to unpleasant and emotional words (Murgatroyd, Rushton, Apter, & Ray, 1978)
- A greater likelihood of displaying obsessional behavior (Fontana, 1978, 1981a)
- A less acute sense of humor (Martin, 1984; Ruch, 1994)
- Less variety of sexual behaviors indulged in and less use of pornography (Murgatroyd, 1983, 1985b)
- Less likelihood of teenagers being delinquent (Bowers, 1985)
- Less interest in gambling and smaller odds when gambling (Anderson & Brown, 1987)
- Less likelihood of taking drugs (Doherty & Matthews, 1988; Loonis, 1999c, Loonis & Apter, 2000)
- Less likelihood of being addicted to alcohol or tobacco (Loonis, 1999c)
- Greater muscle tension build-up during tasks (Svebak, 1984; Svebak & Murgatroyd, 1985)
- Greater care and precision and less vigor in dealing with difficult psychomotor tasks (Svebak, 1984; Svebak & Murgatroyd, 1985)
- Greater heart rate increases in response to threat (Svebak, Nordby, & Ohman, 1987)
- Faster and deeper breathing in response to threat (Svebak, 1986b)
- A more focal and localized pattern of cortical activation (Svebak, 1985b)
- Greater feelings of stress as a response to negative life events (Martin, Kuiper, & Olinger, 1988)
- Greater feelings of stress as a response to daily hassles (Lafreniere, 1997; Martin, Kuiper, & Olinger, 1988)
- Greater tendency to use problem-focused coping strategies (Baker, 1988; Howard, 1988; Murgatroyd, 1985b)
- Greater likelihood to associate work with life satisfaction (Mamali, 1990)
- More intense work motivation (Mamali, 1990)
- Less orientation to intrinsic motivation (Mamali, 1990)
- A preference for endurance rather than explosive sports (Svebak & Kerr, 1989)
- Lesser preference for risky rather than safe sports (Chirivella & Martinez, 1994; Cogan & Brown, 1998; Kerr, 1991b; Kerr & Svebak, 1989)
- More likely, if a police officer, to be a volunteer than a "regular" (Grover, 1999)
- Greater fear of failure and less hope of success (Murgatroyd, Rushton, Apter, & Ray, 1978)
- Increasing age (Loonis, 1999c; Ruch, 1994; Tacon & Abner, 1993)

great interest in themselves, they may also be considered to provide validity for the TDS. (In most cases the total TDS score has been used, although in a few studies the correlation is with one of the subscales.) More details of many of these studies will be found in later chapters of this book.

In addition, Lafreniere and colleagues (1988) and Frey (1990) both reported evidence to show that the scale does in fact predict the amount of time that people spend in the telic and paratelic states over at least short periods of time, when these states are not induced by environmental conditions. Also impressive is the multi-method work of Svebak and Murgatroyd (1985) that validated the TDS against both the qualitative data provided by individuals' self-descriptions and the quantitative data deriving from psychophysiological testing (more detail will be given on this research in chapter 5).

In terms of convergent validity, correlations have been shown, as would be expected, between the TDS and measures of stimulation/sensation-seeking. Murgatroyd (1985b) reviewed a number of studies of the TDS and the Eysenck Personality Inventory (EPI; Eysenck & Eysenck, 1969), which generally showed negative correlations between the Extraversion subscale and the TDS Arousal-avoidance subscale. He also cited evidence of a relation between Zuckerman's Sensation-Seeking Scale (SSS; Zuckerman, 1974) and the Arousal-avoidance subscale but again not with the other two subscales of the TDS. Trimpop, Kerr, and Kirkcaldy (1999) reported on significant correlations in the expected directions between the TDS and its subscales on the one hand and a number of measures of, or related to, sensation-seeking on the other, including all five subscales of Zuckerman's SSS Form V (Zuckerman, 1979), two of the subscales of the Tension Risk Adventure Inventory (TRAI; Keinan, Meir, & Gome-Nemirovsky, 1984) and the Preparation/Prevention subscale of the Desire for Control Scale (DCS; Burger & Cooper, 1979). Murgatroyd et al. (1978), using a measure of need for achievement (Robinson, 1976), showed a relation between telic dominance and fear of failure and telic dominance (negatively) and hope of success (see also Kahn & Kureshi, 1986). This would be consistent with the idea that the telic state involves the absence, and the paratelic state the presence, of a "protective frame."

As far as discriminant validity is concerned, Matthews (1985) examined the relation of the TDS to Cattell's 16PF (Cattell, Eber, & Tatsuoka, 1970) and also Cattell's Motivational Analysis Test (Cattell, Horn, & Sweney, 1970). In both cases there is some overlap that makes sense in theoretical terms, but the various tests also have their own domains. Svebak and Apter (1984) found no significant relationship between TDS scores and Type A/Type B behavior as measured by the total scale scores of the Jenkins Activity Survey (Jenkins, Rosenman, & Friedman, 1967). Murgatroyd (1985b), in his review cited above, also found little evidence for a relationship between the TDS and any of its subscales and the neuroticism dimension of the EPI. These discriminant validity studies show that, although there is some overlap of a kind that might be expected between the TDS and some other well-known instruments, the TDS is also measuring something different and cannot be "assimilated" to these other scales. In addition, O'Connor (1992) showed little relationship between telic and negativistic dominance as measured by the TDS and the Negativism Dominance Scale (see below), respectively.

Unfortunately, a number of psychometric problems have arisen with the TDS over the years, especially as it has started to be used in countries other than that of its origin, the United Kingdom (and, as Shelley and Cohen, 1986, pointed out, the TDS is middle-class in orientation). In particular, correlations between the three subscales, which theoretically are supposed to be high because they are about three facets of the same phenomenon, have tended to drop, especially between the Arousal-avoidance subscale and the other two subscales (Cook & Gerkovich, 1993; Matthews, 1985; O'Connor, 1992; Svebak & Apter, 1984; Tacon & Abner, 1993). This trend is reversed, however, in Trimpop et al. (1999). Factor analyses have also been problematic (see Cook & Gerkovich, 1993; Gotts, Kerr, & Wangeman, 2000; Hyland, Sherry, & Thacker, 1988; Murgatroyd, 1985a). However, some of the difficulties concerning factor analysis are ameliorated if one remembers that the three subscales are not supposed to represent three different independent factors but rather three phenomenologically different aspects of a single process; this would perhaps imply that a single factor would make most psychological sense—which is, incidentally, what is found in Trimpop et al. (1999).

The Paratelic Dominance Scale

The problems with the TDS led to the development of the Paratelic Dominance Scale, which was constructed meticulously through a number of stages (PDS; Cook & Gerkovich, 1993). The resulting instrument consists of 30 items, each of which is a simple statement that the respondent is asked to judge as true or false as a self-description. Most of the items have an explicit temporal component. Examples of items are "I regularly think of the future," "I often take risks," and "I usually take life seriously." The items make up the same three subscales as the TDS, except that they are now scored in the opposite direction, as implied by the name of the scale, and the subscales are also correspondingly labeled in the opposite direction as Playfulness, Spontaneity, and Arousal-seeking. Scores from the subscales may be added to provide an overall paratelic dominance score.

The scale is reported to have satisfactory psychometric properties: Alpha coefficients are good, and the factor structures of the PDS are reported to be consistent with reversal theory (Cook & Gerkovich, 1993). Young (1998), who used the scale in her study of the flow experience in tennis players, obtained alpha values of greater than 0.9 for all three subscales. She also found that telic dominant tennis players liked flow because it helped them reach their goal, whereas paratelic dominant players liked it more because it energized them, which implies some validity for the scale. Lafreniere (1997) reported a significant association between paratelic dominance and mode (as measured by the SSQ, see above) in a study of the appraisal of stressful events. Gotts and colleagues (2000), on the basis of a large cross-cultural study in Australia, the Netherlands, and North America, concluded that PDS items are more satisfactory for cross-cultural work than are TDS items. In fact, on the basis of factor analysis across all three cultures, they suggested a cross-cultural scale consisting of either 21 of the 30 PDS items (representing a three-factor solution) or 14 of the items (representing a two-factor solution, future-oriented and arousal-seeking).

The Nijmegen Telic Dominance Scale

In the Netherlands, Boekaerts (1986) and Boekaerts, Hendriksen, and Michels (1988a, 1988b) have developed the Nijmegen Telic Dominance Scale (N–TDS), a telic dominance scale specifically for children aged 12 and older. The 27 items are based on those in the TDS, modified for use with children. An example of an item would be "Imagine that your parents ask you what you would like to do on Sunday afternoon: (a) go to a large play-garden or (b) visit an interesting museum." The items are divided into the same three subscales as those of the TDS. However, children are asked to respond not just by choosing between alternatives but by rating both alternatives in terms of how attractive they are (on a 5-point scale). The "not sure" option is then dispensed with. This leads to some psychometrically interesting possibilities for scoring. Issues that arise from the development of this scale are discussed in Boekaerts (1988).

The Negativism Dominance Scale

Written by McDermott and Apter (1988) and developed by McDermott (1988a, 1988b), the Negativism Dominance Scale (NDS) is used to measure dominance in relation to negativism–conformity. Norms for this scale are found in Tacon and Abner (1993). This scale, together with information on results from using it, is documented in some detail in chapter 9 in this volume. To give a single example of research using the scale, Vlaswinkel and Kerr (1990) used it in their study of high-level performers in risk and team sports.

The Motivational Style Profile

Unlike other dominance scales, the aim of the Motivational Style Profile (MSP; Apter, Mallows, & Williams, 1998) is to measure by means of a single instrument every type of dominance recognized in the theory. This profile (originally titled the Personal Orientation Profile; Apter & Apter-Desselles, 1993) has a number of advantages over earlier scales and this (or its shorter version, the Apter Motivational Style Profile, see below) may well become the instrument of choice in future research.

1. As noted, it looks at every type of dominance, providing a comprehensive profile of scores for each respondent.
2. Not only does it measure dominance, it also measures the salience of each dimension in comparison with other dimensions, thus also providing a salience profile for each respondent. (It is in fact the first reversal theory instrument to attempt to measure salience.)
3. Respondents make explicit temporal judgments by means of a 6-point rating scale *(never, seldom, sometimes, often, very often, always)*. This emphasizes to respondents the fact that their self-ratings are in terms of frequency, something that is critical to the reversal theory notion of dominance.
4. The instrument is non–ipsative, because each subscale is independent of each other subscale. This presents certain psychometric advantages.
5. Items are, in comparison with some earlier scales, simple and relatively abstract, which should make them easier to translate in ways that make sense in different cultures. (In fact, the scale has already been translated into a number of languages and used in different countries.)
6. Optimism and pessimism subscales are included to provide an assessment of the individual's overall assessment of his or her prospect of achieving satisfaction in each of the metamotivational states. Subscales are also included for arousability (as distinct from arousal preference) and for effortfulness.

There are in fact 14 subscales made up of five items each, producing a total scale of 70 items. The subscales are Telic, Paratelic, Arousal-avoiding, Arousal-seeking, Conformist, Negativistic, Autic Mastery, Autic Sympathy, Alloic Mastery, Alloic Sympathy, Optimism, Pessimism, Arousability, and Effortfulness. (Autic and alloic items are phrased in terms of autocentric and allocentric versions of these states.) For the first 10 of these, which represent metamotivational states (or "motivational styles"), the second is subtracted from the first in each pair to produce a dominance score, and the first is added to the second to produce a salience score. This means that three kinds of overall profile are produced for each respondent: a subscale profile, a dominance profile, and a salience profile. Some examples of the items are "I like to break rules," "I like to be in control of things," and "I hate to feel unpopular."

Apter and colleagues (1998) described in detail the way in which this scale was developed, using participants in both the United Kingdom and the United States. The alpha coefficients for the subscales in the final instrument and the factor structure are satisfactory. As part of her research on sexual risk-taking (see chapter 11 in this volume), Gerkovich (1998) found highly significant correlations between seriousness dominance as measured by the MSP and the three different PDS subscales and PDS total.

A more recent derived version of this scale, the Apter Motivational Style Profile (AMSP; Apter International, 1999a, 1999b), measures just the four dominances (and their related subscales): telic–paratelic, negativistic–conformist, mastery–sympathy, and autic–alloic. For simplicity, salience scores are not included. The transactional subscales are broken down into their components, meaning that the respondent has separate scores for mastery, sympathy, autic, and alloic rather than these being combined as they are in the MSP (see above). In other words, the respondent is provided with eight subscale and four dominance scores, these being standardized in relation to a relevant population (e.g., U.K. managers) and presented in a chart form. This simpler version, which uses only 40 items, is used in workshops for personal development (see chapter 13 in this volume) in conjunction with computer-generated narrative reports. A manual is also available containing various norms (Apter International, 1999e).

STATES OVER TIME

In studying people's states over time, it is necessary to make a distinction between the internal bias that characterizes an individual with respect to a pair of states and the actual amount of time that an individual spends with one or the other of these states being active. We have already referred to the former in this chapter as dominance, and the latter we can think of as *state balance*.

All the dominance instruments described so far are intended to measure the first of these. That is, they aim to measure the bias that is currently "built in" to an individual at the time of testing. Whether this bias is actually reflected in the time spent in each state will depend not only on dominance so-defined but also on factors external to the individual. One general factor here is that of the attitudes embodied in the cultures in which the individual finds himself or herself. For example, some national cultures, and some corporate cultures, would appear to be more mastery oriented than others, which means that they tend to encourage the mastery state. Perhaps an even greater external influence, however, is that of the concrete situations in which an individual actually finds himself or herself, with their various contingencies and frustrations. In other words, the actual time spent in each state may be influenced strongly by situational context. Someone may be paratelic dominant, but they would not be likely to spend much time in the paratelic state if they were, to give an example, confined in a small prison cell. It is reasonable to assume that, in the normal way of things, state balance, especially if tested frequently over a reasonably long period and making some allowance for culture, will approximate to dominance (and this is an assumption made in many of the dominance tests) unless there is obviously something unusual about the individual's situation in life. That is to say, with all other things being equal, and if one can assume that people have a reasonable choice over the situations in which they find themselves, then state balance will give a good indication of dominance.

It is possible to assess state balance directly by getting self-reports from the individual over time by aggregating the reports from state measures actually completed in real time—a technique often referred to as *experience sampling*. Thus Apter and Larsen (1993) asked participants to respond three times a day to a "Mood and Activity Report" for 60 successive days; Walters and colleagues (1982) asked participants to respond to an index of telic or paratelic states at 15-minute intervals during their working day. As mentioned earlier in this chapter, O'Connell and Cook, in chapter 7, report on a study in which participants trying to give up smoking were prompted by a hand-held computer to respond to items appearing on a screen at predetermined times (as well as responding when they felt an urge to smoke).

It is also interesting to assess state balance within particular kinds of situation. We may think of this as *situational state balance*. So it would be possible, for instance, to ask about someone's situational state balance at work (which might be a reflection of the corporate culture of the organization in which he or she works) or his or her state balance while playing cards.

There is obviously some arbitrariness about how one defines a situation, and one has to be clear in doing this. So situational state balance with respect to recreation in general might be different in a given person from situational state balance with respect to sport as a specific form of recreation. This in turn can be different from tennis state balance or golf state balance, which might also differ from each other. If the situation is a *strong* one, then it may overwhelm any influence from dominance, but if it is *weak* then we may expect dominance to reassert itself, over time, in the context of this situation.

The psychometric exploration of the metamotivational states that, for particular individuals, enter into different specific situations, activities, or domains is starting to be taken up in reversal theory research. This exploration has been referred to as *metamotivational analysis* in Apter (1997a) and exemplified by Apter and Spirn (1997) in their study of blood donation, by Apter and Batler (1997) in their research on dangerous sport, by Kerr et al. (2000) in their study of dancing, and by O'Connell and Brooks (1997) in their work, "Resisting urges and adopting new behaviors." Likewise, Lindner and Kerr (1999, 2000, in press), referred to the analysis of *metamotivational orientation* and applied this, among other things, to the study of people's reasons for indulging in recreational sport. Various measures of the metamotives involved in different specific activities, and therefore of situational state balance, are in the course of development.

It is also useful to distinguish situational state balance from what we might call *event state balance*. By this is meant the balance of states over a particular defined occasion, for example, over a round of golf or a game of tennis. Because different forms of state and state balance have been referred to in the course of the chapter, these are summarized for the reader's convenience in Table 3.1.

As well as distinguishing dominance from state balance in its different forms, it is useful to make a conceptual distinction between two types of dominance, namely current dominance and constitutional dominance. What we have been referring to so far is *current dominance*—the bias that an individual currently possesses with respect to a pair of states. *Constitutional dominance* is in a sense a more basic level of dominance and consists of the innate biological bias that one has been born with in relation to each of

Table 3.1.
Different Forms of State Balance

Type	Focus	Timing	Example
State	Active state in the pair	Momentary	Active state at a given moment while shopping
State balance	Balance of time spent in the members of the pair	Defined continuous period of time	Actual overall time spent in the two states during the past month
Situational state balance	Balance of time spent in the members of the pair	Aggregated over iterations of the same defined situation	Actual time spent in the two states while shopping over the past month
Event state balance	Balance of time spent in the members of the pair	Defined short continuous period of time	Actual time spent in the two states on a particular shopping expedition

the pairs. (Some interesting evidence from muscle morphology to support such a built-in temperamental bias with respect to the telic and paratelic states has been provided by Braathen & Svebak, 1990; Svebak, 1990, 1999; and by Svebak et al., 1993).

How is it that current dominance may come to differ in its direction and degree of bias from constitutional dominance? This is a large question yet to be investigated in detail, but it is possible in principle to suggest a number of factors: (a) the individual may be subject to certain critical experiences (physical trauma, loss of love, unexpected good luck) that change the way that he or she sees the world, at least for a period of time (e.g., Girodo, 1985, reported that undercover agents become more telic dominant after their first experience of real undercover work); (b) there may be periods during development when one or another metamotivational state is biologically programmed to come to the fore, for example, negativism during the "terrible twos" and at adolescence (Apter, 1983); and (c) the person may acquire attitudes from their culture (mediated by family, school, and in other ways) that encourage one or another metamotivational state. The relations among these different levels of analysis are summarized in Figure 3.1.

MEASURING STRESS

Svebak (1991a, 1993) has developed a different kind of reversal theory test, the Tension and Effort Stress Indicator (TESI), designed to measure experienced stress over some specified time interval, measuring separately the two types of stress that Apter and Svebak (1989) have defined as tension-stress and effort-stress. Definitions of these contrasting types of stress are found in chapter 6 of the present volume, but basically, *tension-stress* is the feeling of not being where one wants to be on a dimension (like felt arousal), whereas *effort-stress* is the feeling that comes with exerting effort to overcome tension-stress. The TESI measures both forms of stress in relation to all the eight metamotivational states. This indicator has now been used in a variety of investigations (e.g., Svebak, 1997; Svebak, Mykletun, & Bru, 1997). A fuller documentation of this instrument and its use are found in chapter 6 of this volume. We can also note in passing that, although this was not its original intended use, the TESI has been used as a state indicator (Kerr & Svebak, 1994; Males, 1999; Males & Kerr, 1996; Wilson, 1999; Wilson & Kerr, 1999). There is a problem here, which is that as part of the test the participant has to rate emotions on all eight dimensions even though, at a given moment, reversal theory suggests that only half of these will be active. However, if we see such a usage as really about event state balance rather

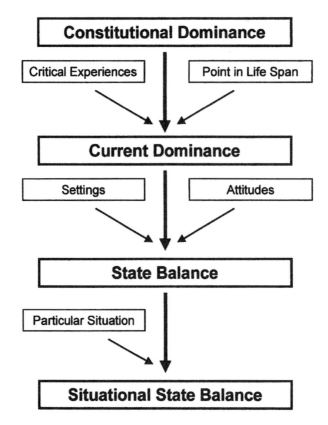

Figure 3.1. Types of dominance and state balance.
Note. Constitutional dominance represents the innate bias that a person is born with, and current dominance represents that person's actual bias at a given time. State balance is the time actually spent in different states, and situational state balance is the time actually spent in different states in a particular kind of situation.

than about state in the strict sense, then this use of the TESI is a meaningful and useful one. The measure itself can be found in Svebak (1991a, 1993).

Wendel (1999), in conjunction with Popkess-Vawter (1998), has developed another approach to tension-stress, the Tension Stress Scale, which is a state measure of tension. Participants respond in two stages. In the first stage, they identify which state from each pair is the operative one by choosing a box containing a list of descriptors. For example, the box representing the negativism state includes sticking up for what I think, bending/breaking rules, angry, stubborn, rebellious/defiant, wanting to be difficult, doing my own thing. At the second stage, for each of the states selected in this way, the respondent indicates the degree of tension being experienced in relation to that state by indicating his or her (a) actual and (b) desired position on a set of 10-point scales representing different ways of experiencing the state. (In the case of the negativistic state, these dimensions are trapped–free, held back–released, caught–liberated, and restricted–unrestricted.) The average discrepancy between the desired and actual ratings over these scales provides an indication of the degree of stress being felt by the respondent in relation to the state concerned, and an overall indication of stress can in principle be provided by averaging over the discrepancies of all four of the active states. The instrument has been found to have satisfactory alpha coefficients and has been validated by testing in real-life situations. It has been used by Wendel (1999) to investigate dieting problems in obese individuals.

CONCLUSION

It is to be hoped that out of this profusion of scales a few will emerge in the future as standard instruments. At the same time, other kinds of tests will need to be developed to test the full range of reversal theory ideas or to use reversal theory in ways that are of practical benefit. Tests that need to be developed include (a) tests of *lability*—the relative frequency with which different individuals reverse between states, (b) tests of how sensitive and aware people are with respect to their states and emotions, (c) tests of the levels of the emotional and feeling variables that will satisfy people in each of the states, (d) tests of the degree to which different activities can substitute for each other within a state (which Loonis, 1999c, has called *vicariance*), (e) tests of the factors that tend to induce different states, (f) tests of the strategies that people tend to use within states and of the skill with which they pursue these strategies, and (g) tests that will identify which states tend to go together in different people and whether there are typical sequences of states and state combinations in different people. The study of the way in which people interact, in small groups (families, teams, offices) or large organizations, will also depend on the further development of psychometric instruments, and one or two of these are documented in chapter 13 of this volume.

The problems involved in developing state, dominance, and other kinds of measures have been emphasized in this chapter. But it is only by recognizing and confronting such difficulties, which are not unique to reversal theory, that we can hope to make real progress. A more detailed examination of some of the problems of developing tests, especially state tests, can be found in Apter (1999b). Meanwhile, it can be said that a set of adequate and useable instruments and techniques, both qualitative and quantitative (as emphasized by Kerr, 1999a; see also chapter 10 in this volume), has been developed and is available for those who wish to pursue reversal theory research. The ways in which these instruments have already been put to use will become evident from the chapters in the rest of this book. A summary of the main measures that have been discussed here is found in Table 3.2.

Table 3.2.
Reversal Theory Measures for the Individual

Title	Type of Test	Domains Involved
Telic State Measure (TSM)	State, Tension	Telic–Paratelic
Somatic State Questionnaire (SSQ)	State	Somatic
Telic/Paratelic State Instrument (T/PSI)	State	Telic–Paratelic
State of Mind Indicator for Athletes (SOMIFA)	State, Tension (in sport)	All domains
Negativism State Measure (NSM)	State	Negativism–Conformity
Autic Mastery–Sympathy State Measure (AuMSSM)	State	Mastery–Sympathy
Metamotivational State Coding Schedule (MSCS)	State	All domains
Telic Dominance Scale (TDS)	Dominance	Telic–Paratelic
Paratelic Dominance Scale (PDS)	Dominance	Telic–Paratelic
Nijmegen Telic Dominance Scale (N–TDS)	Dominance (in children)	Telic–Paratelic
Negativism Dominance Scale (NDS)	Dominance	Negativism–Conformity
Motivational Style Profile (MSP)	Dominance, Salience	All domains (and some other variables)
Apter Motivational Style Profile (AMSP)	Dominance	All domains
Tension and Effort Stress Inventory (TESI)	Stress	All domains
Tension Stress Scale (TSS)	Stress	All domains

4

BASIC RESEARCH ON REVERSAL THEORY

MICHAEL J. APTER AND KEN HESKIN

Many of the studies to be documented in later chapters of this book concern the testing of hypotheses in different research areas, such as smoking cessation, sexual risk-taking, and gambling, where the primary interest is in the research area rather than in reversal theory as such. In these cases reversal theory is used as a tool: It provides a way of explaining the phenomena, some distinctive questions to be asked, a useful structure for framing the hypotheses, and convenient psychometric instruments that can be brought to bear. On the whole, as will be seen, the evidence that has been generated in this kind of research has produced meaningful outcomes that are consistent with reversal theory, and therefore such studies indirectly support the theory. At the very least it could be said that they provide a kind of pragmatic validity in the sense that the theory leads to interesting, useful, and meaningful findings. In other words, reversal theory is a tool that seems to function well for research purposes. (In terms of the hierarchy described in chapter 2, most of these studies are at levels 4 and 5, i.e., the levels of derived hypotheses and conceptual framework.)

However, some research studies are more basic than this in that they do directly address and test some of the fundamental propositions that make up the core structure of the theory and its associated concepts (levels 2 and 3 of the hierarchy as laid out in chapter 2). In many of these cases, the primary concern of the researcher was to test the theory directly; in other cases, this was one of the effects of the research, even if this was not its sole objective. The aim of this chapter is to highlight and review research that deals directly with these foundations of reversal theory. In some cases the research is described here, in others we shall point to the chapter in which the research in question is documented in more detail. For convenience we can group this research under four main headings.

As we have seen, one of the pivotal ideas of reversal theory is that people are inconsistent over time, reversing from time to time between opposite metamotivational states. Walters, Apter, and Svebak (1982) reported the earliest direct study of this dynamic. They used the medium of color preference to gauge arousal preference among participants. The basic premise of the study (based on previous research documented in the paper) was that colors have an influence on arousal and that long-wavelength colors such as red, orange, and yellow tend to have an arousing effect, whereas short-wavelength colors such as blue, indigo, and violet are more relaxing, with greenish colors being relatively neutral. The idea was that if a participant indicates a preference for a long-wavelength color at a particular time, then he or she is likely to be in the arousal-seeking (i.e., paratelic) state, whereas if the participant prefers a short wavelength color, then he or she is likely to be in the arousal-avoiding (i.e., telic) state. The researchers used this association to map arousal preference changes among 75 office workers during their normal working day. Specifically, they asked workers individually, at intervals of either 15 or 30 minutes, to choose the color they liked best from a standard set of seven colors selected from across the spectrum. Testing lasted between 1 day and 8 days. The results were very much in line with reversal theory predictions. People tended to fluctuate in their choices rather than exhibit stability, and they chose between the opposite ends of the color spectrum rather than a neutral (usually green) position. This showed both that high and low arousal can be attractive and that change from one preference to the other can occur with some frequency. A generally bimodal pattern of color preferences emerged both for individuals and subgroups, which is consistent with reversal theory's postulated dual arousal system. (There was also high interpersonal agreement during post-testing on the arousal value of each of the colors, and this was broadly consistent with the study's basic premises.)

In a second study reported in the same paper by Walters et al., 41 participants at work were asked not only to state their color preference at 15-minute intervals, but also to complete an adjective checklist indicating whether they were feeling: (a) playful or serious; (b) spontaneous or planning ahead; and (c) bored, excited, anxious, or relaxed. In respect of participants indicating a choice between bored, excited, anxious, or relaxed, the authors were able to test directly the assumption that color preference and arousal-seeking or arousal-avoiding were systematically related. It was indicated in the first two chapters that these four emotion terms characterize high and low arousal as experienced in the arousal-seeking and arousal-avoiding states in reversal theory's characterization of the relationship between felt arousal and hedonic tone. These emotion terms therefore locate individuals both in terms of which arousal preference state they are currently occupying and also whether or not they are actually experiencing the level of arousal corresponding to their preference. Thus, for example, an individual checking "bored" would be in the arousal-seeking state but not experiencing a sufficiently high level of arousal. (Figure 2.2 in chapter 2 shows these relationships clearly.) By checking one of the playful–serious options and one of the spontaneous–planning ahead options, the individuals are indicating their occupancy of either a telic (serious, planning ahead) or paratelic (playful, spontaneous) motivational state of mind.

The results of the second study produced the same pattern of fluctuations (reversals) between high and low arousal preference, and the same bimodality, as the first study. Furthermore, the data very clearly indicated in all analyses that calming colors tended to be strongly associated with telic adjectives and arousing colors with paratelic adjectives, as one would predict from reversal theory. It was significant in terms of the construct validity of the telic–paratelic distinction that the preponderance of responses from participants indicated a telic state during the study, as one would expect from individuals in the work situation. It was also of interest that participants differed in terms both of their balance between telic and paratelic states and in terms of their frequency of reversal between states (lability). This can be seen from Figure 4.1, which shows the data from two participants who contrast in both state balance and lability.

The Walters et al. studies, conducted within the normal context of adult life rather than in the laboratory, and with working adults rather than with students, are remarkable in the consistency and force with which they support key reversal theory concepts and undermine the tenets of optimal arousal theory (as described in the introductory chapter). Analyses across participants, within participants, and across studies support reversal theory in observations with high ecological validity.

Although reversal theory studies may, in general, be said to have pushed the temporal boundaries of observation in psychological research, the study by Apter and Larsen (1993) stands out within reversal theory research for the duration of observation involved. In this study, 43 undergraduates completed a "Mood and Activity Report" 3 times a day for 60 consecutive days—at noon to summarize their mood and activity that morning, at 6:00 p.m. to summarize their mood and activity that afternoon, and at bedtime to summarize their mood and activity during the evening. The questions covered mood, physiological stimuli (how hungry, pressured, etc.), medical and psychiatric symptomatology, and personal activities. The aim of the study was to create a data set of high ecological validity relating to patterns of change in people's lives and to do this by directly assessing state dominance via the actual reported frequency of states (state balance) assessed over short, successive periods of time. The aim was also to relate these

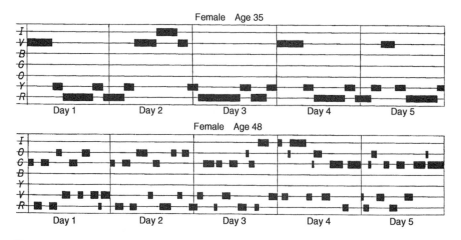

Figure 4.1. Changing color preference data from two representative participants, who were tested every quarter of an hour over five working days.
Note. The horizontal bars represent time spent with each color as the preferred color. The rank position of the colors on the vertical dimension represents their arousal value as estimated by each participant, the least rousing color being at the top and the most rousing color at the bottom. By inference from color preference, it can be seen that arousal preferences tended to reverse over time. I = indigo, V = violet, B = blue, G = green, O = orange, Y = yellow, R = red.
From "Color Preference, Arousal and the Theory of Psychological Reversals," by J. Walters, M. J. Apter, and S. Svebak, 1982, *Motivation and Emotion, 6,* p. 203. Copyright 1982 by Kluwer Academic/Plenum Publishers, New York. Reprinted with permission.

assessments to real-life events in participants' lives and to relate a wide range of personality characteristics measured by conventional questionnaires.

The data were analyzed in various ways, but from the perspective of the present issue, that of individual change over time, the most relevant analysis was that of individual participants over time. This revealed patterns of change within individual participants very much in line with reversal theory's structural characterization of the inconsistency inherent within us all. Differences across participants in the frequency of reversal (lability), the balance of time in one state as opposed to its opposite (state balance), and ways of behaving in particular states were all evident in the data. The analysis of the individual over time may be said to be the heart of reversal theory, and the data illustrate very clearly and elegantly the reversal process in action in the everyday life of individual participants, as is shown in Figure 4.2. We can also note in passing that a within-subject analysis over all participants showed a significant relationship between arousal-seeking/ arousal-avoidance measures and the telic–paratelic measures, as predicted by reversal theory.

Some of the results of the Apter and Larsen study show outcomes that reversal theory would not have predicted, such as a relationship between

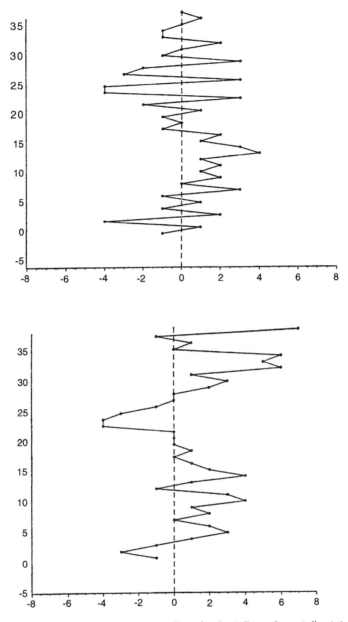

Figure 4.2. The two graphs represent readings for the telic and paratelic state variable for two single participants, corresponding to 37 sequential ratings for each participant. *Note.* The chronological sequence goes from bottom to top on the vertical axis in each case. The horizontal axis represents telic values as positive and paratelic values as negative.

From *Advances in Reversal Theory* (p. 114), by J. H. Kerr, S. Murgatroyd, and M. J. Apters (Eds.), 1993, Amsterdam: Swets & Zeitlinger. Copyright 1993 by Swets & Zeitlinger. Adapted with permission.

paratelic states and positive moods. It is also true that some of the correlations in the study might comfortably have been higher, but this is probably an artefact of the design and the protracted periods (5–6 hours) covered by the participants' reports, when many varied activities occurred and participants may have reversed between states a number of times. The averaging effect would then inevitably have reduced the correlations between variables compared to what would have emerged on a more fine-grain analysis with shorter reporting times (e.g., every quarter of an hour). The Apter and Larsen research does demonstrate, however, the importance of studying people over extended time periods in order to subject theoretical ideas to the rigors of ecologically meaningful analysis. Reversal theory emerges from this severe test creditably well, although future time-extended studies will probably need to sacrifice duration against the desirability of shorter reporting timeframes for participants.

Many studies using repeated measurements of state over a shorter period of time have demonstrated reversal. An example would be Pilon (1998), who found that reversal took place in some participants over the short period of a 30-minute trial (a mock clinical diagnosis situation). Many examples will be found in studies of sports, for which the reader is referred to chapter 10 in this volume; these studies involved observation of players over the course of sporting events (e.g., Purcell, 1999a).

In addition to these studies that directly track people over time, many studies imply change in everyday life in the sense that when the same people are asked about different situations or different specified moments, they report different metamotivational states and state combinations. For instance, Wendel (1999), in developing the Tension Stress Scale, tested the items in three different settings—a social gathering, summer and fall enrollment at a college, and nursing students before taking a major examination—and she found telic–paratelic differences. Likewise, the work by Cook, O'Connell, Gerkovich, and others in Kansas City on smoking cessation (to be reported in detail in chapter 7) shows that individuals display different metamotivational states (selected from all eight states) at different times and under different circumstances.

In fact, although a great deal of research, to be reported later in this book, has been carried out in this way on the pair of metamotivational states that were identified first in reversal theory—the telic–paratelic pair—there is an increasing amount of attention being given to other pairs of states. An example of this kind of research is that of Rhys (1988), who has applied reversal theory to the experience of nurses as they interacted with patients, specifically nurses working with dying patients in Continuing Care Units (CCUs) or hospices. Using semistructured interviews, Rhys talked to 41 CCU nurses about their work. The results indicated that the bulk of nurses' work experience concerns the autic–mastery state combination and the alloic–sympathy combination. Autic–mastery is associated with the traditional role of the nurse, competent in the administration of drugs and the practical aspects of patient management, with the nurse controlling and the patient complying. It was evident from the nurses' interview responses that many derived considerable pleasure from the application of their skills in this way. Alloic–sympathy involved nurses deriving pleasure from devoting attention to the personal care of the patient and seeing that attention have a positive effect. (The study revealed, incidentally, that this was often the most rewarding aspect of nursing for some nurses but is sometimes fraught with difficulty because of insufficient time to devote to any one individual.) It can be inferred that nurses reverse between the autic and alloic and between the mastery and sympathy states in the course of their work.

REVERSALS ARE INDUCED IN THREE WAYS

According to reversal theory, as we have seen in earlier chapters, reversals may be brought about in three main ways: (a) external events and situations, which we refer to as *contingencies*; (b) frustration; and (c) satiation. In the following studies, participants were observed undergoing the reversal process.

Contingency

Contingency reversal is seen in many of the studies to be reported in later chapters in which metamotivational states are induced by means of experimenter manipulations. For example, in Svebak's psychophysiological work (see chapter 5), the telic state was induced in some studies by means of the threat of an electric shock for poor performance and the paratelic state by means of exposure to a comedy film. The outcome of these laboratory studies demonstrates clearly the existence of contingent reversals.

Contingent reversals have also been observed in real-life settings. For example, Apter and Batler (1997) carried out a questionnaire study of the "gratuitous risk" involved in sport parachuting. Participants were 61 members of parachuting clubs. As part of the questionnaire, members were asked to specify what they experienced as the moment of maximum danger. For the majority of participants, this was identified as occurring at some point during the period of time between jumping from the aircraft and the parachute opening. The questionnaire also presented them with a line representing time in minutes over the course of the activity, with their personal moment of experienced maximum danger shown as a point at the center of the line. They were asked to indicate on this line the point at which they felt maximum anxiety and also the point at which they felt maximum excitement. The pattern of responses is shown in Figures 4.3 and 4.4. It shows that for the majority of participants, the moment of maximum anxiety was just before the moment of maximum danger, and the moment of maximum excitement was the moment just after the moment of maximum danger. In fact, the most common pattern in individual parachutists was for anxiety to build up to a peak just before the parachute opened and then excitement to be experienced at its strongest immediately or shortly thereafter. The conclusion seems unavoidable that a reversal occurs as danger turns to safety, this reversal resulting in high arousal being experienced as highly pleasant instead of as highly unpleasant. In other words, we see a contingent telic-to-paratelic reversal. A similar pattern has been reported by Kerr, Kawaguchi, Oiwa, Terayama, and Zukawa (2000) for dancers, where "curtain up" represents the moment of maximum threat.

Males (1999), who investigated the experience of slalom canoeing, gives us another study that documents contingent reversals occurring in real-life settings. Reading the interview transcripts that he provided and the reversal theory interpretation that he added, it is possible to follow the reversals that occur in response to the changing challenges that confront the athletes in this situation. (In fact, these transcripts bring the theory to life in a colorful and realistic way and would make an excellent introduction

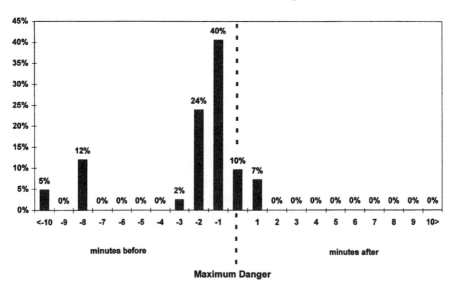

Figure 4.3. The percentage of parachutists reporting the moment at which they felt most anxious before or after the moment of perceived maximum danger.
Note. From *Stress and Health: A Reversal Theory* (p. 127), by S. Svebak and M. J. Apter (Eds.), 1997, Washington, DC: Taylor & Francis. Copyright 1997 by Taylor & Francis. Reprinted with permission.

Moment of Maximum Excitement

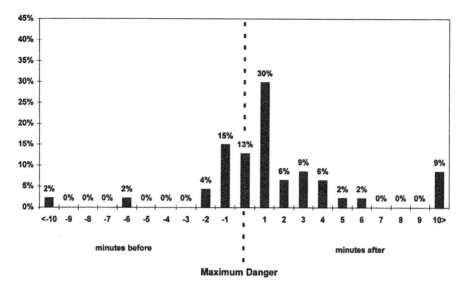

Figure 4.4. The percentage of parachutists reporting the moment at which they felt most excited before or after the moment of perceived maximum danger.
Note. From *Stress and Health: A Reversal Theory* (p. 127), by S. Svebak and M. J. Apter (Eds.), 1997, Washington, DC: Taylor & Francis. Copyright 1997 by Taylor & Francis. Reprinted with permission.

to the theory.) Interestingly, Males also provided evidence that some athletes are able to control their states by, for example, changing their settings immediately before the event in which they are to take part. This is consistent with the reversal theory postulate that, although reversals are involuntary, they may be brought under indirect voluntary control.

Tacon and Kerr (1999) and Kerr and Tacon (1999) also showed that different locations could induce contingent reversals (or serve to maintain ongoing states). Students entering one of four locations were asked to complete the Telic State Measure (TSM). Two of these settings, the university library and a lecture theatre just prior to a lecture, were hypothesized to be telic locations. The other two settings, the university sports center and a party at the students union building, were taken to be paratelic locations. The results strongly supported this relationship. Kerr and Tacon (2000) showed something similar.

Frustration

Barr, McDermott, and Evans (1993) used a children's puzzle for their study because it could be experienced in the telic state as a task and in the paratelic state as a game. The puzzle was presented as being extremely difficult to solve (which it was) so that frustration was likely, and participants were instructed to spend as much or as little time on the task as they pleased, being allowed to stop at any time for any reason. There were a number of hypotheses, but the key hypothesis for present purposes was that the frustration involved would cause participants to undergo a reversal from their original state (whether telic or paratelic) during the trial.

Thirty nonpsychology students participated in the study (15 men and 15 women), and trials were undertaken in the participants' own homes. Participants completed a modified version of the TSM before and at the completion of the task. At the end, they also reported on their boredom, frustration, and interest levels on 4-point Likert scales and were interviewed about their impressions and thoughts concerning the activity and their approach to it. Six of the participants actually completed the puzzle success- fully against the odds of 300,000 to 1 claimed by the manufacturer of actually doing so. This level of success was unexpected, as the experimenters really wished to focus on the frustrating effects of failure in the activity. As a result, these participants were dropped from the main analysis, leaving the remaining 24 who failed to solve the puzzle.

The majority of participants (19) reversed on before-and-after measures using the TSM. Ten participants began the activity in the paratelic state and finished in the telic state, 9 began telic and finished paratelic, 2 started and finished in the telic, and 3 started and finished in the paratelic. Fisher's exact probability analysis showed that this outcome was statistically signifi- cant and provided strong support for the hypothesis that participants would, under these conditions of frustration, reverse during the trial.

In general, those participants who started in the paratelic state reported significantly more boredom than frustration at the end, whereas the converse was true for those who started in the telic state. In other words, frustration in the telic state was reported as such, whereas it took the form of boredom (frustration in achieving excitement) in the paratelic state. Of even greater interest was the finding that participants who began in the paratelic state spent more than twice as long on the task as those who began in a telic state. The mean persistence time for paratelic starters was 42 minutes compared to 20 minutes for telic starters, and the difference was statistically significant.

Reversal theory puts an emphasis on wanted or preferred arousal as opposed to actual arousal, and preferred arousal was measured among the participants by means of the TSM. Theoretically, the telic state involves low preferred arousal, and the paratelic state involves high preferred arousal. Barr et al. investigated the pattern of preferred arousal in the two reversing groups and found a statistically significant pattern exactly as the theory would predict. Those participants who started in the paratelic state had a mean arousal-seeking score at the start that was significantly higher than those starting in the telic state. After reversal, however, they finished the task with a mean arousal-seeking score significantly lower than for the other group of participants who had by the end reversed to the paratelic state.

Evidence for frustration causing reversal in real-life settings comes from the work of Purcell (1999a, 1999b), who argued that the spoken monologues that he collected from golfers during play displayed examples of frustration leading to reversal—these reversals being mainly from the conformist to the negativistic state.

Satiation

As we have seen, one of reversal theory's most distinctive tenets is that people are in some sense fundamentally inconsistent. In particular, the idea that for no particular reason other than satiation, with simply being in one state for a period of time, metamotivational reversal will occur, is a unique reversal theory proposition. Reversal theory departs most radically from either dispositional or situational approaches to personality in its claim that reversals will sometimes occur without situational triggers to provoke them and despite, perhaps, an individual's dominance in the original state. Lafreniere, Cowles, and Apter (1988) investigated the phenomenon of spontaneous reversal in an empirical, well-controlled, and replicable laboratory setting to better understand the reversal process itself, particularly satiation-induced or spontaneous reversal.

In this study, a stratified sample of 36 students drawn from a larger sample of 311 Canadian psychology students was involved. The larger group had completed the Telic Dominance Scale (TDS; Murgatroyd, Rushton, Apter, & Ray, 1978), and the subsample consisted of an extreme telic-dominant group ($n = 10$), an extreme paratelic-dominant group ($n = 10$), and an intermediate group ($n = 16$). Participants were observed for periods of 2 hours, in a comfortable room. The "cover story" was that they were there to evaluate different kinds of computer programs.

Participants in the study were given access to two kinds of program, namely video games and statistics teaching programs. They were advised that they could choose any kind of material to use on the computer for any length of time and change programs at any time or stay with the same one if they wanted to. The basic assumption of the study was that psychology students in the telic state would want to work on the statistics programs, whereas those in the paratelic state would choose video games. Pilot work had indicated that these two types of materials were indeed experienced in these ways, and the participants were asked to complete the TSM for each of the two kinds of programs at the end of their 2-hour involvement to confirm their expected experiential mode.

To ensure that reversals were not inferred erroneously (where an individual found a particular program unsatisfactory or simply wanted a change of material), participants were supplied with a number of alternatives for each type of material. In addition, to make sure that satiation-induced reversals were not inferred where participants became frustrated or simply made a voluntary decision to try to change state (both theoretical possibilities), questionnaires completed by the participants at the conclusion of the study required them to identify their reasons for changing types of computer program. Interviews were also conducted with each participant on completion of the questionnaire to further investigate the reasons for the actual reversals that were inferred from observations.

The data indicated that the basic premises guiding the design of the study were sound. Poststudy, 29 of the 36 participants reported that they had been in the telic state when working on statistics and in the paratelic state when playing video games, and the statistical analysis of results was based on these 29. Telic dominance was not found to be a confounding factor, because evaluations of the games and statistics programs were not significantly correlated with dominance.

Lafreniere et al. (1988) hypothesized that spontaneous reversals would occur, including satiation-induced reversals. The results showed that over the 2-hour period, approximately three reversals per participant occurred on average. The fact that a few participants showed no reversal at all indicated that reversal was not somehow an artefact of the situation itself. Furthermore, a proportion of the reversals observed were clearly satiation-induced as indicated by the participants' descriptions of the event (during poststudy interview) as occurring "for no obvious reason." This conclusion was reinforced by the fact that satiation-induced reversals increased proportionately over the 2-hour period of observation, as one would expect from a satiation-driven phenomenon. Finally, as also hypothesized, the total amount of time spent on each type of material was related to dominance in the way that reversal theory would predict, with paratelic-dominant individuals spending longer periods of time playing the video games, and telic-dominant individuals spending longer working on statistics programs.

Lafreniere et al. pointed out that there are some important implications of their study for psychological research methodology in general. Specifically, the generally short duration of many psychology experiments may exclude the emergence of important psychological phenomena, such as satiation-induced effects. Conversely, when longer studies are involved, the premise that individuals can act as their own controls (within-subject design) is problematical, because they may change in significant ways in the course of observation. Similarly, assumptions about participants' uniform experience as they interact with experimental tasks are also problematic and need to be checked in poststudy investigations. The lessons from this study support the basic premises of reversal theory and highlight the fundamental importance of taking into account individual inconsistency in an understanding of human experience and motivation. In this respect, reversal theory challenges conventional assumptions about the nature of personality.

Frey (1990) observed 20 participants reading over a period of 2½ hours. They had available to them six types of reading materials that had been previously evaluated by 18 independent judges to be either of the kind that one would like to read in the telic state or the kind that one would like to read in the paratelic state. Three types of reading materials were of the first kind and three of the second. Participants could read from any of the materials for any period of time that they liked, provided only that they did nothing but read for the 2½ hours. Participants were also asked to report on their arousal preferences at 6-minute intervals throughout the whole period. Frey found that participants did indeed switch from time to time between telic and paratelic types of reading materials, even though there was no external prompt or reason to do so, and they also reported different levels of preferred arousal. In fact, the levels of preferred arousal largely corresponded with the type of reading material chosen at the time, lower levels of arousal preference being associated with the telic state.

IT IS POSSIBLE TO BE IN A STATE THAT IS OPPOSITE TO ONE'S DOMINANCE

Although individuals may be dominated by one state in each pair of metamotivational states, they will normally be expected to spend at least some periods of time in the opposing nondominant state (unless they have certain types of mental illness, as is discussed in chapter 14). In other words, everyone is normally subject to reversals and to intra-individual change with respect to a pair of states, even if they are strongly dominated by one state in that pair; it is this notion of the dynamic nature of human experience that distinguishes reversal theory from any kind of trait theory. We have already seen some evidence for this in studies reported above in which participants were seen to reverse whatever their dominance level appears to be. We also saw the study by Lafreniere et al. on the phenomenon of satiation, in which most participants spent time in both the telic and paratelic states, whatever their dominance.

An unusual example of this phenomenon comes from a study by Weinberg (1998) of athletes taking part in the Western States 100-Mile Endurance Run, an "ultra run" that takes place annually in California. Among other questionnaires that she administered to 166 participants were the Motivational Style Profile (MSP) and the State of Mind Indicator for Athletes (SOMIFA). She found that the hypothesis of a relationship between the two kinds of measure—one a dominance measure and the other a state measure—could not be supported. This means that many of the athletes were competing in a state of mind different from their dominant state of mind, across all four pairs of states.

Likewise, in the context of sports, Young (1998) carried out a study of "flow" experiences (experiences involving total absorption in the task) in 31 Australian women who were professional tennis players. Interestingly, she found that these experiences, when they occurred, could be categorized as either telic or paratelic. What is perhaps even more interesting, in terms of the present argument, is that she found no relationship between telic dominance (as measured by the Paratelic Dominance Scale; PDS; Cook & Gerkovich, 1993) and the type of flow, telic or paratelic, experienced. In other words, many players were reporting experiences during play that represented a state different from their direction of dominance.

Svebak and Apter (1987), in a laboratory study on laughter, found not only that it was possible to induce the paratelic state (as measured by the TSM; Svebak & Murgatroyd, 1985) by means of exposure to a comedy film, but that it was perfectly possible to do this with participants who were strongly telic dominant, consisting of the top 10 scorers from a group of 116 students, as measured by the TDS (Murgatroyd et al., 1978). In fact 9 of these 10 individuals reversed to the paratelic state in response to the experimental manipulation. It was also found, consistent with reversal theory, that for all participants in the paratelic state, the frequency of the laughter response, indicating the degree of positive hedonic tone, was positively correlated with felt arousal. Furthermore, this was just as true of the telic-dominant participants in the paratelic state as it was for the paratelic-dominant participants in the paratelic state.

Apter and Svebak (1986), in an experimental study of the effect of metamotivational state on electromyographic (EMG) gradients, found that although they were comparing groups of telic- and paratelic-dominant participants, some of the participants were in a metamotivational state during the experiment that did not match their dominance group. This was an extreme groups design, in which only the highest scoring participants on the TDS were included in the telic extreme group, and only the lowest scoring participants in the paratelic extreme group. In other words, some extreme telic participants were in the paratelic state during the experiment, and vice versa. In this study, state of mind during the experiment was ascertained by a detailed interview after the experiment, carried out by an interviewer who was blind to the participants' TDS scores and their performance during the experiment (for further details, see chapter 5 in this volume). Particularly interesting here was the fact that clear differences in EMG gradients emerged when the ongoing state during the experiment was used as the criterion rather than dominance, even extreme dominance. The authors pointed out that if the analysis had been carried out in the traditional way of comparing people with different scores on a personality variable, nothing would have been found: The effect was state dependent and not an effect of more enduring characteristics. And of course the idea of people being in a state opposite to their "personality," as was found here, would be difficult to explain by mainstream dispositional (i.e., trait) theorists.

Lafreniere (1997) administered a state test, the Somatic State Questionnaire (SSQ; Cook, Gerkovich, Potocky, & O'Connell, 1993), to student participants who were about to take a package of tests, including the PDS, that measured dominance. Although a significant association was found between dominance and ongoing state, as measured in these ways, there were also substantial switchovers, with 22% of telic-dominant participants being in the paratelic state and 10% of the paratelic-dominant participants being in the telic state. (Dominance here was determined by being in the top, middle, and bottom third of scorers on the dominance scale.) The data in this respect are shown in Figure 4.5. Again this shows that dominance may influence the likelihood of being in a given state at a given time but that people are able to switch to the state opposite to their dominant state. (Note that, for this reason, we would not expect dominance scales to predict state at any given moment with great accuracy but that we would still expect

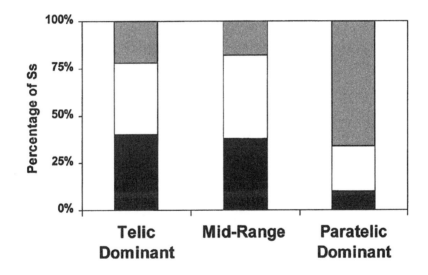

■ Telic Mode □ Mid-Range Mode ▨ Paratelic Mode

Figure 4.5. The relationship between metamotivational mode and dominance in a study of students.
Note. From *Stress and Health: A Reversal Theory* (p. 42), by S. Svebak and M. J. Apter (Eds.), 1997, Washington, DC: Taylor & Francis. Copyright 1997 by Taylor & Francis. Reprinted with permission.

dominance scales to predict the most prevalent states for a given individual over a reasonable period of time.)

An interesting, possible complication that arises from all this is that people who are telic dominant and people who are paratelic dominant might, in some respects, experience the telic and paratelic states differently. Spicer and Lyons' (1997) study on cardiovascular reactivity exemplifies the possibility for future research into this area. One of their principal findings was that the greatest increase in diastolic blood pressure during experimental sessions (3–6 minutes of conversation) occurred in participants who were telic dominant but in the paratelic mode at the time (as measured by the TDS and the TSM, respectively). They suggested that such dominance/state "misfits" deserve further investigation.

AROUSAL SYSTEMS ARE BISTABLE, NOT HOMEOSTATIC

According to reversal theory, as was explained in earlier chapters, there are two arousal preference systems, with the individual reversing from one to the other over time. (We have also seen that one of these is associated with the telic and the other with the paratelic state.) In this respect, the predictions of reversal theory are clearly different from those of optimal arousal theory and indeed from those of any kind of homeostatic motivational theory (which includes nearly every theory of motivation). We have already seen, earlier in this chapter, some convincing evidence for the idea of swings between arousal-seeking and arousal-avoidance as shown in the work of Walters and colleagues (1982). A more dramatic and focused study of reversal itself is that of Apter and Batler (1997) on the experience of parachuting, cited earlier in the chapter. It will be recalled that this study showed that before the moment of maximum danger, most participants reported experiencing anxiety; after that moment, when the danger has been overcome (the parachute has opened), most participants reported experiencing excitement. This implies that they experienced the same high arousal, in quick succession, in opposite ways. First it was extremely unpleasant, and then, after the reversal had occurred, it was experienced as highly pleasant.

Apter (1976) wrote the earliest journal article flagging the subsequent campaign against traditional notions of arousal and motivation. This was a small but seminal study whose aim was to test the validity of the notion that organisms typically experienced optimal arousal at intermediate levels (Hebb, 1955).

Apter simply asked a sample of 67 British undergraduate psychology students to rate 50 varied situations on 7-point scales for the degree of felt arousal that the situations induced and the degree of pleasantness or unpleasantness experienced (hedonic tone). The study revealed that the most experientially pleasant situations (situations averaging greater than 5 on the 7-point scale of affective tone) were more or less equally distributed across the 7-point range of the arousal scale. Some very pleasant situations were associated with very high levels of felt arousal (e.g., "arriving on holiday in a foreign country"), some with very low levels of felt arousal (e.g., "relaxing after a hard day's work") and some with intermediate levels (e.g., "going for a walk").

As Apter pointed out, these data are inconsistent with the idea of a single, intermediate optimal level of arousal. They are also inconsistent with elaborations of this basic idea, such as those proposed by Fiske and Maddi (1961), suggesting that the optimal level of arousal may vary, for instance, with what is required in the nature of the task. Apter's results showed, for example, that a task invariably judged to be highly arousing and in which high arousal would appear to be useful and appropriate to the organism (e.g., avoiding an accident) was rated as very unpleasant. The results clearly indicated the need to reconsider conventional homeostatic explanations of arousal and motivation and to contemplate alternative concepts of the kind offered by reversal theory whose theoretical explanations appear to be better aligned in this respect with the complexities of human motivational data.

One of the hypotheses tested by Pilon (1998) was that individuals in the telic state would experience a negative relationship between arousal and hedonic tone, and those in a paratelic state would experience a positive relationship. His participants were 113 Canadian psychology students taking part in an experiment on the effects of ambiguity. Their task, presented by computer, was to make mock clinical diagnoses on the basis of information presented to them, which varied in difficulty and ambiguity. Telic dominance was measured using the PDS, metamotivational state by the Telic/Paratelic State Instrument (Calhoun, 1995), hedonic tone by five 6-point bipolar items, and felt arousal by a 6-point Likert-type item. The hypothesis was tested by a standard multiple regression analysis using hedonic tone as the criterion variable, predictor variables being metamotivational state, self-reported arousal, and the interaction of the two variables. The hypothesis was confirmed. Figure 4.6 provides a visual representation of the interaction, in which the data has been divided into two groups on metamotivational state by means of a median split, each group then being subjected to a multiple regression procedure giving rise to a regression line on the graph. This shows strikingly the inverse relationship of arousal and hedonic tone for the two states—the classic "crossover" of reversal theory. Interestingly, and in line with reversal theory, this relationship did not occur where telic dominance was used in place of telic state to predict the relationship at a given moment.

However, where telic dominance is used to predict a more general relationship between arousal and hedonic tone over time, we see essentially

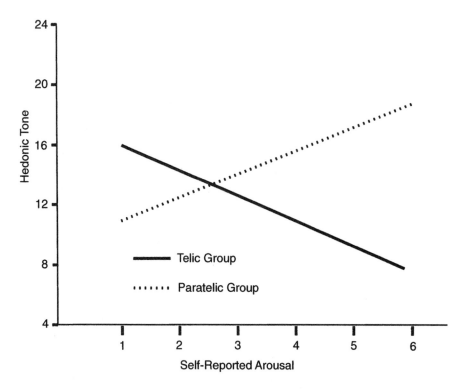

Figure 4.6. Interaction effect of metamotivational state and felt arousal on hedonic tone.

Note. From *Reactions to Arousal and Ambiguity: An Application of Reversal Theory* (p. 57), by P. Pilon, 1998, Windsor, Ontario, Canada: University of Windsor. Copyright 1998 by the University of Windsor. Reprinted with permission.

the same pattern. Martin, Kuiper, Olinger, and Dobbin (1987) showed that for telic-dominant people, the higher the stress reported over time (and therefore presumably the higher the arousal over time), the more unpleasant the feelings, whereas for paratelic-dominant people the reverse is the case, at least up to a certain level of stress. This study is strongly supportive of reversal theory in this respect, again showing the crossover effect. This and related studies are described in more detail in chapter 6.

Frey (1990), in the study mentioned earlier, looked at the distribution of arousal preferences that participants reported during the 2 1/2 hours that they were observed reading. Because there is no statistical test of bimodality, it is not possible to provide statistical support, but Frey found that the distributions he obtained were not normal in almost all cases, and many of them had a bimodal appearance.

In all of this, we should note that arousal preference is assumed by reversal theory to be different from arousability, which is the ease with which someone can actually be aroused (whether they want this or not).

This is of course a distinction that tends not to be made in other theories of personality. This distinction implies that it would be perfectly possible to have a high preference for arousal and a low arousability and conversely a low preference for arousal and a high arousability. Lafreniere (1993) has provided direct evidence for this, which is described in chapter 14 of this volume.

Before leaving this section, we should also draw attention to the fact that clinical evidence also supports the idea of reversals with respect to arousal. For example, Murgatroyd and Apter (1986) reported on the treatment of patients with agoraphobia by helping them induce the paratelic state when they felt anxiety coming on (see chapter 14 in this volume).

CONCLUSION

The preponderance of the studies cited under the four headings above have dealt with the telic–paratelic pair alone. A number of other studies, however, have involved all the states postulated in the theory, and to the extent to which it has proved possible to identify and track the states, the structure of the theory in this respect has been supported. Of particular importance is the evidence provided by O'Connell, Gerkovich, and Cook (1997) that the four pairs of metamotivational states are independent and orthogonal in their effects. In this study of smoking cessation, which is reported in more detail in chapter 7, a logit modeling procedure was used on data derived from the Metamotivational State Interview, and this showed that, as reversal theory would suggest, the four pairs of states were largely unrelated to each other. This means that the telic state did not co-occur more often with the conformist than with the negativistic state, or with the sympathy than with the mastery state, and so on; in other words, generally there was a lack of association in this respect between states across pairs.

In reversal theory research we see a trend toward an interest in all the eight states postulated in the theory rather than in the telic and paratelic states alone. Indicative of this is the way in which the newest generation of psychometric instruments, such as the MSP (Apter, Mallows, & Williams, 1998), the TESI (Svebak, 1993), the TSS (Wendel, 1999), and the SOMIFA (Kerr & Apter, 1999)—all of which are described in the previous chapter— engage with all eight states or dominances.

In conclusion, a further point is worth emphasizing. There is evidence that metamotivational states, at least the telic and paratelic pair, even though identified phenomenologically, do have some kind of objective "reality." This has been shown particularly by Svebak in his work on the psychophysiology of the telic and paratelic states, in which he and his colleagues have shown that these states are associated with different patterns of functioning in a number of physiological, especially autonomic, systems. Svebak, Cook, and others have also shown differences in cortical functioning associated with these two states. We shall not go further into this area here, because Lewis and Svebak review this psychophysiological work in the following chapter.

Of particular interest is the way in which psychophysiology, phenomenology, and psychometrics articulate with each other in many of these studies. An especially good example of this is the work by Svebak and Murgatroyd (1985), which "triangulated" psychophysiological data, psychometric data from use of the TDS, and phenomenological data from interviews (blind to the other two types of data). Such blending of qualitative and quantitative data means that psychometric and physiological data can be related to the richness of real-life experience, interview data can be tied rigorously to objective measurement, and psychometric tests can be validated at both the biological and ecological–social levels. This study is described in more detail in the next chapter.

5

THE PSYCHOPHYSIOLOGY OF METAMOTIVATION

GARETH LEWIS AND SVEN SVEBAK

It is essential to the development of any theory that it be tested empirically. In particular, if a theory can be shown to have a predictive value outside of its initial scope of study, then this is the most powerful form of verification. In relation to reversal theory, powerful support for the arguments of reversal theory would be gained by demonstrating a relationship between metamotivational and psychophysiological states. This chapter is a review of the evidence for just such relationships.

Reversal theory has been developed using an approach described elsewhere in this book as structural phenomenology (see also Apter, 1981c, 1989b; Murgatroyd & Apter, 1984, 1986). Its primary approach is to examine the deep structure of subjective experience. To do this, it examines how the different aspects of subjective life are related to each other, and it interprets behavior in the light of this experience. In this respect, the approach of the theory can be characterized as "inside out" in that it starts from subjective meaning. This in itself contrasts with the prevailing methodology in psychophysiological research that tends to make inferences from external or objective measurements alone. However, reversal theory has also always worked on the assumption that this subjective experience is connected with physiological phenomena. There are good grounds to believe that the different ways of organizing our subjective experience are related to the way in which the physiological responses of the body are organized.

In the same way that mental processes have a structure and that such processes change over time, the underlying neurophysiological and biochemical processes also have such a structure determined by similar principles. In this respect, reversal theory treats mental processes as epiphenomena of biological processes (Apter, 1982a, chap. 13). In this way mental life is seen as providing a unique perspective on the underlying neurophysiological functioning and one that has not been given due attention in research to date. The contention from the reversal theory perspective, therefore, is that physiological processes cannot be meaningfully or fully studied in isolation from the experience of the study participant.

Most of the research to be described in this chapter deals in one way or another with arousal. It is the claim of reversal theory (see chapters 1 and 2) that there are two distinct ways of experiencing arousal, these being associated with the telic and the paratelic motivational styles. From this the question becomes whether the measurable physiological responses that are associated with arousal differ between these two styles. If such a relationship could be found, this would provide strong support for the phenomenological arguments of reversal theory and for the "reality" of states that were initially identified in purely subjective terms.

METHODOLOGY AND DESIGN OF THE EXPERIMENTS

What we describe below is a linked series of experiments and investigations that provide a coherent set of data and results, addressing the primary issues that we have just discussed. Because of this linkage, and because there are some novel aspects to this series of experiments, we first describe some of the key features of the whole program.

To investigate physiological changes, it makes sense to consider evidence from each of the main areas of concern in psychophysiological research. These areas include the major regulatory pathways for brain control of motor functioning throughout the body. As such, the research deals with (a) somatic functioning (skeletal muscle tension), (b) autonomic functioning (cardiovascular and respiratory arousal), and (c) cortical activity.

Alongside this, a primary consideration is to isolate which metamotivational variables account for the relationships discovered. Recorded physiological changes could be related to (a) mode dominance; (b) state; and (c) some other factor such as arousal, effort and so on.

With this agenda in mind, in the late 1970s, Professor Sven Svebak and his colleagues at the University of Bergen, Norway, conducted a series of experiments and investigations to study the relationships between metamotivational factors and concomitant physiological responses. Svebak, in his earlier work on the psychophysiology of humor (Svebak 1985a), had already established empirical evidence to suggest that some people would experience high arousal as pleasurable rather than as stressful. This led him to eventually organize his research around a reversal theory interpretation of arousal rather than the prevailing optimal arousal theory (Svebak & Stoyva, 1980).

The resulting investigations involved task-induced physiological changes arising from what is known as the *continuous perceptual-motor task paradigm*. That is, the task was selected to make demands involving both perceptual monitoring and related motor responding. Such changes had been studied in the 1950s and 1960s by Malmo (e.g., see Malmo, 1965). The principal task adopted by Svebak made use of a commercially available video game that simulated cars racing. This involved the participants using a joystick to control a car without crashing into other cars on the screen. In the standard version of the task, the participant's car moved at twice the speed of other cars, and those other cars appeared at random. Each crash was considered as an error and by speeding up the rate at which the other cars appeared the task could be varied. Such tasks can be used for fun and enjoyment as well as for more serious purposes. This makes them ideal as they can in principle be performed in either the telic or the paratelic mode (Apter & Svebak, 1992).

During the course of the experiments, various means were used to manipulate the main variables of the experiment such as arousal and motivational factors. As well as the ability to control the speed of the cars, and therefore the difficulty of the task and the likelihood of errors, other manipulations were used. One important manipulation used was that of threat. It was expected that this would increase arousal and also induce a telic state. The particular threat used in this case was that of electric shock, and participants were told that this would be administered if they failed to reach a preset (but unspecified) standard in their responses. The level of shock was designed to be uncomfortable but not painful, and as such it was introduced to the participants before the task began. It should be noted, however, that it was the threat of shock here that was the manipulation, and the shock was never in fact administered during experimental trials. Applying or not applying the threat condition could manipulate motivation in the experiments. An added and related manipulation, in contrast to the threat, was the promise of a reward (e.g., monetary). Other manipulations were also used in the experiments, as reported below.

Two instruments were used to obtain data about metamotivation in the program reported here. These were the Telic Dominance Scale (TDS; Murgatroyd, Rushton, Apter, & Ray, 1978) and the Telic State Measure (TSM; Svebak & Murgatroyd, 1985). Both of these scales are described in chapter 3. It should be noted that scales 1, 2, and 4 of the TSM are the state versions of the TDS subscales. Also, a measure obtained by computing the difference between the scores for items 3 and 4 of the TSM represents a discrepancy between preferred and felt level of arousal. This difference constitutes a measure of *tension*. It will be appreciated that standard psychometric anxiety measures are not appropriate here, or elsewhere in reversal theory research, because they assume that high arousal and anxiety are the same thing, which means that the participants are not given the opportunity to indicate pleasant high arousal in the form of excitement (this problem has been discussed further by Spicer & Lyons, 1997).

This then describes the factors and the approaches taken to both manipulate and measure those factors in the program of experiments. The account of these studies is the story of the step-by-step unfolding of the relative importance and influence of these interacting variables.

SKELETAL MUSCLE TENSION

The initial experiments were based on the approach established by the work of Malmo (1965). He investigated physiological changes induced by task performance. In these experiments he showed that electromyographic (EMG) activity, which can be recorded graphically, fluctuates over time. This activity reflects what one might think of as the degree of tension in the muscles. He drew attention to the tonic (or slow) build-up of this activity in passive muscles, which continues over the course of a task and then falls away as soon as the task is completed. Passive muscles are those not directly used in the task involved. This resulting build-up of muscle tension is referred to as the electromyographic gradient.

Evidence suggested that steep gradients could improve performance for some tasks. However, steep gradients experienced over long periods of time can cause fatigue. There is also substantial commonsense evidence to suggest that muscle tension can lead to problems like backache and headache. It was suspected that the telic state tends to produce muscle tension. This notion is reinforced by common experience in the sense that worry and anxiety (i.e., high arousal experienced in the telic state) are commonly associated with muscle tension (Svebak, 1991a).

In the first experiment by Svebak, Storfjell, and Dalen (1982), measurements were taken from the passive forearm flexor muscle (*carpi radialis*). Manipulation was introduced by applying or not applying the threat of electric shock. The threat itself was considered enough to induce the telic state. The threat clearly worked as participants rated themselves as more serious minded and planning oriented in the threat condition than in the nonthreat condition. The result of the experiment was that the gradients were significantly steeper under the threat condition. Similarly, felt arousal was also higher in the threat condition. This was strong evidence that EMG gradient can be manipulated by threat, which was an important methodological consideration.

However, the significance of the results is unclear because using threat was found not only to induce the telic state, but also to tend to raise arousal.

It is therefore possible to interpret the steeper gradients as being a function of the higher arousal rather than a function of the telic state. These two variables needed to be separated.

Thus, as a consequence, in Svebak's (1984) next experiment, another means was used to manipulate metamotivational mode. Participants were recruited to form extreme groups in relation to telic dominance. The 10 highest and 10 lowest scorers on the defining TDS subscale for serious-mindedness were chosen from a group of 180 students. These extreme scorers were chosen on the basis that they were more likely to be in their preferred state at the time of the experiment than those who were not extreme, and no other manipulation was used. Participants performed the task five times at 2½ minutes per run in sequence and then a sixth time at high speed to induce more crashes. The mean EMG group scores on each run are shown in Figure 5.1.

For each run, five scores were sampled at equal intervals, together with baseline measures taken before and after the task. These graphs clearly illustrate that for the telic group, the gradient rises steeply during the task and then falls away on completion. In contrast, for the paratelic group the pattern does not really constitute a gradient. A learning or practice effect can be seen, in that the gradients flatten for the telic group run by run, and the difference between the groups diminishes. The exception is the case of the last run when the difficulty again increases.

From this, and the fact that arousal levels (as measured by the TSM) were not significantly different between the two groups, we can conclude that the build-up of muscle tension is a telic phenomenon. That is, it is the telic–paratelic distinction, rather than arousal, that is significant in determining EMG gradient. However, telic-dominant participants tended to be in the telic state for the duration of the task, and paratelic-dominant participants also tended to be in a state corresponding to their dominance (as shown by TSM scores). Although this was the intention of the extreme group's manipulation, the consequence is that it is not then possible to know for sure whether it is dominance or state that accounts for the steepness of the EMG gradients.

Further interesting results in this study came from measurements taken in the forearm flexor in the active arm, the one controlling the joystick. These measurements represent phasic (or short-term) changes that relate to the direct movements involved in the undertaking of the task. The paratelic group produced higher averaged amplitudes, but in the final run (when the task was made more difficult) their amplitudes increased, whereas those of the telic group decreased. These strongly contrasting response tendencies are illustrated in Figure 5.2.

One possible interpretation here is that there are distinct musculo-skeletal response styles that relate to the telic–paratelic distinction. The

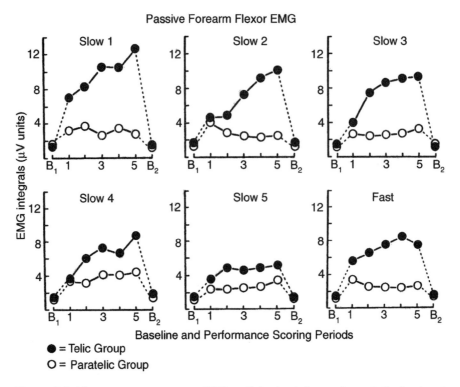

Passive Forearm Flexor EMG

● = Telic Group
O = Paratelic Group

Figure 5.1. Mean group scores on EMG activity for telic- and paratelic-dominant participants.
Note. EMG = electromyographic. Measurements were made at half-minute intervals for 2½ minutes as well as pre- and posttask. The task was performed six times, the final time at a relatively fast speed. All recordings are from the forearm flexor of the passive arm.
From "Active and Passive Forearm Flexor Tension Patterns in the Continuous Perceptual-Motor Task Paradigm: The Significance of Motivation," by S. Svebak, 1984, *International Journal of Psychophysiology 2,* p. 172. Copyright 1984 by Elsevier Science. Reprinted with permission.

telic participants were making increasingly careful and precise movements (suggesting a narrow response range and tighter control) under extreme pressure. In contrast, the movements of the paratelic participants became more uncontrolled and intense (suggesting greater intensity and a wider range of volitional responses).

This experiment was followed up by a further similar experiment by Svebak and Murgatroyd (1985), and resulted in similar findings. To resolve the problem of distinguishing between the respective influence of dominance and state, Svebak (1986a) conducted a further experiment in which he mixed participants with extreme dominance as well as the threat manipulation in

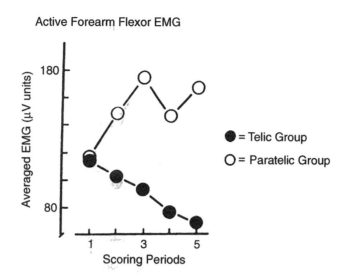

Active Forearm Flexor EMG

Figure 5.2. Mean group scores on EMG activity for telic- and paratelic-dominant participants and from the same task as shown in Figure 5.1.

Note. EMG = electromyographic. The recordings are from the forearm flexor of the active arm and for the sixth, faster version of the task.

From "Active and Passive Forearm Flexor Tension Patterns in the Continuous Perceptual-Motor Task Paradigm: The Significance of Motivation," by S. Svebak, 1984, *International Journal of Psychophysiology 2,* p. 173. Copyright 1984 by Elsevier Science. Reprinted with permission.

the hope that some participants would "crossover" or reverse state during the experiment. Substantial crossovers did not occur, as the threat appeared not to be strong enough. However, a positive outcome was that the connection between EMG activity and the telic–paratelic distinction was reinforced and the evidence strengthened.

To overcome these difficulties, in the next experiment 12 students were chosen from a sample of 222. Six each were chosen for being telic and paratelic dominant, using the TDS, but this time their dominance was less extreme. (These students were in fact recruited from a larger scale psychophysiological experiment on 20 telic- and 20 paratelic-dominant individuals.) The rationale is that these 12 moderately dominant individuals would be more likely to cross over when subject to manipulations. State was measured by a postexperiment blind structured interview rather than TSM. Threat of shock and reward were used respectively for good and poor performance. As a result, four from each group did in fact cross over and perform the task in a state opposite to their dominance. This enabled Apter and Svebak (1986) to study the influence of state and dominance separately. The results can be seen in Figure 5.3. This demonstrates clearly that it is state rather than dominance that is the key factor in determining EMG gradient.

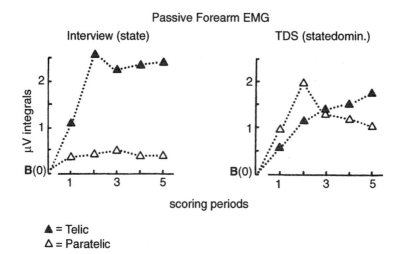

Passive Forearm EMG

Figure 5.3. Mean group scores on EMG activity for telic and paratelic participants, averaged over four trials, for a 2½-minute task.
Note. EMG = electromyographic. The recordings are from the forearm flexor of the passive arm. The terms *telic* and *paratelic* refer in the graph on the left to state at the time of the task (as assessed by interview) and on the right to dominance as measured by the Telic Dominance Scale.
From "The EMG Gradient as a Reflection of Metamotivational State," by M. J. Apter and S. Svebak, 1986, *Scandinavian Journal of Psychology 27,* p. 215. Copyright 1986 by the University of Bergen. Reprinted with permission.

To generalize these findings, Rimehaug and Svebak (1987) used a stratified sample of 19 participants from across the telic–paratelic dominance range as measured by the serious-minded subscale on the TDS. This time the task was a cognitive one, and state was manipulated by the possibility of monetary reward or its absence. The state of the participants during the experiment was assessed by a postexperiment interview. Behavioral evidence of distress was also recorded during the task by picking up participants' spontaneous utterances on audiotape. The resulting distress scores turned out to be positively related to EMG activity. Just as important, but as expected, metamotivational state was strongly related to EMG gradients. In fact, the best predictor of EMG scores was an index score comprising the telic state and distress measures. It was observed that EMG gradient increased as arousal increased, although it was difficult to distinguish the effects of increased arousal as against increased effort in performing the task. However, the results of the earlier experiments were generalized in the sense that the effect worked in a new type of task. Also, by using measurements in both arms and in the biceps and triceps muscles, it was possible to establish that the effects are not local to the forearm flexor.

CARDIOVASCULAR AND RESPIRATORY FUNCTIONING

Cardiovascular activity is one of the most important and well-researched areas in psychophysiology. This is partly because of the obvious connection between heart attacks and other cardiovascular diseases and stress. In the experiments reported here, heart rate was the measure used as an indicator of cardiovascular activity, with the intention of testing for a possible relationship between heart rate and telic–paratelic dominance or state.

Heart rate is controlled by the autonomic nervous system and neuroendocrine influences. Respiration is controlled by cardiovascular processes and brain sensors of oxygen and carbon dioxide concentrations that regulate muscle contraction in the diaphragm and the muscles of the rib cage. Respiratory dysfunction can have an adverse effect on performance and well-being. An example would be hyperventilation (overbreathing), which can be associated in everyday life with psychosomatic complaints such as dizziness, nausea, and a pounding heart. If it could be shown that such dysfunctions were related to telic dominance or telic state, this could prove useful both for future research in the field and for patient counseling.

In the first experiment reported earlier in the chapter (Svebak et al., 1982), heart rate was also recorded. It was found that there was a significant difference between the heart rate responses in the threat and no threat conditions, in that heart rate was considerably higher in the threat condition (see Figure 5.4). The same problem pertains to this study, however, as to the studies reported earlier on the EMG gradient, in that threat increased arousal (and potentially, effort) as well as inducing the telic state, making it difficult to distinguish the influences of the two.

Similarly, it was found in this study that respiration rate, which was also recorded, was on average twice as high as baseline at about 30 seconds into task performance and significantly higher in the threat than in the no-threat condition. Participants not only increased their respiration rate but also breathed more deeply. Put simply, increased arousal, together with the telic state, caused breathing to become deeper and faster. In the Svebak and Murgatroyd study (1985), the different respiratory amplitude response patterns of telic- and paratelic-dominant participants can be seen clearly. These are shown in Figure 5.5.

Svebak (1986b) also found that in the threat condition, telic-dominant participants breathed more rapidly and more deeply than did paratelic-dominant participants. In this case he took measurements from the thorax and the abdomen rather than the thorax alone, which was the source of measurement in the Svebak and Murgatroyd study.

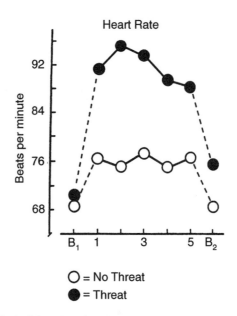

Figure 5.4. The effect of threat on heart rate.
Note. Heart rate is measured at half-minute intervals throughout the 2½ minutes
of the task and averaged over all participants. Pre- and posttask baseline levels
are shown.
From "The Effect of a Threatening Context Upon Motivation and Task-Induced
Physiological Changes," by S. Svebak, O. Storfjell, and K. Dalen, 1982, *British Journal
of Psychology 73,* p. 509. Copyright 1982 by the British Psychological Society.
Reprinted with permission.

Thus, the telic–paratelic distinction has a physiological concomitant
in respiration as it does in the other functions previously discussed. In
support of this, Svebak and Grossman (1985) have reported an association
between the telic state (as measured by the TSM) and the number of
psychosomatic complaints reported when participants were asked to hyper-
ventilate. In this way the results supported specific cardio–respiratory–
somatic interactions for the telic versus the paratelic dominance and states.

Returning to the heart rate variable, Svebak (1986a) used both an
extreme group as well as a threat manipulation. The results are depicted in
Figure 5.6. These show that in the no-threat condition both dominance
groups display moderate heart rate increase, whereas the acceleration of
heart rate is considerably greater for the telic group in the threat condition
than for the paratelic group in this condition. Because arousal level was
broadly similar for the two groups (as measured by the TSM), we can
conclude that it is the telic–paratelic factor that is the key variable rather
than arousal. As already mentioned, this result is important, but it has
significant implications for future research on cardiovascular psychophysiol-

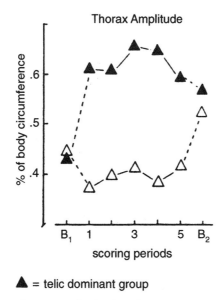

Thorax Amplitude

Figure 5.5. Mean group scores for thorax amplitude for telic- and paratelic-dominant participants.
Note. Measurements were taken at half-minute intervals over the 2½ minutes of the task. Pre- and posttask baseline levels are shown.
From "Metamotivational Dominance: A Multimethod Validation of Reversal Theory Constructs," by S. Svebak and S. Murgatroyd, 1985, *Journal of Personality and Social Psychology 48,* p. 112. Copyright 1985 by the University of Illinois. Reprinted with permission.

ogy. As before, however, it is not possible, on the basis of this data, to distinguish between the influence of state and dominance.

Until roughly the time of this research, it was generally supposed that Type A behavior influenced susceptibility to coronary heart disease. Despite substantial research, this broad connection has not been established empirically and is now in some doubt. We do know that telic–paratelic dominance is unrelated to Type A and Type B behavior (Svebak & Apter, 1984). It could be that telic–paratelic dominance, either alone or in interaction with Type A or Type B behavior, could provide some explanation for cardiovascular over-responsiveness and vulnerability to heart disease.

Consequently, Svebak, Nordby, and Ohman (1987) tested the heart rates of 40 participants during task performance. The participants were split equally into the combinations telic–Type A, telic–Type B, paratelic–Type A, and paratelic–Type B. The results suggested that there was a cardiovascular responder type with the combination telic–Type A who were especially high in heart rate reactivity (see Figure 5.7). This combination may well

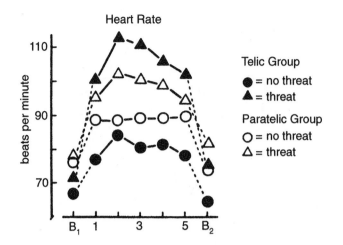

Figure 5.6. The effect of threat on heart rate for telic- and paratelic-dominant participants.
Note. Heart rate measurements were taken at half-minute intervals over the 2½ minutes of the task, with and without threat of shock for inadequate performance, and averaged over dominance group for each condition. Pre- and posttask baseline measures are shown.
From "Cardiac and Somatic Activation in the Continuous Perceptual-Motor Task: The Significance of Threat and Serious-Mindedness," by S. Svebak, 1986, *International Journal of Psychophysiology 3*, p. 159. Copyright 1986 by Elsevier Science. Reprinted with permission.

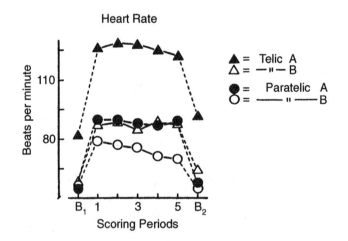

Figure 5.7. Mean heart rate group scores for telic–Type A, telic–Type B, paratelic–Type A, and paratelic–Type B participants.
Note. Measurements were taken at half-minute intervals over the 2½ minutes of the task. Pre- and posttask baseline levels are shown.
From "The Personality of the Cardiac Responder: Interaction of Seriousmindedness and Type A Behavior," by S. Svebak, H. Nordby, and A. Ohman, 1987, *Biological Psychology 24*, p. 5. Copyright 1987 by Elsevier Science. Reprinted with permission.

be an excellent predictor of cardiovascular disease. Consistent with this is some evidence from the work of Gallacher and Beswick (1988) that Type A participants in the telic mode show significantly greater increases in diastolic blood pressure in response to mild stress than do the other combinations of telic–paratelic state with Type A or B behavior.

Svebak and Apter (1987) have provided further evidence in support of reversal theory that showed a high heart rate acceleration generated in response to mirthful laughter (which occurs only in the paratelic state). This was an interesting study because it showed the effects discussed above but in relation to shorter term phasic responses. The effect occurred equally for telic- and paratelic-dominant participants, emphasizing again that state and not dominance is the critical factor. As with cardiovascular activity, paratelic state induced by laughter also caused phasic respiratory responses. In fact the phasic respiratory and heart responses go together hand in hand.

Although not carried out in Svebak's laboratory, another study should be mentioned here. Spicer and Lyons (1997) measured systolic and diastolic blood pressure and heart rate in female participants (N = 102) involved in 3–6 minute conversations about themselves. Readings of both blood pressure and heart rate were taken during the conversation and during a rest period before the conversation began. The TSM was used to assess telic–paratelic state, and participants also took the TDS to measure dominance. The main result, using analysis of covariance, was that telic-dominant participants showed greater blood pressure increases than did paratelic-dominant participants. But there was no corresponding difference in heart rate. There were also a number of interaction effects. The most striking and interesting of these was that blood pressure increase was greatest for telic-dominant participants who happened to be in the paratelic state during the conversation. Spicer and Lyons suggested that such misfits between dominance and state deserve more attention in future research.

CORTICAL ACTIVITY

It has long been taken for granted that arousal is associated with concomitant activity in the cortex of the brain. For psychologists, the study of cortical activity has always had a special interest because conscious processes are held to be epiphenomena of neurobiological processes in this part of the brain.

Svebak (1982) had extreme telic- and paratelic-dominant participants perform the standard task already described under both threat and no-threat conditions. Electroencephalographic (EEG) activity was recorded by placing electrodes on the parietal area of the cortex. Power spectrum scores were recorded on-line in the alpha, beta, and theta frequency bands. Interestingly, threat and no-threat conditions had little effect, suggesting that arousal, effort, or metamotivational state had little influence on cortical activity. Paratelic-dominant participants, however, consistently produced significantly higher power spectrum scores in the theta and beta bands. They also produced higher scores in the alpha band but only in baseline scores and only for the left hemisphere. Other than this, hemispheric differences were minor, contradicting the trend to attribute a wide range of psychological effects to the differences between hemispheres. In this study, then, dominance effects were the only ones found.

Svebak (1985b) sought another manipulation to examine changes in cortical activity, as threat was found to have little effect. *Hyperpnea* is a respiratory change induced by breathing as fast and as deeply as possible (in this case for 30 seconds). *Hypopnea* involves holding the breath. The experiment involved 10 participants in each of the extreme telic- and extreme paratelic-dominant groups (drawn from a group of 110 students). For overbreathing, power scores increased in the theta and beta bands, and for underbreathing they were lowered.

In both conditions, scores were significantly higher for the paratelic-dominant than for the telic-dominant participants. The most marked difference (in the theta band) is shown in Figure 5.8. Again, this reinforces the conclusions of the previous experiment that the effects relate to telic–paratelic dominance. (This whole topic of cortical activation in relation to breathing is taken up again in chapter 7 on smoking and smoking cessation.)

These higher scores are displayed across all bands by paratelic-dominant participants and are characteristic of a "cortical information-processing style" (Apter 1989b). Svebak argued, in line with current theory (e.g., Cooper, Osselton, & Shaw, 1980), that these high amplitudes of the cortical activity of the paratelic-dominant participant are global and diffuse, whereas those of the telic-dominant participant are more focal and localized at a number of points in the cortex. It is tempting to see a connection here between the freedom and spontaneity of the paratelic state and the focus and planning of the telic state. Perhaps there also might be a connection with the different behaviors of telic- and paratelic-dominant participants in the EMG experiment by Svebak (1984) reported earlier in the chapter, in which telic participants made precise responses, and paratelic participants made rather wild and generalized responses in the face of an increasingly difficult task.

Further evidence of the concomitance between the activity of the brain and motivational state comes from a measure of cortical activity called P300, which is a form of event-related potential, so-called because its peak occurs roughly 300 milliseconds after stimulus onset. It is understood to relate to the ability to attend purposefully to task-relevant stimuli. If so, we might expect P300 scores to be higher in the telic state; Svebak, Howard, and Rimehaug (1987) tested this proposition. They compared the reactions

Theta

Left hemisphere   Right hemisphere

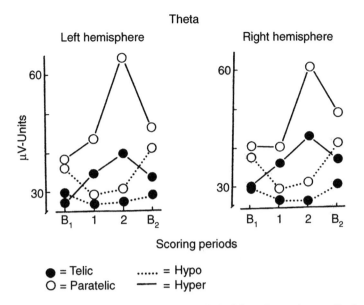

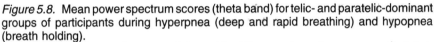

● = Telic   ...... = Hypo
○ = Paratelic   —— = Hyper

Figure 5.8. Mean power spectrum scores (theta band) for telic- and paratelic-dominant groups of participants during hyperpnea (deep and rapid breathing) and hypopnea (breath holding).
Note. Breathing instructions were followed for 30 seconds and measurements taken after 5 seconds and 20 seconds. Pre- and posttask baseline scores are shown. Scores for right and left hemispheres are shown separately.
From "Serious-mindedness and the Effect of Self-Induced Respiratory Changes Upon Parietal EEG," by S. Svebak, 1985, *Biofeedback and Self-Regulation 10,* p. 57. Copyright 1985 by Kluwer Academic/Plenum Publishers. Reprinted with permission.

of participants in a task performance in which they had to respond quickly to "Go" and "NoGo" prompts (i.e., prompts to the participants to respond or not to respond). The participants were split between telic and paratelic extreme groups. As predicted, P300 scores were higher for telic-dominant participants. Once again this demonstrates the strong association between metamotivational mode and an important psychophysiological measure. (Other evidence concerning cortical activation in relation to metamotivation is found in chapter 7.)

PSYCHOPHYSIOLOGY AND LIFESTYLE

It is worth revisiting one of the experiments already cited, because this study shows clearly that there is a relationship among psychometric measures, psychophysiological measures, and phenomenological accounts in the form of personal descriptions of everyday life as it is lived. In the study by Svebak and Murgatroyd (1985), participants were not only classified in terms of telic and paratelic dominance by means of the TDS (serious-mindedness subscales), they were also interviewed about their lifestyles by an interviewer who was blind to both their TDS scores and their psychophysiological results. The style and content of the telic- and paratelic-dominant participants were markedly different.

Here is an extract from the account by a telic-dominant participant of how he started his previous day:

> I got up at 10:00, went to the bathroom and washed my hands, then I went to the toilet, washed my hands again, and then decided to have a shower. I brushed my teeth, then dried myself very thoroughly. I went to the gym for some weights and other training, but because it was closed due to a problem with water I could not get exercise. This upset my routine. I went to the bank to collect my loan, and then I telephoned my father to ask his professional advice about what to do with the money.

Here, by contrast, is the account by a paratelic-dominant participant of how she started her day:

> Yes, well . . . er . . . I overslept . . . hadn't felt well the day before . . . and, er, I needed sleep . . . so, er, I just slept in . . . I don't think my clock worked . . . but I slept in. I got to the reading room at 10:00. I was supposed to go to a lecture and to two tutorial groups, but I did not bother. Instead I talked to a man who fancies me. I agreed with him that I would go to the pictures, so I went home and had a shower, washed my hair and sat in a sauna—it was good.

The difference between these two accounts is stark. The telic-dominant participant reports doing things because they will be good for him and imply forward planning, like going to the gym to exercise and asking for advice on his loan. The paratelic-dominant participant does things more because they are enjoyable, like chatting and having a sauna, and with little awareness of consequences, as in the consequences of missing a lecture. Interestingly, Svebak and Murgatroyd pointed out that the two *styles* of the accounts are also different and also reflect the difference in dominance, and in this these participants exemplify the accounts of all the participants in their respective groups. Thus, the accounts of telic-dominant participants tend to be detailed, precise, and given in the correct chronological order. The accounts of paratelic-dominant participants tend to be more haphazard, impressionistic, and exaggerated. As Svebak and Murgatroyd succinctly described it, the telic-dominant participant "provided a descriptive account with occasional evaluation," whereas the paratelic-dominant participant "offered an evaluative account with occasional descriptions" (p. 113). Again, it is tempting to make connections with the local versus diffuse nature of cortical functioning observed in the participants representative of these two types of dominance as reported in the study on cortical functioning reported above (Svebak, 1985b).

This study is also important because it shows how one can triangulate among psychometric, psychophysiological, and phenomenological evidence. Thus, the psychophysiological data is shown to be tied to a world of personal meaning, the phenomenological accounts are shown to be grounded in physiological functioning, and the psychometric instrument is validated by reference to both "soft" and "hard" data.

CONCLUSION

Because of the complexity of the experiments and the weight of technical data involved, it is possible that some of the more important messages may get lost in the detail of this narrative. For this reason, it may be important to summarize some of the most salient conclusions.

First, it is clear that EMG gradients can be manipulated by threat. It also, as expected, increases felt arousal. It is also clear (from Svebak, 1984) that state is predicted by dominance. Because there is no difference between telic and paratelic groups in terms of felt arousal, we can conclude that the telic–paratelic distinction is a crucial factor in determining EMG gradients. Further, we can conclude that high EMG gradients, and therefore muscle tension, are a telic phenomenon (Svebak, 1988b). The Apter and Svebak study of 1986 is critical in demonstrating that state rather than dominance appears to be the key factor.

Svebak (1986a) showed that heart rate can also be manipulated by threat, and in rather the same way as skeletal muscle tension, it is a telic phenomenon. Threat not only increases arousal and induces the telic state, it is also related to a faster and deeper respiratory rate. Thus, the evidence from studies of respiration reinforces the previous results. In particular, overbreathing (hyperventilation) and its associated complaints can be viewed as a telic phenomenon.

The evidence from the cortical studies also replicated the patterns shown in relation to other psychophysiological measures in that they demonstrate a distinction in physiological response between metamotivational states. They also help confirm that arousal and other contingent factors are not as significant as the motivational ones (Svebak, 1983).

Taken as a whole, we can say with reasonable confidence that there are clear and strong relationships between motivational experience and identifiable physiological and neurophysiological processes. Svebak (1985a) has organized his results in the way shown in Table 5.1.

It is easy to see in this table the association between the telic state and strong tonic changes, opposed by the strong phasic changes that go with the paratelic state. Interestingly, this would appear to be consistent with the phenomenological definitions of the telic and paratelic states—

Table 5.1.
Physiological Features of Telic and Paratelic Characteristics
(States or Dominances)

Dependent Measures	Telic	Paratelic
Skeletal muscles		
Tonic changes (passive)[a,b,c,d,e,f,m]	High	Low
Phasic changes (active)[b,c,m]	Low	High
Fibre composition[l]	Type I	Type II
Cardiovascular measures		
Tonic heart rate changes (threat)[a,c,g]	High	Low
Phasic heart rate changes (comedy)[h]	Low	High
Pulse transit time[g]	Short	Long
Respiration rate (threat)[a,i]	High	Low
Respiration amplitude		
Tonic changes (threat)[a,d,i]	High	Low
Phasic changes (comedy)[h]	Low	High
Cortical activity		
Area in synchrony[j]	Small	Large
P300 amplitude[k]	Large	Small

[a]Svebak, Storfjell, & Dalen (1982).
[b]Svebak (1984).
[c]Svebak (1986a).
[d]Svebak & Murgatroyd (1985).
[e]Apter & Svebak (1986).
[f]Rimehaug & Svebak (1987).
[g]Svebak, Nordby, & Ohman (1987).
[h]Svebak & Apter (1987).
[i]Svebak (1986b).
[j]Svebak (1985b).
[k]Svebak, Howard & Rimehaug (1987).
[l]Svebak et al. (1990).
[m]Braathen & Svebak (1990).

the telic being the long-term, planning, and goal-seeking state, as against the paratelic state, which is concerned with the present moment, intensity, and spontaneity.

Finally, we should mention two things. First, this series of experiments has strongly established the claims made in the introduction to this chapter about relationships between the organization of our subjective experience and the concomitant organization of our physiological responses. However, this leaves, as always, a number of interesting but unanswered questions still to be explored. One example would be the challenge of disentangling the relative effects of effort and arousal alluded to in these experiments.

Second, there is no doubt that this series of experiments particularly and the wider discourse concerning reversal theory in general will influence the methodology of psychophysiological research. One key theme here will surely be the importance of subjective experience and the need to take into account the way that the participant is experiencing, and giving meaning to, what is happening to him or her in the laboratory.

Looking to the future, as Spicer and Lyons (1997), among others, have pointed out, we may expect studies to include all eight metamotivational states rather than the telic–paratelic pair alone and to use new techniques in neuro-imaging. It will be fascinating to see what will be disclosed by such research.

III
RESEARCH APPLICATIONS

6

STRESS

ROD A. MARTIN AND SVEN SVEBAK

The concept of stress has occupied the attention of a large number of psychological researchers and theorists for several decades. Despite, or perhaps because of, the thousands of articles and books that have been published on this topic, there is still considerable disagreement concerning how best to conceptualize and study stress and its related phenomena. Early researchers (e.g., Holmes & Rahe, 1967) took a stimulus–response approach, assuming that external, objectively defined stressful events will have a predictable impact on physical and emotional health. However, it soon became apparent that different individuals respond to similar life events in different ways; some become ill following relatively little stress, whereas others seem able to remain healthy despite high levels of aversive experience (cf. Rabkin & Struening, 1976). These observations have given rise to vigorous research into the personality traits and coping processes that allow some people to resist the deleterious effects of stress better than others. Thus, researchers have investigated the stress-buffering effects of such variables as hardiness (Maddi & Kobasa, 1984; Orr & Westman, 1990), hope (Snyder et al., 1991), optimism (Scheier & Carver, 1987), sense of humor (Grover, 1999; Lefcourt & Martin, 1986; Martin & Lefcourt, 1983; Svebak & Martin, 1997), learned resourcefulness (Rosenbaum, 1990), and sense of coherence (Antonovsky, 1987). As we show in this chapter, measures of metamotivational state dominance, derived from reversal theory, may be added to this list of potential stress-moderating variables.

Richard Lazarus (e.g., Lazarus & Folkman, 1984) has long emphasized the importance of examining the ways in which individuals subjectively appraise the meaning of environmental events in order to understand such individual differences in responses to stress. More recently, Lazarus (1993) has called for a greater integration of research on stress and emotion, arguing that theories of psychological stress should be considered a subset of emotion theory. He pointed out that an analysis of an individual's emotional responses

119

to a situation, such as guilt, anger, panic, happiness, or joy, provides a richer understanding of the person–environment transaction than simply focusing on the narrower concept of stress. He proposed a *cognitive–motivational– relational framework* that examines core relational themes and their associated appraisal processes that give rise to a range of emotions.

The conceptualization of stress provided by reversal theory is generally consistent with Lazarus's approach, while adding several innovative components. Like the approach taken by Lazarus, reversal theory emphasizes the importance of attending to the subjective, phenomenological experience of the individual (Apter, 1991a, 1997a; Apter & Svebak, 1989). In addition, the formulation of stress provided by reversal theory is closely tied to the conceptualization of emotions more generally. Furthermore, the importance of motivational (or more accurately, metamotivational) states is emphasized, as well as the relevance of the individual's relational concerns. However, reversal theory goes beyond Lazarus's approach in providing a structural– phenomenological framework for understanding the dynamic processes involved in the person–environment interactions that are involved in various forms of stress and their emotional sequelae. A brief overview of the reversal theory conceptualization of stress is presented, followed by a summary of the empirical research that has been conducted to date.

TENSION-STRESS AND EFFORT-STRESS

A distinction is made in reversal theory between two fundamentally different types of stress, referred to as *tension-stress* and *effort-stress* (Apter & Svebak, 1989). Tension-stress refers to the feelings that arise when one perceives a discrepancy between the preferred and actual level of some salient motivational variable. For example, if one is in the telic state, where preferred arousal is low, tension-stress would arise if one's perceived arousal level became high. Similarly, tension-stress occurs if one is in the mastery mode and cannot achieve the feelings of power that are desired in this state. The term *tension* is used here in a manner consistent with the everyday use of the term to refer to feelings of unease, a sense that "things are not what they should be" and that "one needs to do something" (Apter & Svebak, 1989, p. 41).

In contrast, effort-stress has to do with the feelings accompanying the expenditure of effort to reduce tension-stress. Thus, effort-stress relates to what is commonly referred to in the stress literature as coping, which involves efforts to reduce, tolerate, or master a stressor, without any assumption being made about whether or not these efforts are successful. Effort does not necessarily refer to physiological activation or the actual expenditure of energy. Rather, it refers to the subjective experience of striving and determination captured by such phrases as "pushing oneself," "exerting willpower," "not giving up," and "working at it" (Apter & Svebak, 1989, p. 41). It should be noted that these definitions are phenomenological, relating to the individual's mental state, and cannot be assessed directly by means of physiological measures or behavioral observations.

To clarify the distinction between tension- and effort-stress, Apter (1989b) suggested the analogy of physical illness, which may involve both symptoms resulting from infection by a microorganism (comparable to tension-stress), and symptoms resulting from the body's defenses against the infection (comparable to effort-stress). Effort-stress often occurs as a consequence of tension-stress, and the two are typically expected to be positively correlated—the more the tension, the more the effort to overcome it. However, this correlation will not be perfect. At some times, a person may become resigned to tension-stress, suffer in silence, and not exert any effort to cope with it. Or a low-effort strategy may be deliberately adopted, and sometimes enforced by the medical doctor, in the form of some drug that takes away the tension-stress pharmacologically. Alcohol, tranquilizers, opiates, and many other drugs act to take away tension-stress without the expenditure of much effort-stress. This low-effort strategy may be the only one available despite the fact that it may boost the potential of subsequent external stressors, including problems at work, with spouse, finances, and one's own health. Effort-stress may also sometimes occur in the absence of tension stress, as a consequence of efforts to avert or avoid potential tension stress before it occurs. For example, a person with many work responsibilities may exert a great deal of effort to fulfill the necessary tasks in order to avoid the feelings of tension and anxiety that would arise if he or she failed to complete the tasks.

There are a number of types of effort (Apter & Svebak, 1989). Effort may be required for physical or psychological action, such as struggling to find a solution to a problem, working hard physically, or running away. Effort may also be required for concentration, to focus attention on the task at hand (e.g., problem-solving), or to divert attention away from an unpleasant situation (e.g., avoidance, distraction). The amount of effort required to cope with a particular situation may be a function of various factors, including task factors (difficulty, duration, intensity), physiological factors (fatigue, sleepiness), psychological factors (importance and significance of a goal, self-confidence in attaining the goal), and contextual factors (distractions, appropriateness of the social and physical environment).

STRESS IN RELATION TO METAMOTIVATIONAL STATES

Both tension-stress and effort-stress may be experienced in any of the metamotivational states or modes described by reversal theory (Apter, 1991c;

Svebak, 1988a, 1991b). In each pair of states, there is a salient variable for which the preferred level is high in one mode and low in the other. As noted above, tension-stress results from a discrepancy from the preferred level of the relevant variable in each state. Depending on the combination of modes that the individual happens to be in at a given time, the tension-stress has its own affective quality. For example, the telic–paratelic and negativism–conformity pairs of modes give rise to so-called somatic emotions and thus to four types of somatic tension-stress. Here, the salient variable is felt arousal, and the preferred level is high in the paratelic state and low in the telic state. Thus, when an individual is in the telic state, tension-stress occurs when the person is experiencing high levels of felt arousal. This tension is experienced as anxiety if the person also happens to be in the conformity mode and as anger if the person is in the negativistic state. In contrast, in the paratelic state, tension-stress occurs when the person is experiencing low levels of felt arousal. Here, the tension is experienced as boredom if one is concurrently in the conformity state and as sullenness if one is in the negativistic state.

The mastery–sympathy and autic–alloic pairs of modes contribute to conditions that give rise to the experience of transactional (interpersonal) tension-stress. Here, the relevant variable is *felt transactional outcome* (Apter, 1991a) rather than arousal (i.e., the degree to which the person perceives himself or herself to be "winning" or gaining vs. "losing" in relational transactions). Again, different levels of this variable are preferred in the different states. When a person is in the autic mode, perceptions of losing in an interpersonal transaction are experienced as tension-stress, whereas in the alloic state, tension-stress occurs when one perceives oneself to be gaining or winning over the other. Again, the emotional tone of the tension-stress differs depending on whether one is also concurrently in the mastery or sympathy mode. When a person is simultaneously in the autic and mastery modes and perceives that things are not going his or her way, the person experiences tension-stress in the form of humiliation. In contrast, in the autic and sympathy modes, tension-stress occurs in the form of resentment when one perceives oneself to be losing. On the other hand, in the alloic and mastery modes, winning in transactions creates the tension-stress experienced as shame, whereas in the alloic and sympathy modes, the perception of winning gives rise to tension stress that is experienced as guilt. Thus, tension-stress is always experienced as unpleasant in any state, but for different (and even opposite) reasons, and the tension-stress is experienced in the form of qualitatively different emotions or moods depending on the current metamotivational state of the individual. In this way, reversal theory provides a structural–phenomenological framework for conceptualizing a broad range of negative stress-related emotions.

Although it is not clearly spelled out in writings on reversal theory and stress, it would appear that, in each of these last four combinations of states, one would also need to be in the telic state in order for the tension-stress to be experienced as unpleasant or stressful. This is because the paratelic state gives rise to parapathic emotions (typically designated by enclosing emotion terms in quotation marks, e.g., "shame," "guilt," "anger"), which are experienced as enjoyable rather than unpleasant. It is only in the telic state that these emotions are truly distressing and therefore likely to be experienced as aversive or stressful. This is to say that anxiety or anger may blend with any of the four transactional forms of tension-stress.

Although there are several forms of tension-stress relating to the various combinations of metamotivational states, effort-stress is assumed to be similar in all of these cases (Apter, 1989b). The only distinction is whether it occurs in the telic or paratelic state. In the telic state, effort-stress is always felt as unpleasant—it involves expending effort in performing an activity that one does not desire to perform for its own sake. It is a serious-minded activity. In fact, telic effort-stress seems to be what most people think of when referring to stress. In contrast, in the paratelic state, effort-stress is experienced as pleasant and invigorating, because it involves expending effort in relation to a task that is intrinsically enjoyable. In this state, effort is carried out with enthusiasm and is accompanied by perceptions of challenge rather than threat.

In the case of telic effort-stress, there are several possible outcomes with regard to the relation between tension-stress and effort-stress. First, the individual may be successful in exerting effort to remove the threat or achieve a goal, thus reducing the level of anxiety associated with the tension-stress. Alternatively, the person may give up trying to exert effort and may therefore experience intense anxiety, such as a panic attack. Finally, the person may exert a great deal of effort to overcome the stressor but may be unsuccessful, therefore experiencing both tension- and effort-stress.

EMPIRICAL INVESTIGATIONS

Research With the Tension and Effort Stress Inventory

Svebak (1993) developed the Tension and Effort Stress Inventory (TESI) to assess variables relevant to the reversal theory conceptualization of stress described above. The TESI is divided into three sections to measure the experience of (a) sources of stress, (b) related coping efforts (effort stress), and (c) moods and emotions relating to the experience of tension-stress in various combinations of metamotivational states. The TESI may be modified to focus on any particular time period in which the researcher is interested (e.g., the past week, the past 30 days, etc.). More specifically, the first part includes four items assessing the experience of sources of stress (defined as pressure, stress, challenge, or demand) over a particular time period as related to work, family, finances, and the person's own body, respectively. The second section consists of four items (relating to the same four areas of functioning) that ask about the degree of effort that the individual has put into coping with these sources of stress over the same time period. Finally, tension-stress is reflected in the third section of the TESI, in which eight items assess the degree of unpleasant moods or emotions (relating to eight combinations of metamotivational states) during that time: anxiety, boredom, anger, sullenness, humiliation, shame, resentment, and guilt. Another eight items in this section assess the range of positive emotional experiences or moods associated with a lack of tension-stress in each combination of metamotivational states: relaxation, excitement, placidity, provocativeness, pride, modesty, gratitude, and virtue. All items are scored on 7-point Likert scales.

Svebak, Mykletun, and Bru (1997) described several studies that investigated the relationship between the scales on the TESI and various forms of back pain. In one study (Svebak, Ursin, Endresen, Hjelmen, & Apter, 1991), 96 female bank employees were recruited on the basis of their responses to the Standardized Nordic Questionnaire (Kourinka et al., 1987), a measure of musculoskeletal pain symptoms. Their study focused specifically on pain from the neck, shoulders, and lower back. These participants all reported some degree of musculoskeletal complaints over the previous month, in one or more of these three areas, ranging from mild to severe. All were examined by a rheumatologist to exclude cases of fibromyalgia, damage due to accidents, or previous hospitalization for back trouble due to neurological or osteological diseases.

Analyses of the correlations between emotions on the TESI and back pain scores yielded some interesting findings. Among the unpleasant tension-stress emotions, anxiety, boredom, and sullenness were unrelated to pain scores. However, anger did show some association with scores on pain in the neck and shoulders ($rs = .26$ and $.29$, respectively). Interestingly, unpleasant transactional emotions due to failure to cope with interpersonal relations (humiliation, shame, resentment, and guilt) were more associated with pain in the back over the past year. For example, resentment and guilt were particularly related to pain in the neck and shoulders and, to a lesser extent, pain in the lower back. Humiliation and shame were related to pain in the shoulders. With regard to positive emotions, relaxation was negatively related to pain in the shoulders ($r = -.28$) over the past week, whereas pride was positively related to pain in the shoulders ($r = .37$) over the past year. These researchers concluded that the pattern of findings from this study indicates a risk of neck and shoulder pain in particular among individuals dominated by telic and negativistic modes (thus reporting frequent anger), the sympathy and autic or alloic modes (frequently experiencing resentment and guilt, respectively), or the mastery and autic modes (experiencing pride).

With regard to sources of stress and effort-stress as measured on the TESI, few correlations were found with measures of back pain. A weak correlation was found between neck pain and effort invested to cope with stressors due to work ($r = .22$). Scores on stressors and related efforts to cope that were attributed to one's own body were significantly correlated with pain in the neck, shoulders, and lower back. Svebak et al. (1997) concluded from these findings that "body complaints may be caused by extrinsic stressors and then themselves become stressors, thus triggering a vicious circle of events" (p. 62).

Another study relating the TESI to back pain by Bru, Mykletun, and Svebak (1994) involved 547 female staff in different departments of a regional hospital in Norway. On the TESI, significant correlations were found between scores on overall stressors and degree of effort ($r = .83$), providing support for the prediction that tension- and effort-stress tend to be positively correlated. Tension-stress scores (as measured by the negative emotion scales) also correlated significantly with the total stressor and effort-stress scores. With regard to back pain, the positive emotions were unrelated to any type of pain, whereas overall tension-stress scores (total of the eight negative mood items) were significantly but relatively weakly correlated with neck pain ($r = .26$), shoulder pain ($r = .17$), and lower back pain ($r = .14$). Correlations of similar magnitude were found between back pain and scores on sources of stress and effort-stress. A path analysis was also conducted to test a model in which tension-stress (dysphoria) mediates the relationship between work-related effort-stress and overall back pain, whereas positive moods (euphoria) moderate this relationship. The results provided support for this theoretical framework.

Svebak (1997) described two prospective studies that examined the role of tension- and effort-stress as predictors of academic performance. The participants in these studies were students who were scheduled to complete a major, highly competitive examination in psychology that would determine whether they could continue in a professional psychology training program. In the first study, four weeks before the exam, the participants were given the TESI to complete in terms of how stressful they perceived the exam to be and how much effort they put into coping with this stressor. Analyses were conducted to determine the degree to which scores on the TESI could be used to predict participants' subsequent performance on the exam. For this purpose, the participants were divided into five groups on the basis of their performance (high, medium, low, failure, and no-show). There were only marginal differences among the groups in their perceptions of the magnitude of the stressor. However, the amount of effort invested in coping with the stressor produced a significant predictive effect, due to the fact that those who failed to attend the exam exerted less effort in coping than did the other groups. The discrepancy between the perceived magnitude of the stressor and the efforts to cope (defined as an index of tension-stress) also predicted group membership. In particular, those who did not attend the exam showed large discrepancy scores, whereas those who obtained the highest scores on the exam showed the lowest discrepancies.

In the second study, conducted one year later, the participants completed the full version of the TESI before the examination, in terms of the past year and also the past week. In this study, those who failed the exam or did not attend, as compared to the more successful students, reported lower levels of work-related stress and also lower levels of efforts to cope with this stress both over the past 12 months and during the preceding week. In addition, efforts to cope with stressors attributed to one's own body were significantly related to better performance on the exam. Those who did less well on the exam also reported lower anxiety, higher excitement, and higher provocativeness. Thus, tension-stress in the form of anxiety (reflecting the telic state of goal-directedness) was a positive predictor of success, whereas paratelic excitement (indicating the paratelic state of playfulness) predicted poor performance.

Shelley (1999) reported on another investigation using the TESI. This study investigated stress among teachers by means of classroom scenarios of different kinds of disruptive behavior and asked the teachers how they would feel when faced by them. First, however, she induced either the autic–mastery state (by means of an induction script emphasizing the need to control unruly children whose behavior is an affront to their authority) or the alloic–sympathy state (by means of a script emphasizing the emotional needs of children and the way in which disruptive behavior can be a cry for help). She then measured their tension stress by means of their responses to the TESI. As predicted, she found that their tension-stress was considerably less when they were in the alloic–sympathy than the autic–mastery state. The state nature of this response was emphasized by the fact that it applied regardless of the general level of stress the teachers actually reported experiencing in their classrooms.

Telic Versus Paratelic Dominance as a Moderator of Stress

In extending the reversal theory conceptualization of stress to a consideration of metamotivational dominance rather than states, Martin and his colleagues (Dobbin & Martin, 1988; Martin, 1985; Martin, Kuiper, & Olinger, 1988; Martin, Kuiper, Olinger, & Dobbin, 1987; Martin & Svebak, 1997; Martin-Miller & Martin, 1988) conducted a series of studies investigating the stress-moderating effects of telic versus paratelic dominance. Although this research followed the tradition of previous studies of stress-moderating variables, their predictions based on reversal theory were rather unusual. In general, investigations into stress-moderating variables assume that the positive relation between stressful life events and disturbances of mood and health will be weaker among individuals who are more resistant to stress due to particular personality traits or coping styles. It is not generally expected that the correlation between stressors and illness outcomes will be negative for certain individuals, for example, that some people will actually reveal improvements in emotional or physical functioning as stressful events increase in frequency or severity. However, Martin and colleagues, based on a reversal theory conceptualization, made precisely this sort of prediction.

Martin (1985) suggested that the concept of stress as typically conceptualized relates particularly to telic stress (i.e., frustrations, pressures, conflicts, etc.) that interferes with the achievement of important goals and would therefore be likely to be experienced as aversive when one is in the telic state. For example, most of the events listed in the typical life events measures represent a threat, frustration, or obstacle with regard to academic, work, or relational goals (financial difficulties, loss of a job, death of a loved one, breaking up of a relationship). Martin suggested that these events are likely to produce increases in felt arousal as individuals attempt to cope with them. Based on the reversal theory framework outlined above, Martin hypothesized that different patterns of emotions would be found for paratelic-dominant versus telic-dominant individuals in relation to the levels of such stressful events that they are experiencing at a given time. He suggested that telic-dominant individuals, by definition, are likely to remain in the telic mode for longer periods of time and, therefore, feelings of anxiety, dysphoria, and distress are likely to predominate in these individuals when they experience the arousal associated with coping with ongoing stressors. Thus, for telic-dominant individuals, he predicted a positive linear relationship between the frequency and severity of stressors and mood disturbance. These individuals are likely to report feelings of relaxation and calmness when stress is low or absent, but as stress levels increase there will be a proportionate increase in feelings of tension, anxiety, depression, and so on.

In contrast, a more complex pattern was predicted for paratelic-dominant individuals. When stress is very low or absent in their lives, paratelic-dominant individuals are likely to experience feelings of lethargy, boredom, or dysphoria, because low levels of arousal are unpleasant in the paratelic state. When faced with moderate stress, these people, by definition, are more likely to reverse into (or remain in) the paratelic state more frequently and, as a result will experience an increase in excitement and exhilaration as the intensity and frequency of the stressors increases. However, there is a limit to the amount of stress that will be experienced in this way. It is likely that if stressors become highly threatening or frequent, even the most paratelic-dominant people will reverse into the telic state, becoming serious-minded and arousal-avoidant. At that point, the felt arousal will become unpleasant, and these individuals will begin to experience feelings of distress proportionate to the severity of the stressor. Thus, for paratelic-dominant individuals, Martin predicted a curvilinear relation between the severity of stress and mood disturbance, with greater levels of dysphoria occurring when stress is either very low or very high and lower levels of dysphoria occurring when stress is of moderate intensity. Thus, paratelic-dominant individuals are viewed as being most happy when they have a degree of stress and problems to deal with, whereas telic-dominant people are seen as becoming easily disturbed by stressors.

Martin and colleagues conducted several studies that tested these hypotheses by examining the relationship among telic dominance, severity of stressors, and the psychological effects of the stress. Telic versus paratelic dominance was measured throughout by means of the Telic Dominance Scale (TDS; Murgatroyd, Rushton, Apter, & Ray, 1978), but different measures were used for severity of stressors and for the psychological effects or adaptational outcomes. In one study (Martin et al., 1987; also reported in Martin et al., 1988), involving 48 male and female undergraduate students as participants, stressors were assessed by means of the Recent Stressful Event Questionnaire, which was based on the first part of Folkman and Lazarus's (1980) Ways of Coping Scale. Participants were asked to provide a written description of their most stressful event of the past month. Events typically reported included interpersonal difficulties (arguments with friends and family members) and various academic and vocational concerns (time pressures related to course assignments and studying for exams). Trained judges rated these event descriptions as being either resolved or ongoing. An event was rated as resolved if the participant used the past tense, described the event as having occurred during a specific time period, or otherwise indicated that it was no longer a problem. An event was rated as ongoing if the participant used the present tense or described the event as continuing to be an aspect of his or her current life situation.

It was assumed that participants whose most stressful recent event was resolved were not experiencing significant ongoing stress, inasmuch as any ongoing stressors they may have had were not recalled as being the most stressful of the past month. It was also assumed that the stressful events experienced by students during a given month would be of moderate intensity. Although severity of the stressors was not measured, an informal examination of the event descriptions suggested that this was indeed the case. The adaptational outcome in this study consisted of scores on the Beck Depression Inventory (BDI) (Beck, Ward, Mendelson, Mock, & Erbaugh, 1961). It should be noted that the mean score of the BDI was 5.7 for this sample, which is well below the clinical range, and the results were discussed in terms of dysphoria rather than clinical depression.

The results, analyzed by means of a hierarchical multiple regression analysis, revealed nonsignificant main effects for both the dichotomous resolved–ongoing variable and telic–paratelic dominance, as predicted. However, also as predicted, the interaction between these two variables was significant, indicating that the magnitude of the relationship between telic dominance and dysphoria varied as a function of whether the event was resolved or ongoing. When simple correlations were computed between telic dominance and BDI for participants with resolved and ongoing events separately, a positive correlation was found for those whose event was ongoing ($r = .40$, $p = .05$), indicating that telic-dominant participants reported higher levels of dysphoria than did paratelic-dominant participants when the event was ongoing. On the other hand, the correlation for those whose event was resolved was negative but nonsignificant ($r = -.15$), indicating that telic- and paratelic-dominant participants did not differ in stress level when the event was resolved.

More important, when the regression lines for the two groups (resolved vs. ongoing event) were plotted on a graph, it showed that telic-dominant participants were more disturbed if the stressor was ongoing than if it was resolved, whereas paratelic-dominant individuals were more distressed if the event was resolved than if it was ongoing. Thus, in support of the hypotheses, the results showed that paratelic- and telic-dominant participants show opposite responses to stressors. Telic-dominant individuals are most distressed when their most stressful recent event is ongoing, whereas paratelic-dominant individuals are most distressed when the event is resolved, suggesting that they prefer to have moderate levels of stress.

A second study was conducted that was essentially identical to the first, except that the dependent measure was now a biochemical index of stress, salivary cortisol (Martin et al., 1987; also reported by Dobbin & Martin, 1988). Cortisol is an adrenocortico steroid that is secreted during sympathetic nervous system activation and is considered to be a measure of physiological arousal associated with stress. The participants were 42 male and female undergraduates who were asked to provide saliva samples immediately before completing the TDS and the Recent Stressful Event Questionnaire. In this study, the participants themselves were asked to indicate whether the event was resolved or ongoing. The saliva was subsequently assayed for cortisol using radioimmunoassay procedures.

The results were again analyzed by means of hierarchical multiple regression, and the interaction between the dichotomous resolved–unresolved variable and TDS scores in predicting cortisol levels was again significant, indicating that the relation between telic dominance and cortisol varies as a function of whether the event was resolved or ongoing. When recent stressors were ongoing, the correlation between TDS and cortisol was nonsignificant ($r = .02$), whereas when recent stressors were resolved, the correlation was $-.53$ ($p > .05$). Thus, if their most stressful recent event was resolved, paratelic-dominant individuals had higher cortisol levels than did telic-dominant individuals.

When the results were plotted on a graph, it revealed that, as participants' scores on the TDS became more extreme in either the telic or paratelic direction, their salivary cortisol levels became increasingly divergent as a function of whether the event was resolved or ongoing. In particular, those at the more paratelic-dominant end of the dimension revealed higher salivary cortisol levels when their recent stressors were resolved rather than ongoing, whereas those at the more telic-dominant end had higher cortisol levels when their recent stressors were ongoing rather than resolved. Thus, as with the previous study, these results indicate that paratelic- and telic-dominant individuals experience stress in very different ways.

In a third study, Martin et al. (1987) conducted a laboratory experiment in which stress level was manipulated. Martin and colleagues had 27 undergraduate participants perform an experimental task (a 10-minute video game) in either a no-stress or a mildly stressful condition. In the no-stress condition, the participants were instructed to play the game simply for fun. In the moderately stressful condition, they were instructed to try to do the best they could, as their performance would be evaluated by the experimenter and compared to that of other participants. All the participants completed the task in both conditions, in counterbalanced order. The results revealed that the paratelic-dominant participants obtained significantly higher scores on the video task in the stressful condition than in the nonstressful condition, whereas the telic-dominant participants obtained higher scores in the non-stressful than in the stressful condition. In addition, on a set of rating scales, telic-dominant participants reported feeling significantly more unpleasant and more dissatisfied with their performance and perceived the experimenter as more hostile in the stress than in the no-stress condition. In contrast, the paratelic-dominant participants did not differ between conditions on any of these variables. Also, physiological recording of skin conductance indicated that telic-dominant participants showed a higher mean frequency of spontaneous skin responses (increases of skin conductance of at least .05 μmhos within a 1-second period) in the stressful than in the no-stress condition, whereas this measure did not differ between conditions for paratelic-dominant participants. Thus, using a laboratory manipulation and a variety of measures, this study provided additional support for the hypothesis that telic-dominant individuals are more adversely affected by moderate stress than are paratelic-dominant people, whereas the latter tend to perform better under conditions of moderate stress as compared to no stress.

The previous three studies reduced the stress variable to a dichotomy and studied only stressors ranging from low to moderate intensity, so it was not possible to examine the way in which telic- and paratelic-dominant participants might react across a range of stressor intensities including stress of greater severity. In a fourth study, Martin (1985; also reported by Martin et al., 1987) had 74 male and female undergraduates complete the College Student Life Experiences Survey (CSLES; Sandler & Lakey, 1982) and the Daily Hassles Scale (DHS; Kanner, Coyne, Schaefer, & Lazarus, 1981). The CSLES consists of a list of potentially stressful events that are germane to students (e.g., breaking up with a boyfriend or girlfriend, failing an exam). Participants were asked to indicate which of these events had occurred in their lives during the previous year and to rate whether they had had a negative or positive impact on them. A total score was computed by summing the number of negatively rated events checked by each participant. The DHS comprises a list of minor distressing demands such as misplacing or losing things or having too many things to do. The participants were instructed to check off the hassles that had happened to them during the preceding month and to indicate the degree of severity of each on a scale from 1 to 3. A total hassles score was obtained by summing these values. The adaptational outcome variable in this study was the Profile of Mood States (POMS; McNair, Lorr, & Droppleman, 1971), which contains scales for five negative moods (tension, depression, anger, fatigue, and confusion) and one positive mood (vigor). A total mood disturbance score was computed by summing the five negative moods and subtracting the vigor score. Participants were instructed to complete this measure in terms of how they had generally been feeling over the past month. In addition, the participants were asked to complete the TDS.

As noted above, it was predicted that telic-dominant participants would show a direct linear relation between stressors and mood disturbance, whereas paratelic-dominant participants would show a curvilinear relation between these variables, with higher mood disturbance at both low and high levels of stress and lower mood disturbance at moderate levels of stress. The data were analyzed by means of hierarchical multiple regression analyses, using each of the two stress measures separately. The results supported the predictions. Telic- and paratelic-dominant participants did not differ significantly in their reported overall levels of negative life events or hassles or in their overall mood disturbance scores. However, as predicted, there were significant interactions between TDS scores and the quadratic (curvilinear) component of both of the stressor measures, indicating that the shape of the regression curve predicting mood disturbance from stressors changes as a function of telic dominance scores. The pattern of results is shown in Figures 6.1 and 6.2.

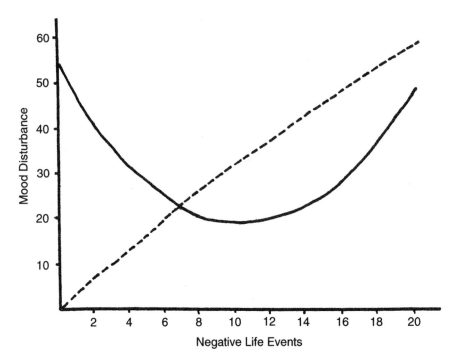

Figure 6.1. Regression curves for telic-dominant (dashed line) and paratelic-dominant (continuous line) participants showing the relationship for each of these groups between level of stress as measured by negative life events and mood disturbance. *Note.* From "Telic Dominance, Stress, and Moods," by R. A. Martin, 1985, in M. J. Apter, D. Fontana, & S. Miller (Eds.), *Reversal Theory: Applications and Developments,* Cardiff, Wales: University College Cardiff Press. Copyright 1985 by M. J. Apter. Reprinted with permission of the author.

As seen in Figure 6.1, when the CSLES was used as the stressor measure, the telic-dominant participants showed a strong linear relationship between life events and mood disturbance, such that those with high levels of negative life events reported more disturbed prevailing moods than did those with fewer life events. In contrast, the paratelic-dominant participants showed the expected curvilinear relationship, such that moods became less disturbed as negative life events became more frequent, and then curved back in the unpleasant direction as the frequency of life events increased still further. Figure 6.2 shows that essentially the same pattern of results was found when the daily hassles score was used as the measure of stressors. Overall, then, the results of this study provided additional empirical support for the hypotheses. With both the measure of major life events and the daily hassles scale, the patterns observed at low to moderate levels of stressors were similar to those obtained in the previous studies. For telic-dominant participants, a positive linear relation was found between stressors and mood disturbance, whereas

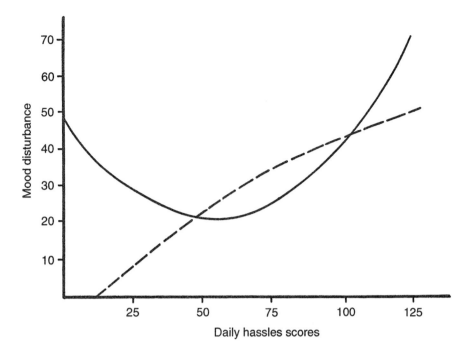

Figure 6.2. Regression curves for telic-dominant (dashed line) and paratelic-dominant (continuous line) participants showing the relationship for each of these groups between level of stress as measured by daily hassles and mood disturbance.
Note. From "Telic Dominance, Stress, and Moods," by R. A. Martin, 1985, in M. J. Apter, D. Fontana, & S. Miller (Eds.), *Reversal Theory: Applications and Developments,* Cardiff, Wales: University College Cardiff Press. Copyright 1985 by M. J. Apter. Reprinted with permission of the author.

for paratelic-dominant participants this relationship was negative. On the other hand, as predicted, when levels of reported negative life events and hassles were in the moderate to high range, the relation between stressors and mood disturbance was found to be positive for both telic- and paratelic-dominant participants.

Thus, paratelic-dominant participants appear to display the least negative (or most positive) affect when they are experiencing moderate levels of stressors, whereas telic-dominant participants are least negative with little or no stress. Presumably, paratelic-dominant individuals, who seek arousal and challenge, perceive their lives as being unstimulating and unchallenging when they are experiencing very few negative life events or hassles, and they therefore feel more bored and dissatisfied. On the other hand, it is clear that these individuals have a limit to their tolerance for stress, as their mood levels become increasingly disturbed when the number of stressors increases beyond a certain optimal level. As discussed earlier, it may be that paratelic-dominant individuals reverse into the telic state when they are faced with higher levels of stress (although this hypothesis was not directly tested in this study).

A study reported by Summers and Stewart (1993) and by Stewart, Summers, and Thorne (1995) with a sample of 50 semiprofessional and university baseball players confirmed the findings of Martin's (1985) study. The DHS and the Athletic Life Events Scale were used to assess levels of stressors. The POMS was used to measure moods. Analyses of the data indicated that telic-dominant baseball players exhibited a positive linear relationship between severity of stressors (both life events and hassles) and mood disturbance. In contrast, paratelic-dominant baseball players were found to exhibit a curvilinear relationship between severity of stress and mood disturbance similar to that found by Martin.

Kiernan (1997) also reported a study that replicated these findings with a sample of 48 participants who completed the BDI, the Paratelic Dominance Scale (PDS; Cook & Gerkovich, 1993), and the DHS. As in the Martin (1985) study, a U-shaped relationship was found between daily hassles and depression scores for paratelic-dominant participants, whereas the relationship for telic-dominant participants was linear. In an attempt to determine whether these findings are due to changes in individuals' metamotivational state, as predicted by reversal theory, rather than to stable trait differences (such as would be explained by a sensation seeking explanation, for example), Kiernan also had three participants (one highly telic, one highly paratelic, and one intermediate, as determined by scores on the PDS) keep daily records of their telic–paratelic state, arousal level, and mood states using Likert-type scales. In two of the three individuals there was a significant difference between the correlations of arousal and mood in the telic and the paratelic states. In the third case, the difference was not significant but was in the predicted direction. These results were interpreted as supporting a reversal theory explanation over an optimal arousal one.

In a partial replication of the Martin (1985) study, Lafreniere (1997) conducted a study with 141 university students. Telic versus paratelic dominance was measured by means of the PDS. The Inventory of College Students' Recent Life Experiences (Kohn, Lafreniere, & Gurevich, 1990), a measure of daily hassles designed for use with college students, was used to assess stress levels. In addition, the Perceived Stress Scale (PSS; Cohen, Kamarck, & Mermelstein, 1983) was administered as the outcome variable. These participants also completed the Somatic State Questionnaire (SSQ; Cook, Gerkovich, Potocky, O'Connell, & Hoffman, 1991) to determine their current metamotivational state. The results revealed a significant interaction between PDS and the hassles measure in predicting perceived stress. As predicted, under low levels of hassles, paratelic-dominant participants reported higher levels of perceived stress than did telic-dominant participants, whereas under high exposure to hassles, telic-dominant individuals reported more distress on the PSS than did those who were paratelic dominant.

Further analyses were conducted to relate hassle levels to the metamotivational states of the participants at the time of participation in the study. Individuals in the negativistic state, as compared to those in the conformist state, were more likely to report higher levels of hassles overall, as well as more hassles related to social mistreatment, romantic problems, and friendship problems. The direction of causality here is unclear: It may be that exposure to these types of hassles causes individuals to be more likely to reverse into the negativistic mode or, alternatively, being in the negativistic mode may lead to greater perceptions of oneself as having experienced these types of hassles. Finally, a two-way interaction was found between gender and paratelic dominance in predicting hassles having to do with romantic problems. Men who were paratelic dominant reported more romantic hassles than did men who were telic dominant. In contrast, women who were telic dominant reported more romantic hassles than did women who were paratelic dominant. According to the author, these results suggested, "individuals who operate outside of stereotypical gender roles with regard to relationships (women who are playful and men who are serious) fare better romantically than those who adopt a more traditional approach" (Lafreniere, 1997, p. 41).

Telic Dominance, Coping, and Type A

Consistent with the reversal theory formulation of stress described earlier, Apter (1989b) suggested that telic-dominant individuals may react to stressors and threats in a more effortful way than do paratelic-dominant individuals. This is because telic-dominant individuals are more likely to perceive the arousal associated with the stressors as unpleasant and are therefore likely to engage in more strenuous efforts directed at eliminating the cause of the stress. Paratelic-dominant individuals, on the other hand, who are more likely to experience stress-related arousal as challenging and exhilarating, may be less concerned about efforts to eliminate the source of the stress. Some support for this hypothesis is provided by several studies that have been conducted to investigate the relationship between telic–paratelic dominance and ways of coping. Murgatroyd (1985b) administered the Ways of Coping Inventory (Folkman & Lazarus, 1980) to 100 students about to take a degree examination. Howard (1988) administered a revised version of this coping measure to a group of telic-dominant and a group of paratelic-dominant respondents who were instructed to respond in terms of their most stressful experience of the previous week. Baker (1988) selected a group of extreme telic-dominant and a group of extreme paratelic-dominant participants (15 in each) from a sample pool of 107 participants ranging in age from 17 to 70. She asked them to rate "the most bothersome event of the day" every day for seven days, using a questionnaire adapted from Stone and Neale (1984).

Despite the differences in measures and research design, essentially similar results were found in each of these studies. This was that the telic-dominant participants were significantly more likely than paratelic-dominant participants to use problem-focused coping strategies involving direct action against the source of the stress. In contrast, paratelic-dominant participants tended to use a variety of other strategies, such as wishful thinking or distraction. Thus, telic-dominant individuals are more likely to exert effort against the source of the stress. Apter (1989b) interpreted these findings as suggesting that the effortful coping of telic-dominant individuals may place them at greater risk for psychosomatic illness.

There has also been some interest in the relationship between telic dominance and the Type A coronary-prone behavior pattern, as there appear to be some similarities between the two constructs. Apter and Svebak (1989) linked Type A conceptually to telic effort-stress, suggesting that Type A personality may relate to the degree to which the individual is willing to expend effort in dealing with stressors. Svebak (1988a, 1988c) expanded on this by suggesting that the Type A individual may be conceptualized as one who is dominated by a combination of the arousal-avoiding (telic), negativistic, autic, and mastery modes. However, empirical investigations into the relation between Type A and telic dominance have been mixed. In a study of 222 Norwegian students, Svebak and Apter (1984) did not find a significant relationship between the TDS and Type A, as measured by a Norwegian translation of the Jenkins Activity Survey (JAS). In contrast, Gallacher, Yarnell, and Phillips (1988), using a sample of 99 middle-age British men, found weak but significant correlations between total scores on the TDS and Type A as measured by both the JAS and the Framingham Scale ($rs = .25$ and $.26$, respectively, $p > .01$). However, the correlation with the Arousal-avoidance subscale of the TDS was negative for the JAS ($r = -.21$, $p > .05$), and nonsignificant for the Framingham Scale ($r = .03$). Thus, further clarification is needed for the way in which the Type A coronary-prone construct fits into reversal theory.

CONCLUSION

Consistent with its approach to other domains of psychology, the reversal theory conceptualization of stress emphasizes the importance of examining the way in which individuals subjectively experience life situations. An event or experience that is perceived as threatening and produces negative emotional consequences in one person might be perceived as a positive challenge and experienced as exciting or exhilarating by someone else (or by the same person at a different point in time). Thus, stress is clearly in the eye of the beholder. Reversal theory makes further contributions to our understanding of stress by positing a distinction between tension- and effort-stress, and by providing a comprehensive framework for analyzing the dynamic interplay of metamotivational states, environmental events, and stress-related emotions. Thus, reversal theory has anticipated the recent call by Lazarus (1993) to bring to bear broader theories of emotion and motivation to enrich our understanding of stress. A considerable amount of empirical research has been conducted to investigate the reversal theory conceptualization of stress and, in general, the results have provided encouraging support for the theory.

As we have seen, reversal theory has already generated research on many aspects of stress with a focus upon understanding individual differences in the appraisal of a stressor and ways of coping with potential stressors. These differences reflect the probabilistic nature of the concept of dominance, rather than the traditional trait approach to individual differences. In addition, these differences offer a sophisticated theoretical conception of seeming paradoxical relations between motivation, emotion and arousal that have caused much debate and confusion for decades of stress research. However, although interesting results have been obtained within the domains of musculoskeletal back pain, stress hormone mechanisms of importance to immune function, and mental health reflected in a range of dysphoric states, much remains to be seen from this approach to stress and coping. One example is the field of psychosomatic (psychophysiological) disorders including gastrointestinal, immunological, and cardiovascular functions in relation to stressful life events. In addition, most of the studies so far have focused upon how university students cope with stressors, and the debate regarding the generalizing of these findings to adult populations coping with stressors at work and within the family across the lifespan has not been settled.

7

SMOKING AND SMOKING CESSATION

KATHLEEN A. O'CONNELL AND MARY R. COOK

Humility is required for smoking cessation researchers (Lichtenstein, 1985). In 1985, we had come to know the truth of this statement. We conducted a 4-year study of more than 1,000 people who were trying to quit smoking. The results showed that the best set of our theory-derived predictors accounted for only 10% of the variance in long-term success. The need for humility became even more apparent, because some of the variables in the model actually were significant predictors in the opposite direction from what we hypothesized (O'Connell, 1986). For instance, on the basis of the Health Belief Model (Rosenstock & Kirscht, 1974), we hypothesized that people who were feeling higher threat and more vulnerability to getting a smoking-related disease, who saw more benefits and fewer barriers to quitting, would be the most likely to succeed. Our findings actually showed that both threat and benefits predicted a *lack* of success and that barriers were not important to the process of quitting. Participants who had high threat of illness scores and those who knew that their pulmonary function tests were abnormal were less likely to succeed in quitting than people who had a lower threat of illness scores and people who knew that they had normal pulmonary-function tests. Although perceived barriers to smoking cessation were unrelated to success at cessation, those who perceived more benefits from cessation at the beginning of their cessation attempt were more likely to have relapsed by 12 months as compared to those who expected fewer benefits. The findings were opposite to our predictions. Not only were the results humiliating, but they were also irrational.

While mulling over these perplexing results, the authors of this chapter simultaneously and independently stumbled across reversal theory. One of us had read a review of *The Experience of Motivation* (Apter, 1982a) in the journal *Addictive Behaviors* (Miller, 1985). The other had encountered the reversal theory-based psychophysiological research of Sven Svebak (e.g., Svebak, 1984, 1985b, 1986a) while serving as the editor of *Biofeedback and*

Self-Regulation. Our further explorations of the theory revealed something remarkable: Reversal theory addressed irrational behavior (O'Connell, 1991, 1996). In addition, reversal theory made interesting predictions about, and promised to address, both the motivational and the psychophysiological issues in smoking (O'Connell, 1988). Because one of us had an abiding interest in motivation and health behavior, and the other was entranced with the confusing psychophysiological effects of nicotine, we embarked on a collaborative effort to use reversal theory as an explanatory model of processes in smoking behavior and cessation. This chapter describes the outcomes of that effort, the paths we followed, and what we believe these efforts have taught us about reversal theory, smoking, and health behavior.

Our approach has had two thrusts. First, we have applied reversal theory concepts to the attempt to quit smoking and especially to the highly tempting situations experienced by those who were trying to quit. Second, we have used reversal theory concepts to make predictions about the effects of smoking on physiological variables such as brain waves, muscle tension, and heart rate. Although there were times when these two thrusts seemed to be going in unrelated directions, we continued to bring the results of each research effort to bear upon the other in order to interpret results and develop better designs for subsequent studies. Although our approaches have been theory based, we have not limited ourselves to testing theories; rather, our interest has been in addressing the significant health care problem of smoking and its consequences.

RESEARCH ON HIGHLY TEMPTING SITUATIONS

Previous work in smoking cessation had indicated that trait variables and those measured before the initiation of a cessation attempt were not predictive of success in smoking cessation. Because there was a growing interest in relapse prevention and the process of smoking cessation (Brownell, Marlatt, Lichtenstein, & Wilson, 1986), we focused our research on highly tempting situations experienced during a cessation attempt. Our own work (O'Connell & Martin, 1987) and the work of others (Baer, Kamarck, Lichtenstein, & Ransom, 1989; Baer & Lichtenstein, 1988; Cummings, Gordon, & Marlatt, 1980) had indicated that lapsing during a cessation attempt was related to experiencing negative affect states during a highly tempting situation.

Reversal theory offered a comprehensive way to understand the experiences of individuals who were tempted to smoke during cessation. Reversal theory suggested that there were several different types of metamotivational states that could be experienced at any given time. The theory suggested that, although smoking lapses could take place in any of the states, the reasons for the lapse would differ. For instance, lapses in the telic state might have to do with the need to lower arousal levels, whereas lapses in the paratelic state might have to do with the need to raise arousal levels. Although lapses could occur in each state, reversal theory also suggested that some states would be more vulnerable to lapsing during temptations than other states (O'Connell, 1988). Specifically, we reasoned that paratelic, negativistic, and sympathy states would be associated with lapsing more than would the opposing telic, conformist, or mastery states. The following sections outline our research findings with respect to these hypotheses.

Research Methods

Two types of studies were undertaken to test these hypotheses. One type involved interviewing individuals who were attempting to quit smoking about their most highly tempting situations. These tape-recorded interviews took place from 2 weeks to 15 months after the cessation attempt began. The interviewers asked participants to describe their first lapse (if any) since the last interview session and their most highly tempting situation since the last interview. These interviews were then coded using the Metamotivational State Coding System (Potocky, Cook, & O'Connell, 1993) that we had developed for this purpose (see chapter 3 in this volume). Results of these studies have been reported in Cook, Gerkovich, O'Connell, and Potocky (1995); Gerkovich, Cook, O'Connell, and Potocky (1993); Gerkovich, Potocky, O'Connell, and Cook (1993); O'Connell, Cook, Gerkovich, Potocky, and Swan (1990); O'Connell, Gerkovich, and Cook (1995, 1997); and Potocky, Gerkovich, O'Connell, and Cook (1991). Table 7.1 summarizes these studies.

The second type of investigation that we have undertaken uses Ecological Momentary Assessment (EMA) techniques (Stone & Shiffman, 1994) to study, in near real time, the experiences of individuals who are quitting smoking. Participants used a tape recorder to report on the coping strategies they used when they were tempted to smoke or actually did smoke. In addition, the participants completed computerized assessments administered by a hand-held computer they carried with them. The computer-administered questionnaire included assessments of reversal theory states.

Telic–Paratelic Pair

Although we expected that lapses would occur in all states, we reasoned that paratelic states would be more vulnerable to lapses than telic states for three reasons. Paratelic states are characterized by being playful and sensation oriented rather than serious and goal oriented. The serious goal to quit smoking would not be salient in the paratelic state. Second, the paratelic

Table 7.1.
Reversal Theory Studies of Lapsing in Smoking Cessation That Use the
Retrospective Report Method

References	Methods	States Studied	States Associated With Lapses
O'Connell, Cook, Gerkovich, Potocky, & Swan, 1990	Cross-sectional; Study 1: 3 months after quitting Study 2: 6–15 months after quitting	Telic–paratelic Negativistic–conformist	Study 1: paratelic, negativistic Study 2: paratelic, negativistic
Potocky, Gerkovich, O'Connell, & Cook, 1991	Within-subjects; 3–6 months after quitting	Telic–paratelic Negativistic–conformist	Paratelic, negativistic
Gerkovich, Potocky, O'Connell, & Cook, 1993	Cross-sectional; 3–15 months after cessation	Telic–paratelic Negativistic–conformist	Elaboration of O'Connell et al., 1990; paratelic, negativistic
Gerkovich, Cook, O'Connell, & Potocky, 1993[a]	Cross-sectional; 2–26 weeks after cessation	Telic–paratelic Negativistic–conformist Mastery–sympathy	Paratelic, sympathy
Cook, Gerkovich, O'Connell, & Potocky 1995[a]	Cross-sectional and within-subjects; 2–6 weeks after cessation	Telic–paratelic	Paratelic
O'Connell, Gerkovich, & Cook, 1995[a]	Cross-sectional; 2 to 26 weeks after cessation	Mastery–sympathy	Sympathy
O'Connell, Gerkovich, & Cook, 1997[a]	Cross-sectional; 2–26 weeks after cessation; study of combinations of states	Telic–paratelic Negativistic–conformist Mastery–sympathy Autic–alloic (Intra-autic–autocentric versions of autic)	Paratelic Intra-autic sympathy Autocentric mastery

[a]Overlapping data sets.

state is associated with preferences for high arousal; increasing physiological arousal is one of the well-known effects of nicotine. Third, paratelic states are associated with a preference for low felt significance, that is, people in paratelic states want to believe that what they are doing is not important. They want to believe that "one little cigarette won't hurt."

In three studies of retrospective reports of highly tempting situations (Cook, Gerkovich, O'Connell, & Potocky, 1995; Gerkovich, Potocky, O'Connell, & Cook, 1993; O'Connell et al., 1990), the above hypotheses were confirmed. We found that paratelic states are significantly more likely to be associated with lapses than are telic states. In two studies (Potocky et al., 1991; Cook, Gerkovich, O'Connell, & Potocky, 1995), we used within-subjects designs. We found that this effect was due to differences in states between lapse and abstain episodes for the same participants and not to lasting trait differences that might exist between participants who lapse and those who do not.

We also predicted that participants in the paratelic state would be more sensitive to cigarette availability than would those in the telic state. If cigarettes were not available to participants in the paratelic state, they would be unlikely to seek them out because doing so might require a reversal to the more goal-oriented telic state. Participants in the telic state, on the other hand, would already be goal oriented and would seek out cigarettes whether they were available or not. Therefore, lapses in the paratelic state would be more likely to occur when cigarettes were available than lapses in the telic state. This hypothesis was supported in two of the three studies (O'Connell et al., 1990) in which it was tested.

Ecological Momentary Assessment Studies

Although these findings suggest that people in the paratelic state are more vulnerable to lapses than those in the telic state, lapses are still likely in the telic state. For instance, we found in our first EMA study (O'Connell, Gerkovich, Bott, Cook, & Shiffman, 2000) that approximately 75% of the lapses occurred in the telic state. These telic lapses may be due to being in the other vulnerable states, described below. However, the overall findings point to the need to cope with urges in both telic and paratelic states. Our own work (O'Connell, Potocky, Gerkovich, & Cook, 1993) and that of others (Baer, Kamarck, Lichtenstein, & Ransom, 1989; Bliss, Garvey, Heinold, & Hitchcock, 1989; Shiffman, 1984) indicates that failing to use coping strategies during a highly tempting situation is significantly related to relapse. Lapsing in the paratelic state may be due to the failure to use coping strategies.

In ongoing work we have used EMA techniques described above to study the coping strategies of individuals who are attempting to quit smoking.

Preliminary findings on 36 participants who carried the equipment for 3 days during their first 10 days of cessation indicate that fewer coping strategies were reported during episodes when participants were in the paratelic state than when they were in the telic state. Within-subject assessments of the 11 participants who experienced lapse episodes while on the study also revealed that episodes in which the participants lapsed were significantly more likely to be experienced in the paratelic state than episodes in which participants resisted smoking (O'Connell et al., 2000). This observation supported the findings from our retrospective studies.

Negativistic–Conformist Pair

We hypothesized that being in the negativistic state would be associated with lapsing, whereas being in the conformist state would be associated with abstaining. Individuals in the negativistic state are interested in breaking rules, and smoking a cigarette during a quit attempt can be an example of rule-breaking behavior. The hypothesis was supported in our first two studies (Gerkovich, Potocky, O'Connell, & Cook, 1993; O'Connell et al., 1990) but not in the third study (Cook et al., 1995), which focused on experiences that occurred earlier in the cessation process than those of the first two studies. We found that although participants lapsed in the negativistic state, they also lapsed in the conformist state. One reason for the lack of replication of this finding may be that negativistic states occurred relatively infrequently early in the cessation process. Our EMA data revealed that participants were negativistic in only 14% of all episodes, indicating a relatively low amount of negativism shortly after quitting (O'Connell et al., 2000). Therefore, the power to detect an effect may not have been adequate. It may also be the case that the negativistic state is a more important predictor of lapsing later in the cessation process.

Mastery–Sympathy Pair

Reversal theory holds that individuals reverse from the mastery state, in which they are oriented toward control and competition, to the sympathy state, in which they are oriented toward caring and cooperation (Apter, 1988b; Apter & Smith, 1985; O'Connell, 1993a; O'Connell & Apter, 1993). Although these orientations usually involve controlling or caring for individuals, objects, or situations external to the self, sometimes it is the self that one wants to control or care for. We hypothesized that the sympathy state would be associated with lapsing, whereas the mastery state would be associated with resisting the urge to smoke in highly tempting situations. This hypothesis was supported (Gerkovich, Cook, O'Connell, & Potocky, 1993;

O'Connell et al., 1995). The typical situations in which the sympathy state operates to undermine smoking cessation efforts are those in which the individual is feeling deprived and sorry for himself or herself. Lapses in abstinence can bring relief from such feelings. In their study of responses to instances of failing at behavior change, O'Connell and Brooks (1997) showed that individuals failing to resist urges to carry out established behaviors were much more likely to be classified in the sympathy-gaining state than those failing to carry out a new behavior. Classification in the sympathy-gaining state required endorsing items such as affectionate, appreciated, cared about, tender, and kind to self. This finding implies that lapsing during a cessation attempt can bring positive sympathy-related outcomes.

Although we are convinced that the mastery–sympathy states have important implications for smoking cessation, we have had trouble developing self-administered instruments to measure these states, and we have yet to be able to identify psychophysiological correlates of them.

REVIEW OF PSYCHOPHYSIOLOGICAL STUDIES

Arousal and its associated hedonic tone are key concepts in reversal theory as well as in many models of smoking behavior. If the paratelic and telic states reflect differences in arousal or activation systems (see the work by Svebak and his colleagues in chapter 5 in this volume), and smoking alters either arousal or activation, smoking should have different effects on physiology, depending on the state the individual is in at the time.

The literature on the physiological effects of smoking suggests that one reason smoking is maintained is that smokers learn to use cigarettes to both increase and decrease central nervous system arousal (e.g., Gilbert, Robinson, Chamberlin, & Speilberger, 1989; Golding & Mangan, 1982; Pomerleau & Pomerleau, 1984). Arousal, however, is not a unitary construct. Pribram and McGuiness (1975) postulated an arousal system that produces a phasic response to perceptual input, a more tonic activation system that maintains readiness for action, and an effort system that coordinates the other two. Tucker and Williamson (1984) concluded that the arousal system is most dense in the frontal cortex and on the right side of the head and is noradrenergic, whereas the activation system is dopaminergic, with maximal distribution in the left frontal region. Although few studies had directly addressed the question of differential physiological effects of smoking as a function of state, the limited data available were supportive of the hypothesis because they indicated that smoking in highly arousing, anxiety states reduced arousal (e.g., Gilbert, 1995; Gilbert et al., 1989; Herning, Jones, & Bachman, 1983; O'Connor, 1982).

Spectral Analysis

Our first psychophysiological study tested the hypothesis that the effects of smoking on electrophysiological measures of arousal, as reflected in the spectral analysis of the electroencephalograph (EEG), would depend on whether the individual was in the telic or paratelic state. We also expected that state dominance would be reflected in spectral analysis of the EEG but would provide weaker support for the hypothesis than the state analysis. Smokers, selected on the basis of their scores on the Paratelic Dominance Scale (PDS; Cook & Gerkovich, 1993), came to the laboratory after abstaining from smoking since bedtime the night before. Sensors were attached to measure EEG, heart rate, and muscle tension. They then participated in a battery of tasks and measures under three conditions; while deprived, after puffing on an unlit cigarette of their own brand, and after smoking. State was measured frequently during this process. Analysis focused on the relationship between state and physiological measures.

EEG frequency has traditionally been divided into bands. The delta band represents activity below 4 Hz (cycles per second) and is associated with sleep. The theta band, 4–7.5 Hz, is associated with relaxed low arousal and reverie. When the person is relaxed but alert, EEG frequency is predominantly in the alpha band (8–12 Hz). Higher levels of arousal produce beta 1 and beta 2 bands (i.e., frequencies above 12 Hz). We analyzed the EEG using a technique called Discrete Fourier Transform, which produces two measures for each band: the frequency of the brain waves and their power or magnitude. As arousal increases, frequency in and across the bands can increase. Because the delta band is rare in the waking EEG and because the delta band also contains a great deal of "noise," we did not include it in our analyses.

The results of this study, as reported in Cook, Gerkovich, Hoffman, et al. (1995), revealed the first indications of gender differences in regard to smoking, state, and physiology. For men, increases in alpha peak frequency as a function of smoking were greater in the telic than in the paratelic state; although smoking increased alpha peak frequency in women, no differences as a function of state were observed. Beta 1 frequency was reduced by smoking (primarily due to participants in the telic state) and was more prominent from the frontal than from the parietal sites. No effects on beta frequency were found when participants were in the paratelic state. Analysis of alpha, theta, and beta 1 power led to the same conclusions. The results indicate that, as expected, participants in the telic state smoked in such a way as to decrease arousal, whereas participants in the paratelic state smoked in such a way as to increase arousal. However, support for the hypothesis was found primarily in men. This gender difference may be due to the recent observation (Perkins, 1996) that men respond more to nicotine, and women respond more to the context in which smoking occurs.

Analysis of EEG differences among telic-dominant, paratelic-dominant, and nondominant individuals also proved interesting. As expected, scores on the PDS did not significantly predict the actual state the participant was experiencing during the experiment. No significant differential effects of smoking in the three dominance groups were found for theta, alpha, or beta 1 power; paratelic-dominant participants, however, showed a marked increase in beta 2 power as a function of smoking. Dominance is thought to be reflected in the amount of time an individual spends in the telic versus the paratelic state, whereas state measures are aimed at determining the state that is in effect for a given individual at a specific time. We have previously speculated (Cook et al., 1997) that EEG differences among dominance groups might be due to relatively "hard-wired" neural mechanisms, whereas difference between state groups should reflect an underlying mechanism that is capable of brief, phasic response.

Contingent Negative Variation

Another way to evaluate the effects of smoking on EEG activity and to test whether they are modified by state or dominance is to record the *contingent negative variation* (CNV). To collect CNV data, the participant is first presented with a warning stimulus (S1), followed after a fixed amount of time by a second stimulus (S2) that indicates to the participant that he or she should respond as rapidly as possible by pressing a button. The CNV is the electrically negative brain potential that occurs between S1 and S2. Because the CNV is a hard-wired system, we expected telic-dominant participants to show larger amplitude CNV and that this would occur earlier in the interval between S1 and S2. We expected paratelic-dominant participants to show a delayed increase in CNV amplitude, that is, the CNV would occur later in the interval between S1 and S2. In the task we used (Cook, Gerkovich, Hoffman, McClernon, & O'Connell, 1996) the pitch (high or low) of the warning signal indicated whether the participant was to respond (Go trials) or not respond (No-Go trials) to S2. This allows a comparison between trials in which the participant is preparing to make a quick response and trials during which the participant knows that no further action is required. Data analysis indicated that participants in the telic state had larger CNV responses to Go stimuli than those in the paratelic state. During No-Go trials, participants in the telic state had a larger early response and a smaller late response, whereas those in the paratelic state had a larger late response. Smoking did not affect the CNV and did not interact with state.

When analysis of the CNV data was based on dominance rather than state, smoking and dominance did not differentially affect the CNV unless gender was taken into account, and the significant effects were limited to the No-Go CNV. Smoking, compared to sham smoking, increased the amplitude of the No-Go CNV more for paratelic-dominant men than for telic-dominant men. As expected, this effect was particularly strong during the late portion of the CNV. The pattern for women was quite different. Telic-dominant women showed a decrease in both the early and late portions of the No-Go CNV after smoking. Paratelic-dominant women had increased amplitude during the early portion and decreased amplitude during the later portion of the CNV curve. This finding is directly opposite to the observations made in men.

The pattern of changes observed in the CNV indicates that a need to perform the CNV task quickly and accurately dissipates differences between the telic and paratelic dominance groups, as significant effects were found primarily for the No-Go task. Of particular importance are the gender differences we found; they once more indicate the necessity to include both women and men in studies of the effects of smoking on physiology.

Heart Rate and Muscle Responses

Another way to study arousal and smoking in the laboratory is to measure heart rate and skeletal muscle responses to smoking (Gerkovich, Cook, Hoffman, & O'Connell, 1998). As expected, smoking resulted in increased heart rate, and these changes were significantly different for the three dominance groups. For paratelic but not for nondominant or telic individuals, heart rate was increased significantly. Unlike the EEG measures discussed previously, men and women did not differ in their heart rate responses. Smoking significantly decreased muscle tension for both men and women, but no significant effects of dominance group were found.

Results of physiological studies of the effects of smoking provided convincing information that, at least for men, reversal theory can play an important role in understanding smoking behavior. Because differential effects on EEG activity occurred when men smoked in the telic and paratelic states, we next sought to find another behavior that might produce similar alterations in the EEG. As described below, respiratory maneuvers were selected for this purpose.

A REVERSAL THEORY–BASED SMOKING CESSATION INTERVENTION

The results of our field studies suggested that succeeding at smoking cessation required skills to cope with the urge to smoke in a variety of metamotivational states. Our laboratory research suggested that smoking in telic states causes different effects than does smoking in paratelic states.

Our laboratory studies also showed that different breathing maneuvers could mimic some of the effects of smoking in telic and paratelic states. We measured the EEG before and after smoking in the telic and paratelic states and before and after the volunteers performed each of a set of breathing maneuvers designed to alter the EEG. We also measured changes in carbon dioxide as a function of each of the breathing maneuvers. The maneuvers had the expected effect on the EEG. We therefore designed a randomized clinical trial of these methods in a group of individuals who were interested in quitting smoking. The experimental group received instructions on how to determine whether they were in the telic or paratelic state. In addition, they received instructions on how to do four different breathing maneuvers. The telic maneuvers were the breath-hold and the three-part-breath, both of which were designed to increase carbon dioxide levels in the blood and slow EEG frequency. The paratelic maneuvers were the laugh breath and overbreathing, both of which were designed to decrease carbon dioxide and to speed the EEG (O'Connell, Cook, & Gerkovich, 1997). Participants in the experimental group were taught to assess their metamotivational state (telic vs. paratelic) and choose the appropriate breathing maneuver in order to cope with urges to smoke. Participants were tested during the training session to ensure that they understood the procedures. The control group received general instructions and practice on how to do a deep-breathing exercise, which they were instructed to use to cope with every urge. Both groups were also given a standard smoking cessation intervention, based on materials developed by the American Lung Association. Each participant met individually with the same nurse–intervener for two sessions. They also received three follow-up telephone calls from the nurse.

CHALLENGES OF DEVELOPING A REVERSAL THEORY INTERVENTION

The trial is still under way, and results are not yet available. However, developing and testing the intervention has forced us to address several questions that may be similar for all interventions based on reversal theory. The first question was whether to separate the arousal-seeking/arousal-avoidant component of the telic–paratelic pair from the serious-minded–playful component. Most of the prior measures have assessed both components. Strictly speaking, our intervention was most directed at arousal-seeking and arousal-avoiding. We reasoned that we might want to separate these components during the training. However, a pilot study of the training technique revealed that teaching participants two separate pairs of states increased the complexity of the training, causing participants to make errors in identifying states (O'Connell, Kakolewski, Goings, Gerkovich, & Cook,

1997). Furthermore, although the two pairs of states should move together (i.e., one should be arousal-avoidant when telic and arousal-seeking when paratelic), they can differ. For instance, under some circumstances it is possible to be playful and arousal-avoidant. If individuals decided that they were both playful and arousal-avoidant, we did not know what breathing maneuver to tell them to use. When we revised the training and combined the components of the telic–paratelic states, we found that participants made fewer errors on the test and that the training could be simplified considerably (O'Connell, Kakolewski, et al., 1997).

Another question that we dealt with early in our work with reversal theory, and which resurfaced in our intervention study, was whether urges to smoke during a cessation attempt would always be experienced in the telic state. If someone were serious about quitting smoking, would not an urge to smoke cause a reversal to the telic state because it represented a threat to a valued, perhaps life-saving, enterprise? But the premise of reversal theory is that individuals reverse between states, and this should hold even for those who are quitting smoking. Our early work convinced us that this is a major insight of reversal theory. No matter how serious or important one's long-term goals are, one is not always focused on them. Indeed, the results of our recent EMA study described above give the most conclusive answer to this question. Approximately 29% of urges to smoke were experienced in the paratelic state (O'Connell et al., 2000). Although most urges to smoke were in the telic state, our data demonstrate that indeed people do have urges to smoke in paratelic states.

From a conceptual perspective, we also wondered whether a person could ever resist the urge to smoke in a paratelic state, or did resisting the urge always indicate a reversal to the telic states? After examining our own behavior in a variety of situations, we concluded that just because one is playful and spontaneous does not mean that one submits oneself to unnecessary danger. People in the paratelic state do not generally jump off buildings for the fun of it. In fact, some activities in the paratelic state might be aimed at preserving the paratelic state. If someone is quitting smoking, is paratelic, and has the urge to smoke, he or she could also have the realization at some level that smoking a cigarette will lead to a significant loss of self-esteem, causing a telic reversal. One might seek to avoid the telic reversal that smoking could cause just like one might seek to avoid the telic reversal that getting caught speeding could cause when driving fast in a paratelic state.

Apter (1989a) has pointed out that there are two ways to deal with negative affect: One is to reverse to the opposite state and the other is to change the level of the underlying motivational variable (e.g., arousal, felt significance). Our reversal theory analysis suggested that we needed to develop strategies that were consistent with the needs of each state rather than strategies that cause reversal. The tendency to want to reverse is not symmetrical. When a person is in the telic state, he or she can think of telic reasons for having a reversal. For example, a person might understand that efforts toward achieving a significant goal would be enhanced if he or she took the evening off and went to the theater. Thinking of good reasons for reversal is more difficult to do when a person is in the paratelic state because it is more difficult to see how switching to the telic state could meet paratelic needs.

It is interesting that most strategies recommended for resisting the urge to smoke are consistent with the telic state. These include reminding oneself of the negative consequences of smoking, planning alternative activities, or taking deep breaths in order to relax. We are unaware of strategies recommended by smoking cessation experts other than ourselves that are consistent with the needs of the paratelic state. Methods for raising arousal levels like two of the respiratory maneuvers we designed would be consistent with the needs of the paratelic state.

EXPLAINING REVERSAL THEORY CONCEPTS

Some of the problems we have encountered in training our participants relate to problems we have encountered in explaining reversal theory to our professional colleagues. Convincing participants that their states alternate between being telic and paratelic has sometimes been difficult. Like many psychologists, a number of our participants were "trait theorists," telling us that they were always in one state or the other and therefore, there was no need to learn the maneuver for the state they perceived as irrelevant. This response may have been an effort to simplify the demands of the training or to simplify reality, or it may represent the reaction of a person who is extremely telic or paratelic dominant. We have had similar problems when we try to inform behavioral scientists about reversal theory.

Another problem in communicating reversal theory to participants and colleagues alike is that telic and paratelic states are not necessarily related to affect. There is a tendency, even among reversal theorists, to associate telic states with negative affect and paratelic states with positive affect. Our participants have the same tendency. However, reversal theory clearly posits that one can experience both positive and negative affect in either telic or paratelic states. Nevertheless, the confusion is easy to understand, because it is probably true that most negative moods (except boredom arising out of the experience of low arousal) are experienced in the telic state and that most paratelic states are associated with positive mood.

Perhaps the most overriding problem that we face in explaining reversal theory to participants and colleagues is the complexity of the theory. Although many people (especially those who are not behavioral scientists) find the idea that one is sometimes serious and sometimes playful intuitively understandable and even appealing, grasping the more complex implications of reversal theory takes a great deal of study. It is our responsibility to simplify our explanations of the theory as much as possible. However, we must also recognize that a theory that explains human motivation and behavior is unlikely to be simple.

PROBLEMS THAT REVERSAL THEORY DOES NOT ADDRESS

Reversal theory has been a valuable tool in helping us understand smoking cessation and relapse. However, there are some questions that we have not yet been able to address with reversal theory. If one is more likely to lapse in the paratelic state, why doesn't one resume abstinence when one reverses to the telic state? People who experience a single lapse during a cessation attempt have a 90% probability of returning to regular smoking. Thus far, we have not been able to explain why smoking often continues after individuals reverse back to the telic state. Although there is a strong affect management function of smoking, it is also true that smoking involves addictive and habitual components that may operate independently of affect and metamotivational state. A lapse may predispose the individual to abandon a cessation attempt in order to achieve the benefits of smoking in the telic state as well as in the paratelic state. It is also possible that lapses in paratelic states may not lead to immediate relapse and that, in fact, people who lapse in paratelic states do regain abstinence when they reverse to telic. However, the experience of a lapse reinforces the addictive and habit components, making resisting more difficult the next time a highly tempting situation occurs.

Finally, although we have shown that lapses are more likely in paratelic than in telic states, the fact remains that most lapses occur in telic states, because ex-smokers spend most of their time in the telic state. Our EMA study showed that participants were telic in over 70% of episodes (O'Connell et al., 2000). What factors predispose lapsing versus resisting in telic states? It is possible that telic states that are associated with relapse coincide with negativistic or sympathy states. In an analysis that included telic–paratelic, negativistic–conformist, mastery–sympathy, and autic–alloic pairs, we have shown that combining the pairs improves their predictive power (O'Connell, Gerkovich, & Cook, 1997). However, more conceptual and psychometric development is needed with respect to the negativistic–conformist, mastery–sympathy, and autic–alloic states to be able to address this issue adequately. We have often speculated that the pairs of states may vary in terms of how salient they are at any given time. The sympathy state may be more important than the telic state and may have a greater effect on behavior at certain times. Adding this level of complexity to an already complex theory has seemed daunting.

CONCLUSION

Despite its limitations, reversal theory has led us to a better understanding of several issues in smoking cessation. Reversal theory is a promising framework in which to address the differential effects of smoking in different states on arousal levels and on psychological states. The theory has led us to a number of important discoveries in the laboratory. Second, reversal theory addresses the irrationality of smoking and lapsing by suggesting how irrationality and impulsivity are sometimes appealing to even the most rational and self-disciplined individuals (O'Connell, 1991, 1996). A participant in one of our studies described his urge experience this way:

> I was working late one night, really trying really hard to get a project done. I was on my way to the printer when I passed the reception area of the building. Suddenly I noticed a pack of cigarettes and a lighter. I couldn't believe it. I was so excited. It was like finding a Ferrari in your garage. I felt it was a gift from heaven specifically for me.

In this case, the discovery of a cigarette appeared to cause paratelic and sympathy reversals and impulsive behavior in someone who had been goal oriented and self-disciplined (telic–mastery) up to that point.

Finally, reversal theory explains why it is so difficult to quit smoking or to maintain any health behavior change. Usually such changes demand that one must cope with the urge to lapse in a variety of states and situations. Smokers have been able to use one primary method—smoking—for managing their arousal in both directions. Without smoking, they must learn a variety of strategies. This makes smoking cessation both difficult to achieve and to study and reminds us again how much remains to be learned and that we should keep a firm grasp on humility.

8

ADDICTIONS

R. IAIN F. BROWN

In 1985, William R. Miller, one of the most creative and prolific writers in America on the psychology of addiction and the originator of motivational interviewing, which has swept the world as an intervention strategy for all addictions, made a very positive appraisal of the potential of reversal theory to guide and inform research and treatment of the addictions. He identified the most obvious types of reversal pathology as *excessive lability* of reversals and *rigidity and imbalance* of states that he described as an unhealthy preponderance of one state over another. He also wrote that reversal theory might demonstrate an underlying unity between addictive behaviors and other forms of psychopathology. Probably unknown to him at that time, the role of all of these dysfunctional reversals in mental health problems, in general, had already been identified and written about by Murgatroyd and Apter in a series of papers beginning in 1981 and then summarized and reviewed in Murgatroyd (1988; see also chapter 14 in this volume).

Miller suggested a further dysfunctional type of reversal, namely the reliance on addictive behavior to accomplish a reversal. He also focused on the potential of reversal theory for the explanation of relapse, the very area of studies in addictions that has had the most extensive, thorough, and fruitful empirical exploration by reversal theorists, as reviewed by O'Connell and Cook in chapter 7 of this volume. Perhaps most perceptively of all, he predicted that the theory would finally help in the clarification of what it is that addictive behaviors have in common, mentioning specifically pathological gambling, certain compulsions, and sexual deviations.

EARLY FOCUS ON GAMBLING ADDICTIONS

Long before I knew of the existence of the Miller paper, I had already seen some of the uses of reversal theory adding richly to possible explanations for the processes of normal gambling and for the explanation of my own specialization, the phenomena of gambling addictions. And I had discovered for myself the capacity of the theory to stimulate fresh insights in the understanding of the field of addictions in general.

In 1984, George Anderson and I published a pioneering piece of research on normal gambling that demonstrated for the first time that greatly elevated levels of autonomic arousal were a central feature of casino gambling among normal gamblers. Michael Apter had been present as we presented this to the British Psychological Society in April 1982 and he had persuaded us to revisit our original sample of gamblers and test their telic dominance. The results were presented at the 2nd International Conference on Reversal Theory in Wales in 1983 but not published until much later (Anderson & Brown, 1987). This was followed by a first rudimentary attempt to advance a theory of gambling addictions (Brown, 1986) and some implications for therapy (Brown, 1987a).

The gambling environment was seen as satisfying most of the requirements for paratelic arousal. This was partly because of its inherent great uncertainty, but also because of the strict rules, familiarity, and security that surrounded it in a framework of safety. In other words, the situation involves what Apter (1992) later called a "protective frame" and which he argued is essential for the paratelic state and for experiencing high arousal as excitement (see chapter 11). Entering that gambling environment and beginning to play was seen as providing powerful paratelic state-inducing, or state-maintaining, cues. Entry to an episode of gambling could thus be used deliberately by the individual already in a paratelic state to transform a negative experience of boredom into a hedonically positive one of excitement. More important, we argued that such an entry could be used by the individual who did not happen to be already in the paratelic state as a deliberate means of inducing a reversal from telic to paratelic. In this way, high arousal experienced with negative hedonic tone as anxiety could instead be experienced with positive hedonic tone as excitement. It is obvious that similar decisions to take drugs, legally prescribed and illegal; to smoke tobacco; or to drink alcohol would be taken with similar expectations of improving hedonic tone (Brown, 1987b, 1989; Donovan & Chaney, 1985).

The subjective experience of the gambler during the course of an episode of gambling was interpreted as a series of rapid switches between telic and paratelic states—an emotional roller coaster. These switches, the cues inducing them, and their consequent effects on the gambler's hedonic tone and behavior are described within a reversal theory analysis in more detail in Anderson and Brown (1987). It is assumed in the analysis that, when clearly losing, gamblers normally revert to a telic state and, when clearly winning, continue in a paratelic state but that, overall, the dominant state in which they continue to play is a paratelic one. It is again obvious that such an analysis can be applied to virtually any addictive activity, provided only that it be remembered that in gambling the gambling action itself provides the focus of attention and therefore mostly determines both the hedonic tone and also the course of reversals. This is probably not the case with other addictive activities, where attention may range more freely during the course of the activity concerned over a variety of aspects of the situation, including social happenings. Thus, even when in a predominantly paratelic state, the reversals, and therefore the states, of the drinker are more influenced by the ongoing social situation around him or her, whereas the gambler is focused on the process of play. Such an analysis has yet to be applied in strictly reversal theory terms to addictions other than gambling, although both Donovan and Chaney (1985) and Brown (1987b, 1989) in their analyses of the rise and fall of arousal in drinking episodes pave the way toward it.

Finally, Anderson and Brown found that the ending of the episode of gambling was more often, but not always, occurring in a telic state. This state was sometimes induced by losing and sometimes by some reminder of the increased felt significance of the sums of money involved in relation to larger telic concerns outside the casino, such as paying the rent or debts. Again, the usual telic state ending of an episode of addictive activity is obviously generalizable to other addictive activities. Most episodes of addictive activity end simply with an increasing physical inability to sustain the action, either physically (e.g., in drinking) or financially (as in gambling). This has the consequence of a reversal to the telic state and, as with gambling, a realization of the real and possibly dismaying significance of the behaviors that have been performed.

In Anderson and Brown's 1987 paper, the addictive pathology was seen in gambling as the causal product of the experience of intermittent reinforcement from very high arousal in a paratelic state. The person with an addiction who loses but who is influenced by this reinforcement schedule may continue to gamble in the telic state in the face of the most distressing anxiety. This is because of his or her learned expectation that a big win will bring a powerful reward in pleasurable excitement when eventually that high arousal, which is experienced as anxiety now, will be reinterpreted in a paratelic state as a correspondingly great surge of excitement and triumph. Paradoxically, both winning and losing, therefore, can lead to a prolongation of the addictive activity.

With important variations, this analysis of the factors determining the damaging prolonging of the episode can be applied to other addictive activities (e.g., as in Donovan & Chaney, 1985, and Brown, 1987b, 1989). However, in other addictions, the "end game" of the episode of action is more likely to be dominated by the need to avoid, for as long as possible, the low hedonic tone of a painful telic state of physical and psychological withdrawal. Again, given Miller's prediction that something like it would emerge from reversal theory, it may seem surprising that this analysis has not yet been applied more widely to other addictions.

EARLY EXPLORATIONS INTO PERSONALITY CHARACTERISTICS OF VARIOUS ADDICTIONS

Anderson and Brown (1987) had found that, as might have been predicted, scores on the Telic Dominance Scale (TDS; Murgatroyd, Rushton, Apter, & Ray, 1978) were significantly and negatively correlated with scores on Zuckerman's (1979, 1994) Sensation Seeking Scale and that, in the gambling behavior of normal regular gamblers, there was a significant negative correlation between telic dominance and bet size. Doherty and Mathews (1988), in exploring the characteristics of other addictive behaviors, found that people with an opiate addiction in a Personality Disorder Unit were significantly higher than control participants in scores on Eysenck's Psychoticism Scale but significantly lower on both Eysenck's Extraversion Scale (Eysenck & Eysenck, 1975) and the TDS with respect to all three subscales. Turner and Heskin (1998) found that, among a sample of Australian secondary-school students, self-labeling as a heavy drinker and as a heavy smoker were both significantly associated with paratelic dominance and that self-labeling as a heavy smoker was further significantly associated with negativism dominance. Wicker, Hamman, Hagen, Reed, and Wiehe (1995) found, in a sample of university students required to imagine hypothetical bets in various situations, that bet size, particularly in imagined low-income situations, was related to telic dominance. Those who were telic dominant took smaller bets, especially in imagined low-income situations, and this was interpreted as loss aversion rather than risk aversion. Kenealy (1981) reported that a sample of people labeled alcoholics living in a half-way house scored significantly higher on the Serious-mindedness and Planning-orientation subscales of the TDS when compared with social drinkers. She interpreted this as indicating that recovering alcoholics were more concerned with goals related to themselves and with planning ahead in order to achieve them than were the social drinkers with whom they were compared.

EXTENSION OF THE REVERSAL THEORY ANALYSIS OF GAMBLING ADDICTIONS

In Brown (1988), the findings of the papers by Anderson and Brown (1984, 1987), especially those which reported a high negative correlation between the TDS and the Sensation Seeking Scale, were seen as supporting a reversal theory explanation of gambling activities rather than the traditional optimal arousal/optimal stimulation theory or even Gray's two-system biological hedonism model (Gray, 1971) such as is used by Zuckerman (1979). More important, the understanding of the complexity and unpredictability of the human subjective experience, which is so effectively highlighted by reversal theory, gave rise to a new appreciation of the significance and importance of subjective experience in the development and maintenance of an addiction.

One of the great strengths of reversal theory is that the complex structural phenomenology that it has developed serves as a constant reproach to simple behaviorally minded empirical experimentalists. Unless the role of subjective experience, with its associated messy emotionality, is to be disregarded altogether (and there can be few since Skinner who have "kept their scientist heads" in that particular stretch of desert sand), then it must be acknowledged that good feeling and awareness of personal well-being are not just the byproducts of some blind instinctual blundering. Rather, it is actively sought and managed by even the most naïve of the hedonists that we all, inevitably, from time to time are. Reversal theory demonstrates that, for all of us, the maintenance of good or even tolerable hedonic tone is potentially a very sophisticated enterprise indeed, even if it is one that, sadly, has little chance of consistent success.

In his seminal book, Apter (1982a) suggested several ways in which we attempt to control arousal, but he assumed that many reversals are spontaneous in the sense that they occur in an unplanned and often unexpected way. Yet, if it is possible to manipulate or induce reversals also, it is immediately obvious that in any really sophisticated attempt to maintain good hedonic tone, both arousal and reversals can and will be manipulated.

In the Brown (1988) paper, after quoting some of Apter's (1982a) ways of manipulating arousal, the case was made for the "butterfly effect." The idea that the fluttering of the wings of a single butterfly has an effect on the total system of the known universe is, of course, a gross exaggeration of the observation that

> attempts to induce reversals by seeking out specific environments or engaging specific activities may fail to induce the required reversal and have unpredictable effects upon arousal, which may even have the opposite effect on hedonic tone to those desired. Similarly attempts to maintain good hedonic tone through the manipulation of levels of arousal are equally likely to have unpredictable effects in the induction of unexpected reversals. Both means of short term control of the arousal/hedonic tone system are extremely uncertain and inefficient, especially when the chance effects on the system of spontaneous reversals from

both satiation and external contingencies are added. (Brown, 1988, p. 200)

A GENERAL THEORY OF ADDICTION

This problem of hedonic management became clear to me in the summer of 1987 when I was reading Apter's (1982a) book. The passage that finally illuminated it and summed it up was

> it is hardly to be wondered at that high levels of positive hedonic are not typically maintained for extended periods. To put this in everyday terms, it is not surprising that people have difficulty in remaining happy for very long. (p. 330)

This "uncertainty principle of subjective experience" is further elaborated to the point of caricature in Brown (1993b), where the near impossibility and potential absurdity of attaining good hedonic tone simultaneously in five dimensions is illustrated. Although this may seem to expose the predictive emptiness of reversal theory, it certainly illustrates its potential sophistication in contrast to the "methodological vandalism" (Apter, 1989b, p. 2) and naïve experimentalism of much of 20th-century psychology. Above all, it provides the point of departure for a fundamental insight into the nature of addiction, which stimulated me to develop a general theory of addiction—a theory that restored subjective experience to a central role in the explanation of the development and maintenance of addictions.

This insight was that the short-term maintenance of good hedonic tone is a difficult business for normal people, but that an addictive process, by contrast, represents a reliable and effective method by which a person can reach and maintain high positive hedonic tone, at least in the short term (Brown, 1988). Further, using the chosen addiction, high hedonic tone becomes for a period so achievable that, just as Bejerot (1972) pointed out, it becomes an acquired drive in its own right. Characteristic of this drive is the kind of frenzied pursuit of a single activity that was displayed by the rats in the experiments of Olds and Milner (1954) after the rats discovered how to reward the pleasure centers of their brains directly by pressing bars. They continued to repeat this activity, ignoring all opportunities to eat or drink, until they dropped with exhaustion. It can be argued that

> the whole range of addictive activities, from the ingestion of substances such as alcohol, food and legal and illegal drugs to engaging in activities such as gambling, sexual conquest or even antique buying, can all be seen as methods for manipulating hedonic tone. (Brown, 1988, p. 201)

Furthermore, the unreliability of the chosen addictive behavior, although superior to the relative uncertainty and chaos of the normal search for

positive hedonic tone, gives rise to an intermittent schedule of reinforcement. This makes for great resistance to extinction and a tendency to
ready reinstatement, not just in gambling, as is well known, but also in
all addictions.

This theory was developed in a series of applications to various specific
problems within the general field of the study of addictions, for example,
to the phenomena of gaming and gambling (Brown, 1991, 1993d, 1993e),
to short-term crisis management as a feature of hedonic goal seeking in
addictions, and to addictions as ultimately a flight from the telic (Brown,
1993a).

This general theory of addiction, which I also call the "hedonic management model of addiction," inspired by reversal theory and grounded in
cognitive–social learning theory, is detailed in Brown (1997). It contends
that "the factor in all . . . currently accepted models which has not been
given enough importance is the role of conscious subjective experiences,
beliefs and decisions of the addicted person" (p. 16).

The theory starts from the observation, grounded in reversal theory,
that

> all individuals manipulate their arousal, mood and experiences of subjec-
> tive well-being to sustain good hedonic tone (states of relative pleasure
> and euphoria) for as much of the time as possible. In the normal pursuit
> of happiness some regularly reproducible feeling states become secondary
> goals or drives. (p. 23)

And it continues by first acknowledging that each individual may have
predisposing vulnerabilities to addiction. Some of these vulnerabilities may
be at least partially genetically determined, which may leave the individual
with a large conscious difference for much of the time between the amount
of negative hedonic tone they can tolerate and the amount they normally
experience. This is what I refer to as the "hedonic gap." Other vulnerabilities,
perhaps in lack of social skills or in poor learning from damaged human
relations, may narrow the range of easily accessible rewarding activities
normally open to an individual.

Drawing on the cognitive social learning theory of Rotter (1982), the
individual is seen as having, at any point in time, a repertoire of easily
accessible rewarding activities and a hierarchy of preferences among them.
The origin of addictions is seen as either a gradual development of the
importance of an activity or in the sudden discovery of an activity that
provides a relatively powerful and effective means of manipulating hedonic
tone to sustain long periods of euphoria or relief from dysphoria. In either
case, it brings the addictive activity to the top of the preference hierarchy
in most, or even all, situations. Why any one activity becomes the addiction
and not another is seen as depending, along with other factors, on the

power of its reinforcement effects and on the skill with which the person with the addiction learns to use it to manipulate hedonic tone.

Thus, an addiction is seen as developing through a positive feedback loop that leads to an acquired drive for particular feeling states as goals and so to the salience (dominance of thinking feeling and behavior) of a single activity as a source of reward. This feedback loop always involves a series of cognitive failures such as deficient self-awareness (vigilance), short-term planning, crisis management, and faulty decision-making. It also usually involves conflict with others and within the self, thus leading again to the further narrowing of the repertoire of easily accessible rewarding activities. Increasing salience leads to increasing tolerance, to withdrawals and to further action to relieve or avert these withdrawals, which, in turn, leads inevitably to yet greater salience.

During the later stages of its development, the engagement in the addictive activity comes in repeated cycles or in episodes that make up a serial. At the beginning of each episode of addictive activity, dysfunctional cognitive distortions and belief systems and, later in the serial, rituals inducing the sought-after feeling states (and perhaps routines facilitating entry to partially or wholly dissociated states) make it possible for the person with the addiction to see the entry to the episode as desirable, and to expect periods of high hedonic tone, even if only in the short run.

At the point of full development of an addiction, it can be described as a motivational monopoly or reward specialism. This is because a single addictive activity so dominates thinking, feeling, and behavior (i.e., has such salience) that it becomes virtually the sole source of reward and is used to maintain a near-continuous subjective mood or feeling state. Hedonic management is now mere crisis management. Decisions are now made solely on a basis of extremely short-term reward or expected relief to avoid withdrawals.

Recovery comes through a change in cognitive systems especially in the background of beliefs that formerly supported the addictive activity. This always involves a radical change in the policy and style of the management of hedonic tone. Improved self-awareness and vigilance is developed, often against a necessary background of increased tolerance of acute short-term dysphoria. A better quality of decision-making is cultivated through better planning for the medium- and long-term manipulation of hedonic tone. This leads simultaneously to both the reduction, or extinction, of the addictive activity and the revival and regeneration of a wide repertoire of easily accessible rewarding activities. These activities result, in turn, in a wider range of sources of reward and so to an improved overall rate of reward or quality of life.

As the sources of rewards become more dispersed and the overall rate of reward rises, so the vulnerability to cross addictions decreases and the risk of a reversion to the old pattern of behavior at the height of the addictive activity, that is, of a relapse to the full addiction, diminishes. Nevertheless, after any addiction there always remains a residual vulnerability to the reinstatement of that old pattern of behavior.

This general theory of addictions defines addictions in a way that clearly distinguishes them from obsessions, compulsions, or attachments, and it seeks to study addictions as a meteorologist would study depressions and hurricanes, seeing them as motivational monopolies that are almost value-free. Indeed, some positive addictions may be very constructive for individuals and societies, for example, jogging and transcendental meditation (Glasser, 1976) and some but not all forms of addiction to work. The costs of addictions are well known but the hidden benefits are seldom acknowledged. Even the most destructive have some secondary beneficial effects such as reliable control of changes of mood and subjective experience (escape from pain, boredom, etc.), coping with social anxiety and hostility, and as a source of identity (e.g., "I am someone who has overcome an addiction"). Most addictions can be mixed blessings or mixed curses, with both valuable and undesirable consequences, both socially and individually.

Obviously this new theory of addiction is fundamentally a theory of addiction as an acquired drive. But the goal of that drive may be much more than just what is often colloquially called "a mood change" or even a desirable state (of intoxication or of arousal or of insulation from negative feelings). Rather it is the long-term maintenance of high positive hedonic tone, a much more sophisticated concept than any of these.

Unfortunately the full sophistication that reversal theory could bring to this new general theory of addiction could seldom be presented. This is because it was difficult enough for the normally cognitive–behavioral and empirically oriented audience or readership of psychologists to absorb a new theory of addictive activities without also requiring them to absorb an equally new and, to them, even stranger, new theory of reversals all in the same operation. So the new general theory of addictions had to gain its independence from its origins so that it could stand on its own and be presented without reference to reversals. This theory is presented in print (Brown, 1997) in the specific context of, and with special reference to, addictive elements in criminal offending. But, once again, this general theory stands on its own without any necessary confinement to the context within which it is presented.

The full reversal theory analysis of the nature of the multiple and varied goals of the acquired drive still needs to be completed. And, when it is, it will be as sophisticated in comparison to the colloquial "mood management" view of addictions as the reversal theory analysis of arousal is in comparison to the old optimal arousal theory of, for example, Zuckerman (1994).

Based on the work of Zuckerman (1994), Apter (1989b, 1992), and Brown (1988, 1997), Eric Loonis, in France, developed further a general theory of addiction as a hedonic management model, involving some new concepts (Loonis, 1997, 1998, 1999a, 1999b, 1999c; Loonis, Apter, & Sztulman, 2000; Loonis & Sztulman, 1998). First of all, Loonis suggested continuity between Zuckerman's (1979) concept of sensation seeking and Apter's (1992) work on *The Dangerous Edge*. The sensation-seeking trait, as described by Zuckerman, is elaborated by Apter by means of a number of cognitive and behavioral strategies (such as the creation of protective frames, as described in chapter 11 in this volume), which are used by the individual to regulate their psychological states. Loonis observed that all our activities in daily life could, in one way or another, serve the management of hedonic tone. This suggests the need to propose a principle as fundamental as that of the double articulation of language in linguistics: the principle of the double function of activities. This means that all of our daily activities serve two functions: a pragmatic function of adaptation to the world and a hedonic function concerning the management of psychological states. This double function explains the great variety of hedonic and addictive sources of stimulation. For Loonis, addictions represent extreme methods of hedonic management within the framework of the second function of activity. Addictions are defined on two orthogonal axes:

1. the axis of type of addiction, from substance addictions to those in which cerebral arousal is obtained by means of behavior
2. the axis of severity of addiction from minor everyday addictions to those that are pathological.

Every type and level of addiction can in this way be placed in relation to these two axes (consumption of drugs, alcoholism, gambling, sexuality, interpersonal relations, including compulsive activities, obsessions, and the addictive use of erotic fantasies; Loonis, 1999b).

Loonis considered the function of hedonic management of activities to represent a set of motivations that are superimposed on the classical motives (such as hunger and thirst) and that relate to the concept of metamotivation as proposed by Apter. For Loonis, our activities, considered as actions of hedonic management (the second function), are organized as an "action system." This action system is characterized by three variables: salience, variety, and vicariance. Loonis's concept of salience corresponds to Brown's concept, and Loonis's concepts of variety and vicariance together correspond very closely to Brown's concept of "easily accessible rewarding activities." Loonis proposed that the distinguishing characteristics of an addictive action system would be high salience, low variety, and vicariance. Using a new and ingenious method of measuring, Loonis, Apter, and Sztulman (2000) demonstrated that these characteristics do indeed distinguish a group of people with addictions from a comparison group of people without addictions and are correlated with paratelic dominance and dysphoric characteristics. This provides some empirical verification of the usefulness of the concepts and theories of addiction that are developing around reversal theory.

With a hedonic management theory such as that of Loonis, it is possible to go beyond the traditional concept of addiction—addictivity being recognized as an aspect of the general functioning of all individuals. As Loonis argued (1999a), we are moving toward an "ecology of action" and a "state psychology." He continued that it is possible that the concept of hedonic management within the framework of a basic metamotivational system will turn out to be as significant for the new century as Freud's concept of the unconscious was for the last. In any case, Miller's (1985) original positive predictions about the potential contributions of reversal theory to the study of addictions, as set out at the beginning of this chapter, are in the process of being fulfilled.

9

REBELLIOUSNESS

MARK R. McDERMOTT

Rebelliousness, or *negativism* as it is called in reversal theory, despite being conspicuous during the two developmental periods of infancy and adolescence (Braman, 1995), is a relatively neglected psychological construct. Within the post–World War II North American experimental social psychology tradition, empirical work focused primarily on elucidating the conditions under which people conform. With the exception of the work of Gamson, Fireman, and Rytina (1982), comparatively little attention was directed at those sociocontextual conditions under which people rebel and as to whether a disposition or personal readiness to rebel could be identified as an individual difference variable (Brown, 1986). Reversal theory's focus on negativism and conformity has provided a forum in which much work has been done to redress this imbalance. This chapter reviews the ways in which rebelliousness has been measured and investigated within reversal theory both as a psychological state and as a form of metamotivational dominance.

Apter (1982a, p. 198) defined being in a *rebellious or negativistic state* as "wanting or feeling compelled to do something contrary to that required by some external agency"—appropriately the emphasis being on the actor's self-perception and experience (rather than on a value judgment of an external observer) and on the necessary precondition of an external "requirement." The reference to a requirement places appropriate emphasis on the role of social conditions and recognizes that negativistic phenomena cannot be conceived in purely intrapsychic terms, a point well explicated by Stenner and Marshall (1995) in their Q methodological study of rebelliousness. The term *requirement* also emphasizes that the pressure or influence is in the nature of something contextual like a rule, expectation, or convention. This distinguishes negativism from mastery in the reversal theory sense, the latter being about the attempt to control rather than defy and to control some specific entity (like a machine or another person). Thus, a tennis player will want to resist the influence of his or her opponent (this desire being an expression of the mastery state); the tennis player would be in the negativistic state only if he or she felt the desire to break some rule like wanting to cheat or wanting to contravene some form of etiquette while playing (e.g., swearing).

It should also be noticed that the negativistic state, like all metamotivational states, defines a desire, not an action. As far as action is concerned, if the individual perceives himself or herself to be actually acting in a way that is contrary to some external source of influence to conform, then he or she is said, in reversal theory terms, to be experiencing *felt negativism*. When the individual perceives himself or herself to be acting in accordance with the influence, then he or she is said to be experiencing *low felt negativism* or *felt conformity*. (Where the terms *negativism* and *conformity* are used without qualification in what follows, they are referring to the whole area of experience and behavior without distinguishing such different aspects as the negativistic state and felt negativism.)

Apter and Smith (1976) proposed that the negativistic state can serve a variety of functions, including gaining independence, performing attention-seeking behavior, experiencing excitement, and breaking up the status quo. Further, Apter (1983) also has proposed that the negativistic state is often activated in the service of identity development. In particular, he has suggested that felt negativism serves to enhance a sense of personal distinctiveness from others, a sense of personal autonomy and control, and a sense of continuity of self over time (something that a longitudinal study has yet to confirm). By negating specific values and behaviors it is argued that we come to know who we are *not* and thereby who we *are* as individuals. Thus, some forms of negativistic action may be envisaged as being of prosocial worth and not always as having pejorative psychological connotations. This point will be returned to later in the chapter.

As well as conceiving of the negativistic state as a desire that arises in response to a requirement of an external agent, Apter (1982a) also noted that it is possible to experience *self-negativism:* "a desire or compulsion to act against some requirement of the self, rather than against some requirement of an external agency" (p. 368). Braman (1988, 1995) has noted that some children set out deliberately to prevent themselves from doing what they want to do. Braman (1988) has called these telic self-negativistic children "oppositional" children. He argued that they have internalized the same values and aspirations as their parents. Thus, when reacting against the requirements of a parent, Braman argued that such a child is in effect rebelling against his or her own perceived needs in an attempt to avoid the anxiety and criticism that can be engendered by trying and sometimes failing to comply with the wishes of parents whose standards are being revised constantly upward and whose unqualified praise is never forthcoming. Thus, it is as if "youth to itself rebels, though none else near," as Laertes warns Ophelia in Act I, Scene III, of William Shakespeare's (1623) *Hamlet, Prince of Denmark*. Apter (1983) argued that self-negativism comes about when all attempts at being negativistic toward external requirements have been frustrated, and so rebelliousness is displaced onto the self. Despite these cogent analyses, self-negativism has not been examined extensively in reversal theory empirical research. Thus, this chapter focuses on the forms of negativistic behavior and experiences that arise in response to externally imposed requirements and expectations.

Before documenting how negativism has been investigated in applied research settings, first considered are how reversal theory conceptions of the negativistic state and negativism dominance have been operationalized and measured—apposite measurement being an essential prerequisite of high-quality applied research.

MEASURING NEGATIVISM

State Measures

Four psychometric tools have been developed that involve attempts to identify or measure aspects of the negativistic and conformist states. The first three of these measures regard negativism as a one-dimensional construct. However, as is seen in consideration of negativism dominance in the ensuing section, a multidimensional approach (specifically, two forms of negativism as detailed later, *proactive* and *reactive*) may be more appropriate when conceiving of the negativistic state and when developing further measures.

Tension and Effort Stress Inventory

State measures of negativism are included as components in a subsection of the Tension and Effort Stress Inventory–State version (Svebak, 1993). Respondents to this inventory are asked in its last and third section to indicate how they are feeling presently on semantic differentials for 16 emotions.

In reversal theory, terms the emotions stipulated here that are relevant to being in a rebellious metamotivational mode are

- Anger (i.e., unpleasant felt arousal in the negativistic state)
- Provocativeness (pleasant felt arousal in the negativistic state)
- Sullenness (unpleasant felt arousal in the conformist state)
- Placidity (pleasant felt arousal in the conformist state)

Provocativeness is particularly interesting here because it is an emotion often overlooked in psychological research, and related to the idea of mischievousness (the term used for this emotion in chapter 2), the German concept of schadenfreude which means taking pleasure in others' misfortunes, and the feeling of gleeful pleasure in causing trouble or (in the case of children) being naughty.

Metamotivational State Coding Schedule

O'Connell, Potocky, Cook, and Gerkovich (1991; see also Potocky, Cook, & O'Connell, 1993) developed the Metamotivational State Coding Schedule in part to elicit retrospectively, via structured interview questions, instances of negativistic experience and to code these in terms of relevant descriptors: stubborn, difficult, rebellious, angry, guilty, conformist, wanting to break rules, and wanting to follow rules (see chapter 3 in this volume).

Somatic State Questionnaire

Cook, Gerkovich, Potocky, and O'Connell (1993), in developing the Somatic State Questionnaire (SSQ), have produced four bipolar self-rating scales that measure the negativistic–conformist states: feeling rebellious/not feeling rebellious, not feeling angry/feeling angry, feeling compliant/feeling defiant, and wanting to break rules/not wanting to break rules (more details are found in chapter 3 of this volume).

Negativism State Measure

O'Connor (1992) constructed the Negativism State Measure to measure the extent that participants maintained their dominant mode during experimental situations. This measure required participants to respond to four items, 6-point scales being used with defining adjectives at each end: rebellious–conforming (purportedly measuring what McDermott, 1987, termed *proactive rebelliousness*), vengeful–accepting (purportedly measuring what McDermott, 1987, termed *reactive rebelliousness*), low arousal–high arousal, and preferred high arousal–preferred low arousal. Additional instructions are provided that define each of these terms. Arousal items were included in this measure because of an empirical relationship between proactive negativism and arousal.

Dominance Measures

Athough reversal theory is primarily state based, the investigation of dominance has received considerable attention. Notably much of the attention has focused on the telic–paratelic pair of metamotivations, telic dominance having been investigated extensively. The three remaining metamotivational pairs, by comparison, have been investigated to a lesser extent, perhaps because the playful–serious-mindedness distinction has so much resonance and face validity within individualistic, goal-oriented cultures. It is evident that theoretically, and in terms of ecological validity, the negativism–conformity pair also are of fundamental importance to an understanding and full delineation of the structural phenomenology of everyday life. In response to the relative neglect of negativism, McDermott and Apter (1988) and McDermott (1986, 1987, 1988a, 1988b) developed the Negativism Dominance Scale (NDS).

Negativism Dominance Scale

During the development of the NDS, two forms of negativism were identified: *proactive* and *reactive rebelliousness* (McDermott, 1986, 1987, 1988a). The proactive form of rebelliousness is a form of the negativistic state in which the feeling is one of wanting to oppose a perceived requirement in order to obtain fun and excitement. It involves the proactive pursuit of such somatic and hedonistic goals. In reversal theory terms it can be best described as *paratelic negativism*, because it is about the heightening of pleasurable arousal through often gratuitous and provocative oppositional behavior. An example of an instance of proactive negativism is driving down a one-way street in the wrong direction just for kicks. The reactive form of negativism is a form of the negativistic state in which the feeling is one of wanting to oppose a perceived requirement that is judged to be unfair, unreasonable, or unjust. This form then, is often a reaction to an interpersonal frustration, affront, indignity, disappointment, or rebuff and is characterized by feeling vengeful, retaliatory, or vindictive. Unlike the proactive form, it is not actively pursued but is an unpremeditated response to problematic interpersonal circumstances. In reversal theory terms, reactive rebelliousness can best be described as *sympathy negativism*, because the individual in such a state is in the position of a relatively disempowered supplicant who has been dealt with unsympathetically—negativistic behavior being engaged in order to exert countercontrol. As such this form of negativism is transactional in kind. An example of an instance of reactive negativism is telling a charity to "go to hell" after getting turned down as a volunteer.

These two factorially derived subscales of the NDS have been shown to be cross-culturally replicable in North American and British samples (coefficients of congruence ranging from 0.89 to 0.9) and to have construct validity and internal reliability (McDermott, 1987). Among 132 16–17-year-old adolescents in Illinois, reactive rebelliousness was found to correlate positively with unexcused absences (truancy) and excused absences from school, and reactive rebelliousness correlated negatively with academic achievement as measured by semester grade-point average and positively with the number of referrals to the head teacher in a semester for disruptive behavior (McDermott, 1987). Thus, the subscales have good criterion related validity and have been shown to have reasonable levels of internal reliability, Cronbach's alpha ranging from 0.61 to 0.78, and ecological validity (McDermott, 1988b). Extending this work into the occupational domain, Hawes (1998) prospectively examined over a one-year period the predictive utility of an adapted version of the NDS with regard to one- to two-day attitudinal absences and turnover in 658 newly employed retail staff, but she did not find supporting evidence for the application of the NDS in this context. However, in Robinson, Weaver, and Zillmann's (1996) study of rock music video preference, they replicated the factor structure of the NDS, and its utility in other arenas of application has been demonstrated, as considered in more detail later in this chapter.

In addition to these covariates, the two forms of rebelliousness have been found by McDermott (1987) to correlate with various other psychological constructs such as need for power over others (in young men) with reactive rebelliousness; rugged individualism (in men) with reactive rebelliousness; irritability (in a female subsample) with reactive rebelliousness; extraversion (in men) with proactive rebelliousness; liking to speak and entertain (in men) with proactive rebelliousness; somatic symptomatology, anxiety and insomnia, and depressive affect (in a male subsample) with proactive rebelliousness; an external locus of control and the belief in the role of *chance* in determining positive outcomes (in men) with proactive rebelliousness; and whether or not young women self-report a willingness to take a sociopolitical lead with scores on the proactive rebelliousness subscale.

Regarding norms for the NDS, Tacon and Abner (1993) gave the 14 items (and the Telic Dominance Scale [TDS]) to 1,400 Canadians ages 25 to 65 of diverse socioeconomic status. Interestingly, they found negativism dominance to decline with age and proactive negativism to be less prevalently reported among higher socioeconomic groups. Thus, as indices of occupational status and family income decrease in magnitude, self-reports of spending proportionately more time in a proactive rebelliousness state increase in number, a reciprocal and circular relationship being likely to exist between them. Negativism then, as a psychological construct, is profoundly patterned, sociostructurally and demographically. As such, it is an important constituent of the reversal theory framework, addressing how individuals experience and respond to social influence.

McDermott (1987, 1988b) has provided evidence that further supports and extends the validity of the distinction between proactive and reactive negativism. In a sample of British undergraduate students, interviews were carried out with a group of high-scoring and low-scoring respondents to the NDS with three men and three women in each group. In interviews, participants were asked about their previous day and in particular about their responses to any perceived requirements that they had experienced. In this way, interviewees spoke of how they had responded to various forms of social influence and thereby referred to instances of conformity and rebellion. Independent judges then rated each of these recorded interviews for the degree to which the verbal reports indicated proactive and reactive rebelliousness. It was found that ratings correlated positively with NDS subscale scores for male interviewees. Thus, this finding illustrates the ecological validity of these two forms of the negativistic state—that is to say that among young men in particular, they are identifiable and conspicuous in everyday life. Young women's rebellion may take subtler, less obtrusive forms, and so the raters may have found them more difficult to recognize and quantify reliably.

A further qualitative analysis by McDermott (1987, 1988b) of self-reports extracted from these interviews also illustrates and supports the ecological validity of the NDS. One high-scoring proactively rebellious male interviewee, for example, spoke of his feelings about going out for the evening when he knew he should have been studying for an imminent exam:

> Actually it gave me great pleasure going out. I suppose I enjoy doing things I know I shouldn't do. Also, if I can't afford to do something, I'll do it. Well, I think I spoil myself sometimes and just go out. I enjoy things better though if I'm not supposed to do them than if I'm supposed to do them or if it's OK to do them, because I get more excitement out of doing them then. Course you're a bit guilty about it, but that was OK that was. I wasn't bothered at all. (McDermott, 1988b, p. 322)

Another high-scoring NDS respondent, but on the reactive negativism subscale, spoke differently of how she was responding oppositionally to the same perceived requirement, namely the need to study for impending exams:

> Well, I'm not bothered to revise at the moment, 'cause I don't give a shit about exams, so I didn't mind at all. I've always thought that way. I just don't have any respect for some reason. I've always walked out of exams. I've always done it. I don't know why. I just think there are better things I should be worrying about and better things to be doing. (McDermott, 1988b, p. 320)

Thus, one interviewee responds to the need to study for exams by not doing so and engaging instead in social behavior ("going out"), which is experienced as oppositional and as serving the function of heightening pleasurable arousal ("get more excitement"), namely proactive negativism. The second interviewee responds to the need to study also by not doing so but in addition by expressing bitterness, anger, and disillusionment with exams as a form of assessment. She goes on to denigrate their worth and by recalling previous instances of sudden in vivo withdrawal from examinations, such spontaneous outbursts of oppositional behavior being entirely consistent with reactive negativism as previously defined.

As a measurement device, the utility of the NDS extends beyond the immediate domain of reversal theory. In this vein, Brown (1986) argued that for individuals who are being subjected to a malign authority to rebel, as in Milgram's (1965) experiments, two conditions need to be present: (a) the opportunity for collective and shared definition of a situation as unjust and (b) an individual within the group who has, as Brown called it, an above-average "readiness" to rebel and oppose what is perceived as unjust— thus, an individual who will act as the catalyst for the others in the social group. The NDS, it is contended then, can be used to examine both the role of negativistic and conformist dominances within reversal theory and to address the role of these interindividual differences in readiness to rebel as implicated by Brown (1986) in the social psychology of social influence processes.

Since the time of its initial development, the NDS has been utilized in a variety of applied contexts that are considered in later sections of this chapter.

Motivational Style Profile

Another measure of negativism dominance is contained within the Motivational Style Profile (MSP; Apter, Mallows, & Williams, 1998), a questionnaire designed to assess all pairs of metamotivational states in reversal theory (see chapter 3 in this volume).

However, the content of the negativism items in this measure are about the paratelic form of negativism (proactive rebelliousness) with items pertinent to the reactive form not being evident. Also, the number of items in the negativism and conformity scales is less than those in the NDS. Thus, although the MSP is comprehensive in terms of measuring all the pairs of metamotivational states, it is not as conceptually or as operationally well elaborated as the NDS in so far as the measurement of negativism is concerned.

NEGATIVISM AND APPLIED RESEARCH

Negativism has been explored in a variety of applied contexts that are considered in the remainder of this chapter.

Music Preference and Negativism Dominance

Within the context of societal concern about the possibility that various kinds of rock music might have adverse consequences for those who listen to it, Robinson, Weaver, and Zillmann (1996) explored the relationship between personality and the appreciation of rock music. In particular, they examined preferences for and the psychological effects of various kinds of rock music videotapes. Specifically, they examined scores on extraversion, neuroticism, psychoticism, and reactive and proactive rebelliousness and their relationship with preferences for soft/nonrebellious versus hard/rebellious rock music videotapes. Sixty male and 78 female undergraduates completed the relevant personality questionnaires and then watched rock music videotapes as supplied. Participants then rated their enjoyment of these videos. Robinson et al. found that respondents scoring high on psychoticism or high on reactive rebelliousness enjoyed hard/rebellious rock music videotapes more than did those scoring low on either of these dimensions. The reverse was found for enjoyment of soft/nonrebellious rock music videotapes. Scores on extraversion, neuroticism, and proactive rebelliousness did not relate to enjoyment ratings.

The authors concluded that these findings suggest vindictive and vengeful negativism (i.e., reactive rebelliousness) that arises from disappointment, frustration, rejection, and deficient care "fuels the enjoyment of defiant rock" (p. 268). That the proactive form does not covary with such enjoyment indicates that hedonistic, sensation-seeking oppositionalism for its own sake is relatively unimportant as a concomitant of identification with rock music. Rather, young people who are disaffected for a variety of reasons would appear to enjoy such videos most, with all of the quasi-aggressive posturing and acting out that they often contain and model.

In addition to these findings, and in the course of carrying out preliminary checks on the psychometric properties of the NDS, they examined its factor structure and found that the two-factor model as proposed by McDermott (1986, 1987, 1988a) was entirely replicable, the pattern of item loadings aligning with those previously specified for the proactive and reactive rebelliousness factors.

Humor, Disgust, and Negativism

Oppliger and Zillmann (1997) carried out a similar study of the psychological concomitants of preferences for viewing various products from television. In particular, they video-recorded episodes from MTV's program *Beavis and Butt-Head* and classified them as involving strongly disgusting humor that was focused on excretion of body fluids in socially inappropriate scenarios; humor with weak disgust, such as food-related jokes; and humor with no-disgust, for example, that involving derogation.

They asked 65 college students to watch these episodes, measuring their disgust-sensitivity and rebelliousness using the NDS at the outset of the experiment and eliciting ratings of funniness and disgust after exposure to each episode. They found that highly rebellious respondents were less disgust sensitive than were more conformist-dominant individuals, a negative correlation between these two sets of scores being observed. Also, they found that highly rebellious respondents found the episodes involving disgust to be funnier than did participants who reported little negativism, an analysis of the variance of amusement ratings producing a main effect of rebelliousness that approached significance. Likewise, there was a modest, positive correlation between amusement ratings and rebelliousness scores. The analysis of this data, however, did not report the separate effects of the proactive and reactive rebelliousness subscales, which individually may have proved to be more informative concerning the enjoyment of disgusting humor. Oppliger and Zillmann (1997) suggested that disgusting humor is something particularly enjoyed by adolescents. Given that as many as one in five adolescents go through a period of rebelliousness (Balswick & Macrides, 1975), it may well be that negativism mediates the association between this developmental period and the enjoyment of disgusting humor. Perhaps it is because disgusting humor often involves irreverent depictions of the flagrant breaking of the rules and the niceties of social etiquette, so that as a genre of humor it resonates well with negativistically dominant individuals, many of whom may be found amongst people in their teenage years.

Substance Use, Health, and Negativism

Turner and Heskin (1998) examined cigarette and alcohol use in a sample of adolescents (14–17-year-olds) as a function of differences in motivational dominance. In particular, they investigated differences among "heavy," "moderate," and "nonsmokers/drinkers" on paratelic and negativism dominance, the latter being measured by the NDS. They found significant differences among the three smoking categories, with heavy users being more negativistic and paratelic dominant than either moderate smokers or nonsmokers. However, differences in the negativism means among the three drinking categories were not statistically significant, although in the direction as hypothesized (i.e., heavy drinking being associated with higher negativism). This study did not report subscale scores from the NDS and so did not look at the differences among the groups in terms of reactive and proactive rebelliousness for either cigarette or alcohol use. However, McDermott (1989) did find that scores on reactive rebelliousness correlated more substantively with the number of cigarettes smoked per day ($r = .34$,

$p > .001$) than did scores on items measuring proactive rebelliousness ($r = .26, p > .002$), although the difference between the strength of these correlations was not large. Thus, it may be that the smoking of cigarettes is more associated with coping with feelings produced by responding to what are perceived to be unjust or unreasonable interpersonal requirements than with feelings associated with the need to engage in oppositional behavior for the sake of heightening arousal and gaining excitement. Such a contention, however, is in need of examination through further empirical research.

The role of the negativistic state has been investigated extensively however in relation to smoking cessation and regarding smoking relapse. In relation to the latter, O'Connell, Cook, Gerkovich, Potocky, and Swan (1990) examined situations in which ex-smokers were at risk of smoking. They found that among those ex-smokers who experienced such a relapse crisis, those who were in either a paratelic or negativistic state were more likely to smoke than those in a telic or conformist state. These findings were replicated longitudinally within participants by Potocky, Gerkovich, O'Connell, and Cook (1991), who found that maintaining abstinence during a crisis was associated consistently with being in telic and conformist states, whereas smoking in crises covaried with being in paratelic and negativistic states. Thus, the negativism state represents a psychological vulnerability in so far as smoking relapse is concerned. In combination with the paratelic state and cigarette availability, these three variables are powerful predictors of relapse and thereby are suggestive of how to evolve preventative coping strategies for those who wish to quit.

Taking this work one step further, Cook, Gerkovich, O'Connell, and Potocky (1995) sought to understand how metamotivational state might predict the outcome of tempting situations that occur in the first 6 weeks of a smoking cessation program. Independent groups and repeated measures analyses of interview data from 68 program participants indicated that the telic–paratelic metamotivational states and the amount of effort needed to obtain cigarettes significantly predicted abstinence and relapse. Surprisingly, removal of the negativistic–conformist pair of states did not significantly reduce the goodness-of-fit of the model, indicating that these states as measured were not important predictors of smoking relapse. Thus, the conclusions drawn from this study are at variance with those of earlier studies. One possible explanation for this inconsistency lies in the problems associated with the measurement of negativism. In each of these studies, interview methods were used that did not incorporate the distinction between proactive and reactive negativism, which as has been stated already, may be differentially related to smoking behavior. Further research utilizing interview protocols that incorporate this distinction may produce a more consistent set of findings. In overview, however, this body of work suggests negativism is likely to be of further utility for explaining the occurrence of smoking behavior and smoking relapses during attempts to quit. Certainly the study of negativism and conformity is relevant to the prediction of other health behaviors and outcomes.

In this vein, O'Connell and Brooks (1997) examined whether or not metamotivational state as measured by the SSQ (see chapter 3 in this volume) was related to changing habits, as recommended by health promotion experts and clinicians. To such an end they randomly assigned 242 participants to one of four recall tasks: (a) an occasion when they had succeeded in resisting an urge to carry out an old habit, (b) an occasion when they had not succeeded in doing so, (c) an occasion when they had been able to carry out a new behavior, and (d) an occasion when they had not been able to do so. Also, they asked all participants to complete the SSQ so as to indicate the metamotivational state they recalled experiencing during their success or failure. A chi-square analysis of the negativistic–conformist states in relation to the four conditions was statistically significant. Of participants recalling success scenarios, only 18% indicated that they were in the negativistic state, whereas for failure scenarios 38% of participants recalling these reported the negativistic state. Being able to resist an urge to carry out an old behavior and to instigate a new one was associated with being in a conformist state. The results of this study suggest that negativism is an important psychological construct for explaining failure to resist engaging in maladaptive health habits and adopting new ones.

It is likely then, that the negativistic and conformist states are of predictive value not just in relation to the prediction of healthy and unhealthy behaviors, but also with regard to the more substantive issue of major health outcomes. In such a vein, Ratcliffe, Dawson, and Walker (1995) found that social conformity is independently associated with an increased risk of death within five years among patients with Hodgkin's disease and non-Hodgkin's lymphoma. Thus, the significance of negativism dominance as a predictor of health behavior and health outcomes cannot be understated and is worthy of further empirical investigation.

Participation in Sport and Negativism

A significant amount of empirical work has been conducted on the role of negativism and conformity in relation to participation in various types of sport. Vlaswinkel and Kerr (1990), using a Dutch translation of the NDS, investigated the hypothesis that participation in sports involving risk of injury would be associated with high negativism dominance scores and that participation in cooperative team sports would covary with lower scores, indicating conformist dominance. They found that student performers of risk sports scored significantly higher on reactive negativism than did performers of safer team sports. They found also however, that professional soccer players scored more highly on this subscale than did long-distance runners. Why participants in risk and contact sports should report a tendency to spend more time in a reactively negativistic state is not clear, and the reasons for this are in need of further investigation. Differences in negativism dominance between participants in various forms of sports also have been found by Braathen and Svebak (1992), who examined the motivational styles of Norwegian teenage men and women who performed endurance, explosive, and team sports (more details are found in chapter 10).

A further study by Chirivella and Martinez (1994) examined motivational dominance among tennis players, karate practitioners, and parasailers. Tennis players were found to score more highly on NDS reactive negativism than were karate practitioners and parasailers. The authors posited that this result is explainable by the notion that the breaking of rules during tennis carries less risk of a threat to physical integrity than does the operation of such a motivational style during participation in the risk sports of karate or parasailing. They found also that scores on the proactive rebelliousness subscale correlated negatively with time in months spent previously practicing the sports.

The findings of Vlaswinkel and Kerr (1990), Braathen and Svebak (1992), and Chirivella and Martinez (1994) suggest that the experience of the negativistic and conformist states are patterned across participation in different types of sport and that such motivational styles are adaptive or maladaptive in terms of achievement and persistence, depending on the particular type of sport. Further work is needed to identify the properties of these sports that account for the motivational styles associated with them.

Whether or not the sport involves risk of injury is one such property that has been examined carefully by Cogan and Brown (1999). They looked at the motivational dominance of snowboarders and badminton players who had been matched in terms of educational level, employment status, ethnicity, enthusiasm for their primary sport of choice, and age, the average age of respondents in each group being 21–22 years. The two groups differed, however, in the amount of injuries they had sustained in the past through participating in their respective primary sport; as was expected, snowboarders reported significantly more broken bones, muscle strains, and serious cuts than did badminton players. Thus, unlike in previous studies, snowboarding was confirmed objectively as a risk sport, whereas badminton was confirmed as a comparatively very safe sport. With this important element of study design in place, they found on the psychological measures that the snowboarders reported significantly less arousal avoidance and less serious-mindedness than did the badminton players and further that they scored higher on proactive negativism than did their racket-wielding counterparts. Thus, from this study it is apparent that taking part in this risk sport is associated with a proactively rebellious form of excitement seeking in which fun and arousal are sought for their own sake. In addition, when respondents were also asked about injuries sustained through participation in secondary sports activities, a significant correlation was found for the number of muscle strains and episodes of concussion with scores on the proactive negativism subscale, risk-prone respondents thereby demonstrating a proclivity for sports that are congruent with this motivational style.

From the review of the preceding four studies, it is evident that the investigation of negativism and conformity in relation to participation in different types of sports is producing findings that may be of value to both practitioners and coaches.

Soccer Spectating and Negativism

In Europe, sporadic violence between police and groups of rival supporters outside soccer stadiums and inside on the terraces has been a lamentably frequent feature of soccer spectating for many years. Kerr (1988c), in his research and in his book *Understanding Soccer Hooliganism* (1994), has provided an articulate analysis of clashes between police officers and soccer spectators in terms of negativism, notably of the excitement-seeking proactively rebellious kind. He reminded us that for negativism to be experienced three elements have to be present: (a) a set of perceived requirements to behave in specified way; (b) a source of these requirements, such as appointed authority figures; and (c) the desire to act against such requirements, perhaps for the sake of heightening pleasurable arousal. Kerr's (1994) analysis found that police and stewards at soccer games act as sources of requirements and that attempts to impose tighter controls on the movements of soccer fans in an effort to prevent escalating violence paradoxically provides an exaggerated set of requirements against which fans in a negativistic state all the more want to rebel. Such requirements thus become appraised as challenges, with successful opposition of these challenges then simply enhancing the reputations of the negativistic spectators within their peer group (Emler, 1984) and reinforcing such behavior. In combination with social psychological modeling of group and social influence processes, this analysis offers intriguing empirical possibilities and once again points to the ecological validity of the negativism construct in everyday life situations.

Antisocial Behavior and Negativism

As has been seen from a brief consideration of substance use and soccer spectating, the sequelae and connotations of negativistic experience and behavior are often socially undesirable, maladaptive, and even antisocial in kind. In such a vein, the proactive form of negativism is a sensation-seeking form of hedonistic oppositional behavior. Although some manifestations of this state covary with the taking of risks in socially sanctioned settings such as those associated with the practice of various sports, others covary with provocative, antagonistic, and potentially confrontational behavior. Thus, rebelliousness in some contexts can constitute a form of challenging play, a thesis developed by McDermott (1991). Although this paratelic, playful negativism can be harmless and enjoyable in its effects, and indeed productive in the formation of whistle-blowing protest groups and youth countercultures, on occasion it can be involved in aggressive acts of civil disobedience such as rioting or as a marker of disaffection in school settings and as an antecedent of school truancy (as McDermott, 1987, has found). It can also be involved as a covariate of juvenile offending (delinquency), of oppositional defiant disorder as defined in the *Diagnostic and Statistical Manual of Mental Disorders* (4th ed.) (American Psychiatric Association, 1994), and psychopathy in later life.

Jones (1981) and Jones and Heskin (1988), writing within a reversal theory framework, pointed to the connection between delinquency and negativism, arguing that for many young people, conformist options such as success at school or employment are denied them, thereby directing adolescents toward negativism rather than such experience and behavior being the product of an active choice. Jones (1981) noted, however, that oppositional behavior can promote prosocial change, whereas Apter and Smith (1976) contended that it could serve to break the status quo and disrupt an existing unhappy situation such as a dysfunctional marital relationship in which a child is neglected or exposed to the specter of frequently conflicting parents or to severe inconsistent disciplinary behavior. The association of negativism with delinquency and other forms of antisocial conduct should not imply that a negativistic adolescent is at fault or is displaying an inherent psychological deficit.

Doherty and McDermott (1997) have empirically examined the role of rebelliousness as a component in a multifactorial model of delinquency. Fifty-one young women and 50 young men ages 15 to 17 years old in a high-school in north London completed a self-report based juvenile offenses checklist, the NDS, the TDS, and two subscales measuring psychopathic withdrawal and belligerence (Blackburn, 1987), these being constructs that have been cited as covariates of antisocial law breaking. It was found, from a multiple regression analysis, that of the seven subscales entered into the equation, reactive negativism was the pre-eminent statistically significant predictor of self-reported delinquent acts ($\beta = .33$, $t = 3.32$, $p > .001$). The latter included events ranging in severity from ones such as viewing a film which is not permitted to be viewed by those under the age of 18 and trespassing to stealing a car but not returning it and using a weapon in a fight. Thus, many of the offenses that are predicted by reactive rebelliousness are by no means trivial. Given that reactive rebelliousness involves interpersonal disaffection and, as suggested by the work of Dodge and Coie (1987), a cognitive readiness to misinterpret ambiguous interpersonal situations in a way that assumes malign intent, the conceptual rationale underpinning the empirical association between offending and negativism is evident and clear. However, the roots of such disaffection and cognitive bias may be more socially learned than individual in origin, particularly when the antisocial behavior among boys is nonaggressive in kind (Eley, Lichtenstein, & Stevenson, 1999).

Negativism also has been linked with offending during adult years. Thomas-Peter (1993a) reported a study in which he examined NDS scores across three sets of respondents: individuals with personality disorders who have committed criminal offenses detained in a special hospital under mental health legislation ($N = 31$); nonincarcerated offenders resident in community hostels ($N = 30$); and control participants without records of offending from administrative, domestic, and nursing staff employed in the health and probation service ($N = 30$). A number of analyses were carried out. Firstly, offenders with personality disorders and nonincarcerated offenders scored significantly higher on proactive negativism than did control participants. In an ensuing analysis, the participants from the two offender groups were subdivided on the basis of other psychometric scores into one of the following three groups: primary (not socially withdrawing) psychopaths, secondary (socially withdrawing) psychopaths, and overcontrolled and inhibited offenders. Both proactive and reactive rebelliousness scores from the NDS differed significantly across all three experimental groups and the control group ($p > .0001$ and $> .0048$, respectively). On proactive negativism the primary psychopath group scored highest ($M = 8$), followed by the secondary psychopath group ($M = 5.72$), then the control group ($M = 3.73$), and last the overcontrolled and inhibited offender group ($M = 2.73$). For reactive rebelliousness the order of the differences was the same (means for each group being 5.44, 4.28, 3.63, and 1.86, respectively).

The results of this study provide a useful caveat to those from the work of Doherty and McDermott (1997): It is notable that once again high scores on the NDS covary with offending, but this time on both subscales. However, overcontrolled and inhibited offenders in fact scored below the control group means on both reactive and proactive negativism. This shows that conformity dominance as well as negativism dominance is also associated with offending behavior. Thus, as reversal theory contends, it is not necessarily the properties of just one of the metamotivational states in a pair that inevitably lead to social pathology or psychopathology. Rather it is when dominance becomes extreme and individuals spend highly disproportionate amounts of time in one state or the other, being unable to reverse from one to the other, that maladaptive coping occurs, which in turn may contribute to the development of social pathology such as offending behavior. We see here that conformity as well as negativism can have antisocial connotations and sequelae. So, just as Rotter (1975) warned against the use of an oversimplifying good-boy–bad-boy dichotomy in relation to his internal versus external locus-of-control construct, the same caution is needed here with regard to negativism and conformity (and indeed to other pairs of metamotivational states in reversal theory).

Creativity, Prosocial Outcomes, and Negativism

Both the terms *rebelliousness* and *negativism* have pejorative connotations, implying that there is little positive to say about feeling oppositional, despite negativism on occasion providing fun, excitement, relief from boredom, and the possibility of countercontrol and interpersonal empowerment. (It was in fact this realization that led to the term *challenging* being used instead by Apter International, see chapter 13, in management consultancy and workshops.)

It was with this in mind that Griffin and McDermott (1998) sought to explore a potentially prosocial facet of negativism by examining the utility of the NDS subscales with respect to self-reported creative acts and creative interests in a sample of 67 first-year undergraduates. Scores on the NDS were found to correlate with just 3 of 16 indices of creative interests and creative activities undertaken during the past 12 months: Proactive rebelliousness was associated with number of creative literary activities and with interest in domestic arts, and reactive rebelliousness was associated with interest in the visual arts. However, given that multiple tests were used, there remains the possibility of Type I errors. Thus, from this study it can only be safely concluded that creativity as measured is not associated with negativism of either the proactive or reactive form.

Why should this be so? One possibility is that the measure of creativity used by Griffin and McDermott (1998) is not an apposite index of this construct. However, also in this study scores on Costa and McCrae's (1985) Openness to Fantasy and Openness to Aesthetics subscales from the NEO Personality Inventory were found to correlate on 14 out of 16 occasions with indices of creative acts and interests, openness in previous studies having been shown to be highly predictive of creative involvement. Nevertheless, it is also possible that the measure of creativity as used was not accessing the kind of creativity into which negativism taps, that is to say, originality, innovativeness, and a tendency to repudiate traditional lines of thought, values, and experience in favor of unconventional, alternative ones. Thus, further research might usefully explore the proposition that the experience of negativism is associated with this form of prosocial, creative behavior.

Despite these findings, there is some indication that rebelliousness is of prosocial worth in specific contexts and circumstances. Mallows (1999) reported findings from a study of the motivational styles of school teacher trainees in which these participants were divided into two groups: (a) those whose management of classroom behavior was problematic and not reaching required standards and (b) those who were seen to be deploying effective classroom behavior management skills. Mallows found that teacher trainees with behavior management weaknesses scored highly on the conformity subscale of the MSP as compared with their more effective trainee colleagues. She observed that these failing trainees were unable to improvise in the classroom when children behaved in unexpected and challenging ways. The less-effective trainees were rule bound, inflexible, and uninventive in response to classroom misbehavior, relying on prototypical scripts of how they thought teachers should behave. Conversely, more negativistic teachers in these situations were more likely to come up with new and creative solutions because they were less fearful of breaking the perceived rules of good teacher behavior and more disposed to trying novel solutions that were tailored to the particularities of individual classroom situations. Thus, evidence is emerging that the negativistic state may well be associated with specific forms of creative problem-solving and prosocial outcomes.

Relational Compatibility and Negativism

O'Connor (1992) has applied a reversal theory framework to an analysis of mother–child compatibility. In so doing, she conducted three studies involving negativism and conformity, the first of which is described here as an example of this work. O'Connor examined whether conformist-dominant, negativistic-dominant, and reversible mothers felt most compatible with children whose dominant mode matched their own. She found that conformist mothers rated themselves as more compatible with a conformist child than with a negativistic child. However, negativistic-dominant mothers did not rate themselves as more compatible with a negativistic child than did conformist mothers. Reversible mothers rated reversible children as most compatible with themselves, followed by conformist, and then negativistic children. Overall, mothers rated highly reversible children, followed by conformist, and then negativistic children as most compatible with themselves. Thus, O'Connor's (1992) findings suggest that mother–child compatibility and indeed relational compatibility more generally is not a simple matter of mode similarity facilitating attraction, of "like" being drawn to "like," or of mode opposition inhibiting compatibility. Rather, mothers rated metamotivationally flexible (reversible) children as most compatible irrespective of the mother's own dominant mode, and likewise all mothers rated negativistic children as least compatible. These findings lend support to the view that negativism is not valued as an interpersonal attribute as highly as others such as adaptability, irrespective of the prosocial properties of this metamotivational style.

CONCLUSION

It is evident from the preceding review that the negativistic and conformist metamotivational states are recognizable in many realms of human behavior and experience. It is also apparent that both negativism and conformity have socially desirable as well as undesirable connotations. Furthermore, the capacity to alternate between negativistic and conformist states is more functional than being exclusively committed to either, such psychodiversity being, as reversal theory contends, highly adaptive. No doubt, in the future, researchers will continue to expand on the explanatory range and power of these metamotivational states and further underscore their importance for reversal theory.

10

SPORT AND EXERCISE

JOHN H. KERR

One of the core features of reversal theory is the concept of metamotivational states and the reversals that are thought to occur between those states in any individual over time. The concept of states and reversals contributes to a view of human behavior which is considered inherently inconsistent. This means that a person may experience a given situation at different times with different operative states. Thus, a person's motivation for taking part in an activity, such as long-distance running, may be very different on different occasions (Frey, 1993, 1999; Kerr, 1985b). Such a theoretical backdrop makes research an interesting challenge, whether sport and exercise or some other aspect of human behavior is at focus (Apter, 1999b; Kerr, 1999b).

Over the past 15 years, reversal theorists interested in sport and exercise have adopted and implemented a multimethod approach to discerning aspects of motivation, personality, and emotional experience specific to human behavior in the sport context. Using a variety of sport and exercise settings, quantitative and qualitative research has involved studies of metamotivational dominance; metamotivational states (and reversals between states); changes in important metamotivational state variables, such as felt arousal and felt transactional outcome; and the experience of somatic and transactional emotions (see Figure 10.1).

This chapter sets out to review the results obtained from reversal theory sport and exercise research. However, some reversal theory work on sport is described in other chapters. Soccer hooliganism is discussed in chapter 9 (on rebelliousness), and studies that focused on risk or dangerous sports are reviewed in chapter 11 (on risk-taking). In addition, some sport and physical activities that can be described as "play" are discussed in chapter 15 (on reversal theory from a humanistic perspective).

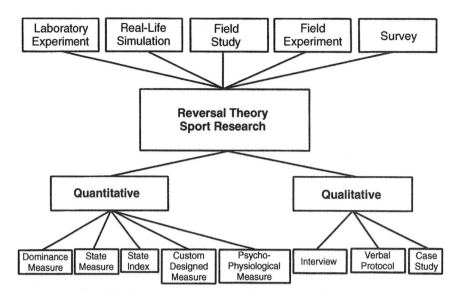

Figure 10.1. An overview of reversal theory sport research.
Note. From *Experiencing Sport: Reversal Theory* (p. 214), by J. H. Kerr, 1999, Chichester, England: Wiley. Copyright 1999 by John Wiley & Sons Ltd. Reprinted with permission.

METAMOTIVATIONAL DOMINANCE RESEARCH

Telic–Paratelic Dominance

Kerr (1987b) used the Telic Dominance Scale (TDS; Murgatroyd, Rushton, Apter, & Ray, 1978; see also chapter 3 in this volume) to examine the telic dominance characteristics of 120 male sports performers participating in professional (cycling and soccer), serious amateur (field hockey, table tennis, and show jumping), and recreational (various activities) sports. A control group of nonsports participants was included in the study. Members of the professional group were dependent on sports for their income; members of the serious amateur group were all involved in regular practice, training, and competition; and members of the recreational group participated only infrequently in sport activities for fun. The results of statistical analysis showed the professionals to be more telic dominant than were the serious amateurs, recreational participants, and control group. The professional group scored significantly higher than the serious amateur, recreational, and control groups on two TDS subscales, Planning orientation and Serious-mindedness, as well as total telic dominance score. The professional group had the lowest group mean score on the TDS Arousal-avoidance subscale, with group differences approaching significance (see Figure 10.2).

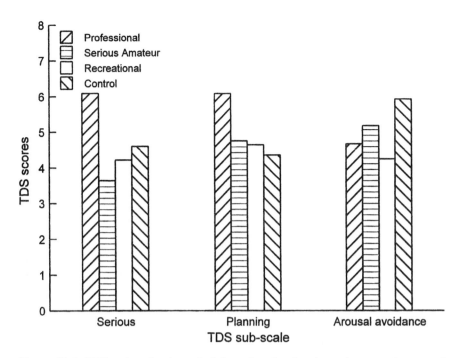

Figure 10.2. TDS subscale characteristics of professional-, serious amateur-, and recreational-sports performers and control participants.
Note. TDS = Telic Dominance Scale.
From *Motivation and Emotion in Sport: Reversal Theory* (p. 34), by J. H. Kerr, 1997, Hove, England: Psychology Press. Copyright by Pergamon Press Ltd. Reprinted with permission.

Male and female professional and amateur triathletes were the focus of Sell's (1991) TDS study. Both professional groups had competed for a longer period, spent more time training, and participated in more competitions than did the amateur group. Male amateurs scored significantly higher (i.e., more telic) than did the male professionals on the Arousal-avoidance subscale, but differences in the Serious-mindedness and Planning orientation subscales and total TDS scores, although similar in direction to the findings of Kerr's (1987b) study, were not significant. Young (1998), however, using the Paratelic Dominance Scale (PDS; Cook & Gerkovich, 1993), did find that female Australian professional tennis players were significantly more telic than paratelic dominant.

In an extension of Kerr's (1987b) study, the telic dominance characteristics of 38 male and female Masters swimmers (former elite-level athletes who continue to train seriously and compete against other top athletes in age-group competition) were examined (Kerr & van Lienden, 1987). This group included 8 former national, 12 former international, and 5 former

Olympic-level swimmers. Their TDS scores were compared with the different groups from the earlier study (Kerr, 1987b). No significant differences were obtained between the Masters swimmers and the professionals for total TDS and subscale scores, but the Masters swimmers were found to be significantly more telic dominant (planning orientation, serious-mindedness, and total telic dominance scores) than were those in the serious amateur and recreational groups. Masters swimmers' telic dominance scores were similar to those of professional sports performers.

The results obtained from the above studies generally support reversal theory arguments (Apter 1982a, 1990b) that professional and other highly committed sports performers will be more telic dominant than sports participants who are less serious about their involvement. Furthermore, there may be a relationship between telic or paratelic dominance and the types of sports that people prefer or choose to participate in. On the one hand, paratelic-dominant individuals, who generally prefer unplanned, spontaneous, and impulsive activities, seem to be attracted to sports like baseball or basketball, which allow for spontaneous, impulsive, and explosive action ("explosive sports"), and they attempt to avoid sports that involve the repetitive, monotonous activity associated with endurance sports, like long-distance running or rowing. On the other hand, telic-dominant individuals, with their general preference for planned goal-oriented activities, appear to prefer endurance sports and tend to avoid explosive sports.

In a study of three independent Australian sports samples, Svebak and Kerr (1989) analyzed responses on the TDS and the Barratt Impulsiveness Scale (BIS; Barratt, 1985) in an attempt to show differences in preference for and participation in certain sports among telic- and paratelic-dominant respondents. First, a group of top tennis players from Sydney and members of the Australian Universities women's field hockey team (explosive sports) were compared with high-level runners competing at the New South Wales Cross-Country Championships (endurance sport). As shown in Figure 10.3, TDS results indicated that the explosive-sport performers were significantly less planning oriented and arousal avoiding than were the endurance-sport performers. However, these results were confounded by age and gender differences, with women in the explosive group and men in the endurance group in the majority. Balancing the explosive and endurance groups for age produced even greater differences on these TDS subscales.

Gender differences between explosive and endurance groups were dealt with in a second analysis involving 64 Human Movement Education students from the University of Sydney (Svebak & Kerr, 1989). In order to identify which sports were performed by telic- or paratelic-dominant individuals, participants were asked to list up to three winter and three summer sports that they actually performed regularly during their leisure time. In addition,

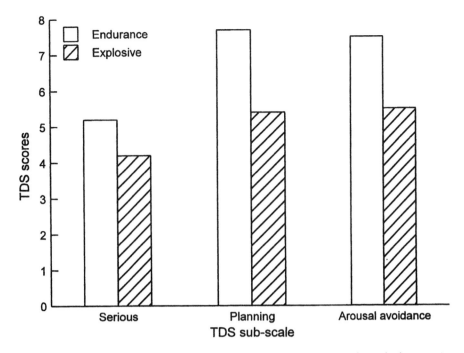

Figure 10.3. TDS subscale characteristics of endurance- and explosive-sports participants.
Note. TDS = Telic Dominance Scale.
From "The Role of Impulsivity in Preference for Sports," by S. Svebak and J. Kerr, 1989, *Personality and Individual Differences 10,* p. 53. Copyright 1989 by Pergamon Press Ltd. Reprinted with permission.

they completed the TDS and the BIS. Highly paratelic-dominant respondents performed baseball, cricket, touch football, surfing, and windsurfing regularly, and highly telic-dominant respondents performed long-distance running and rowing regularly.

Using a random recruitment procedure, a so-called *nonparatelic* group (balanced for age and gender) who did not perform explosive sports in their leisure time was selected for comparison with the paratelic-dominant group. TDS subscale results again proved to be significant, as were results from the BIS Non-planning subscale, which indicated that a less planned lifestyle was a personality characteristic of students who performed baseball, cricket, touch football, surfing, and windsurfing.

The participants in the second analysis were specialist students of Human Movement Education. Would the significant differences in telic–paratelic dominance found with them also be apparent for students from other courses who participated in paratelic-oriented sports? Also, would there be a difference among other student groups in the link between telic–paratelic dominance and preference for participation in certain sports and actual participation in those sports? The third analysis attempted (Svebak & Kerr, 1989) to answer these two questions by examining sport preference and participation among 116 female and 65 male students following courses in arts, economics, education, science, and engineering and others. Again, students listed up to three winter and three summer sports that they actually performed, as well as up to three winter and three summer sports that, if given a free choice, they would have preferred to perform. They also completed the TDS and BIS.

Of the Human Movement Education students in the second analysis, 37.5% reported actually performing the paratelic sports identified above but only some 20% of the general student population did so. Only about a third of the women from this 20% participated in these sports, whereas in the Human Movement Education sample participation was split equally between genders. To allow comparison with the paratelic sport participants, a random recruitment procedure was used to form a group from the remainder of the student population who indicated that they did not perform any of these sports and did not wish to do so. No significant differences were found between these groups on TDS and BIS subscales, suggesting that telic–paratelic dominance was not related to the actual performance of paratelic sports. However, further analysis indicated that gender played an important role. TDS and BIS scores for those students who performed baseball, cricket, touch football, surfing, and windsurfing were compared with 35 other students who had reported that they would have liked to participate in one or more of them but, in reality, did not actually perform them. Women who would have preferred to perform these sports had paratelic-dominant TDS scores similar to those of male students who actually performed such sports. It was concluded that social norms related to gender roles associated with these traditional male sports (baseball, cricket, touch football, surfing, and windsurfing) in Australia explained why female students in this study did not actually take part in the sports they preferred. The above results do provide some evidence that people may prefer and perform certain sports because they are telic or paratelic dominant. Other related studies include Braathen and Svebak (1990), Chirivella and Martinez (1994), Kerr (1988e, and Kerr and Cox (1988).

Negativism–Conformity Dominance

Negativism dominance was explored, using the Negativism Dominance Scale (NDS; McDermott & Apter, 1988; see also chapter 3 in this volume), in team and individual-sport performers (Vlaswinkel & Kerr, 1990; see also chapter 9 in this volume). No significant differences in NDS subscale and total scores were found between 22 professional and 22 recreational soccer players. However, the same group of professional soccer players did score significantly higher on the Reactive Negativism subscale when compared with a group of 38 long-distance runners.

A sample of talented teenage Norwegian athletes, which included 228 young men and 124 young women, took part in a study aimed at examining the relationships among motivational characteristics, gender, type of sport, and level of excellence (Braathen & Svebak, 1992). In terms of negativism dominance, endurance- and explosive-sport performers scored significantly higher on the Reactive Negativism subscale than did team-sport performers. Also, male performers of explosive sports were found to score highest, and female team-sport athletes lowest, on the Reactive Negativism subscale. Athletes from team sports scored lowest and those from explosive sports highest on the Proactive Negativism subscale. It may be that negativistic lifestyles are in conflict with the social demands for the development of excellence in team sports. Also, national- or international-level athletes scored significantly higher on proactive negativism than did athletes who performed at a local level. Differences in negativism dominance appear to be important for those who reach a high level of excellence, but in some cases, these are mediated by gender differences.

Following the testing of the majority of the talented teenage athlete sample on two further occasions, using the NDS among other measures, Torild Hellandsig (1998) reported additional results. These findings confirmed results from the previous Braathen and Svebak (1992) study that skilled explosive-sport performers score significantly higher than did endurance- and team-sport athletes on the NDS Proactive Negativism subscale. However, the results of this study also found that discontinuation from competitive sport could be predicted from performers' scores on the NDS. Specifically, those who stopped competing at ages 18–19 scored significantly higher on the Reactive Negativism subscale than did those who continued to compete. This is an important finding that suggests that the threshold for negativistic responses to disappointment and frustration is relatively low for athletes who discontinued their involvement in competitive sports when compared to those who carried on competing.

Other interesting findings involving negativism dominance have been reported by Cogan and Brown (1998, 1999), who found a link between proactive negativism and injuries incurred in sport (see chapter 9 in this volume). In addition, Wilson and Phillips (1995) found that, among losers in a squash competition, the more negativistic dominant a player was, the greater the unpleasantness he or she experienced after losing. This showed that game outcome could be a mediator of metamotivational state, which, in turn, is also related to aspects of dominance.

Metamotivational Orientation: An Indicator of Dominance?

Lindner and Kerr (1999) adopted a different approach to examining metamotivation and sport participation and preference by using a large-scale survey study to investigate metamotivational orientation. They achieved a 90% response rate from a group of 2,387 incoming students at the University of Hong Kong, who were asked to complete a self-administered questionnaire comprised of three sections.

The first section was concerned with the frequency of past participation in sport or exercise at school (excluding physical education classes) and the frequency of intended participation at university. This section also dealt with motives for past and future participation, and students were asked to indicate the "deciding reason" for their intended participation. Based on their answers, 630 male and 734 female students from the overall sample were classified in terms of their metamotivational orientation toward sport participation. Those who rated health-related fitness highest made up the telic-oriented group, leisure and relaxation the paratelic-oriented group, to be with or make new friends the sympathy-oriented group, for character-building or for better personal image the autic-oriented group, and for sport-related skills and fitness the mastery-oriented group. No statements in the questionnaire represented conformist, negativistic, or alloic orientations.

The second section asked students to indicate their preferences for 39 sports and activities offered at the University of Hong Kong, and the third section was concerned with self-perceptions of physical ability, physical fitness, and their own ability to swim a distance of 50 meters. The findings related to the first two sections are discussed here.

Most students wanted to participate to become or stay fit and healthy or for leisure and enjoyment and, therefore, most students were classified in the telic- or paratelic-oriented groups. There were significantly more men in these groups than in the autic- and sympathy-oriented groups and significantly more women in these groups than in the autic-, sympathy-, and mastery-oriented groups. There were significantly more men than women classified as mastery oriented, although the numbers in these groups were, in comparison to the telic- and paratelic-oriented groups, relatively small.

In terms of sport preference, men rated basketball, badminton, tennis, swimming, table tennis, cycling, and football (soccer) as their preferred activities, and women rated badminton, tennis, squash, swimming, and cycling as their preferred activities. For male basketball, the telic-oriented group, and for male fitness training, the paratelic-oriented group had significantly lower numbers of responses than did the other groups. For male tennis, the number of autic-oriented participants was significantly lower than for the other groups. For the women, the telic-oriented group scored significantly higher, and the paratelic-oriented group scored significantly lower, in their preference for fitness training and diet and exercise activity than did the other groups. Given the characteristics of the telic and paratelic states, these results for orientation are in accord with predictions from reversal theory.

Significant differences between groups were also obtained in preference for some individual sports for the female mastery- and autic-oriented groups, but relative group numbers were small. With respect to past and intended participation rates, both male and female students classified in the mastery-orientation group had significantly higher past participation than did their respective telic- and paratelic-oriented groups. For intended future participation, the male mastery-oriented group's mean score was significantly higher than the male telic- and paratelic-oriented groups, and the female mastery-oriented group's score was also significantly higher than the female sympathy-oriented group's score.

This preliminary data on metamotivational orientation and sport preference generally support previous metamotivational dominance results (Kerr & Svebak, 1989; Svebak & Kerr, 1989), and the results for past and intended participation rates are in line with reversal theory predictions. However, further research is necessary before the possible link between metamotivational orientation and dominance and links among dominance, orientation, and sport preference and participation can be firmly established.

Reversal theory dominance research in sport has been useful for testing predictions from reversal theory. For example, the establishment of differences in telic–paratelic or negativism–conformity dominance between athletes performing at different levels in different sports, athletes performing at different skill levels within the same sport and between different groups of individuals (e.g., athletes and students) in terms of their preference for or participation in certain types of sports has supported reversal theory arguments concerning the nature of motivation that underlies human behavior in sport and elsewhere. Findings related to links among negativism dominance and aspects of athletic performance such as discontinuation, injuries, and increased negative experience after losing also confirm expectations and predictions made on the basis of reversal theory. With the recent development and publication of the Motivational Style Profile (MSP; Apter, Mallows, & Williams, 1998), metamotivational dominance research in sport can now include mastery–sympathy and autic–alloic as well as telic–paratelic and negativism–conformity dominance. Indeed, two studies (Evans, 1994, using an earlier version of this scale, and Weinberg, 1998) have already been completed.

However, consistent with the underlying principles of reversal theory, it should also be kept in mind that other explanations of preference for and participation in sports are possible. For example, telic-dominant individuals may reverse to the paratelic state in order to enjoy paratelic-oriented sports like baseball or may deliberately participate in paratelic-oriented sports in order to induce reversals and allow them the occasional experience of pleasant high arousal as excitement (Kerr, 1989, 1997b).

METAMOTIVATIONAL STATE REVERSALS

In one reversal theory study on sport and exercise, a series of three specially arranged but ecologically valid squash tournaments were used to measure club-, county-, and international-level athletes' psychological reactions to winning and losing (Cox & Kerr, 1989, 1990; Kerr, 1988a). Each tournament involved 10 players of similar ability who each played four games, after which the two best players progressed to the final. Athletes completed the Telic State Measure (TSM; Svebak & Murgatroyd, 1985) and the Stress Arousal Checklist (SACL; Mackay, Cox, Burrows, & Lazzerini, 1978) before and after each game, and data from these measures were collapsed across tournament groups to form different groups of the most successful (winners) and least successful (losers) athletes.

Across-tournament scores on the TSM Serious–Playful subscale showed only one difference between the winners and losers. This was after game 2, during which the losers scored significantly higher than did the winners on this subscale. The mean scores for the winners suggested that the majority were in the telic state during the tournament. For the losers, who were generally more balanced between telic and paratelic states across the tournament, the significant finding after game 2 suggested that many of them reversed to the paratelic state after this game. Perhaps, having lost two games, they realized that progress to the final was unlikely, and this prompted a reversal from the telic to the paratelic state for some. These findings are presented here as an example of a study that examined reversals in sport. Additional findings can be found in Cox and Kerr (1989, 1990), Kerr (1997b), and Kerr and Cox (1988, 1990, 1991).

Another study investigated long-distance running and part of the study sought to identify reversals in metamotivational state induced by running (Kerr & Vlaswinkel, 1993). The participants were 67 male and female Dutch students who exercised regularly. Data were collected before, during, and after a running session in which women ran 5.0 km and men ran 6.6 km. Runners indicated their color choice (red or light blue) on several occasions during the run. Walters, Apter, and Svebak (1982) had found a close association between color choice and arousal preference. Choosing red indicated a preference for high arousal and the paratelic state being operative, and choosing light blue indicated a preference for low arousal, which was characteristic of the telic state. Runners were also categorized into equal groups of fast or slow runners based on their running times.

The results showed that, as the run progressed, both male and female runners increasingly reversed from the telic to the paratelic state (i.e., changed from a preference for low arousal to a preference for high arousal) and at the end of the run, the majority were in the paratelic state. For fast and slow runners, fast male runners' reversals followed a similar pattern, but the pattern for slow male runners was more evenly split between telic and paratelic metamotivational states. The majority of the fast female runners stayed in the telic state longer than did the fast male runners, but most had reversed to the paratelic state by the end of the run. In contrast, the majority of the slow female runners began the run in the paratelic state and did not reverse (see Figures 10.4 and 10.5).

In addition to making a color choice, runners also completed the TSM (Svebak, 1985a; see also chapter 3 in this volume) and the SACL(Mackay et. al., 1978) before and after running. Findings from the TSM Serious–Playful and Planning–Spontaneous subscales confirmed the change from telic to paratelic state with running for the women only. Significant decreases from pre- to postrunning were obtained on these subscales for female runners. (Additional findings concerning TSM Felt Arousal and Preferred Arousal subscale scores and SACL Stress and Arousal subscale scores are reported in Kerr, 1997b, and Kerr & Vlaswinkel, 1993).

The results of the studies described above, and those carried out by Hudson (1998), Hudson & Bates (2000), and Weinberg (1998), as well as the anecdotal reports of the athletes themselves (Kerr, 1985b), have shown that athletes do experience reversals when performing. Indeed, Weinberg's (1998) study included the use of an early version of a new scale, the State of Mind Inventory for Athletes (SOMIFA; Kerr & Apter, 1999), which can identify reversals in all four pairs of metamotivational states over time. It was thought that if athletes and their coaches could identify which metamotivational states were operative at different stages of performance then it might assist them both in pre-event preparation and in understanding ongoing changes in metamotivation during performance (Kerr, 1987a, 1987c, 1993a). The next section also explores this theme but focuses on metamotivational variables that have been found to be important in performance.

PERFORMANCE-INDUCED CHANGES IN FELT AROUSAL AND FELT TRANSACTIONAL OUTCOME

Felt arousal, an important variable with respect to the somatic metamotivational states, is generally defined as how worked up or emotionally intense a person feels about what he or she is doing. *Felt transactional outcome*, the key variable with respect to the transactional metamotivational states,

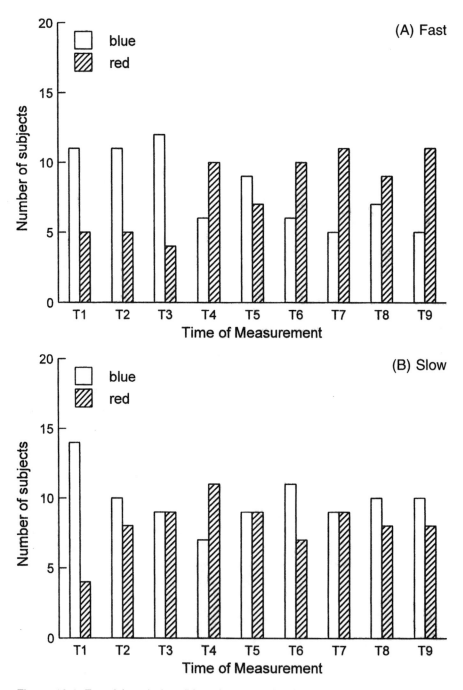

Figure 10.4. Fast (a) and slow (b) male runners' color choice on nine occasions during the run.

Note. From "Self-Reported Mood and Running Under Natural Conditions," by J. H. Kerr and E. H. Vlaswinkel, 1993, *Work and Stress, 7,* p. 173. Copyright 1993 by Taylor & Francis. http://www.tandf.co.uk. Reprinted with permission.

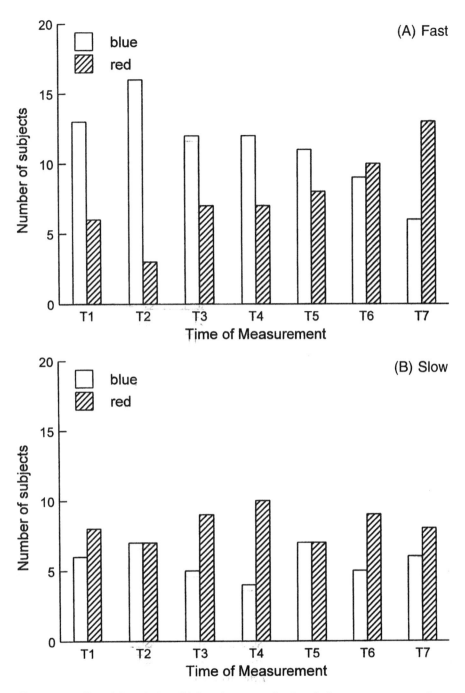

Figure 10.5. Fast (a) and slow (b) female runners' color choice on seven occasions during the run.
Note. From "Self-Reported Mood and Running Under Natural Conditions," by J. H. Kerr and E. H. Vlaswinkel, 1993, *Work and Stress, 7,* p. 174. Copyright 1993 by Taylor & Francis. http://www.tandf.co.uk. Reprinted with permission.

is the degree to which a person feels that he or she has gained or lost in an interaction.

Research linked to the earlier Kerr and Vlaswinkel (1993) running study used a slightly different approach to assess the impact of the intensity of sport activity on participants' psychological states (Kerr & van den Wollenberg, 1997). A field experiment was designed that allowed direct comparison of the effect of intensity of exercise on the psychological responses of the participants. Using a within-subject crossover design, pre–post measurement, and the TSM and SACL measures, the researchers asked two groups of regularly exercising Dutch students to run either 5.0 km or 1.7 km at two intensities: high intensity (as fast as possible) and low intensity (at a comfortable easy speed). Runners were also divided on the basis of time, recorded during the high-intensity condition, into fast and slow running groups.

Kerr and van den Wollenberg (1997) found that runners' experienced arousal levels increased pre- to postrun to a significantly greater extent under the high-intensity condition for both distances than under the low-intensity condition. Under the 1.7-km high-intensity condition, stress and serious-minded scores also increased significantly, and effort scores were also found to be significantly higher (see Figure 10.6).

When fast and slow running groups were compared, no significant differences were found for the 5.0-km distance at either intensity. However, under the 1.7-km high-intensity condition, fast runners were more highly aroused and generally achieved higher levels of arousal than did slow runners, even though slow runners' arousal levels did increase pre- to post–high-

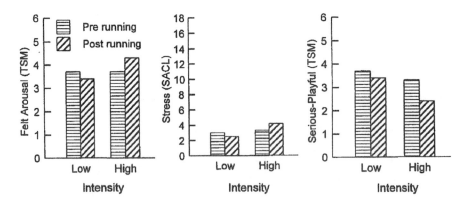

Figure 10.6. Pre- and postrunning mean TSM felt arousal, SACL stress, and TSM Serious–Playful scores for low- and high-intensity running.
Note. TSM = Telic State Measure; SACL = Stress Arousal Checklist.
From "High and Low Intensity Exercise and Psychological Mood States," by J. H. Kerr and A. E. van den Wollenberg, 1997, Psychology and Health, 12, p. 612. Copyright 1997 by Overseas Publishers Association/Gordon & Breach Publishers. Reprinted with permission.

intensity running. At low intensity, fast runners were more spontaneous and less planning oriented and did not have to invest as much effort as did slow runners. Again, fast runners' experience of running was found to be different from that of slow runners. Some runners did experience increases in stress along with the increases in arousal under certain conditions. However, these increases in stress were not sufficient to have had much influence on runners' overall pleasant experience of high arousal. The authors argued that the increase in experienced arousal that accompanied running is the source of exercise-induced psychological changes, including improvements in mood and hedonic tone, in those who exercise regularly.

A further study examined the possible changes in metamotivational state and arousal levels in 17 top-level Dutch rugby players as a result of winning or losing matches (Kerr & van Schaik, 1995). Players completed the TSM and SACL measures at four rugby matches just before and just after playing. Two games were won and two lost, but after winning, players reported significantly higher arousal (SACL) scores and significantly lower stress (SACL) scores than after losing games. As one might expect from everyday experience, when games were won, players' experience was much more pleasant than when games were lost. It was also apparent that players' scores after winning were significantly less serious (TSM) and more spontaneous (TSM) than after losing. These results suggest that, although losing tended to maintain the telic state as players' operative metamotivational state, winning induced reversals to the paratelic state in some players. (Other sport and exercise studies examining felt and preferred arousal include Kerr & Pos, 1994; Kerr & Tacon, 1999; Wilson, 1993; Wilson & Phillips, 1995).

The studies mentioned above examined performance-induced changes in levels of felt arousal. However, although felt arousal can be measured using the TSM, no state measure has been developed that directly measures felt transactional outcome. Wilson and Phillips (1995), extending previous squash studies, were able to measure felt transactional outcome indirectly by use of a mood checklist. The checklist included the eight somatic mood adjectives (relaxation, excitement, placidity, provocativeness, anxiety, boredom, anger, and sullenness) and the eight transactional mood adjectives (pride, modesty, gratitude, virtue, humiliation, shame, resentment, and guilt). Sixty male Australian squash players, who played in five-set competitive squash matches, were asked to choose the adjectives from the mood checklist that best fit their feelings 2–3 minutes pre-game, after the second set, and postgame. They also rated performance, strength of opponent, pleasant–unpleasant, satisfied–dissatisfied, and match close–not close on 10-point rating scales with descriptive adjectives at each end. Players had previously completed the TDS and NDS (Wilson, 1999).

Of interest in this chapter are the results for responses to the mood checklist and especially for the transactional emotions that are concerned with felt transactional outcome. Wilson and Phillips (1995) compared the responses of winners and losers. Winners were found to experience more pleasant than unpleasant, and losers more unpleasant than pleasant transactional emotions. Of the transactional emotions that the winners experienced, significantly more were those associated with high rather than low felt transactional outcome. Winners had strong feelings of net gain from their successful interaction with the losers in squash matches, although winners and losers both experienced significantly more mastery than sympathy emotions. This was the first study in the context of sport that underlined the importance of felt transactional outcome as an important variable in metamotivation. In this case, game outcome provoked important differences in players' experience of felt transactional outcome, or feelings of having gained, from their interaction with other squash players during competitive play. The results indicate that the transactional emotions and felt transactional outcome also have an important role to play in the psychological experience of sport performers.

EXPERIENCE OF EMOTIONS, STRESS, AND EFFORT

The development of the Tension and Effort Stress Inventory (TESI; Svebak, 1993; Svebak, Ursin, Endresen, Hjelmen, & Apter, 1991; see also chapter 3 in this volume) provided researchers with the opportunity to measure the full range of 16 emotions associated with reversal theory's metamotivational state combinations. In particular, the state version, which monitors current emotional experience, could be used in sport and exercise research with athletes before, during, and after performance.

Kerr and Svebak (1994) conducted the first study using the TESI in the sport and exercise context. They used the state version of the measure to examine the experience of 109 Dutch students performing recreational sports. The recreational sports under investigation were easy running in small groups, basketball, and rugby. The experimenters had noted that team sports involve differing degrees of inter- and intrateam interaction, competitiveness, and confrontation (physical contact), whereas individual activities and sports tend not to involve these elements. This they termed *antagonistic physical interaction* (API), defined as "certain aspects of the individual's perception of the cognitive and social consequences that occur naturally in competitive sport settings" (p. 160). Easy running, basketball, and rugby were chosen for this investigation because they were considered to have low, medium, and high levels of API, respectively. API was also manipulated among activities so that in rugby (high API) students participated in a warm-up, intensive tackle practice, and a period of full contact competitive play. In basketball (medium API), students completed periods of warming up, skills practice, and competitive play and, in easy running, small groups of participants were asked to run at a comfortable pace in a noncompetitive way. The volunteer male students were randomly allocated to the experimental conditions within their regular university physical education classes, and they completed the TESI before and after performing each activity.

The findings indicated that mean pleasant-emotion scores for all three sport activities were approximately double unpleasant-emotion scores. Changes in emotions were linked to the level of API. The strongest changes in emotions were found with rugby, which had the highest level of API. Pleasant emotions were reduced and unpleasant emotions were increased pre- to postparticipation, apparently as a consequence of participating in tackle practice and full-contact competitive play. A significant relationship was also found between level of API and stress. Taking part in rugby, basketball, and easy running produced different stress responses in the students. The smallest pre- to postactivity changes were associated with running (low API) and the largest with rugby (high API). A significant group by time-of-testing interaction indicated reduced external stress scores after running and increased scores on external stress after rugby. Also, highly significant changes pre- to postactivity were obtained for internal or bodily stress. Pre- to postactivity significant group differences in internal effort scores were again found to be greatest with rugby (high API) and least with running (low API). External effort scores decreased after running and increased after rugby, with basketball providing only a minor change. It would appear that recreational-sport participants in this study (Kerr & Svebak, 1994) generally experienced participation as pleasant, but the type of sport and level of API influenced the degree of stress experienced and the effort required to cope with that stress (Kerr, 1990a, 1990b).

In an extension of the Kerr and van Schaik (1995) rugby study described above, Wilson and Kerr (1999) again assessed the emotional effects of winning and losing with high-level Dutch rugby players in a similar research design, but used the TESI in place of the TSM. The SACL measure was also used in this study, but the results are not reported here. Scores were thus obtained for the eight individual pleasant emotions and the eight individual unpleasant emotions, which were subsequently also aggregated into groups of total pleasant and unpleasant emotions.

With regard to winning and losing and total pleasant and unpleasant emotions, even though the prematch pleasant emotions means were similar, losers had significantly more unpleasant emotions prematch than did winners. Postmatch, the mean score for total pleasant emotions was larger for winning than for losing. Conversely, the total unpleasant emotions score was significantly greater for losing than winning and, with losing, a significant reduction in total pleasant emotions and an increase in total unpleasant emotions occurred pre- to postmatch. These findings were consistent with results from the previous investigation of emotions in recreational sports (Kerr & Svebak, 1994; see Figure 10.7).

For somatic emotions, pregame means for winning or losing showed no important differences. Winning produced higher scores than did losing for the pleasant somatic emotions and lower scores than did losing for the unpleasant somatic emotions. These differences were significant for relaxation, anger, and sullenness. Postmatch, significant reductions in excitement and provocativeness were prompted by both winning and losing. Relaxation increased in the winning condition from pre- to postgame. For sullenness, winning decreased and losing increased the players' ratings from pre- to postmatch.

For the transactional emotions, prematch means for winning or losing were not significantly different. Winning produced higher scores than did losing on the four positive transactional emotions and lower scores than did losing on the negative transactional emotions postmatch. For humiliation, shame, gratitude, and resentment, these differences were significant. From pre- to postmatch, winning and losing produced significant reductions in pride and significant increases in humiliation, shame, and guilt. Also, at both winning and losing matches, external and somatic stress and effort scores demonstrated highly significant decreases from pre- to postmatch.

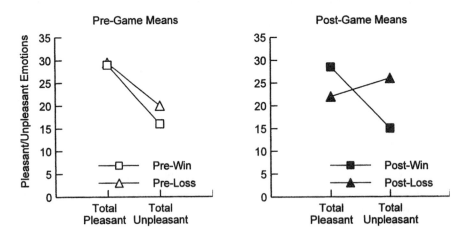

Figure 10.7. Effect of game outcome on total pleasant and unpleasant emotions in rugby.
Note. From "Affective Responses to Success and Failure: A Study of Winning and Losing in Competitive Rugby," by G. V. Wilson and J. H. Kerr, 1999, *Personality and Individual Differences, 27*, p. 91. Copyright 1999 by Elsevier Science. Reprinted with permission.

The two rugby studies (Kerr & van Schaik, 1995; Wilson & Kerr, 1999) have shown that players' prematch mental states, in terms of experienced emotions and arousal levels, were consistent across matches. This suggested that players' mental preparation before games was effective for achieving the players' desired states. However, the studies also revealed the strong emotions that are experienced by players and the role that winning or losing plays in provoking changes in their motivational experience postmatch. Reversal theory's systematic structure of 16 primary emotions provided a useful theoretical base for these studies. In this way, reversal theory provides reversal theory–based research with a distinct advantage over those other studies investigating sport or exercise-induced changes in mood or emotion that have been atheoretical.

BEYOND TESI QUANTITATIVE STUDIES: SLALOM CANOEING AND GOLF PERFORMANCE

Slalom canoeing provided the setting for a combined quantitative and qualitative investigative approach (Males, 1999; Males & Kerr, 1996; Males, Kerr, & Gerkovich, 1998). This study also marked a change in focus from group- to individual-based study in reversal theory sport and exercise research. The participants in the study had been involved in slalom canoeing for just over 10 years on average and spent an average of 13 hours per week in training. They were nine of the top canoeists in their country, and three of them had won individual and team medals at the World Championships. In slalom canoeing competitions, competitors usually have two separate attempts at the slalom course against the clock with time penalties added for any mistakes made on their descent down through the gates placed along the course. In this study, canoeists completed the TESI and the arousal items from the TSM before each descent and also took part in postrace semistructured interviews. Data were collected at local, national, and World Championship events over a whole season.

To compare canoeists' best and worst performances, data from the modified TESI were treated as a collection of individual case studies and analyzed according to time-series analysis (Males & Kerr, 1996). Official race results were used as a measure of performance.

Slalom Canoe TESI Results

Although there were no significant changes in TESI items across performances, consistent with other studies (Kerr & Svebak, 1994; Wilson & Kerr, 1999), levels of pleasant emotions were found to be consistently higher than levels of unpleasant emotions. Null or low levels of arousal discrepancy (TSM) preceded all of the best performances. Two successful Olympic canoeists' profiles provided an interesting contrast and were high-lighted by Males and Kerr (1996). One (canoeist F) performed best in a local canoeing event and worst at the World Championships, and the other (canoeist G) performed best at the World Championships and worst in a local event. Both canoeists experienced both pleasant and unpleasant emo-tions (e.g., excitement, pride, relaxation, virtue, and anxiety). For canoeist F, there were no significant differences between scores for any emotion before best and worst performances, and for canoeist G, only scores on anger revealed a significant difference between best and worst performance. These findings indicated that a stable pattern for precompetitive emotions was typical for these experienced high-level performers. However, both canoeists experienced mismatches between preferred and felt arousal (TSM) levels before their worst performances, in contrast to matched preferred and felt arousal (TSM) levels before their best performances. Kerr (1985a, 1985b, 1987a, 1987b) has underlined the importance of the athlete's experience of felt arousal for optimal performance. Canoeist F's worst performance, at the World Championships, was preceded by reported levels of felt and preferred arousal higher than his season's average. Even though he would have preferred a felt arousal level close to his average for the season, an arousal level significantly lower than that reported at his best performance in the World Championships preceded canoeist G's worst performance at a local event.

As shown in Figure 10.8, TESI stress and effort scores for the two canoeists were also strikingly different. At canoeist F's best performance, his internal stress score was matched by his internal effort score but was below his mean score for the season. His external stress score was higher than his mean score for the season and his external effort scores higher still. At his worst performance, his stress scores were similar to his scores at his best performance, but both internal and external effort scores were higher than the stress scores. This may have reflected a desire to try harder on the part of canoeist F and may have been related to his desire for a higher-than-average arousal level at the same event. As a result, coping efforts (effort-stress), as reflected by TESI scores, exceeded tension-stress. A discrepancy between stress levels and coping efforts was thought to be important because this preceded this canoeist's worst performance (Males & Kerr, 1996).

At canoeist G's best performance, he also reported the season's highest levels of internal and external stress (tension-stress) before competing. In response, his level of internal effort was greater than internal stress, but his reported external effort was considerably less than external stress. At this race canoeist G's bodily state may have been more important to him than

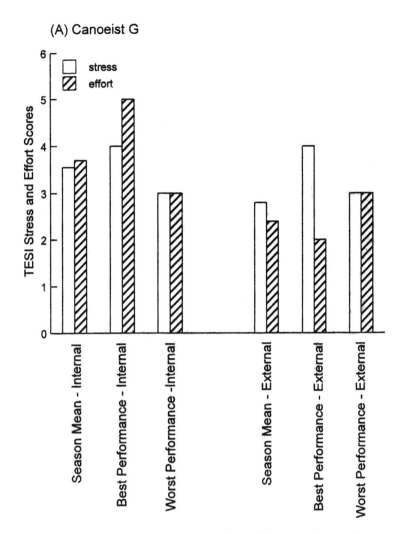

(A) Canoeist G

Figure 10.8. TESI stress (tension-stress) and effort (effort-stress) scores for canoeists G (a) and F (b).
Note. TESI = Tension and Effort Stress Inventory.
From "Stress, Emotion, and Performance in Elite Slalom Canoeists," by J. R. Males and J. H. Kerr, 1996, *The Sport Psychologist, 10,* pp. 30–31. Copyright 1996 by Human Kinetics Publishers. Reprinted with permission.

external considerations. Consequently, his efforts to cope (effort-stress) were directed toward dealing with bodily stress rather than external factors.

The essence of reversal theory is individual experience, and these results illustrate the importance of that approach. The motivational experience of two highly skilled performers operating at the highest level has been described. Even though their emotional experiences were rather similar, their

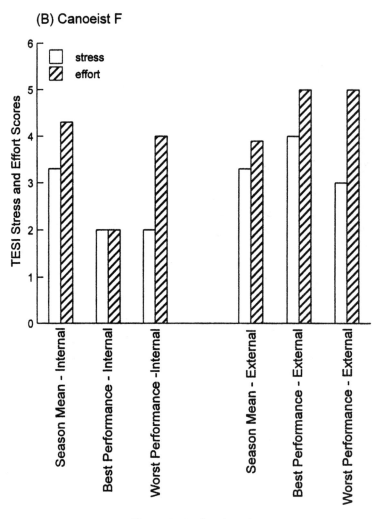

(B) Canoeist F

Figure 10.8. Continued

individual experiences in terms of felt arousal, stress, and effort and their performances were remarkably different.

Slalom Canoe Interview Results

Interview transcript data from the postcompetition semistructured interviews were categorized using a modified version of the Metamotivational State Coding Schedule (MSCS; Potocky, Cook, & O'Connell, 1993). The interviews concerned canoeists' thoughts and feelings preevent, during performance, between runs, and postevent. The task in this part of the study

(Males et al., 1998) was to identify operative metamotivational states rather than individual emotions. (Individual emotions are, of course, considered to be directly linked to combinations of operative metamotivational states in reversal theory.)

In the MSCS, coding units are defined as distinct periods of time, in a given environment, during which the participant reported a single goal and experienced only one combination of metamotivational states. A change in environment, a change in objective, or a change in reported emotional experience marked a change in coding unit. The first stage of the coding process was to identify the different coding units. There were between five and seven coding units in a typical interview. Full details of this metamotivational coding process are provided by Males and colleagues (1998).

Included below is an example of an interview excerpt, concerning the during-performance period of canoeist C, which shows a reversal from the paratelic–conformist to the telic–negativistic state combination following a mistake at a gate:

> C: That broke my concentration a little bit—I got a penalty on (gate) seven and dropped low and I thought 'oh shit—out of the window' and I started to evaluate really. For that one second after you have made a mistake you are thinking about the mistake and not where you should be going next and things like that—what happened then is that I lost the run of the boat a little bit—I started to eddy out a little bit, and it had an avalanche effect sort of thing.
>
> I: So what was happening to your mood as these mistakes were building up?
>
> C: I was getting a bit blasé toward the end really, as soon as I took the penalty, then I knew that I wasn't going to win .... (Males et al., 1998, p. 193)

Following analysis of the results, consistent patterns in operative metamotivational states were found, especially with regard to the transactional pairs (see Figure 10.9). The autic–mastery combination was operative in 100% of coding units pre-event and during performance. Between the two runs, just over 80% of coding units were categorized as autic–mastery with the remainder, just under 20%, categorized as autic–sympathy. Finally, post-race, over 95% of coding units were categorized as autic–mastery. Clearly, autic–mastery was the predominant operative transactional state combination. Among the somatic states, the same was largely true for conformity, but the pattern was less clear for the telic and paratelic pair. Pre-event telic–conformity comprised over 70% of coding units, with just under 20% paratelic–conformity and the remainder telic–negativism and paratelic-negativism. During the race, paratelic–conformity increased to 35%, and telic–conformity decreased to 59.9% of coding units. The remaining 5.1%

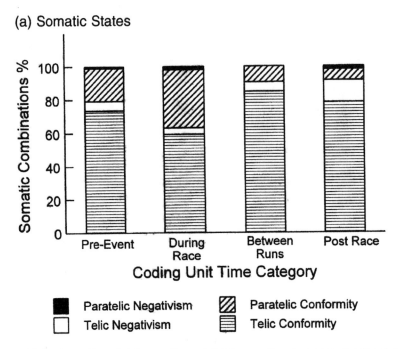

(a) Somatic States

Paratelic Negativism   Paratelic Conformity
Telic Negativism   Telic Conformity

Figure 10.9. Proportion of (a) somatic and (b) transactional metamotivational state combinations reported pre-event, during the race, between runs, and postrace.
Note. N = 103 for pre-event, N = 57 for during race, N = 32 for between runs, and N = 70 for postrace.
From "Metamotivational States During Canoe Slalom Competition: A Qualitative Analysis Using Reversal Theory," by J. R. Males, J. H. Kerr, and M. M. Gerkovich, 1998, *Journal of Applied Sport Psychology,* 10, pp. 195–196. Copyright by the Association for the Advancement of Applied Sport Psychology. Reprinted with permission.

was split between telic– and paratelic–negativism. Telic–conformity was highest between runs at just over 84%. Postrace, increases in telic–negativism resulted in a total for negativism of 14.3% coding units.

In general, the elite canoeists were consistent in their operative metamotivational state combinations; however, it should be noted that occasionally some canoeists had atypical state combinations operative that did not appear to facilitate performance at the elite level. Some examples of occasions when this occurred and what athletes did to change their mental state, along with further excerpts of interview material, can be found in Kerr (1997a) and Males (1999).

Golf Performance

Purcell (1999a, 1999b) and Purcell, Kerr, and Pollock (1996, 2000), adopted a combined quantitative and qualitative approach to a study of decision making, motivation, and emotions in golf. Fifteen highly skilled

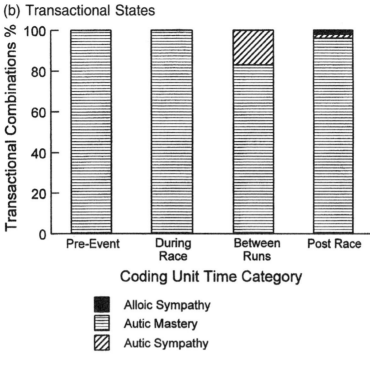

(b) Transactional States

Figure 10.9. Continued

(low-handicap) and 15 low-skilled (high-handicap) male amateur golfers, matched for age and experience, played a round of nine holes involving nonadversarial stroke play. In an attempt to capture the golfers' thoughts as they played, think-aloud protocols were collected at the first and ninth holes, followed by brief structured interviews to supplement the think-aloud data. In addition, after playing each of the nine holes, golfers completed the same modified version of the TESI used by Males and Kerr (1996). Testing followed equipment and procedure checks and a 30-minute warm-up. The limited space in this chapter precludes a discussion of the TESI results from this study (for a full account, see Purcell et al., 2000).

The think-aloud protocols were analyzed using Miles and Huberman's (1994) interactive model and managed using the QSR NUD.IST 4.0. software program (SCOLARI Sage Publications Software). Following the flexible application of inductive and deductive analyses, a general model was constructed using coding procedures. The information-processing approach was used as a framework for the model, which shows the concepts, categories, and the four components of golf performance (planning activities, premotor execution, motor skill execution, and postmotor execution; Purcell, 1999a). In addition, the contents of think-aloud reports were used to examine the cognitive experience and metamotivational states of golfers and to identify events that appeared to induce changes in metamotivational state.

Summarizing the verbal protocol results relating to motor skill aspects of golf performance, low-handicap elite golfers reported higher frequencies of the use of conditional cues (e.g., par, hole length, bunkers), elements of shot analysis (e.g., direction, flight-shape), technical aspects of the golf swing (e.g., grip, body position), and the use of higher order mental skills in the action preparation stage of their performance than the high-handicap, low-skilled golfers. The content and structure of elite golfers' verbal protocols were generally more consistent than those of the less-skilled golfers and showed that elite golfers were less concerned with intrusive extraneous factors than their lesser skilled peers.

With respect to the motivational and emotional aspects of golf performance, the presence of goal-directed (lower and higher order goals) and planning-ahead statements in the think-aloud reports and the retrospective interviews underlined the importance of the telic state for elite golfers. For example, planning involved the use of either attacking or defensive strategies, depending on risk assessment, and was flexible enough to be changed with ongoing performance on a particular hole. For many of the high-handicap, low-skilled golfers, in contrast to the elite golfers, planning was not a feature of golf performance. A good example of flexible planning with a goal-directed focus during the motor execution is shown in the following interview quote from an elite golfer:

> My plan was to keep the ball in play. I knew I wouldn't get there in two with the wind coming left to right and into me. So I played the hole to try to knock my second shot as close as I could to set myself up for my third shot. However, I always put this out of my mind when I'm playing each shot. It's there but I could come unstuck if I think about it when I have to hit the present shot. It's important to have a general plan but to stay focussed on the shot you're playing. (Purcell, 1999a, p. 88)

Specific emotions were also expressed in the golfers' think-aloud reports. These tended to confirm the telic-oriented nature of golf performance. For example, the frequency of the use of the pleasant and unpleasant affective words *relaxation* and *anxiety* (or similar terms) indicated the salience of the telic–conformity state combination. Both groups reported experiencing positive and negative emotions, but negative emotions were less prevalent for the elite than for the lesser skilled golfers. In reversal theory terms, shot outcome, especially when performance was poor, could be considered as a contingent event that was likely to cause reversals in metamotivational states and resulting emotional experience. This occurred for both groups, but was especially true for lesser skilled golfers, who hit more poor shots.

The comments of one high-handicap golfer following a poor performance, which suggest that the telic–negativistic state combination had become operative, provide a good illustration:

> First hole. Two hundred and twenty metres to the bunkers. Into a fairly strong breeze. Use a three wood to draw the ball back into the center. It's a three shot—par five. There's no point in hitting the driver 'cause I can't get on for two. Three wood will allow me to hit the fairway with confidence. See the shape of the shot. Couple of practice swings. Set up. Easy. Oops! Maybe not. Not happy at all with that. That's dead. It's gone right in the gunga. It's not good in here. Glad this isn't a tournament. Jesus. Think I've got it. Ah, Jesus. Yep. Take an unplayable. Um, I'm pissed off about it, but I'll get on with it. I now have a three iron to lay up short of the water. (Purcell, 1999a, p. 89)

This use of verbal protocol reports and retrospective interviews provided qualitative data that could be used to identify the experience of particular emotions and therefore operative metamotivational state combinations, as well as contingent performance events likely to provoke psychological reversals.

CONCLUSION

In comparison with other areas in which reversal theory has been applied, the research work carried out in sport and exercise has been considerable. A number of important questions and topics have been addressed using almost the full spectrum of research strategies and techniques. Not only have the results of these studies helped confirm the value of concepts and viewpoints in reversal theory, but also much more has been learned about the personality and motivation of sport performers and their experience of emotions while performing.

The studies reported here were chosen as representative of reversal theory work in sport and exercise. However, in one short chapter it has only been possible to provide the basic details of a few studies. Readers who are interested in discovering more about reversal theory-based work in sport and exercise are encouraged to read *Motivation and Emotion in Sport: Reversal Theory* (Kerr, 1997a), *Experiencing Sport: Reversal Theory* (Kerr, 1999a), and *Counseling Athletes: Applying Reversal Theory* (Kerr, 2001), as well as search out the appropriate references from the reference list for this book. Applied work in sport and exercise makes a major contribution to the biennial international conferences on reversal theory and is the only topic under consideration in the workshops that are organized by the reversal theory special-interest group in sport approximately once every two years.

11

RISK-TAKING

MARY M. GERKOVICH

Why do people take risks? Why do they take chances with their health, their wealth, and even their lives? One of the most fascinating aspects of human behavior is the paradox between the actions people choose versus the actions that would appear to be in their own best interests. What is it about risk? Not only does it not prevent people from acting in certain ways but it can actually encourage behavior that could lead to disaster. This chapter focuses on an explanation of the appeal and function of risk in the choices people make in their everyday lives. This discussion includes examples of risk-taking behavior concerning health behavior, sports participation, gambling, and even criminal activities.

SALIENT REVERSAL THEORY STATES

One of the strengths of reversal theory is its ability to address such paradoxical behavior as risk-taking. The explanation for why people not only do not avoid risks but also often seek them out is based on certain fundamental reversal theory constructs. Although chapters 1 and 2 in this volume and earlier reversal theory references (Apter, 1982a, 1989b) contain more detailed explanations of the relevant reversal theory concepts, constructs that are specifically related to risk behavior are reviewed here.

Whether a given situation is experienced as pleasant or unpleasant is determined by the metamotivational state in effect at the time. The activities to be discussed in this chapter have in common the fact that they are enjoyed while the person is in the paratelic state. What Frey (1991) stated regarding sexual behavior applies equally to the risk behavior being discussed in this chapter; the purpose of the activity matters less than the manner in which the activity is experienced. The different aspects of the paratelic state, arousal-seeking preference and playfulness–spontaneity, are critical in understanding choices and actions involving risk. In the paratelic state, high-arousal situations are experienced as pleasant (i.e., exciting), and low-arousal situations are experienced as unpleasant (i.e., boring). Risk serves the needs of the paratelic state by increasing arousal, therefore, increasing the positive hedonic tone that is experienced. Anyone who has ridden an amusement park thrill ride has found out that fear can be fun. Apter (1992) stated that risk could actually cause a more intense experience of a high-arousal situation. The relation between increased arousal and the enhancement of the paratelic state is the primary reason risky decisions and actions are taken. In an interview study reported by Gerkovich (1997), a young woman reported being scared about being discovered while having sex in a park, within sight of her boyfriend's home. Her recollection, however, was that this experience was different enough to make it even more exciting.

The playfulness–spontaneity aspect of the paratelic state also contributes to choices involving risk behavior. While in the paratelic state, the person is oriented to what he or she is experiencing at that moment and is not focused on the outcome or the long-term consequences of actions and decisions. When one is on the amusement park roller coaster, one realizes that it is the experience of the ride and not the destination that matters. Decisions may be made on the spur of the moment, however, that could have far-reaching consequences. This aspect of the paratelic state is especially relevant to decisions about sexual activity, which can result in failure to practice disease and pregnancy preventive measures. A common excuse given by people who have unprotected sexual intercourse is that they did not want to interrupt the moment in order to get and use a condom; the potential long-term consequences of disease and pregnancy could not overcome the focus on the current experience. An example of this experience was reported by a young woman who said that she had a fleeting thought that she and her partner should be using a condom, but they were so caught up in the moment that she just did not care enough to stop and use one (Gerkovich, 1997).

The negativistic state is another metamotivational state that is related to risk behavior. The negativistic state, and acting in a negativistic manner, can be used to increase arousal. While in the negativistic state, people feel rebellious or even angry; it feels pleasant to act against expectations. Expressing anger or breaking rules, whether internally or externally defined, increases arousal. This, in turn, enhances the arousal experience in the paratelic state. Frey (1991) described how negativistic rule-breaking serves the needs of the paratelic state by increasing arousal. Apter and Smith (1979b) described the use of mild barriers as a method of increasing arousal during sexual activity; for instance, social taboos can be viewed as mild barriers to be broken during sex. Data from an interview study reported by Kerr, Frank-Ragan, and Brown (1993) provided additional support for the part negativistic behavior plays in increasing arousal. A gay man reported feeling that having sex with another man was made more attractive by the perception that it was "forbidden and evil."

PROTECTIVE FRAMES

From the above description, it is clear that experiences in the paratelic state are enhanced when arousal level is increased. Engaging in risk behavior is one of the most common methods of increasing arousal levels. Being in the negativistic state and acting in a negativistic manner are also methods of increasing arousal. How is it possible to recognize risk and yet still experience it as an enhancement of a positive emotion rather than a negative emotion? Reversal theory accounts for this phenomenon by proposing the concept of protective frames (Apter, 1989b, 1991b, 1992).

The term *protective frame* refers to a way in which we interpret our experience. It is a psychological structure, a kind of frame for viewing the world and our experiences in it. A protective frame is subjectively determined and is not a permanent feature of any given situation. The frame is protective because it allows risk or danger to be viewed as controllable and within the person's ability to deal with it. When the protective frame is intact, a high arousal situation is experienced in the paratelic state as excitement. If something occurs that violates the protective frame, a reversal to the arousal-avoiding telic state occurs, and the high arousal situation is experienced as anxiety. Within the parameters of the protective frame, increasing risk results in increasing arousal that enhances the pleasant hedonic tone (e.g., excitement) experienced in the paratelic state.

In order to understand protective frames, the reader needs first of all to be familiar with what Apter (1992) described as the four phenomenological *zones* that encompass our everyday experiences (see Figure 11.1). The *detachment zone*, which is the furthest removed from trauma, is a subjectively defined area of experience in which the person perceives himself or herself to be no more than an observer of what is going on and therefore completely safe. The *safety zone* is a subjective area of experience in which the person, while an actor in the ongoing situation, still perceives no immediate likelihood of danger or injury. Next is the *danger zone* in which the individual is aware of the real possibility of danger but feels removed to some degree from actual injury or trauma. Finally, the *trauma zone* refers to experience when actual injury or damage occurs. The point at which one moves from the danger zone into the trauma zone is called the *dangerous edge*. The distance between where one is currently and the dangerous edge is referred to as the *safety margin*. When in the telic state, a person tries to make the safety margin as large as possible. The perception that bad things "won't happen to me" contributes to the perception of a large safety margin. Because

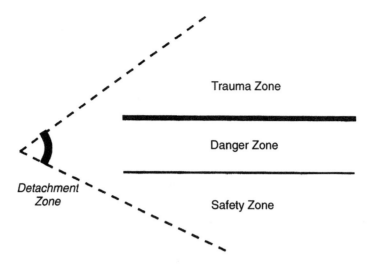

Figure 11.1. The three zones of experience with respect to danger.
Note. The schematic eye, observing the safety, danger, and trauma zones, represents the attachment zone. Each zone has associated with it the possibility of its own type of protective frame which, when present, is experienced as a shield against real trauma. From *The Dangerous Edge: The Psychology of Excitement* (p. 61), by M. J. Apter, 1992, New York: Free Press. Copyright 1998 by M.J. Apter. Reprinted with permission of the author.

the parameters of these zones are subjective, they will differ both between individuals and within an individual over different situations. For a complete description of these four zones of experience, refer to Apter (1992).

Protective frames make it possible for the high arousal experienced with risk behavior to be experienced in the paratelic state as excitement rather than as anxiety. Apter (1989b, 1992) has described three different kinds of protective frame (see Figure 11.1), each corresponding to one of the zones other than the trauma zone. The *safety-zone frame* is experienced when people view themselves not only to be in the safety zone but also to be protected from slipping over into the danger zone; it provides a sense of being removed from the possibility of danger and trauma. Within the safety-zone frame no thought is given to the possible negative consequences of actions. Sexual behavior usually requires the safety-zone frame; while engaged in sex, one feels removed from real-world responsibilities and problems and unlikely, at the time, to have to face them. Without the safety-zone frame, increasing levels of arousal would be experienced as increasing levels of anxiety; this would have deleterious effects on the sexual activity.

The *confidence frame* is associated with the danger zone. It reflects the confidence a person feels in being able to cope with the danger or risk that is present. The influence of this protective frame is demonstrated by attitudes concerning participation in risk sports. Participants who acknowledge the inherent risk in the sport they participate in but who do not personalize the risk may be reflecting the influence of the confidence protective frame; they feel they know how to handle themselves and have the skills to manage any risk or danger that may occur.

The third protective frame proposed by reversal theory is the *detachment frame*; this arises when the person feels detached or removed from the ongoing activity (while in the detachment frame) and unlikely to be drawn into any of the other zones. (The detachment zone is symbolized by an eye in Figure 11.1 to represent the fact that the person is, in this frame, no more than an observer and can observe with impunity all the other zones.) The detachment frame can take three alternative forms. A spectator at a sporting event, movie, or play exemplifies self-substitution. The make-believe form of the detachment frame consists of the person producing his or her own fantasy or imaginary experience. Finally, the retrospection form of the detachment frame consists of remembering some past experience and possibly even reliving some of the emotions of that event. Both the make-believe and retrospection forms of the detachment frame involve mechanisms that increase arousal by either inventing or remembering emotional experiences.

Each type of protective frame has a role to play in preserving the paratelic state of mind while engaged in activities that could be perceived as being risky. When in the paratelic state, with a protective frame in effect, it is desirable to be as close to the dangerous edge as possible; the closer the danger, the higher the arousal that is experienced. Apter (1992) has characterized being in the paratelic state and enjoying high arousal as a balancing act between potential danger or risk and a perception of safety or control. If risk or danger is not available to serve as the source of high arousal, the person will look for other methods to increase arousal (e.g., breaking rules, acting out in anger).

Because protective frames are subjectively determined, they will reflect not only differences between people, but can also change over time within the individual. Some people will inherently be better at maintaining a feeling of safety or control in the face of danger. Any protective frame, however, can disappear given the right circumstances. For instance, the large majority of heterosexual people do not perceive themselves to be at great risk from sexually transmitted diseases (STDs), including HIV infection. This feeling of safety could be based on several things, including the perception that "people like themselves" do not get STDs. The safety-zone protective frame will disintegrate, however, if they hear that someone they identify with, possibly even their sexual partner, has become infected with an STD. Another example of how a protective frame can be changed by circumstances involves the confidence frame. A downhill skier can be enjoying a ski run through an out-of-bounds area, confident in his or her ability to handle the terrain. The confidence frame can disappear when the skier has a fall due to an unexpected obstacle. The high arousal resulting from the challenging ski run at high speed had been experienced as excitement when the confidence frame was intact; the fall and failure of the confidence frame will cause the high arousal to now be experienced as anxiety.

CAUSES AND CONSEQUENCES OF REVERSALS

In both of the cases described above, the failure of the protective frame causes a reversal from the paratelic to the telic state. Apter (1982a) described three types of reversals: contingency, frustration, and satiation reversals. (Refer to Apter, 1982a, for a full discussion of frustration and satiation reversals.) The *contingency reversal*, probably the most frequent type of reversal related to risk behavior, occurs as the result of the impact of an event or situation in the environment. The effect of the event or situation is based on the person's interpretation and can cause a reversal from a preference for high arousal (paratelic state) to low arousal (telic state), or vice versa. In the first example, finding out that someone the person identifies with has become infected with an STD is the contingent event. Apter and Smith (1978) listed a number of examples of the types of threats that can cause a reversal. In the second example, the contingent event that causes the reversal is the physical obstacle in the path of the skier. Regardless of the direction of the reversal, either from telic to paratelic or from paratelic to telic, the higher the arousal level, the greater will be the level of excitement or anxiety.

The consequences of the resulting anxiety or fear can be either short term or long term. Although short-term changes in perception may be enough to remove a person from a specific risky situation, long-term changes in perception of vulnerability and risk are necessary in order for consistent changes in health behavior to occur. Reversals are not under volitional control. One can, however, set up the environment or circumstances so that they are more likely to occur. For instance, adding flashing lights and loud music will increase the arousal level at a party and make it more likely that people will enjoy themselves in a paratelic state of mind. Attractions at amusement parks are designed to present the possibility of danger and risk while actually meeting extremely rigid safety codes.

PROTECTIVE FRAMES THAT LEAD TO RISK BEHAVIOR

According to reversal theory, protective frames are essential in order for the paratelic state, with its preference for high arousal, to be fully experienced and enjoyed. Protective frames, however, make it probable that risk behavior, with all its potential negative consequences, will occur. The parameters of protective frames are determined subjectively and risks may be taken when the protective frames are based on false assumptions or there is an incorrect perception of the strength of the parameters (Apter, 1992). Unprotected sexual activity can occur because each partner believes that the other partner is safe from disease, therefore, there is no health risk involved; it could also occur if the partners believe that it is not possible to get pregnant on this occasion. Both of these reasons represent fallacies of the safety-zone frame. The safety-zone frame can also be misleading if it is based on a context greatly removed from reality. For instance, Brown (1991) proposed that gaming and gambling, in general, are exercises in fantasy; the noise, lights, and costuming of casino staff all contribute to creating an amusement park atmosphere. Gambling with chips instead of real money makes it feel more like a game, as if one is not risking real money. The overall atmosphere can mask the impact of losses, even large ones, thus, keeping the gambler from recognizing the real consequences of his or her actions.

Risk behavior can also occur when the protective frame does not adequately take into account real consequences and relationships. For instance, driving while under the influence of alcohol or drugs can occur when the confidence frame is in effect. The intoxicated driver may have no sense of the possibility of an accident or may have an unrealistic sense of control and skill in driving. Apter (1992) described another way in which the confidence frame can lead to risk behavior. He pointed out that many examples of risk behavior have in common a performance aspect; that is, the person either feels on display as the center of attention or wants to maintain an image before others. The feeling that others are serving as an audience can have two different effects. One effect is to lead to an increase in the confidence frame, often to unrealistic levels. A second effect is to make the action seem less real, more like a game or a piece of theater; this effect enhances the safety-zone frame.

Another way the safety-zone frame can be established is if a group uses a system of rules or guidelines to justify actions that are outside what is generally viewed as acceptable behavior. The problems occur if the rules are misunderstood or misinterpreted either by those taking part in the behavior or by observers. Soccer hooliganism, which is widely known in Europe, is an example of this type of behavior. Soccer hooligans are fans who are playing their own game in which violence and aggression plays a central role. There are rules that determine appropriate targets and how much violence should be inflicted on supporters of the rival team. In fact, the purpose of the ritualized violence appears to be primarily to generate excitement; hooligans may look for confrontations with the police because this would increase the risk, therefore, increasing the arousal level. The rules give a structure to the behavior so that the soccer hooligan feels safe within the parameters of the activity (Kerr, 1994).

The detachment protective frame can also mislead a person into more risk than anticipated. The risk can be miscalculated if a person feels that he or she is beyond the reach of the danger. The make-believe, or fantasy, form of the detachment frame can lead to unwanted risk when the make-believe scenario is acted out in the real world with real consequences. For example, sexual fantasies can present unplanned risks if acted out.

RESEARCH SUPPORT OF REVERSAL THEORY CONSTRUCTS

The first part of this chapter provided a theoretical background of risk behavior: the explanation of why risk is an integral part of experiencing the paratelic state, how it can be experienced in a positive manner, and how the search for excitement can lead to real danger and injury. The remainder of the chapter summarizes the research work that addresses a variety of risk behaviors. Although the preceding discussion has focused on understanding risk behavior from the perspective of the state of mind of the individual in the moment, much of the research has examined risk behavior from the perspective of differences in preferences and styles of responding. These two different perspectives for understanding risk behavior are integrated in the discussion of the research.

Sexual Risk Behavior

Failure to practice safer sex methods for disease and pregnancy prevention has serious consequences not only for the individual, but also for society at large. The number of unwanted pregnancies that result from unprotected sexual encounters and the spread of STDs place a burden on the individual and the community. Pregnancy and disease prevention could be accomplished to a large extent with the consistent use of condoms. Despite widespread knowledge about the sources of risk, the majority of sexually active people either use no protection methods or use condoms on an irregular basis (Bishop, 1994; DiClemente, Forrest, & Mickler, 1990; Gerkovich, 1997, 1998; Keller, 1993; Reinecke, Schmidt, & Ajzen, 1996).

Reversal theory–based research has provided support for the validity of the theoretical constructs with regard to sexual risk behavior. Frank-Ragan (1994) interviewed gay men and bisexual men about a situation in which a condom was used (safe episode) and a situation in which a condom was not used (unsafe episode). In the vast majority (88%) of the safe episodes, the participant reported that a conscious decision to use a condom was made. In contrast, in only 50% of the unsafe episodes did the participant report making a conscious decision about condom use. The conscious decision to use a condom was probably made while at least one of the sexual partners was in the telic state rather than in the paratelic state, when the experience is focused on the moment without concern for long-term consequences. Frank-Ragan also reported a trend for a difference between safe and unsafe sexual episodes with regard to the negativistic state; the only negativistic states that were identified from the interview material occurred in the unsafe episodes.

Other research has been conducted that has emphasized the individual difference aspect of sexual risk behavior using the Paratelic Dominance Scale (PDS; Cook & Gerkovich, 1993). The PDS consists of subscales reflecting playfulness, spontaneity, and arousal-seeking, and a total score that reflects paratelic dominance in general (see chapter 3 in this volume). Bishop (1994) collected questionnaire data from a sample of college students at a large midwestern university. Using the PDS, she found that sexually experienced participants scored higher on all of these measures than did participants who were not sexually experienced. She also found a significant positive correlation between the Arousal-seeking subscale score and (a) having had sex with a greater number of partners in the past 6 months, (b) having more casual sexual partners, and (c) experimenting more with same-gender sexual activity. (This is consistent with data reported in Murgatroyd, 1985b.) As an additional test of the relation between paratelic dominance and sexual risk behavior, Bishop found that people who reported having discussed AIDS with their partner were less arousal-seeking than were respondents who had not spoken to their partner about AIDS.

In a questionnaire study that expanded upon Bishop's work, Gerkovich (1997) replicated the above findings that sexually experienced participants were more arousal-seeking in general than were participants who were not sexually experienced and that participants who had discussed AIDS with their partner were less paratelic than those who had not discussed AIDS. In addition, this study found a positive correlation between alcohol consumption and scores on all PDS subscales as well as the total score.

In a new questionnaire study, Gerkovich (1998) used both the PDS and the Apter Motivational Style Profile (MSP; Apter, Mallows, & Williams, 1998) to look for individual differences in sexual risk behavior. Again, the finding that sexually experienced participants were more arousal-seeking and paratelic dominant in general than were participants who were not sexually experienced was confirmed. Participants were grouped into dominance groups based on their scores on the MSP; dominance scores reflect the relative amount of time spent in the paratelic (reflecting playfulness and spontaneity only) versus the telic state, the arousal-seeking versus the arousal-avoiding state, and the negativistic versus the conformist state. Paratelic-dominant participants, compared to telic-dominant participants, were more likely to report having had sex with a casual partner and to report engaging in alcohol and illicit drug use. Arousal-seeking-dominant participants, compared to arousal-avoiding participants, were more likely to report alcohol use and illicit drug use. In addition, negativistic-dominant participants, compared to conformist-dominant participants, scored higher on an overall index of sexual risk behavior that reflected failure to use condoms consistently, having a greater number of sexual partners, and having had sex with a casual partner. Negativistic-dominant participants also reported having had their first sexual experience at a younger age than did the conformist-dominant participants.

Another aspect of this research involved testing a structural model of sexual risk behavior. It was hypothesized that sexual risk behavior would be explained by a combination of variables representing personality characteristics, attitudes and beliefs, and situational factors. Although the hypothesized model did not provide a significant fit of the data, several hypothesized relations were supported. Sexual risk behavior was significantly explained by an attitudes and beliefs factor as well as a factor representing situation risk (i.e., alcohol and drug use). In addition, the situational risk factor was significantly explained by the factor representing personality measures of playfulness, spontaneity, arousal-seeking, and rebelliousness. People who scored higher on these measures were more likely to report alcohol and drug use. In turn, increased alcohol and drug use was related to increased sexual risk behavior. Although more work needs to be done to further refine the model, the results did support the contribution of reversal theory constructs in explaining sexual risk behavior.

Risk-Sports Participation

Much of the research that has been done on risk behavior has focused on risk-sports participation. This body of research has looked at sport preferences as well as actual participation and has examined feelings at the time of activity as well as individual differences in overall arousal preference. In the publications by Kerr (1988d, 1997a), one can find a more detailed review of the research on reversal theory and risk-sport participation.

Reversal theory would predict that participants in dangerous sports should be paratelic dominant (Kerr et al., 1993); that is, they spend more of their time in the paratelic state looking for high arousal experiences to meet the needs of the paratelic state. Kerr and Svebak (1989) collected data on sport preferences as well as actual sports participation using the Telic Dominance Scale (TDS; Murgatroyd, Rushton, Apter, & Ray, 1978) and the Barratt Impulsivity Scale (BIS; Barratt, 1985). They found that participants who chose a risk sport (e.g., canoeing, caving, downhill skiing) as a preference were more paratelic dominant than were participants who selected a safe sport (e.g., archery, bowling, Frisbee). This was also true when the relation between the TDS and actual sport participation was examined; people who participated in risk sports, both summer and winter, were more paratelic dominant than were those who participated in safe sports.

Kerr (1991a) replicated the above findings with comparisons of different types of risk and safe sports. He found that Australian men who were surfers or sail boarders were more paratelic dominant than were a sample of weight lifters. In a second study, he found that Dutch parachutists and motorcycle racers were more paratelic than were marathon runners. In a final study, Kerr found that British male glider pilots were more paratelic dominant than were participants who were not involved with sports.

Chirivella and Martinez (1994) obtained TDS and Sensation Seeking Scale (SSS; Zuckerman, 1979) data from young men and women who engaged in either tennis, karate, or parasailing. The parasailing group scored higher on SSS scores than did the other groups; in addition, the parasailing group was also more arousal-seeking based on the scores on the Arousal-avoiding subscales of the TDS. It is interesting to note that, based on scores on the TDS subscale, the parasailing group was more serious-minded than the other two groups. The need to take seriously the risks and prepare for the real potential danger in this sport may explain this apparent paradox. There was also a strong positive correlation between age and the Experience-seeking subscale of the SSS. The authors also examined the relations among the measures when participants were identified and grouped by the second sport in which they participated. There was consistency in risk level between the first and second sport and in the relations between sport risk level and scores on risk measures. Participants in the highest risk-level sport had higher risk preference scores than did the other groups based on the SSS Experience-seeking and Disinhibition subscales, as well as the total score, and on the TDS Arousal-avoidance subscale.

Apter and Batler (1997; see chapter 4 in this volume) reported a study of parachutists that also supported the relation between risk and the paratelic state. Data from male and female parachutists documented that the most frequently endorsed reason given for parachuting was for arousal-seeking purposes. The authors also asked the participants to report at what point they experienced maximum feelings of fear or anxiety and at what point they experienced maximum feelings of excitement or thrill. The modal point for maximum anxiety immediately preceded the point of maximum danger, and the modal point for maximum excitement immediately followed the point of maximum danger. The authors interpreted this pattern as demonstrating that one emotion (anxiety) becomes transformed almost instantly into the other (excitement) as the perceived danger is passed, and the experience of excitement achieved in this way is in fact the aim of the activity.

Braathen and Svebak (1992) collected data from teenage high-level sports participants in Norway and looked at both sensation seeking (SSS) and negativism dominance (NDS; McDermott & Apter, 1988). They found that participants who engaged in risk sports, compared to participants in safe sports, scored higher on measures of competitiveness, win orientation, and the importance of being the best. There were also gender differences indicating that the young men were more sensation seeking than were the young women, although this was true only for participants in safe sports. The authors also found that the young men had higher reactive negativism scores than did the young women, and this was especially true among participants in risk sports. The measure of reactive negativism reflects an emotional reaction to a frustration or disappointment and involves increased arousal.

Vlaswinkel and Kerr (1990) studied, with mixed results, the relation between risk-sport participation and negativism dominance. In this study of Dutch performers of risk and safe sports, the authors found that student participants in risk sports scored higher on reactive negativism than did participants in safe sports. When elite-level performers were measured, however, the authors found no differences in negativism dominance between groups of motorcycle racers (risky group), Olympic sailors (less risky group), and long-distance runners (safe group; see also the study by Cogan & Brown, 1999, described in chapter 9 in this volume).

Gender differences have been found when studying the relation between risk-sport participation and personality measures. Although this has often been attributed to cultural or sex role differences, Kerr and Vlaminkx (1997) proposed that it might actually be due to gender differences in the actual experience of risk activities. In their study with Dutch high school students, the authors collected data on mood state and stress levels using the Telic State Measure (TSM; Svebak & Murgatroyd, 1985) and the Stress Arousal Checklist (SACL; Mackay, Cox, Burrows, & Lazzerini, 1978). These data were collected both before and after each participant abseiled down a rock face for the first time. There was a significant interaction between gender and pre- versus postactivity on the stress subscale of the SACL. Women's stress levels were higher than men's before the abseiling and decreased markedly after abseiling; men's stress levels did not differ before and after abseiling. TSM measures did not differ with regard to either gender or collection point, so it is unclear from this study whether the gender differences in stress observed in this study were not solely due to comparable arousal levels being experienced by men and women in different states. If the women had high arousal and were in the telic state, they would experience it as anxiety and should have reported higher stress levels than if they were experiencing the same arousal level in the paratelic state. What could be happening is that the male participants had more confidence and less awareness of the potential danger; therefore, their protective frame allowed them to experience the high arousal as excitement within the paratelic state. The female participants may have lacked confidence in either their own abilities or the safety of the equipment and procedures; therefore, they may not have had a protective frame in place that was adequate to withstand the high arousal they experienced while anticipating the activity.

Other Risk Behavior

Reversal theory has also been applied to other forms of risk behavior. Brown and his colleagues have studied gambling and found support for the relations among risk, increased arousal, and the paratelic state. In an early study, Anderson and Brown (1984) found that 50% of Scottish gamblers said they gambled for excitement. Using the TDS, Anderson and Brown (1987) found that regular gamblers were more paratelic dominant than were the population norm. They also found a negative correlation between scores on the TDS and bet size: Paratelic-dominant people made larger bets. A negative correlation between TDS scores and increased heart rate led the authors to propose that the paratelic-dominant person who is in the paratelic state at the time of play will place larger bets in order to increase arousal. Brown (1991) suggested that gambling serves as a method of arousal regulation; less competitive forms of gambling can lower arousal and reduce tension, whereas more competitive forms increase arousal, which increases enjoyment of the paratelic state. (More information on Brown's approach to gambling, which he sees as a form of addiction, is found in chapter 8 in this volume.)

Brown (Kerr, Frank-Ragan, and Brown, 1993) has also discussed the influence of arousal modulation in eating disorders, which is another form of risk behavior. He suggested that people with anorexia are probably telic and mastery dominant, focused on thoughts of food and eating but feeling compelled to not give in to those thoughts. In contrast, Brown suggested that people with bulimia are probably paratelic dominant, and they use eating binges as a way to increase arousal. He sees people with bulimia as acting out a pattern of binge eating to increase arousal when feeling unpleasant, low arousal in the paratelic state; they then experience the high arousal as unpleasant when they reverse to the telic state; finally, they purge as a way of dealing with the unpleasant feelings in the telic state. This pattern of binging and purging can have disastrous health consequences, but these long-term considerations have little impact at the time the unpleasant feelings are experienced in both the paratelic and telic states.

Trimpop, Kerr, and Kirkcaldy (1999) collected data from a number of risk-related scales including the SSS, the TDS, the Tension Risk Adventure

Inventory (TRAI; Keinan, Meir, & Gome-Nemirovsky, 1984), and the Desire for Control Scale (DCS; Burger & Cooper, 1979). Data were collected from 120 Canadian men between ages 16 and 29. Although contradicting the findings of Chirivella and Martinez (1994), the data supported the popular belief that young people take more risks than older people; older participants scored lower on the SSS scale and the TRAI. The authors found the expected relations between the TDS and SSS and also confirmed the finding from previous studies that the TRAI recklessness and risk-taking factors were independent. The authors interpreted this finding as consistent with the fact that some high-risk sports activities require organization and preparation in order to avoid disasters. A final interesting finding involved the relation of the DCS with the risk measures; it appears that some people who engage in risk activity plan ahead and prepare for their risk-taking. This finding probably reflects the influence of the protective frame in allowing the person to feel some control over the risk activity when the risk is actually faced.

CONCLUSION

The goal of this chapter has been to present an argument for the role that risk behavior plays in the normal experience of the paratelic state. Risk serves the purpose of increasing arousal which, in turn, increases the pleasant hedonic tone experienced while paratelic, whether this is within the context of sports, gambling, sexual activity, or other risk behavior. What is important is to allow risk to be experienced while still preventing long-term negative consequences such as serious injury, loss of savings, pregnancy, or infection with an STD. Evidence has also been presented that demonstrates that felt negativism and the negativistic state can be an additional source of arousal that leads to a further enhancement of the paratelic state. For those who are concerned about the consequences of risk activities, however, it will be necessary to develop options that allow the full experience of the paratelic state while protecting people from the negative impact of their behavior.

12

COGNITIVE SYNERGY

ANDREW S. COULSON

As evidenced by many of the chapters in this book, the concept of motivational style can account for an impressively large array of human experience and behavior. At the same time, however, there would appear to be many everyday feelings that cannot be adequately described by simple reference to the metamotivational modes and their accompanying variables such as hedonic tone or felt arousal. The fascination of toys, the excitement of watching sport, the "magic" associated with special times of the year such as Christmas and Halloween, the delight of art and music, the enjoyment of humor—all these are instantly recognizable as paratelic phenomena. Yet to consider them as little more than different types of paratelic pleasure would detract severely from the unique qualities associated with each. In a similar manner, although feelings such as homesickness, disappointment, sorrow, and embarrassment are manifestly telic in nature, the essential character of these experiences is lost if one describes them as merely different forms of telic anxiety.

To capture the distinctive qualities of the feelings listed above, it is necessary to invoke another reversal theory concept known as *cognitive synergy* (hereafter *synergy*). Unlike metamotivation, which applies to the experience of one's motivation, synergy relates to the experience of identities, such as particular people, objects, places, events, situations, statements, or even oneself. Synergy is thus conceptually distinct from metamotivation, although, as will be seen, it is intimately connected with the telic and paratelic states.

This chapter provides an overview of the fundamental nature of synergy, the ways in which it underlies many common experiences, its mechanism, and its close interactions with metamotivational mode. The main concepts, definitions, and distinctions here are those provided by Apter

The material for this chapter was researched and prepared while the author was at the School of Psychology, Cardiff University, Cardiff Wales, United Kingdom.

(1982a) in his original analysis of synergic phenomena. The following discussion also draws together the relevant experimental studies that have been undertaken in this area of reversal theory.

THE PHENOMENOLOGICAL STRUCTURE
OF COGNITIVE SYNERGY

Cognitive synergies can arise in many different forms, from the experience of baseball camp (Kerr, 1991c) to the enjoyment of antique collecting (Smith & Apter, 1977), from the viewing of television news (Coulson, 1991) to the watching of a comedy program like *Fawlty Towers* (Apter, 1982b). However, all types of synergy have a basic common structure that is captured in the following formal definition: *Cognitive synergy* occurs in experience when a given identity is seen to have opposite, mutually exclusive, or incompatible characteristics, either successively or simultaneously.

In the *successive* version of synergy, the meaning of an identity switches to a mutually exclusive one. This effect may be seen to occur in all ambiguity and other kinds of multistability in experience. For example, the opposing three-dimensional interpretations of the Necker cube (Figure 12.1) fluctuate back and forth, giving the impression of a continual metamorphosis, yet the actual two-dimensional figure remains constant. One could thus describe the cube as displaying what has been termed *paradoxical change* (Apter, 1989b, p. 131). By way of contrast, the *simultaneous* version of synergy relates to contradictions that arise from different levels of interpretation, which may therefore be appreciated together. For example, a porcelain ornament of a ballet dancer is experienced neither as a lump of ceramic

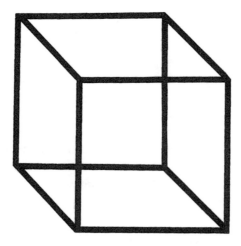

Figure 12.1. The Necker cube, or a reversible perceptual figure.

nor as a real dancer but as both at the same time (cf. Kreitler & Kreitler, 1972, pp. 211–212). In this case, the synergy could be said to involve *paradoxical sameness*: The porcelain is perceived as something else while remaining a piece of porcelain.

The most important aspect of these experiences is that when the incompatible cognitive properties are unified, they produce a striking, dynamic phenomenological effect that none of them could have achieved alone. The word *synergy* is therefore used to describe such conditions because it means a "working together" and applies to any combination in which the result is more than the sum of the individual elements.

It should be noted that, as with other concepts in reversal theory, cognitive synergy is fundamentally both phenomenological and structural in nature. The term refers to an individual's experience of a particular identity and also describes the contradictory structure of the phenomenal field in relation to that identity (Lachenicht, 1988, pp. 30–31). The reality of synergy at an experiential level should therefore not be confused with its reality at a logical level. In fact, synergies cannot exist in formal logic because they contravene the Law of the Excluded Middle, which says that A must be either B or not-B, but not both.

The reader can find discussions that focus primarily on synergy and synergy-related topics in the books and papers by Apter (1982a, chap. 6, 7, 8, and 12; 1982b; 1982c; 1984b; 1989b, chap. 8), Apter and Smith (1977, 1988), Foster (1988, 1993), and Coulson (1991, 1995).

BASIC SYNERGY TYPES

Synergies may be categorized according to their structure in two basic ways. The first, and most important, is the division between *reversal* and *identity* synergies, brief examples of which were given in the previous section. The second way in which synergies can differ cuts across the reversal–identity classes and concerns whether the contradiction results from the presence of one identity or two.

Reversal Synergy

Reversal synergy is the paradoxical-change version of synergy and relates to experiences in which only one level of interpretation is involved. In other words, an identity is interpreted as being either one thing or another. With a reversal synergy therefore, the identity will switch or reverse from one meaning to an opposing or mutually exclusive one, as shown in the Necker cube example. (To avoid any possibility of confusion it should be pointed out that this type of meaning reversal in the experience of identities is not the same as the metamotivational reversals that are the focus in the rest of the theory.)

What happens in such cases is that the focal content of the phenomenal field is replaced by another content but some of the previous meaning carries over for a brief time. The opposing properties therefore appear in succession but overlap for a short period as one meaning gives way to the other. It is the awareness of this temporary coexistence of opposites that constitutes the essence of the synergic effect here. Logically, of course, there is no paradox: The identity is one thing or another. But psychologically there is a feeling of paradox because of the momentary carrying over of meaning.

Reversal synergies tend to fall into two categories. The first type occurs when the reversal goes in one direction only. Apter (1982a, p. 142) gives the examples of hearing that a colleague has been promoted, a bright student has failed, or a friend has gotten married. These situations elicit momentary feelings of bewilderment as the alternative past and present views of the person compete in experience. Similar experiences may occur when one's self-concept changes, for example in the case of a newly qualified doctor, newly married couple, recently imprisoned person, or someone who has mastered a skill for the first time. In all these cases, the pleasantly or unpleasantly bewildering feelings only remain until the new identity is fully accepted and the old one left behind, after which time the synergy disappears. Such one-way changes are also recognized at a cultural level, in that transition periods across major life boundaries, for example from child to adult, unmarried to married, or living to dead, are typically marked by special rituals or ceremonies—the "rites of passage" (Apter, 1982a, p. 149; van Gennep, 1960).

Reversal synergies of the second type occur when the meanings fluctuate between the two interpretations, as happens with all ambiguity. The overlap at the point of transition is continually re-experienced, and even if this is not appreciated consciously, there will at the very least be a general synergic effect at an apperceptual level. For example, whenever a Necker cube reverses, one will continue for a moment to be strongly aware of having just experienced the alternative interpretation. In addition, the repeated switching between meanings may give rise to a general feeling that the contradictory elements are interacting with each other.

In everyday life, perhaps the most commonplace occurrences of ambiguous reversal synergies involve those phenomena that give rise to a disgust or revulsion response. For example, it has been proposed that insects, snakes, and certain other creatures may be experienced as repulsive by native speakers of English because they cut across that culture's basic conceptual categories for edible animals (see Apter, 1982a, p. 148; Leach, 1972). Similarly, virtually all bodily products such as feces, urine, sweat, spittle, and so on are seen as filthy because they attain the ambiguous status of being both part of the body and separate from it. And dirt in general can be viewed as essentially "disorder" or "matter out of place," again giving rise to the experience of ambiguity (e.g., Douglas, 1966). So food is dirty if it contains strands of hair, and hair is dirty if food becomes embedded in it.

In contrast to these examples, one can also note that ambiguity is not always experienced as threatening and unpleasant. Many ambiguous stimuli are very much sought after in the paratelic state, as can be seen from the pervasiveness of ambiguity in many areas of aesthetic production (Apter, 1984b), the enjoyment of experiencing both impossibility and actuality in magic shows (Zajonc, 1966), and the fascination that many people have for uncertain phenomena such as flying saucers and ghosts (Apter, 1982a, p. 147). Even material that evokes a disgust response may be enjoyed as an expression of paratelic negativism, for example when used in humor (Oppliger & Zillmann, 1997). More generally, it may be said that the effects of ambiguity, uncertainty, and other forms of reversal synergy can only be fully understood if one takes into account whether the telic or paratelic mode is operative at the time.

Identity Synergy

As opposed to reversal synergies, identity synergies involve paradoxical sameness, as with the porcelain figurine example. In such cases there are two perspectives or two levels of interpretation that can apply simultaneously to the identity. In other words, the identity is interpreted as being both one thing and another. Thus, as mentioned earlier, one experiences the ballet dancer figure as ceramic and human at the same time.

In this form of synergy, the opposing characteristics repeatedly exchange places between the focus and fringe of our awareness and will, like reversal synergies, overlap at the focus when a changeover takes place. In fact, this focus–fringe structure is what truly differentiates identity synergy from the reversal case (where the opposing property disappears from the phenomenal field after the reversal). Otherwise, the dynamics of the two synergy types are the same.

The term *identity synergy* is used because the incompatible elements apply to the same identity throughout the experience, as opposed to the reversal synergy case, in which the identity switches to a different psychological category. As Apter has noted (1982a, p. 154), having two levels of interpretation also allows for the possibility that no logical conflict has to take place in identity synergies. Nevertheless, even here we continue to remain fully aware of the opposing elements playing off against each other, and thus there is still a phenomenological contradiction involved.

One major class of identity synergy relates to those situations in which an identity is invested with various imaginary characteristics, resulting in real/imaginary or make-believe synergies. For example, a stick of wood may be imaginatively experienced as a sword, or a toy airplane as a "real" airplane. The synergy arises from the phenomenological union of the two different levels of interpretation—the reality and the fantasy. Experientially therefore, the imaginary sword is useless and useful, worthless and valuable, meaningless and a symbol of power and bravery. Certain areas of academic activity may provide the same compelling synergic effects precisely because of the imaginative qualities involved. For example, meteorologists may experience their computational models as "real" weather systems in action, and psychologists may obtain a similar sense of fascination by pretending that people operate like rats or machines (Apter, 1982a; Apter & Smith, 1988). Other types of make-believe synergies occur in relation to the self. An example would be the way in which children derive particular enjoyment from dressing up and "becoming" cowboys, nurses, teachers, and shop assistants (e.g., Bateson, 1973; Caillois, 1961), and adults may obtain similar pleasure from acting, taking part in fancy dress competitions, or living out a fantasy (see Kerr, 1991c). Finally, real/imaginary synergies also pervade the arts, as will be considered later.

Another area in which identity synergies play a major role is religion. In particular, the experience of sacredness could be said to result from a natural/supernatural synergy. In such cases, an object, being, place, or time is perceived as belonging both to the natural, everyday world and to the supernatural, divine one. As with make-believe synergies, the special feeling associated with this synergy may also apply to the self, for example when one is reciting prayers or participating in holy rituals (Coulson, 1995, pp. 34–36). Apter (1982a, pp. 288–291) has elaborated on the ways in which both identity and reversal synergies occur in many aspects of religious thought and experience (also see Foster, 1988).

Synergies of Single and Dual Identities

A second general way of distinguishing between synergy types involves whether the synergy is based on a single identity or on two independent identities.

In the single identity case, the synergy results from one identity displaying contradictory characteristics. For example, in the reversal synergy version, one's knowledge that an unemployed friend has just become a lottery millionaire results in a conflict between the characteristics "poor" and "rich" in relation to the same person. In the identity case, the incompatible qualities are assigned to a single identity from different perspectives. Thus, an antique may be experienced as something both commonplace in the past, and rare in the present (Smith & Apter, 1977).

Dual identity synergies are more complex in nature, in that two incompatible identities are brought together, as opposed to a single identity displaying contradictory qualities. An example of the reversal type would be the ambiguity that arises when someone telephones without giving his or her name, and the voice sounds like it could belong to either of two friends. In the identity case, most make-believe synergies fall into this category. For example, a toy airplane will have its real characteristics as a small useless lump of plastic (identity A) fused with its imaginary characteristics as a large functional aircraft (identity B).

THE MECHANISM OF SYNERGY

Cognitive synergy appears to produce its unique phenomenological effects in two ways: (a) by increasing felt arousal and (b) by enhancing the intensity with which the identity is experienced.

First, it would appear that synergies possess some inherent arousal-increasing characteristics. In common with the experience of many structural stimulus properties such as complexity, novelty, variety, and asymmetry, synergy causes a psychological conflict. More formally stated, its contradictory nature sets off two or more opposing processes in the nervous system, and such activity typically has a motivating effect on the recipient (cf. Berlyne, 1960, 1971, 1978; Coulson, 1995, chap. 5).

In addition to this basic arousal effect, synergies also appear to boost felt arousal as a result of the way in which we respond to such conflict, either in the telic or paratelic mode. As Apter (1982a, pp. 173–174) has discussed, all synergies can be seen as types of puzzles or paradoxes. In the telic state, one will usually want to solve or avoid such contradictions, because the resulting indecision and ambivalence will block action toward one's goal (cf. Storr, 1976, p. 279). Synergy therefore constitutes a frustrating threat in the telic mode, and the incapacity to reconcile the contradictions increases anxiety in this state. In contrast, in the paratelic state the paradoxical aspects of the synergy are enjoyed precisely because of its puzzling qualities, which may also cause pleasant feelings of mild bewilderment. Also, the heightened arousal in this case tends to stem primarily from the way in which the contradictions give a feeling of release from everyday logical thinking (Apter, 1982a, p. 174; also cf. Arnheim, 1966, p. 125).

Increasing felt arousal is one major way in which synergy has its effect. Another is how the whole synergy "comes to life" as a result of the way that the contradictory properties play off against each other. Apter (1982a, pp. 174–176) has described this process as being similar to the numerous perceptual contrast effects that have been demonstrated in experimental psychology. For example, when complementary colors such as red and green are placed next to each other, the red appears redder and the green greener. In a similar manner, synergies can be seen as producing conceptual contrast effects. The opposing meanings in a synergy are brought together in the strongest possible way, with the result that each one becomes more vivid and striking, and the overall experience of the whole identity is strongly intensified as a result.

Because synergies increase felt arousal and heighten the intensity with which the contradictions are perceived, they will generally be avoided in the telic, arousal-avoiding mode and sought in the paratelic, arousal-seeking one. In the telic state, a synergy will characteristically be experienced as "disturbing," "irritating," or "upsetting," whereas in the paratelic state the effect can be described as "fascinating," "magical," "pleasantly bewildering," or even "funny" in the case of humor, as will be discussed. The following three sections expand on these links between synergy and metamotivation, particularly with regard to emotional experience.

SYNERGY AS A REVERSAL-TRIGGERING MECHANISM

Under certain circumstances, synergies can help set up the appropriate environmental conditions that promote a reversal to the paratelic mode. As we shall see later, one of the most pervasive examples of such contingent reversals by synergies may be found in humor. For the present though, it is particularly interesting to note that many cultures create specific synergic environments or rituals that induce precisely these triggering effects.

One prevalent means by which reversals are brought about is via what have been termed secure-context/risky-content synergies. These synergy types are more or less intrinsic to all forms of institutionalized sport, art, or entertainment. In sport, for example, a secure context is provided by the stadium itself, which physically marks off an area in which one is encouraged to feel protected from the threats and worries of the outside world. This sense of security is enhanced by the numerous and unvarying rules, judging methods, time limits, and rituals of the game being played. Yet within such safe and predictable environments, there is a large degree of uncertainty, surprise, conflict, change, and possibly even danger involved in the sport itself. Such factors are often also intensified by the presence of additional synergies that are specific to the particular form of entertainment being experienced (e.g., Apter, 1989b, pp. 135–136; Coulson, 1991). A complex effect therefore takes place in these cases. The *secure context* provides the encapsulated setting that promotes a reversal to the paratelic mode, the *risky content* supplies the excitement and uncertainty to be enjoyed in that mode, and the context and content fuse synergistically to provide yet another source of paratelic enjoyment.

Foster (1988, 1993) has considered a number of other ways in which cultures may encourage the use of synergies to trigger metamotivational reversals. In particular she has discussed Leach's (1961) division of time into profane and sacred time. *Profane time* characterizes everyday life, whereas *sacred time* refers to special solemn or festive events that mark transition points in the yearly cycle or in the life of an individual. One of the special aspects of sacred time is that it is typically marked by various kinds of ritual inversions. For example, at Christmas a tree is taken indoors, or at Halloween people allow their children to beg for treats from strangers. Furthermore, religious rituals at sacred time may involve synergic inversions that would normally be considered licentious, defiling, or sacrilegious. An example here is the "cannibalism" in the Catholic tradition of eating and drinking the body and blood of Christ during Holy Communion (Foster, 1988, pp. 63, 67). For Foster, such cultural synergies are triggers to reverse from the telic, profane time to the paratelic, sacred time. Additionally, these synergies are of course enjoyed in the sacred time, and their paradoxical nature contributes to the special feel or magic associated with cultural or religious occasions.

SYNERGY IN THE TELIC MODE

The majority of examples considered so far relate to the pleasant experience of synergy in the paratelic state. This is not perhaps surprising in that synergic stimulation is actively sought in this mode. Nevertheless, one can also identify a number of synergies that occur in the telic state— one example being that of disgust, as considered earlier. In such cases, the synergic experiences tend to occur as an unwanted side effect of the particular situation.

Apter (1982a, pp. 169–173) has listed a number of such telic phenomena. In the identity synergy case, these would include many make-real synergies, where a fantasized dreaded event—for example, being robbed, having a relationship end, losing one's job—comes true, causing an unpleasant overlap of the real and the imaginary (also see Apter, 1982a, p. 163). Homesickness is another example of a telic identity synergy, where stimuli that remind one of home combine in experience with others that emphasize its distance. Finally, the act of telling lies may cause considerable discomfort in the telic state because it constitutes a double synergy of the real/imaginary kind. Not only does the imaginary falsehood ("I was working late") conflict with the reality of the situation ("I was out having a good time"), but there is a concomitant conceptual attempt to reverse the real and the imaginary. The power of such a double synergy may of course account for why lying may also provide much paratelic enjoyment, for example, to children and pathological liars.

With regard to telic synergies of the reversal type, one particularly noteworthy category here is what has been termed an acceptable/unacceptable synergy. In this case, an acceptable property of an identity is unexpectedly replaced with an unacceptable property, and the first meaning carries over to produce a synergy with the second. Apter (1982a, p. 171) has given the example of disappointment, whereby the displeasure stems from one's expectation of something acceptable suddenly turning into something unacceptable: for example, one is given a cheap watch as a present after anticipating an expensive one. Such synergies also occur in the identity synergy case, as happens when one has to come to terms with an unpleasant truth that one has been making "acceptable" by avoiding or denying it.

There is one further interesting aspect to acceptable/unacceptable synergies. When associated with a concurrent telic–paratelic switch in either direction, and in the presence of high arousal, such synergies tend to result in crying (Apter, 1982a, pp. 172–173). For example, one may cry tears of guilt if one's frequently damaging playful behavior toward another person is recognized for what it truly is. In this case, sorrow is felt because the formerly acceptable playful behavior is seen as unacceptable, and a concomitant reversal to the telic mode takes place. Similar effects take place when the raw, unacceptable reality of a relative's death truly "sinks in" (telic grief) and overlaps with the unreal, "dramatic," acceptable version (paratelic, parapathic grief) that one may have experienced on first hearing the news. Crying also arises when the switch goes in the opposite direction—when the unacceptable gives way to the acceptable. K. C. P. Smith has noted how, for example, weeping is typically induced in mothers at clinics when they are praised for the way they have brought up a problem child (personal communication, May, 1985). In this "relief" version, the synergy tends to be accompanied by a reversal from the telic to the paratelic state.

Finally, it can be seen that some of the classic areas of academic psychology also address the effects of reversal synergies in the telic mode (see Apter, 1982a, pp. 170–171; Coulson, 1995, chap. 2). Examples here include Festinger's (1957) theory of cognitive dissonance, Bateson's (1973) concept of double-bind ambiguities in interpersonal communication, and the conflict-related emotional reactions of the participants in Milgram's studies of obedience to authority (Milgram, 1974, chap. 5, 7, 12). In all of these cases, the synergic effects of the situation are experienced as strongly disturbing, and where possible, action is taken to avoid, reduce, or resolve the conflict.

SPECIAL SYNERGIES IN THE PARATELIC MODE: ART AND HUMOR

There are two areas of paratelic phenomenology in which synergy appears to play a fundamental role. The first of these is aesthetic experience, or how we respond to painting, sculpture, music, dance, literature, poetry, drama, and all other fields that constitute "the arts" or "art" in the broadest definition of the term. Synergies pervade this sphere to such an extent that, "one is forced to suppose that they may be a necessary component of aesthetic experience itself" (Apter, 1984b, p. 419). The second area is humor, the whole structure of which is defined in reversal theory as a form of synergic experience. Synergy may be so essential to these two fields because its paradoxical nature intrinsically provides the strongest possible challenge to our capacity for classifying the environment (Coulson, 1995, chap. 4). When we are not under threat, testing out our conceptual category systems in this way is enjoyable, in that it affords the opportunity to increase our psychological adaptation (see e.g., Humphrey, 1984, chap. 9; Kreitler & Kreitler, 1972, pp. 22–28, chap. 15; Miller, 1988).

Special Paratelic Synergies I: Aesthetic Experience

Although many individual artistic products display their own unique synergic effects, at least seven general classes of synergy occur frequently across all areas of art. Apter (1984b) identified the first five of these classes, and Coulson (1995, chap. 3) identified the remaining two.

Signifier/Signified Synergy

This widespread synergy results from an experiential clash between what an art work represents (the *signified*) and the actual medium that is being used to make the representation (the *signifier*). In that the signified aspect does not actually exist, this synergy type constitutes yet another example of real/imaginary or make-believe synergies. For example, landscape paintings produce an experiential contradiction between the physical attributes of the paint, canvas, and frame (small, flat, enclosed, motionless) and the subject matter of the painting itself (large, three-dimensional, unbounded, moving). Equivalent signifier/signified effects may be seen to occur in every form of figurative art (see Apter, 1982a, pp. 159–162; Apter, 1984b).

Empathy/Alienation Synergy

This takes place when a work of art simultaneously attracts and repels the observer. As Apter (1984b, p. 420) has noted, all art presumably entails a desire on the part of the artist to communicate. Therefore, the specific use of techniques to rebuff the audience may be interpreted as providing yet another source of synergic experience to be appreciated in the paratelic mode. Many devices can be employed to produce this particular synergy, such as the use of uninteresting, repulsive, or disturbing material (see, e.g., Berlyne, 1971, pp. 115–116), or making the subject matter itself strange or bizarre, as in "Theatre of the Absurd" and surrealist art.

Ambiguity Synergy

In addition to being a very common form of reversal synergy in general, ambiguity may be seen as one of the most pervasive characteristics of the arts. For example, Empson (1930/1972) has provided many illustrations of how, when used appropriately, ambiguity and imprecision are the factors that give poetry its greatest strength. The power of multiple interpretations may of course be found in many acknowledged masterpieces such as the *Mona Lisa*, the *Venus de Milo*, and *Hamlet* (for further examples, also see Apter, 1982a, pp. 147–148; Rothenberg, 1979, chap. 7).

Metaphoric Synergy

As with ambiguity, metaphor constitutes a fundamental component of many aesthetic works, occurring not only in the verbal realm, but in art and music as well (see below). Metaphors are dual identity synergies involving two imaginary identities. Although the shared characteristics of each identity fuse, the opposing properties clash with each other, producing the basic synergy effect. As Apter has pointed out, it is precisely this union of contradictions that gives metaphor its impact. Describing a woman as a flower or a military general as a chess player is markedly more striking than saying that the woman is beautiful or the general is clever (Apter, 1984b, p. 422; also see Coulson, 1995, pp. 82–83).

Structural Synergy

This synergy type results from the formal patterns present in the art work. Such effects frequently manifest themselves in the form of structural ambiguity or structural metaphor. In the case of structural ambiguity, a pattern is seen as having two different interpretations. This occurs in "variations on a theme," for example, in that a variation is experienced as both the theme and something other than the theme. The same thing happens in jazz improvisation, because in this genre different musical themes may be related by a common chord sequence and heard simultaneously. Or in a painting, two geometric patterns may overlay each other in such a way that some identity in the picture partakes of both patterns. In contrast, the essence of structural metaphor can be said to lie in the complementary concept of "unity in variety," whereby apparently different things are shown to be related through some unexpected kind of similarity. For example, the buildings in the foreground of a picture may be painted with similar colors or contours to the mountains in the background, thus making an association between the two.

Mass/Space Synergy

This occurs when space is experienced as having a density, shape, or characteristic texture of its own, whereas solid mass can be made to feel transparent, empty, or ethereal in nature. Much abstract sculpture, for example, projects the feeling that space itself is pressuring, shaping or penetrating the material, which in turn is experienced as malleable and rarefied (see, e.g., Arnheim, 1966, pp. 245–255; Kreitler & Kreitler, 1972, pp. 189–194; Rothenberg, 1979, pp. 271–274). Similarly, space may be dynamically "sculpted" by the actions of dancers and mime artists. And music in general can be seen to involve the experience of "space," in that harmony and melody are determined by the intervals between notes, whereas rhythm is defined by the silences between beats (e.g., Kreitler & Kreitler, 1972, pp. 146–147; Storr, 1993, p. 170).

Inner-World/Outer-World Synergy

The final general aesthetic synergy type refers to the way in which our personal inner world of thoughts, images, memories, fantasies, dreams, feelings, and desires may be experientially fused with the external world of objective physical reality. At a superficial level, this synergy occurs when an artistic product "touches something" within us, and there are various ways in which artists may promote such an effect. At a deeper level, the synergy may also be seen to define much of the experience of aesthetic absorption—the sense of fusion that takes place when one has become lost in a piece of music, art, or literature (see Coulson, 1995, chap. 3, 4).

Special Paratelic Synergies II: Humor

Humor constitutes a particularly notable example of paratelic cognitive synergy, in that it is actually defined by the presence of the paratelic mode. Apter (1982a, chap. 8) has provided the most comprehensive explanation of the reversal theory analysis of humor, and discussions of this topic may also be found in the works of Apter and Smith (1977), Apter (1982b; 1989b, chap. 8), Murgatroyd (1987d, 1991), Coulson (1991, 1995), Wyer and Collins (1992), and Svebak and Martin (1997). Palmer (1994) has compared reversal theory systematically with other theories of humor.

Apter (1982a, chap. 8; 1989b, chap. 8) has proposed that all humorous phenomena involve the following five components:

1. The situation displays cognitive synergy.
2. The synergy involved is of a particular type, namely a real/apparent identity synergy. Here an identity appears or purports to be one thing but is "unmasked" or revealed to be another.
3. In this real/apparent synergy, the reality is less than the appearance in some evaluative way, e.g., with respect to ability, power, status, knowledge, importance, monetary value, and so on.
4. The individual who is experiencing the humor is in the paratelic state.
5. The humorous situation should result in increased arousal, which will be experienced as paratelic excitement.

These factors are now examined in further detail.

The Experiential Structure of a Comic Synergy

The first three conditions relate to the basic synergic structure of the humorous situation or joke. To take a typical slapstick example, consider the case of a man walking along the street who spots a banana skin in front of him, deftly leaps over it, and promptly disappears down an open manhole. The synergic real/apparent element here is that the man appears to be perceptive and athletic but turns out to be dreadful at monitoring his environment, as well as accident prone. These characteristics unmask him as being far less than he purports to be.

Three points may be noted about these structural elements in humor. First, there would appear to be two main forms of comic synergy: *transition humor*, in which the real, inferior nature of the identity is suddenly revealed, as in all jokes; and *non-transition humor*, in which one is aware of the real/apparent synergy from the start, for example in comic situations or with comic characters who purport to be more than they are. Transition and non-transition humor are structurally similar to reversal and identity synergies respectively, but because all humor, strictly speaking, involves an identity synergy (different ways of seeing the same thing), the transition/non-transition distinction needs to be retained.

Second, the real/apparent synergies of comedy are different from the real/imaginary or "make-believe" ones discussed earlier. In humor, there has to be some suggestion that the appearance *is* the reality, whereas in make-believe one is aware of the imaginary elements from the outset (see Apter, 1982a, pp. 177–179; Arieti, 1976, p. 127).

Finally, the reversal theory approach should not be confused with the more traditional "superiority theories" of humor, in which the observer feels superior to those who are depicted in the joke or comedy (see La Fave, Haddad, & Maesen, 1976). Superiority and inferiority in reversal theory relate to (the appearance and reality of) the identity, not to the person experiencing the humor.

Research into the structural components of comedy has been limited but has generally substantiated the reversal theory explanation. For example, Deckers and Avery (1994) found that giving jokes illogical punch lines detracted from the humor at least as much as using logical, unfunny conclusions. In both cases the special synergic structure of the joke is lost, and the study demonstrates how the humorous effect cannot be salvaged by the simple addition of incongruity alone (cf., Apter, 1982a, pp. 192–194). Wyer and Collins (1992) performed more direct investigations of the formal properties of humor, the results of which were largely supportive of the reversal theory approach.

Humor and the Paratelic Mode

The presence of the paratelic state (component 4 above) is essential for a humor response. If someone we cared about fell down a manhole in real life, then no matter how comical the situation looked, our reaction would still more likely be one of fright, anxiety, and concern than of amusement. More generally, those in the telic, arousal-avoiding mode will find comedy upsetting, irritating, shocking, sickening, or in some other way disturbing—the "joke at a funeral" reaction. In particular here, the experience of embarrassment has been viewed as a characteristic telic response to a highly arousing real-inferiority/apparent-superiority synergy, which may be felt for oneself (autocentric state) or somebody else (allocentric state). In such cases, the person is shown to be somehow less than the social image that he or she normally projects to others.

The relationship between the paratelic mode and humor appreciation has been supported by a number of empirical studies. For example, Martin (1984) found a significant negative correlation between overall telic dominance (as measured by the Telic Dominance Scale; Murgatroyd, Rushton, Apter, & Ray, 1978) and each of four different measures of sense of humor. Likewise, factor analytic studies on joke appreciation and other measures of humor reveal strong positive loadings of these variables on to a paratelic factor known as *surgency*, which is defined as feeling carefree, playful, and witty (Ruch, 1994; Wicker, Thorelli, Barron, & Willis, 1981).

Comic synergies may also be seen to have inherent reversal-triggering properties. Given that one aspect of a humor synergy is only apparent in nature, the synergy could be said to reveal itself as being only a "pretend" one because it does not involve a genuine contradiction. This removal of the threat of conflict is precisely the type of process that is likely to promote a switch to the paratelic mode (see Apter, 1982a, pp. 184–186). Such reversal-triggering effects have been demonstrated experimentally: Svebak and Apter (1987) found that the presentation of humorous material tended to promote the paratelic state even in telic-dominant individuals.

Humor and Arousal

With regard to the claim that humor boosts felt arousal levels (component 5 above), we are perhaps most conscious of this effect when we try to stifle a laugh, for example when it would be socially inappropriate to show an amusement response. Much of the torture involved in attempting to suppress a fit of the giggles can be traced to the repeated surges of arousal that accompany such states. In addition, a large number of experimental studies, many involving physiological measures, have supported the proposal that the enjoyment or appreciation of humor varies in a positive, linear fashion with the amount of arousal it produces (see Apter, 1982a, pp. 191–192, 194n.; Murgatroyd, 1991, pp. 121–122; Svebak & Apter, 1987; Wilson, 1979, chap. 4) or with how aroused people feel (Wicker et al., 1981). If one may assume that the participants in these experiments were in the paratelic mode, such findings are exactly what would be predicted by reversal theory.

Enhancing the Enjoyment of Humor

In addition to the five criteria for humor given above, there are a number of factors that, although not necessary for something to be perceived as funny, will help intensify the degree of humor that is felt (see Apter, 1982a, pp. 184–190; Apter, 1982b; Apter & Smith, 1977). These include

1. the use of additional arousal-increasing devices such as surprise, sex, violence, taboo, disgust (cf. Oppliger & Zillmann, 1997) and dramatic tension
2. an exaggeration of the opposites involved in the synergy, which is an intrinsic means for enhancing any synergic effect (cf. Deckers & Salais, 1983)
3. the use of multiple synergy, in which a number of comic synergies occur simultaneously or within a short space of time and may also become interconnected or play off each other to produce further comic effects (e.g., Apter, 1982b)
4. the presence of environmental cues such as other people laughing—hence the widespread use of canned laughter in television sitcoms and metacommunicative signals that indicate the paratelic nature of the situation, e.g., particular facial expressions or the use of stock phrases associated with comic material

5. information-processing factors such as comprehension difficulty, whereby the humor is enhanced when it requires a moderate degree of mental effort in order to understand it, and cognitive elaboration, whereby humorous material is funnier if it has more than one way of being read, more implications, more variations, and so on (Wyer & Collins, 1992).

With particular regard to the last point, it may be noted that Wyer and Collins (1992) have expanded on the reversal theory description of humor in several ways. Most notably, they have taken into account the way in which people comprehend information within a social context. Combining this approach with the additional concepts of comprehension difficulty and cognitive elaboration as described above, the authors were able to make a detailed analysis of a rich variety of humor-eliciting events and situations. They also adduced data that largely support both the reversal theory aspect of their account of humor and their additional social and cognitive concepts.

Humor as a Coping Mechanism

A number of writers have argued that humor, when used appropriately, can act as a positive means of coping both with specific psychological problems and with stress in general (see e.g., Lefcourt & Martin, 1986; Murgatroyd, 1987d, 1991; Svebak & Martin, 1997). The reversal theory approach may explain why humor can be so useful as a means of dealing with life's problems. First, the capacity of a humorous synergy to induce the paratelic mode may allow stressful situations to be experienced as challenges that may be approached in a playful way. Second, the real-inferiority/apparent-superiority nature of humor synergies means that comedy may be used to reframe frightening events or worrying problems as less threatening than they first appear (see Murgatroyd, 1987d). Svebak and Martin (1997) have provided empirical evidence that humor can buffer the negative effects of stressors.

EXPLORING THE DEEP STRUCTURE OF SYNERGY

The experimental work reported so far in this chapter has provided much support for the proposed motivational and metamotivational effects of synergy, such as its capacity to increase arousal and, under certain circumstances, induce the paratelic mode. In addition to these studies, some empirical research has also started to probe synergy's fundamental structure. As considered earlier in the mechanism section, there are many types of arousal-increasing phenomena that also produce psychological conflict. What is special about synergy, however, is that it locks opposing psychological processes together into an irresolvable conflict. This dynamic locking factor gives synergy a characteristic phenomenological quality that is not associated with reactions to other forms of conflict such as novelty, complexity, and the like (see Coulson, 1995, pp. 163–165).

Coulson (1995) investigated this distinctive structural property through a series of experiments. The aim here was to see whether empirical evidence would support synergy's theoretical status as a unique form of psychological conflict. Two of these studies examined the way in which synergy influences preference behavior. In the first study, participants were required to make aesthetic ratings of three types of stimuli: (a) pairs of photographs that were visually similar and thereby formed visual metaphors (synergies), (b) pairs of visually unrelated pictures (non-synergies, low conflict), and (c) pairs of visually superimposed pictures (non-synergies, high conflict). In the second study, the period of time participants spent looking at synergic drawings (e.g., those displaying incongruity) was compared with the time they spent viewing pictures that displayed other types of (non-synergic) visual conflict. Factor analyses for both experiments revealed the presence of a synergy factor, suggesting that the participants were reacting to the synergic material in a special way. Furthermore, the different response measures taken in the two experiments indicated that the synergies were eliciting these distinct preference reactions at both an explicit level (in terms of verbal ratings) and an implicit one (in terms of visual exploration time).

The third study in this series addressed the proposal that synergies disrupt cognition—an effect that is likely to occur if synergy truly involves a locking together of competing processes. Participants were required to reproduce time intervals while examining the pictures used in the second experiment. It was found that none of the stimuli significantly lengthened or shortened people's mean experienced duration. However, the synergic material did produce significantly greater variance in people's estimations of elapsed time than did the other conflicting pictures, suggesting that the synergies were having a marked disruptive effect on experience.

The final pieces of empirical work in this series aimed to go even deeper, by examining the structural and dynamic components of synergy that are responsible for the psychological disruption it causes. First, an experiment produced empirical evidence that mutually contradictory identities can be fused in experience. In this study, participants were requested to attempt to see various simultaneously conflicting interpretations of a Necker cube. Not only were people able to perform the tasks, but also a specific pattern of results appeared across the different experimental conditions that could be adequately explained with reference to the perceptual demands required in each case.

Following these findings, a computational neural network model was designed in order to simulate the performance of the participants in the experiment. The network was configured according to the hypothesized local perceptual relationships between the faces of the Necker cube. Connections in the net fatigued and recovered to simulate reversals, and biases were introduced to mimic the different attentional demands in each of the experimental conditions. Across a variety of network versions, the relative frequency of synergic activations—in which mutually inhibitory units were activated at the same time—was found to provide an excellent fit to the data from the participants. A second group of simulations was then performed without the operation of fatigue and recovery in order to capture the synergic moment at which the two opposing interpretations are locked together. Evidence was found for dynamic synergy-like activity in the network in that it displayed simultaneous stability and oscillation. These results suggest that it may well be possible to start investigating synergy's structure and dynamics via computational models.

In the experiments just discussed, as well as in others that primarily address synergy's cognitive effects (e.g., Pilon, 1998), it is typically found that the synergic material does not interact strongly with felt arousal or metamotivational mode. This naturally raises the question of how to devise effective laboratory studies when one does want to investigate the relationship between synergy and arousal or metamotivation. In a discussion of this issue, Coulson (1995) proposed that for valid experimental designs in such cases, the synergic material should (a) be powerful or meaningful enough to induce an arousal or metamotivational response, (b) require some sort of reaction on the part of the participant (cf. Berlyne, 1961; Smith & Principato, 1982, 1983), and (c) be relevant to the metamotivational modes (e.g., by being challenging in the paratelic state or by blocking task completion in the telic state).

CONCLUSION

If there were one general conclusion that could be made from the above overview of synergy, it is that it holds immense potential for continued positive refinement and growth.

At the theoretical level, the concept is proving itself applicable to an ever-widening catalogue of psychological phenomena without overstretching itself (cf. Srull, 1987). Such controlled expansion is possible because of synergy's rigorous phenomenological definition, which allows it to be distinguished from other forms of psychological conflict and thereby prevents its being applied to inappropriate areas of experience.

Progress in the study of synergy appears to be equally promising in terms of empirical investigation. The paradoxical, largely ineffable nature of synergy does not make it an easy phenomenon to study experimentally. Yet, as has been shown, it can still be objectively explored at a number of levels and by a variety of techniques. The results of these studies have not only provided support for the proposed experiential structure and effects of synergy, but have also raised certain important conceptual and methodological issues. Taken as a whole, therefore, such encouraging advances in research on cognitive synergy, at both the theoretical and empirical levels of exploration, are likely to ensure that the future development of this concept will remain a healthy and dynamic one.

IV

PRACTICAL APPLICATIONS

13

MANAGEMENT AND ORGANIZATIONS

MICHAEL J. APTER AND STEPHEN CARTER

Motivation has long been an important topic in management theory and in all those areas—such as employee development, team building, consumer behavior, leadership, and organizational change—that roughly fall under the rubric "management and organizations." As a theory of motivation, reversal theory should, in principle, have something to say in these areas, and this is in fact the case. Indeed, over the years, a number of those working with reversal theory have engaged in management consultancy, often in the form of research, and advice deriving from this research, using the conceptual framework provided by the theory. (Much of this work, unfortunately, is proprietary and cannot therefore be reported in the present chapter.) The interest in using reversal theory in organizations has in fact been growing. Apter International, whose approach is specifically based on reversal theory, has recently been set up as a management consultancy company to fulfill this growing interest. In his book, *Renaissance Management*, Carter (1999) has outlined some of the main ways in which reversal theory can be used in management.

REVERSAL THEORY RESEARCH
IN ORGANIZATIONAL SETTINGS

Although in principle all of the research that has been carried out on reversal theory is relevant in one way or another to the management of business organizations, some papers and reports have specifically used participants in an organizational or occupational setting. For example, in the study by Walters, Apter, and Svebak (1982) described in chapter 4, which tracked metamotivational states over time, the participants were office workers. The research on stress by Baker (1988) and by Svebak, Mykletun, and Bru

(1997), both studied stress explicitly in the work setting. Rhys (1988), also described in chapter 4, studied the transactional states in the occupation of nursing. Grover (1999) studied the ways in which the police handle stress. Kerr (1993b) and Kerr and Vlaswinkel (1995) reviewed research showing the way in which employee breaks for exercise or sport could improve performance at work, interpreting this evidence in reversal theory terms. Tacon and Abner (1993) are among those who have derived norms for different occupations using reversal theory scales.

In a few cases, the research has been conceived from the beginning as being specifically about behavior within organizations. For example, Lin (1996) has provided a detailed study of risk-taking in Chinese miners. Seventeen miners were interviewed at length, and their responses coded in terms of metamotivational states as described in reversal theory. A nonaccident record was found to be related to the arousal-avoidance, conformist, and alloic states. No influence was found for seniority or age. Again, as part of a multidimensional study by Mamali (1990) of 780 electronic and tool machine construction industry workers from five Romanian cities, 152 participants were administered a Romanian translation (by Mamali) of the Telic Dominance Scale (TDS; Murgatroyd, Rushton, Apter, & Ray, 1978). He found, among other things, that (a) the higher the telic dominance score, the more likely the individual was to place work as the most important source of life satisfaction, the less likely he or she was to place hobbies high in terms of life satisfaction, and the more likely he or she was to desire control in his or her life; (b) the higher the telic dominance score, the more intense the work motivation; and (c) the lower the telic dominance score, the lower the orientation to intrinsic motivation.

On the whole, these studies have been focused on individuals within an organization rather than with their interactions or with the organization as a whole. This is likely to change with the advent of such new psychometric instruments as the Apter Work Impact System (see below).

A FRAMEWORK FOR UNDERSTANDING ORGANIZATIONS

It can be argued that reversal theory subsumes many previous psychological theories of management, creating a broader more integrative conceptual structure. Let us look at three examples of seemingly unrelated topics that can be shown within the reversal theory framework to have a common core motivational structure: leadership style, brand image, and corporate culture. These are just three examples of areas that can be understood and related to each other in terms of the common underlying structure of metamotivational states identified by reversal theory, and there are many more.

Leadership Style

From the reversal theory perspective, there can be many different leadership styles, and these can be understood in terms of the eight states or motivational styles. Thus, strategic leaders are those who tend to adopt a telic style, taking the long-term perspective, whereas inspirational leaders tend to be operating in the paratelic style, generating enthusiasm and energy in others. The conformist leadership style is represented by bureaucratic leaders who develop structures and routines in order to improve efficiency and productivity and the negativistic style by leaders who act as "grit in the oyster" to catalyze innovation and change. A mastery-style leader may lead by example, taking professional pride in being able to perform all the skills and handle all the technical problems of those who work for him or her. He or she may also express the mastery state through being highly competitive, framing the needs of the company in terms of a struggle to win markets. In contrast, the sympathy leadership style is associated with an attractive personality and even charisma, with which people easily identify; the leader in the sympathy state also is likely to encourage a caring workplace atmosphere that is people oriented and friendly. The autic leadership style is represented by the prima donna who may also be authoritarian, closely monitoring, and controlling the work of others. The leader who is adopting the alloic style is a collaborative consensus builder who likes to be treated as "one of the team." He or she may also like to empower others in the organization.

All these different leadership styles have their uses, although some may be better suited to particular prevailing cultures and some to different kinds of problems and challenges. The best leaders are presumably those who show some flexibility, so that they can to some degree match the motivational style they display to the demands of the situation. For instance, a team may require a different metamotivational orientation, and hence ideally a different leadership style, depending on the nature of their task at a given time. The requirements of some types of teams, however, may be so different that only different people with different preferred individual leadership styles would suffice—for example, an innovative team compared to a maintenance team or to a project planning team. Using this kind of analysis, Lee and Pease (in press) have developed a 30-item Leadership Orientation Profile to measure the preferred leadership behaviors that athletes desire from their coaches. Interestingly, their first results using this scale suggest that, in general, athletes require psychological diversity in their coaches and the ability to display different metamotivational states in different situations.

Brand Image

Let us take another area, that of brand image or "brand personality." The way that a brand is positioned, advertised, and marketed represents a promise being made to the customer: Buy us, and you will experience this kind of satisfaction. The kind of satisfaction, and hence the brand personality, can be understood in terms of the eight metamotivational states. Thus, some brands promise long-term stability and safety and hence represent the telic state. Others promise immediate fun and gratification (the paratelic state). Some brands promise that you will be doing the fashionable "in thing" (conformist), others that you will be buying freedom and "doing it your way" (negativisim). Some brands promise power and strength (mastery) and others the joys of caring and intimacy (sympathy). Some brands tell you that "you owe it to yourself" (autic) and others that you can enjoy the pleasure of giving (alloic).

From the reversal theory perspective, every promise made in an advertisement or promotional campaign must appeal to one or another of the eight basic needs, although it is possible to promise more than one. In some product categories, some organizations tend to emphasize contrasting metamotivational states. This is true, for instance, of automobiles: Some manufacturers appeal to the feeling of power and ruggedness (mastery), others to utility and safety (telic), and yet others to the needs of caring for the family (alloic sympathy). In some product categories, however, all of the manufacturers or providers use a limited range of appeal that can be described in terms of a single metamotivational state. Thus, beer companies almost universally appeal to the fun motive (paratelic), perfume manufacturers to self-indulgence (autic sympathy), and drug companies to doing what doctors say and what others can be seen to be doing (conformist). These may or may not in fact be the only, or even the best, states to which to appeal for these types of product.

O'Shaughnessy and Guido (1996), in their analysis of reversal theory in relation to advertising and marketing, have highlighted a complication in all this which needs to be taken into account. This is the problem of what they call "marketing consistency," which is that of knowing which state a potential consumer is in while being actually subjected to an advertisement, or the product itself at the point of purchase, especially given that this state is likely to change depending on a variety of contextual and other factors. Also they pointed out that many factors in the pricing, packaging, and display of products can induce different metamotivational states or have different effects in different states. As emphasized by Puntoni (1999) in his exploration of purchase intention and metamotivational state, the situation is clearly complex.

Corporate Culture

To turn to yet another theme, corporate climate can be described in terms of the emphasis placed on the different metamotivational values. Thus, some corporations emphasize the need for keeping to routines, others the importance of a friendly atmosphere, and so on. Further, each corporation will have its own profile in terms of the relative importance placed on the eight states. Sometimes this will be consistent with the brand image of the corporation's product and sometimes not. Changes in the external environment of markets may in turn cause changes in the corporate climate. For instance, Murgatroyd (Athabasca University, 1986) analyzed the experience of Coca Cola in introducing the "New Coke" in 1985. Using published descriptions and detailed interviews with all of the players, he was able to interpret the events from a reversal theory perspective. Pepsi was seen as responding in a paratelic way and Coca Cola in a telic way to the dramatic developments that followed New Coke's introduction. More detailed analysis of the responses to the situation also revealed that mounting public pressure forced Coca Cola's team to become more and more telic while enabling the Pepsi team to become more and more playful in their response (Athabasca University, 1986).

PRACTICAL RELEVANCE

To understand people and to manage or guide their behavior, we have to understand their motives and what they are attempting to get out of life at each moment. Because management, and especially human resource management, is crucially concerned with the behavior of employees, any theory that throws light on their motivation and the way that this motivation changes has enormous potential consequences. It is not too much to say that it is the key to everything else in managing people. When counselors and therapists use reversal theory to help people in self-development (see chapter 14 in this volume), they encourage them to do three things: (a) to experience all the states on a regular basis (i.e., not to get "stuck"), (b) to experience the right states at the right times, and (c) to display appropriate behavior within each state. These three general recommendations can be applied more specifically to people in the work situation and to the organizations that determine the nature of this situation. Let us look at each in turn.

Organizational and Individual Completeness

The first recommendation is that all the metamotivational states need to be brought into play in the workplace. That is, if employees' energies are going to be fully harnessed to the needs of a team or organization, and if employees are going to experience fulfillment from their work, then the whole person needs to be engaged.

From the organizational point of view, the more energy that employees devote to an organization, other things being equal, the better. But beyond this, every motivational state has something distinctive and essential of its own to contribute. In other words, organizations need to develop a performance climate that is "motivationally rich" or, to put it another way, they need to display "psychodiversity." Thus, among other things, the telic state in employees can contribute direction and focus; the paratelic state, infectious enjoyment of the work; the conformist state, compliance with regulations and routines; the negativistic state, needed criticism and innovation; the mastery state, control and professionalism; the sympathy state, a friendly atmosphere; the autic state, personal responsibility and a willingness to take the initiative; and the alloic state, team spirit.

Unfortunately, organizations (and teams) tend to emphasize the serious, compliant, and mastery motivational states at the expense of the playful, challenging, and sympathy states. Among other things, this makes change and innovation more difficult to accomplish and to sustain. For example, as an approach, Total Quality Management, while providing enormous benefits, also has a number of limitations, including a narrow view of employee motivation that exaggerates the telic and conformist states.

Dixon (1993a, 1993b) has argued, as have others (e.g., Apter, 1982a; Fontana, 1985), that the paratelic state is necessary for innovation, but he pointed out that in the organizational context this state is generally not encouraged. Citing results from studies of industrial innovations, he found that few of them had been achieved by the telic method of setting a rigid goal first and then searching for a solution. Most of them resulted simply from someone having an idea and then developing it just to see what happened. Dixon suggested that people with clear-cut ambition to climb to the top of companies may therefore, in psychological terms, be fundamentally different from effective innovators and, because of their telic dominance, are less likely to be original. Dixon (1993a) also cited the experiment by Barr, McDermott, and Evans (1993), described in chapter 4 of this book, which shows that people in the paratelic state are likely to persevere for a longer period in the face of task difficulties. If, as a manager, one wants innovation in a company, therefore, one will do better to frame problems as leisure time diversions for employees than as critical problems for the high fliers.

From the employees' perspective, they need to display all the states on a regular basis if they are to be able to experience a full and satisfying life at work—a life in which they feel that they are doing something of importance (telic) but that is also enjoyable in itself (paratelic), in which they can experience structure (conformist) but are also able to express themselves as individuals (negativistic), in which they can feel competent and in control (mastery) but also be appreciated as people (sympathy), and able to be both individuals (autic) but also part of something larger (alloic). In other words, as Carter (1999) reported from a phrase that he overheard at a workshop, employees want to "bring their whole personality to work." And in doing so, they provide the mirror image of the organization's needs, meaning that there is no basic conflict between the good of the organization and the well-being of the employee—what is good for one is good for the other.

Motivational Matching and Versatility

The second recommendation is that employees (including managers) need to be able to control which metamotivational states they are in and to match the right state to the right situation. In other words, they need to be what Dixon (1994) referred to as *motivationally versatile* or to have what he called a *switchable personality*. Dixon pointed out that because promotion is increasingly limited due to the "flattening" that is occurring in companies, employees may need to think more about fitting themselves to the job they have rather than looking for a job that would ideally suit them. This need for alignment is particularly necessary in motivational terms. Because there are a number of alternative motivations that people experience in the course of their everyday lives, the best way to achieve motivational matches with the tasks that have to be accomplished is to be able to reverse frequently, and as the situation demands, between the opposite motivational states described in the theory.

Hall (1995) put this in a slightly different way by saying that reversal theory makes sense of unpredictable and inconsistent behavior and that inconsistency, when properly harnessed and focused, can be a tremendous asset. Interestingly, this ties in with evidence from reversal theory studies of the family, which suggests that children get on best with their parents when they reverse easily between states (O'Connor, 1992). Apart from anything else, people who are flexible are likely to be able to enter into the same states as those with whom they are interacting.

Fontana and Valente (1993b, 1997) reported on a stress management workshop that they developed to deal with the different kinds of stress that arise when there is a mismatch between the dominance of the employee and the characteristics of the organizational climate of the company for which he or she works (see chapter 15 in this volume). The workshop allowed employees to identify such mismatches and to explore how they can change in themselves or bring about organizational changes so as to reduce the stress that arises from these problems of "fit." Apter International (1999a) has also devised a number of techniques aimed at helping people to improve their personal control (albeit indirectly) over their reversal processes.

Appropriate Behavior

The third recommendation is that each employee needs to learn how to express and satisfy each metamotivational state in ways that are helpful rather than unhelpful to that employee, to the team, or to the organization.

Motivational states can be acted out in various ways, some of them harmful to the individual and the team or organization, some of them helpful. Each employee needs to learn how to inhibit inappropriate behaviors while developing constructive approaches to the workplace. In other words, to use currently fashionable language, they need to develop appropriate "life skills" or forms of "emotional intelligence." This is an obvious point, but what is perhaps less obvious is that the appropriate life skills may be different in each metamotivational state.

The worst problems for organizations seem to be caused by employees who display a limited range of motivational states and express these in disruptive ways; this is particularly true in cases in which the states involved are the paratelic, negativistic, sympathy, and autic states. In the undesirable version of the paratelic state the individual simply "messes around" in an unconstructive way. In the undesirable version of the negativistic state, he or she is no more than disruptive. In the undesirable version of the sympathy state, personal and social issues distract from the work at hand. And in the undesirable version of the autic state he or she is so self-centered that they cannot see, and do not care about, what is for the common good.

In respect to less than fully desirable behavior, Slattery and Apter (1996) have discussed focus group and questionnaire work they carried out on the role of secretaries in a government organization. Secretaries who were seen by their supervisors as unsatisfactory were not necessarily those who did not do what they were asked, but those who did nothing unless asked, who did not anticipate the needs of their bosses, and who were unwilling to play their part in developing a generally friendly and helpful work atmosphere. In other words, they often fulfilled their job descriptions, but they did much less than they might have done, especially in respect of the sympathy and alloic states.

SURVEY AND PROFILING INSTRUMENTS

In order to diagnose different problems at work, various scales, question-naires, interviews, and focus group techniques have been devised. These include in particular three instruments published by Apter International,[1] which have been used in consultancy work in various companies in different parts of the world.

The first of these is the 40-item Apter Motivational Style Profile (AMSP; Apter International, 1999a), which is derived from the longer Motivational Style Profile (MSP; Apter, Mallows, & Williams, 1998) by extracting from the latter the eight subscales dealing with the eight metamo-tivational states (see chapter 3, in this volume, for more details on the MSP). This provides profiles for individual employees, consisting of (a) eight subscale scores representing the amount of time the respondent spends in each state in everyday life and (b) four dominance scores, one for each pair, based on the balance of time the respondent spends in one state rather than the other within each pair. Norms from various sources are available and published in the *Manual for the Apter Motivational Style Profile* (Apter International, 1999e), including norms for managers in the United Kingdom and the United States. A computer-generated report system is available that provides charts of the individual's standardized scores and describes the individual's overall profile in narrative form. It also provides extended narrative on the individual's key states (the states that are important either because they score high on the subscale concerned or because they are strongly dominant) and raises a number of issues for the person to think about in relation to this state. The rationale for this is that if the state occurs frequently in the person's life, then problems in relation to that state are likely to be particularly important for that person and require special attention. There is also a workbook that accompanies the report (Apter International, 1999d). The main intention of the AMSP instrument is to provide a focus for counseling as part of self-development programs.

The second measurement instrument to be described here is the Apter Team Contribution System (ATCS; Apter International, 1999c). The aim of this instrument is to uncover problem areas within team functioning. Team members rate themselves on a set of items. Between them, and in different ways, these items represent each of the eight states. Members are asked to evaluate both how much of a contribution they would like to make to the team with respect to each item and also to rate the item in terms

---

[1] For more information about Apter International, contact The Offices, Glaston Road, Uppingham, Rutland LE15 9EU, England; (+44) 01572 821111; http://www.apterinternational.com

of how much they feel they actually do contribute in this respect. Using similar items, they also assess how far other members of the team contribute and how far each member being assessed behaves in a way that inhibits the team's performance with respect to that item. Normally each team member assesses at least three other members, and the assessments are averaged so that everyone receives information in this way about how they are assessed by others. An example of an item would be "Keeping the team focused on its important goals" (which is clearly a telic item). Team members may gain significant insights about themselves in this way. For example, one person may feel that he is contributing a great deal in some respect, but others see him as "getting in the way." Another may feel that she is not contributing as much as she wants, but others see her as contributing a great deal, and this gives her greater confidence. This kind of information can lead to important change in both team members themselves and in the functioning of the team as a whole.

The third measurement instrument to be considered here is the Apter Work Impact System (AWIS; Apter International, 1999d). This provides a way of carrying out what one might term *motivational mapping* within an organization as a whole, with the aim of identifying motivational–emotional problem areas in the organization that need to be dealt with. The procedure is to have managers on the one hand, and employees on the other, evaluate the same set of items, both of them doing so in two ways: (a) the importance of the item and (b) its degree of satisfaction. The difference between the questionnaire task of the employees and the managers is this: The employees are asked to make these ratings in terms of their importance to them individually and the degree to which they individually feel them to be satisfied. The managers are asked to rate the importance of the items to the organization and the degree to which they think that they are in fact satisfied in employees.

There are 40 items representing, between them, a comprehensive set of workplace aspects of all the eight metamotivational needs and values. For example, the following item is one of those relating to the paratelic state: "I enjoy my work for its own sake." (The managerial version of this item is, of course, put in the third-person plural form.)

On the basis of these four sets of ratings, a series of comparisons can be made constituting a form of "gap analysis." What is being compared in this way is (a) corporate values (the managers' ratings of the importance of items to the organization), (b) employee needs (the employees' personal ratings of importance), (c) employee satisfaction (the employees' ratings of their personal satisfaction), and (d) the manager's perception and understanding of employee satisfaction (the managers' ratings of employee satisfaction). Any lack of alignment points to possible problems in the organization, as shown in Table 13.1.

Table 13.1.
The Structure of the AWIS

	Employee	Organization
Demand	1. Employee values	2. Organizational values
Supply	3. Employee satisfaction	4. Organizational perception of employee satisfaction

Note. A discrepancy between 1 and 3 represents employee frustration. A discrepancy between 2 and 4 represents organizational strain. A discrepancy between 1 and 2 represents value conflict. A discrepancy between 3 and 4 represents delivery conflict.

It is also interesting to see which items are rated low in importance, both by managers (corporate values) and employees (personal needs in the workplace). If some need or value is rated low it implies that it is being undervalued in terms of its potential relevance to the organization, and hence its contribution in the workplace is not likely to be high and the motives involved are not likely to be fully harnessed to the needs of the organization.

It will be realized that comparisons can also be made in these various ways between different departments, offices, divisions, teams, and so forth within an organization, thus providing another set of possible misalignments and differences. All these comparisons can also be made either at the level of the 40 items themselves or in terms of their aggregation into the eight metamotivational states. More information is found concerning the AWIS, and how it can be used, in Carter (1999, chap. 5).

All three of these measuring instruments use the same set of reversal theory categories, meaning that essentially the same structure is being used at the individual, team, and organizational levels, allowing systematic comparisons to be made, if desired, between these levels. The most important thing to realize about these instruments, however, is that they are part of a framework for diagnosing dysfunction in organizations and as such they form the basis for intervention and change. In other words, they are part of a systematic approach to help organizations harness and use to their fullest extent all the metamotivational states. There is a sense in which one could say that this represents a systematic eclectic approach to organizational intervention in a way analogous to the eclectic approach to therapy that the theory provides at the individual level (chapter 14 in this volume).

CONCLUSION

This chapter has shown that reversal theory is relevant to a multitude of different areas of application in organizations. Although we have not looked at all these areas here, it should be clear that it is relevant to many topics from office design to career planning, from stress management to handling diversity, from coping with mergers to understanding the needs of the customer. Activity is already under way in relation to these and other topics. Furthermore, we would suggest that reversal theory is uniquely well placed to offer a framework for understanding the impact that technology and globalization are increasingly having on our working lives and also to suggest practical interventions that will benefit both the organization and the individual.

A number of key areas suggest themselves for further research within the theory. First, what is the nature of workforce commitment when long-term employment is declining? The reversal theory concept of the need for motivational variety and versatility suggests that it may be better seen in terms of the breadth of an individual's contribution rather than its length. Second, does the goal-oriented nature of much performance management lend itself to developing performance within the emerging reality of work— or does performance management need to become a broader concept based on some notion of building a "performance climate" that would accommodate all the motivational states? Finally, what can reversal theory show us about the meaning of work itself, and what are the implications of this for the social, educational, and economic policies through which society shapes its affairs and its future?

14

PSYCHOPATHOLOGY, THERAPY, AND COUNSELING

KATHRYN D. LAFRENIERE, DAVID M. LEDGERWOOD,
AND STEPHEN J. MURGATROYD

As described elsewhere in this book, reversal theory provides a powerful and effective framework for understanding both the dynamics of human emotions and the link between our understanding of such emotions and actions. It also provides a starting point for understanding basic presenting problems of clients who seek counseling and psychotherapy.

In this chapter we briefly review some of the research, case material, and analysis that has contributed to the development of a body of therapeutic practice associated with reversal theory and discuss some of the limitations of this work. In addition, we suggest some additional work that is needed to advance our understanding of how reversal theory can be used by therapists as a framework for decision making in a therapeutic relationship. It should be noted that reversal theory does not at this point provide particular intervention techniques. What it does is to provide a new way of framing the problems of diagnosis and of guiding the strategic decisions that have to be made in therapy.

The reversal theory approach to clinical psychology and psychiatry is a particularly ambitious one, because it involves a new way of understanding and of structuring the field that in many ways cuts across traditional category systems. The general lines of this structure emerge from Apter and Smith (1979a), Murgatroyd (1981a, 1981b), and Apter (1982a, chap. 11) and are developed in Apter (1989b, chap. 9; 1990a) and elsewhere. Murgatroyd (e.g., 1987a, 1987b, 1987c, 1988) has especially drawn out the implications for therapy and counseling that arise from this conceptual structure.

It is interesting to note, incidentally, that reversal theory itself was derived from the child guidance clinic, especially in a family therapy context (Apter & Smith, 1979a), and therefore clinical issues are close to the heart of the theory.

A NEW TAXONOMY FOR DIAGNOSIS

A reversal theory framework has been applied especially to the analysis of neurotic and personality disorders. The theory has not yet been applied in any systematic way to the analysis of psychosis, although in principle it would suggest that psychosis is likely to arise when the core structure of motivation itself (as described in the motivational matrix shown in chapter 1, Figure 1.1) breaks down. In the examples of psychopathology reviewed here, the core structure remains intact, but there are deficiencies in the way in which it operates or expresses itself. (In passing, we can note that Brown, 1993c, has argued that the switches involved in multiple personality disorder are not to be equated with the reversals of reversal theory.)

Apter (1989b, 1990a) suggested that there are two levels of analysis and that pathologies may arise at either level, or in some cases, at both of these levels at the same time.

Structural Disturbances

This category refers to the problems that occur across metamotivational modes, which derive from inadequacies in the mechanics of reversal. Structural disturbances can take two basic forms, that of inhibited reversal and that of inappropriate reversal.

In the case of *inhibited reversal*, the individual tends to be locked into one of the modes in a metamotivational mode pair and is unable to reverse between the two in the way that characterizes most individuals in the course of everyday life. Consequently, the individual who shows inhibited reversal will show extreme dominance in relation to one of a pair of metamotivational modes. For example, an individual may find it very difficult to reverse from the telic mode, with either mild consequences (being serious all the time and unable to ever "lighten up" and enjoy the moment) or more severe psychopathological results, such as experiencing chronic anxiety (in that high arousal is always experienced as anxiety rather than excitement). Murgatroyd and Apter (1984) described the case of David, age 37, whose anxiety disorder involved obsessive thoughts about dangers to himself. David appeared to be locked into the telic mode and spent most of his time in the pursuit of the goal of keeping himself safe, by checking things, washing himself repetitively, and recording all of his symptoms and feelings of ill health. His therapy was aimed at enabling him to reverse and spend some time in the paratelic mode. Scott (1986) writes about a woman trapped in the telic state after her husband left her.

Improved assessment techniques in reversal theory have made it easier to identify whether individuals are displaying the kinds of imbalances between states that would result from inhibited reversal. Notably, the Apter Motivational Style Profile (AMSP; Apter International, 1999a; see also chapter 3 in this volume) can be used in association with software that produces a narrative report drawing attention to such imbalances (as well as directing the respondent's attention to possible areas of inappropriate behavior within the states). The applicability of this instrument for self-development, especially in the work context, is described in chapter 13.

The second kind of structural disturbance involves what Apter has termed *inappropriate reversal* (Apter, 1989b). In this sense, the term *inappropriate* means to convey that the psychological event (in this case, the reversal) produces psychological distress, either for the individual or for others in the social environment, that could have been avoided. An individual who has a tendency to be in a given mode of a metamotivational mode pair at an inappropriate time exhibits this structural disturbance. The person who cannot seem to relax and enjoy himself on a long-awaited vacation and the individual who does not respond with appropriate seriousness to a crisis at work both display mild versions of this problem. More serious and pathological outcomes would include acute anxiety disorders and phobias, in which inappropriate reversals to an anxious telic state occur in response to environmental stimuli that most people would not typically perceive as being threatening.

Murgatroyd and Apter (1986) illustrated this kind of inappropriate reversal in the case of Sally, age 30, who received therapy for frequent anxiety attacks and depression (she had previously been diagnosed by a psychiatrist with agoraphobia). Although she was paratelic dominant, tending to display a preference for playfulness and spontaneity, she showed a pattern of high arousal avoidance that would be more characteristic of a telic-dominant person. Thus it appeared, paradoxically, that Sally preferred to seek satisfaction of the paratelic state without the experience of high arousal. The reason for this, which emerged in the course of therapy, was that situations characterized by heightened felt arousal (e.g., being sexually attracted to someone, shopping in crowded stores, watching an exciting television program) would often precipitate her panic attacks. In other words, while in the paratelic mode she would reverse inappropriately to the telic mode in situations in which she should have been able to experience high arousal as nonthreatening and even pleasurable. This reversal occurred because the sudden increase of arousal in itself was experienced by her as threatening. In the subsequent telic mode she would then be anxious that she would become more anxious, this in turn making her more anxious again, in an ever-tightening vicious circle, thus displaying the classic pattern of a build-up to a full anxiety attack. This meant that she would become even more fearful of arousal and therefore even more likely to respond with a reversal to the telic state in the future. In this way, these inappropriate reversals grew to be habitual, so that it became almost inevitable that she would experience an acute anxiety attack whenever she started to feel any excitement. For this reason she avoided all situations that might be stimulating. But, because she was paratelic dominant, this meant that she was often bored and miserable.

For some individuals, reversals may be fairly easily accomplished in one direction (e.g., telic to paratelic) but involve more difficulty in reversing in the opposite direction (paratelic to telic). Blackmore and Murgatroyd (1980) described the case of Anne, age 6, who showed serious behavioral problems at school, for whom any source of frustration would tend to trigger a switch from a "work state" (telic mode) to a "disrupt state" (paratelic mode), when she would lash out physically or verbally toward the teacher or her classmates. Anne appeared to be paratelic dominant, based on her general absence of goal-directed activity and the spontaneity of most of her actions, and she had considerable difficulty regulating her own behavior. When in the paratelic state, she seemed to require a very high level of arousal and to be generally unsuccessful in satisfying this need through normal and acceptable means. She would switch easily from her work state to her disruptive state when frustrated, which would presumably heighten her experience of felt arousal. Typical strategies used by her teacher to calm her (i.e., to reduce her arousal) would only reinforce her frustration, and she had a great deal of trouble returning to a work state (telic mode). Blackmore and Murgatroyd suggested that her behavioral problems reflected "a pathological inability to regulate reversal" (p. 38).

Inappropriate Strategies

The second level of analysis refers to problems that occur within a particular metamotivational mode, in trying to achieve satisfaction, or to avoid dissatisfactions peculiar to that mode. Apter (1989b, 1990a) identified three kinds of inappropriate strategies: those that are functionally inappropriate, temporally inappropriate, and socially inappropriate.

In using *functionally inappropriate* strategies, the individual is likely to be in appropriate modes at appropriate times, but the strategies used within that mode are likely to achieve a different, or even opposite, effect than what was actually intended. That is, the strategies tend to be ineffective or counterproductive to achieving the satisfaction specifically sought within a particular mode. In the telic mode, for example, a person might become so involved in constructing increasingly complex planning schemes that he or she would actually reduce the opportunities for achievement that are linked to satisfaction in this mode. Similarly, an individual in the paratelic mode might use the same unimaginative strategies repeatedly, in a misguided attempt to achieve excitement, and find that they produce boredom instead (Apter, 1989b).

The clinical work of Braman (1988, 1995) on oppositional children provides a further example of the use of functionally inappropriate or counterproductive strategies within a mode. Braman has described the behavior of this type of child as involving telic self-negativism. According to Braman's observations, the parents of this type of child tend to hold very high expectations for their child's achievement, especially at school. The child comes to realize that displays of ability and intelligence will only exacerbate the parents' drive for them to succeed and will increase the pressure that is placed on them. Consequently, the oppositional child will disguise his or her own ability, refuse to work hard, and generally act in ways to defeat his or her own accomplishments. Although these strategies may be superficially successful to the child at first, in that they deflect parental expectations of high achievement, they are self-defeating over time and run counter to the desire for achievement that these children actually tend to possess. The negativism that is initially directed toward parents and teachers is ultimately directed toward themselves and can lead to habitual self-defeating behavior and a lifelong pattern of underachievement. (For a more detailed treatment of rebelliousness and its problems, see chapter 9 in this volume.)

A second category of inappropriate strategies includes those that are *temporally inappropriate*. This is the case when strategies used within a particular mode are immediately effective in bringing pleasure, relief, or satisfaction and in this sense are functional but have long-term consequences that are negative. Here, the distress that the individual is avoiding in the present is likely to be associated with the presence of greater difficulties in the future that are often made worse by their prolongation. Research on compulsive gamblers (e.g., Anderson & Brown, 1984; Brown, 1988) provides a good illustration of such temporally inappropriate strategies. According to these investigators, gamblers tend to be in the paratelic mode when they play, and as a result, they focus on their short-term excitement and do not think of the long-term consequences of losing significant sums of money. Heavy losses do tend to trigger a reversal to the telic state in compulsive gamblers; however, they tend to continue to play, both in an attempt to recoup their money and to try to attain the "high" or rush that comes with winning again. This means that they will continue to gamble in both the paratelic mode (for the immediate thrill) and in the telic mode (to work to attain higher rewards in the future) and will not see a reason to stop gambling until they ultimately run out of resources. By the time they experience the distress that results from not being able to continue their quest for excitement, it is too late, and the full impact of their losses becomes clear to them. (See also chapter 8 on addiction in this volume.)

Socially inappropriate strategies involve an individual attaining satisfaction inherent to a particular metamotivational mode, but doing so in such a way as to cause some level of difficulty for other people (Apter, 1989b, 1990a). Reversal theory analyses have been applied to socially inappropriate strategies in a number of contexts, including soccer hooliganism (Kerr, 1988c, 1994), in which socially inappropriate behavior results from attempts to achieve the thrill of paratelic high arousal and negativistic defiance and sadistic fantasy leading to actual aggression (Thomas-Peter, 1993b). More subtle forms of socially inappropriate strategies are frequently observed in family therapy (Apter, 1982a; Apter & Smith, 1979a), in which a child tests the parents to see which negative behaviors (swearing, refusing to eat, etc.) will produce the most dramatic and exciting effects. In each of these cases, the individual achieves satisfaction within the paratelic mode (as well as the negativistic mode) but in doing so causes distress to other people.

Murgatroyd (1990, 1993a) described the case of Justin, age 29, who made obscene telephone calls to achieve satisfaction within particular metamotivational modes. As described by Murgatroyd, Justin's case involved a great deal of metamotivational complexity. Justin was an executive who was married and successful and who tended to be generally in the telic, conformist, mastery, and autic states in his daily life. His marriage was described as being based on common interests and providing "a great deal of pleasure and fulfillment, but not too much excitement or disagreement" (Murgatroyd, 1990, p. 373). To achieve the excitement he seemed to lack, he had made a number of obscene telephone calls to women he did not know. He would view pornography and masturbate while making the telephone calls, and he found the whole experience to be very exciting, particularly when the women reacted by crying or complying with his demands to repeat certain words he said. After making the telephone calls, however, he would experience tremendous remorse, anxiety about being caught and punished, and great sympathy for the women he had just victimized. In reversal theory terms, his metamotivational modes during the telephone call were paratelic, mastery, negativistic, and alloic, and his socially inappropriate actions would serve to intensify the experience of achieving satisfaction in each of these modes. After the telephone calls, he would reverse to telic, sympathy, conformity, and autic states, in which his remorse, anxiety, and concern for the women would cause great distress for him. The focus of his therapy was guided by this reversal theory analysis and was aimed at helping him achieve satisfaction in each of these metamotivational modes in ways that were safe, legal, and socially appropriate. He and his wife were then able to explore more exciting ways of expressing sexuality within their marriage, and he no longer needed to engage in socially inappropriate methods for experiencing excitement.

UNDERSTANDING PSYCHOPATHOLOGY

The taxonomy described in the previous section provides a broad framework from which many psychiatric diagnoses (at least in the area of neuroses and personality disorders) can be viewed within the context of a reversal theory analysis. In this section, a number of traditional psychiatric diagnostic categories are discussed in reversal theory terms. Each of these involves some of the five fundamental structures (i.e., the two structural disturbances and the three inappropriate strategies) outlined above, acting solely or in combination.

Chronic Anxiety

Apter (1982a, 1989b) suggested that chronic anxiety generally reflects inhibited reversal, in which the person seems to be trapped in the telic state and therefore experiences high arousal as anxiety rather than excitement. This experience can be exacerbated by functionally inappropriate strategies that fail to reduce the high levels of arousal. If the person is subject to regularly experiencing very high levels of arousal (due to temperamental, metabolic, cognitive, or environmental reasons) and is unable to switch easily to the paratelic mode, chronic anxiety is the likely result (Apter, 1982a).

Some individuals experience high arousal more frequently due to individual features of their temperament that make them higher in *arousability* or resting level of cortical arousal. A number of theories of personality, including those of individual differences in reactivity, strength of the nervous system, and stimulus-intensity reducing and augmenting all posit individual differences in arousability and suggest that arousal avoidance will tend to occur as a result of one's natural tendency to experience greater levels of arousal (Kohn, 1987). Unlike these other theories, reversal theory distinguishes between arousability and arousal preference, where arousal avoidance is likely only in conjunction with the telic state. Reversal theory further suggests, therefore, that anxiety problems arise where there is both high arousability and a tendency to be in the telic state. In a study of the relationship between arousability and telic dominance, Lafreniere, Gillies, Cowles, and Toner (1993) hypothesized that telic dominance would be orthogonal to arousability and that individuals who were high in both telic dominance and arousability would be characterized by high levels of state and trait anxiety. They administered questionnaire measures of arousability, telic dominance (the Telic Dominance Scale; TDS; Murgatroyd, Rushton, Apter, & Ray, 1978), anxiety, and depression to 79 undergraduate university students. Their results indicated that both telic dominance and serious-mindedness were indeed found to be orthogonal to the arousability measures. Individuals who were high in both serious-mindedness and arousability showed the highest levels of trait (but not state) anxiety. In addition, those who were high in telic dominance and arousability manifested the highest levels of depression. These results suggest that trait anxiety and depression might be an outcome for telic-dominant individuals who are subject to experiencing high arousal due to their temperamental levels of arousability and that telic dominance and arousability should be considered in combination to predict psychopathology, not arousability alone.

A reversal theory perspective would suggest that chronic anxiety can be dealt with in one of two ways (Apter, 1982a). The patient can be encouraged to find ways to lower his or her arousal or avoid arousal being raised. This is the focus of many conventional approaches in which relaxation techniques are taught to anxiety patients. The second way would involve facilitating a reversal to the paratelic state if the arousal becomes unpleasantly high, so that the high arousal can be experienced as excitement rather than as anxiety.

Phobia

According to Apter (1982a, 1989b), phobias result from reversing inappropriately to the telic state in response to a stimulus that most people would regard as neutral or benign and experiencing unnecessary anxiety as a result. This might be further complicated by feeling anxious about the anxiety that is experienced (a functionally inappropriate strategy), which can be a vicious circle that eventuates in a full-scale panic attack. We saw an example of this above in the case of Sally (Murgatroyd & Apter, 1986). As with chronic anxiety, the problem of phobias can be approached by either attempting to lower the arousal that is experienced in response to the phobic stimulus or situation or by attempting to induce a reversal to the paratelic state. In the paratelic state, the arousal experienced in relation to the phobic situation will be experienced as excitement or as "fear" that is contained and framed in a safe manner without significant consequences for the individual (like the fear that we may experience when viewing a horror movie; Apter, 1982a).

Depression

Apter (1990a) has suggested that depression results from inhibited reversal, or being "stuck" in one mode or another, and then using strategies that are functionally (and perhaps temporally) inappropriate to achieve satisfaction and to avoid dissatisfaction in that mode: Feelings of helplessness and depression are the likely result. Apter (1982a) identified four specific subtypes of depression, and these are outlined in Murgatroyd (1987c) as follows:

1. *anxiety depression*, in which depressive experiences are layered with anxiety
2. *apathy depression*, in which the person is unable to produce arousal or activate an affective state other than depression and lethargy
3. *overexcitement depression*, which occurs rarely in the case of mania when the person feels unable to escape from a state of chronic overexcitement and experiences depression along with this feeling
4. *boredom depression*, in which the person is unable to attain either the excitement or level of activation he or she desires (Murgatroyd, 1987c, p. 303).

Murgatroyd (1987c) noted that the first two of these occur because the individual is "locked into" the telic mode. They differ from each other in that anxiety depression is characterized by excessive arousal occurring in the telic mode from which the person cannot escape by either reducing the arousal or reversing into the paratelic state, whereas in apathy depression, there is so little arousal that the person lacks the energy to pursue essential goals to which experience in the telic state is oriented. The third and fourth of these types occur within the paratelic mode, when the affective and arousal needs of this mode are not satisfied. In overexcitement depression, inhibited reversal from the paratelic mode suggests that the person is trapped in an excitement-seeking state and subject to being overwhelmed by overly intense sensations that cannot be avoided. In boredom depression, which is characterized by low arousal, the person is locked into the paratelic mode and yet lacks the intensity of experience that is necessary for satisfaction within this mode.

Apter (1989b) developed this whole analysis a little further by suggesting that there may be eight different basic types of depression, one associated with each metamotivational state. In other words, depression arises in situations in which one feels helpless about the possibility of attaining the satisfaction defined by that state or state combination. Thus, autic sympathy depression would arise where one felt that one was unlovable, negativistic depression where one felt trapped and unable ever to break free of certain constraints, and so on. Because the states come in opposites, this means that there are opposite types of depression, too. This also implies that a therapeutic intervention that worked for one type of depression might in fact be counterproductive for the opposite kind.

Murgatroyd (1987c) illustrated a reversal theory approach to the treatment of depression in the case of Gill, age 28, who was employed in retail management and suffered from apathy depression, according to the typology outlined above. Gill was highly telic dominant, and her descriptions of her experiences were characterized by extremely low arousal. Her behavior reflected low energy, going through the motions of everyday life and disengagement from social relationships. Affectively, she described herself as incapable of experiencing excitement and pleasure. She did not appear to be bored or seeking to raise her level of arousal; on the contrary, she was extreme in her arousal avoidance and sought to maintain her low arousal, but expected that she could achieve satisfaction at that level. Based on this information, her depression was categorized by Murgatroyd as apathy depression rather than as boredom depression. While boredom depression is felt to occur in the paratelic state and to involve dissatisfaction through restlessness, apathy depression originates in the telic state and involves a lack of both energy and desire to change things.

Murgatroyd's (1987c) treatment goals for Gill were to help her to see her depression in motivational terms, to encourage her to identify her motivational experiences and their structure, and to facilitate a change in how she experienced her motivation and actions. These goals were directed toward having Gill gain insight into her experience and to increase her level of arousal.

A number of techniques were used to accomplish these goals, including homework assignments to keep a visual diary of her experience between appointments, and attempts to increase her arousal through having her respond to a challenge, as well as attempts to elicit anger. Murgatroyd also noted that Gill's diary material reflected a high degree of *self-negativism*. Through the use of dramatized paradoxical intention, the therapist was able to reduce this negativism directed toward the self, and to increase Gill's arousal, and eventually her depression abated. Thus, reversal theory's typology of depression, which focuses on the interaction of motivation (experienced arousal) and metamotivational mode, was instrumental in guiding an appropriate course of therapeutic intervention.

Delinquency

Reversal theory suggests that delinquency also arises from inhibited reversal, in this case being caught in the paratelic mode (Apter, 1990a). The delinquent individual continually seeks greater excitement and stimulation and tends to spend a great deal of time in the negativistic and mastery modes. Socially (and sometimes temporally) inappropriate strategies are then used to obtain satisfaction within these modes, giving rise to delinquent acts such as vandalism and hooliganism (Kerr, 1994).

Bowers (1985, 1988) compared the TDS scores of adolescent boys who were delinquent (i.e., had experiences with the criminal justice system) with those who were identified as disruptive at school (i.e., showed behavior problems in the classroom), as well as with a control group of boys who did not present either type of problem. His findings lent support to the idea that delinquency tends to be a paratelic phenomenon. The delinquent group of boys scored significantly lower in telic dominance than did either the disruptive group or the control group, and boys in the disruptive group were also less telic dominant than the control group. The delinquent group also differed significantly from both of the other groups on planning orientation and from the control group on arousal avoidance. Interestingly, the serious-mindedness scale did not discriminate significantly between the three groups. Bowers concluded that deterrent strategies aimed at reducing delinquency in youth are probably limited in their effectiveness in that they presume that delinquent acts are committed in a planned, goal-oriented fashion, an assumption not borne out by his results. Instead, he suggested that interventions should focus on helping adolescents who are prone to delinquency develop effective strategies for coping with their low felt arousal, so that their boredom and restlessness does not lead them to engage in criminal acts. Similar conclusions have been reached by Jones (1981) based on his observations of counselor–delinquent interactions in approved schools in the United Kingdom.

Psychopathy

Although at first glance psychopathy would appear to be an adult version of delinquency, and therefore seen as arising from inhibited reversal, the work of Thomas-Peter and colleagues (Thomas-Peter, 1988, 1993b; Thomas-Peter & McDonagh, 1988) suggests that psychopathy does not reflect inhibited reversal from the paratelic mode. In one study (Thomas-Peter & McDonagh, 1988), the hypothesis that psychopaths would tend to score lower on telic dominance (i.e., be more paratelic dominant) than control participants was tested using the TDS. Their results indicated an opposite trend where the broad group of psychopaths (as medically and legally defined) tested as more telic dominant than the control group. When the experimental group was further subdivided into the three categories of primary and secondary psychopaths (roughly, extraverted and introverted psychopaths respectively) and nonpsychopathic offenders, the primary and secondary psychopaths were found to be more paratelic dominant than the nonpsychopathic offenders. There was no significant difference in telic dominance between psychopathic and normal control individuals, and therefore the hypothesis of psychopaths being trapped in the paratelic mode was not supported.

Later work by Thomas-Peter (1993a) investigated the role of negativism. In this study, offenders with personality disorders, nonincarcerated offenders, and a control group completed the Negativism Dominance Scale (NDS; McDermott & Apter, 1988; see chapters 3 and 9 in this volume) along with some other tests. The data were analyzed in a number of ways. Taken as a whole, the results supported the finding that both primary and secondary psychopaths were more negativistic dominant than other offenders and the control participants. (Thomas-Peter suggested, among other things, that his data cast doubt on the traditional distinction between primary and secondary psychopaths.) This implies that if psychopathy is a function of inhibited reversal then this inhibition is on the negativism–conformity as well as the telic–paratelic dimension. Thomas-Peter (1996) went on to argue, on the basis of these data and case studies, that the dominant modes of the psychopath are the telic, negativistic, and autic modes.

Even more interestingly, Thomas-Peter (1996) explained that the difference between psychopaths and normal people who display similar patterns of dominance is that the hypothetical curves representing the relationship between hedonic tone and felt arousal and felt transactional outcome (as shown in Figure 2.2 in chapter 2) take on a different shape from those of normal people. Specifically, he suggested that the curves bow inward rather than outward so that they cross at a point which is low rather than high in hedonic tone. (The shape of the two curves would be the same as taking any one of the hypothetical graphs in Figure 2.2 and turning it upside down.) This also means that at low levels of arousal and at the loss end of the felt transactional outcome dimension, it takes relatively large changes in those variables to make much difference to the improvement of hedonic tone. As Thomas-Peter described it, "The psychopath has an abnormality of construction, or elasticity, in the structure of . . .emotions. The result is that psychopaths are quick to experience negative emotion and slow to experience positive emotion" (p. 33).

Obsessionality

In contrast to the paratelic-dominant orientation that characterizes delinquency, the obsessional personality type reflects high telic dominance. Here, the emphasis is on seriousness, organization, rigidity, cleanliness, and doing things properly. For the obsessional individual, the accomplishment of each of these features becomes a goal in itself (Apter, 1982a). Ironically, this rigid adherence to goals, deadlines, and self-imposed rules may well be counterproductive to the accomplishment of more significant life goals. In reversal theory terms, this represents a functionally inappropriate strategy. In addition, according to Apter (1982a), obsessionality reflects inappropriate reversal, with the telic state being over-facilitated and the paratelic state underfacilitated. Thus, paratelic to telic reversals would be much more readily accomplished than telic to paratelic ones.

The work of Fontana (1978, 1981a) examined the distinction between the obsessive personality (characterized by obsessional traits) and the obsessive neurotic (characterized by obsessional symptoms). Fontana hypothesized that the obsessional personality would show the pattern outlined above, which reflects high telic dominance and difficulty in reversing to the paratelic state. In contrast, the obsessive neurotic was expected to display frequent reversals between telic and paratelic states, as reflective of neurotic ambivalence. Thus, reversals would be overinhibited in the case of the obsessional personality but underinhibited for the obsessive neurotic. Fontana tested these predictions by administering an inventory of obsessional traits and obsessional symptoms to 84 college lecturers. He reasoned that obsessional traits should correlate positively with telic dominance on the TDS and its subscales, but that obsessional symptoms should correlate with neither telic dominance nor any of its subscales. His findings demonstrated clear-cut support for each of these predictions, and these findings are consistent with the reversal theory conceptualization of obsessionality as resulting from inappropriate reversal.

Sexual Dysfunction

Sexual dysfunction (e.g., erectile dysfunction, premature ejaculation, anorgasmia, dyspareunia) is viewed in reversal theory as a case of inappropriate reversal (Apter & Smith, 1978). Because sexual pleasure involves being in the here and now and enjoying the experience of high arousal that precedes and accompanies orgasm, it is clearly a paratelic phenomenon (Apter, 1982a). Although high arousal is experienced as excitement in the paratelic mode, a sudden and inappropriate reversal to the telic mode will recast the high arousal as anxiety, and sexual responsiveness will be inhibited.

Apter (1989b) noted that the reversal theory approach differs from the common conceptualization that anxiety inhibits sexual excitement, in the case of sexual dysfunction. Instead, reversal theory would predict that anxiety is how the sexual excitement is experienced, when one is in the "wrong" mode after an inappropriate reversal has occurred. The reversal theory approach would also serve to explain why the person may feel greatly excited right before the dysfunctional response occurs and why the greater the excitement, the greater the anxiety and subsequent disruption to the sexual behavior.

Frey (1991) outlined three factors that may precipitate an inappropriate reversal in the context of a sexual encounter. One is the presence of a threat, such as getting caught or being interrupted, getting pregnant, having one's self-esteem damaged by not being able to prove oneself, losing control, or being vulnerable. A second cause of dysfunctional reversals in this context is a focus on goal orientation. A number of goals may be superimposed on the sexual situation, including trying to conceive, trying to achieve simultaneous orgasms or multiple orgasms, or trying to outperform a partner's former lovers. Placing emphasis on goals, rather than enjoyment of present experience, is likely to facilitate a reversal to the telic mode. A third trigger for inappropriate reversals comes from a sense of obligation during sexual involvement, in which one person is less motivated toward the sexual encounter or the activities it involves and is primarily acting to accommodate their partner.

The reversal theory approach has important treatment implications for sexual dysfunction (Frey, 1991). Because high arousal is intrinsic to sexual experience and enjoyment, relaxation techniques to lower arousal are not appropriate. Instead, attempts to reduce the individuals' perceptions of threat, goal-directedness, and obligation would be instrumental in helping them remain in the paratelic mode during sexual experiences.

Sexual Perversion

Various types of "sexual perversion" (e.g., voyeurism, exhibitionism, sadomasochism, and various paraphilias) are generally seen as socially inappropriate ways of satisfying the need for increased excitement in the paratelic mode (Apter, 1990a; Apter & Smith, 1978). Although many people use different techniques to achieve high levels of sexual arousal in the paratelic mode, some individuals use techniques that fall outside the bounds of normal sexual behavior. Frey (1991) proposed that the desire for non-normative or extreme sexual techniques can occur for a number of reasons:

1. If the individual habituates too quickly to stimuli, he or she will continually pursue new and extreme sexual strategies.
2. For some individuals, sexual stimulation on its own is unable to achieve the desired level of arousal.
3. The individual may require extraordinarily high levels of arousal during sexual experiences.

When normal sexual behaviors are insufficient to fulfill these needs, the person may look to new and more unusual sources of stimulation to achieve an adequate level of arousal (Apter, 1982a).

In his pursuit of achieving ever greater levels of excitement, the sexual extremist may place himself and others at psychological or physical risk. In such cases, it is likely that the mastery mode (reflected in the need to dominate others) and the negativistic mode (the enjoyment of breaking taboos) are highly involved, in addition to the paratelic mode (Apter, 1990a; Apter & Smith, 1979a). Strategies that are socially inappropriate (even if functionally appropriate) are used to achieve satisfactions inherent to each of these modes. An extreme version of this would be rape (Apter, 1992, chap. 10; Apter & Smith, 1987). (See also chapter 11 of this volume, on risk-taking, which deals with irresponsible sexual behavior.)

INTERPERSONAL PROBLEMS

Psychological problems can result from social interactions that are characterized by incompatible modes, dominances, and strategies of the people involved. When people interact frequently and intensively with others (e.g., with family members), such incompatibilities can lead to the development of psychopathology (Apter, 1990a). Apter and Smith (1979a) have described numerous examples of the consequences of incompatibilities arising from the typically paratelic orientation of the child and the parent's telic orientation. Children will naturally seek to increase arousal in the paratelic mode, often by engaging in noisy, boisterous activity that can be experienced as disruptive by the parent. If the parent is in the telic state and is preoccupied by important goals, this kind of disruption will give rise to stress and anxiety on the part of the parent. In turn, if the parent tries to prevent the child's excitement seeking when they are in the paratelic state, the child is likely to become bored and restless and will seek other (and perhaps more troublesome) ways of achieving their need for high arousal.

Apter and Smith (1979a) also described the overparatelic child, who is "generally wild, excitable and disruptive" (p. 93). This child is extreme in his or her pursuit of excitement, often engaging in thrill-seeking activities that are potentially dangerous. In addition, the overparatelic child may pursue excitement by doing things to raise the arousal level of the entire family, such as engaging in temper tantrums or provoking conflict between the parents. This behavior is likely to be received in the telic mode by the parents, who are concerned with the consequences of their child's actions and the far-reaching goals of effective parenting. The high arousal provoked by the child's actions, then, will be experienced as anxiety by the parent.

Problems can develop not only through such state-incompatibilities and the misunderstandings that can arise from them, but also from people in a relationship using inappropriate strategies in their interactions. Wilson and Wilson (1998) have explored a variety of these issues through a series of case histories involving couples in marital therapy. Thus, some problems arise from inappropriate ways of behaving in the mastery state in a relationship. These include instrumental anger (i.e., blaming), the attempt to dominate in a manipulative way, promiscuity to achieve self-validation, and (in conjunction with the alloic state) willingness to be a scapegoat. Other problems arise from inappropriate ways of being in the paratelic state (Wilson & Wilson, 1999), especially those that involve certain ways of excitement seeking through fantasizing and the acting out of such fantasies. For example, in one couple described in their paper, the husband encourages his wife to have sex with other men. As Wilson and Wilson pointed out, the offense mechanisms that seem to be disclosed in the case histories they report are as distorting and problematic as classic Freudian defense mechanisms. Wilson and Wilson (1996) described a number of common ways of being in each metamotivational state in a negative way (as well as a positive way). They also pointed out (Wilson & Wilson, 1997) that therapists themselves are also subject to these negative ways of behaving, and therefore relationship problems can arise between a therapist and his or her clients that may have some resemblance to those that arise within couples.

Often problems in families involve both incompatible states and inappropriate behaviors resulting in complex systems of maladjustment. Murgatroyd and Apter (1984) illustrated a case of interpersonal problems arising in a family situation in the case of Jake, age 12, who expressed fears about school and manifested a variety of illnesses (which is likely to occur in the telic mode). Jake's mother attempted to protect him, especially from his father, who came across as threatening. Jake's father and sister, who are both paratelic dominant, laughed at the mother's concern and seemed to take pleasure out of the high arousal present in the conflict situation. They accused the mother of babying Jake, whose telic anxiety was further reinforced by this characterization. The mother, like Jake, manifested a physical (and telic) response to these confrontations: She eventually became ill and depressed and required hospitalization. While the mother was hospitalized, the father ran the home in a much more paratelic fashion, taking more time for leisure activities than was the case when the mother was in charge. Jake's symptoms of ill health and telic anxiety began to recede, and he subsequently returned to school. When the mother recovered and resumed the management of the household, the father became bored, restless, and then depressed, and he began to drink and smoke more (as a response to the lack of fit between his paratelic dominance and the return to a telic environment). The father became argumentative with all the members of the family, and this served to consolidate the telic state of the mother and bring about a reversal back to the telic state for Jake. At this point, Jake began to show anxiety about school and an increase in physical ailments again, effectively starting the maladaptive cycle once more. Murgatroyd and Apter (1984) noted that the case of Jake shows how "psychological disturbance in members of a family can be perpetuated by means of a complex interaction between their operative modes at different times, mode dominance, cognitive appraisal and social reinforcements and punishments" (p. 400).

AN APPROACH TO ECLECTIC PSYCHOTHERAPY

Some of the case histories described in the sections above show examples of a reversal theory approach to therapy in action (e.g., those from Murgatroyd, 1987c, 1990, 1993a; Murgatroyd & Apter, 1984, 1986; Wilson & Wilson, 1998, 1999). The therapeutic approaches to these cases illustrate the utility of applying a reversal theory perspective to clinical intervention. Apter (1990a) pointed out that reversal theory provides a conceptual framework that permits evaluation of the nature of the problem, the goals of therapy, and the means for achieving these goals, rather than providing specific intervention techniques per se. In other words, reversal theory provides a "framework for eclectic psychotherapy" (Murgatroyd, 1988; Murgatroyd & Apter, 1984, 1986).

Within the framework suggested by reversal theory, the individual therapist can select from a range of techniques and therapeutic orientations to accomplish the goals of the intervention. In other words, reversal theory provides a systematic framework for making decisions about both strategic goals of therapy and concrete practical intervention tactics. For example, a therapist treating someone suffering from chronic anxiety might first decide that the strategic aim of therapy should be to attempt to facilitate more frequent reversals to the paratelic mode rather than to lower levels of arousal. To accomplish this purpose, he or she might then choose from a variety of more specific tactics. These might include the use of Gestalt therapy to release the "blocked excitement" of anxiety, Frankl's technique of paradoxical intention, or rational–emotive therapy techniques aimed at having clients reinterpret their bodily states so that high arousal comes to be experienced as stimulating, rather than threatening (Apter, 1982a, 1990a). Apter (1990b) has also indicated that encouraging clients to take part in sporting activities can serve the dual purposes of facilitating reversals to the paratelic mode (where anxiety will be experienced as excitement, and threats will be perceived as challenges) and helping to break the fixed pattern of being stuck in the telic mode. A similar effect can be achieved through the use of humor, according to Murgatroyd (1987d, 1991), where creating a paratelic climate in therapy, and highlighting incongruities that can elicit a laugh or smile, can be used by the therapist to help move a client who is trapped in the telic mode.

Should a therapist decide that the main strategic level of intervention with a particular person should be that of dealing with inappropriate strategies within a particular mode, rather than attempting to facilitate mode changing, then again he or she would be able to choose between a variety of different tactics, including the use of behavior modification, cognitive–behavior therapy, or general counseling advice (Apter, 1990a). In addition, humor could be used to help identify socially inappropriate strategies or to point out the tension and contradiction between immediate and future needs to clients who use temporally inappropriate strategies (Murgatroyd, 1987d).

Applying reversal theory to therapeutic decision making has a number of implications, some of which are outlined in Apter (1990a):

1. It is essential for the therapist to know as much as possible about how the client is experiencing a problem, from the reference point of the client. This will permit an examination of how the metamotivational modes are operating for the client and whether the problem involves structural disturbance or inappropriate strategies.

2. If the metamotivational underpinnings of the problem are not clearly understood by the therapist, therapy is likely to be ineffectual and may well be counterproductive. For example, as described in a preceding section, reversal theory outlines different kinds of depression, which arise from different interactions of experienced arousal and metamotivational mode. If an individual is suffering from boredom depression, attempts to increase arousal will be beneficial, but if the depression is experienced in the telic mode as anxiety depression, increasing the levels of arousal will be detrimental.

3. The therapist should be prepared to make strategic decisions involving a choice of different approaches to achieve the same goal. Thus, as we have seen, in attempting to address the problem of a telic-dominant client's anxiety, for example, the therapist is faced with a choice of whether to teach the client methods of reducing arousal in the anxiety-provoking situation or to facilitate a reduction in the client's telic dominance by encouraging more frequent reversals to the paratelic mode (e.g., by the use of humor or sport). An advantage of reversal theory's approach to clinical intervention is that there are always strategic alternatives, and if one approach is initially unsuccessful, new strategies (as well as new tactics) can be used to achieve the same end. In any case, reversal theory helps the therapist to stand back and ask some basic questions about the aims of therapy in relation to particular clients— questions that often go by default.

4. Combining different tactics can be self-defeating if one fails to consider the metamotivational complexity inherent in the reversal theory framework. Different approaches to treating sexual dysfunction might entail trying to reduce arousal (because it is experienced as telic anxiety) or attempting to facili-

tate a reversal to the paratelic mode. The combined effects of these two tactics would be ineffective though, leading to the frustrating consequence of paratelic low arousal.

5. It is instructive to know which metamotivational modes the client is in during therapy sessions, so that these can be used to maximum therapeutic advantage. Clients who are in a paratelic state will be less receptive to attempts to have them explore the serious and long-term consequences of their present behaviors, and clients in a telic state may be unable to detach themselves sufficiently from their problems to see creative and novel solutions. Murgatroyd (1987d, 1991) has suggested that the use of humor to achieve client reversals to the paratelic mode can be especially beneficial in therapy, creating the detachment and spontaneity—the "protective frame"—that is most conducive to creative problem-solving. Apter (1991d) has suggested that hypnosis has the same function of putting people into the paratelic state, in which they can enjoy playing a kind of narrative–fantasy game at the behest of the hypnotist.

6. Therapeutic interventions guided by reversal theory can teach clients to engage in appropriate telic–paratelic reversals, which will then enhance their ability to integrate appropriate information and develop increasing skill and flexibility. Van der Molen (1985, 1986b) has referred to this as a "positive learning spiral." Following Van der Molen's approach to learning, Apter (1990b, 1992) recommended that paratelic dominant individuals who might otherwise engage in unhealthy or risky behaviors be taught open-ended learning strategies that will expand the range of their experiences and skills, rather than limiting them. This can be achieved through encouraging a paratelic-dominant person to master the skills involved in playing a particular sport, for example.

7. A reversal theory approach to assessment and diagnosis can be based on a number of different strategies for gathering information from the client. Some of these are suggested below:

   ▪ *Observation*—some of the structural disturbances and inappropriate strategies are readily observable during the course of a normal therapeutic session. For example, in the case of inappropriate reversal, basic observations made during a session can be checked by asking, "How would you describe your feelings about anxiety or excitement at this time?" (telic–paratelic) or "What do you feel about others versus yourself right now?" (allocentric–autocentric), thus providing an opportunity for clinical observation with self-accounts.

- *Self-report*—the individual is asked to report on situations in terms of the model of reversal theory (following training of the client in the theory). We might note in passing that simply having the ability to talk about their problems in terms of a helpful new language has a therapeutic value in itself, because it helps the client to feel that he or she is coming into greater control of what is happening (Apter & Smith, 1978).
- *Questionnaires*—information may be gained from the use of relevant tests and questionnaires of the kind described in chapter 3. The Apter Motivational Style Profile (Apter International, 1999a) may be especially helpful here, because it deals with all the pairs of states in a single instrument.
- *Diary Keeping*—the client is introduced to the key elements of reversal theory through some brief examples and is provided with a chart to record how they feel at certain key times, either preplanned as diary times or triggered by a pager. They may even respond directly on a hand-held computer (as, for example, in some of the studies described in chapter 7 on smoking cessation). The client may be asked to respond to a simple direct request to indicate which state they are in, or, for instance, an instruction to signify a color that has been pre-arranged as an indicator of a particular state (see Walters, Apter, & Svebak, 1982).
- *Situation Analysis*—the client is asked to recount in detail key situations that they regard as significant in terms of how they understand their presenting problem. In respect of each of these situations, the therapist interrogates the client about their psychological state before and during the situation, determining in this way the pattern of reversals that occurred. The therapist can also explore with the client the behavior that they displayed in each case, both before and during the time that the problem arose.
- *Simulation*—the therapist creates situations in which she or he can test the assumptions being made about the client's reversal patterns in "safe," guided simulations meant to reproduce the basic elements of the client's presenting problems. For example, if the client is unable to experience sexual arousal when presented with sexual images or cannot reverse from an anxious state to an excitement state when presented

with highly humorous situations, then the nature of the reversal pattern can be observed directly. Ethical caution needs to be exercised as to the nature and intensity of these simulations. Fontana, in the next chapter (15) explores simulation further in relation to the powerful technique of drama-therapy (Fontana & Valente, 1993a, 1993b, 1997).

The need to consider metamotivational complexity, structural distur-bances, and inappropriate strategies has been argued in relation to a number of specific treatment contexts, including the treatment of criminal behavior and psychopathy (Apter & Smith, 1987; Thomas-Peter, 1993b), educational psychology (Seldon, 1980), family therapy (Apter & Smith, 1979a), marital therapy (Wilson & Wilson, 1998, 1999), and crisis counseling (Murgatroyd, 1981a, 1981b). In each case, the limitations of therapeutic approaches that fail to recognize this complexity are pointed out and suggestions for incorporating a reversal theory framework are made. Apter (1982a) indicated that a reversal theory approach should be viewed as complementary to a variety of existing therapeutic approaches rather than as a treatment alterna-tive that precludes the use of other approaches. In other words, reversal theory's contribution to therapy is to provide a "framework for eclecticism" (p. 264).

Commentary in response to Murgatroyd's (1987c) account of the case of Gill (described in the section on depression above) provides some valuable insights into how the psychotherapeutic community might evaluate the strengths and weaknesses of reversal theory. In general, the eclectic approach it offers is seen as a strength: Hart (1987) commented that "the therapist managed to blend a variety of techniques in truly ingenious ways" (p. 320). Sollod (1987) suggested that some of the ideas and methods arising from the reversal theory approach to therapy may well prove to be effective, particularly with certain clients and when "integrated into other, more comprehensive psychotherapeutic approaches" (p. 324). The therapist's techniques for encouraging emotional expressiveness and helping the client to challenge long-established and restrictive meanings that she attached to her emotions were also praised (Hart, 1987).

Much of the commentary centered around the use of the theory itself. Although it was acknowledged that the use of theory in therapy can be beneficial in providing a strategic focus and a basis for optimism in the therapist and a nonthreatening structure to facilitate the client to express feelings, recount life events, and try new things, concerns were raised about the characterization of reversal theory as a structural–phenomenological approach (Hart, 1987; Sollod, 1987). Both critics argued that reversal theo-ry's phenomenological approach shares little in common with the approaches of phenomenological and existential theorists such as Heidegger, Husserl,

May, and Gendlin, and they suggested that a truly phenomenological approach would not impose meanings on the client's experiences. They indicated that there is a danger of it then becoming a "prescriptive phenomenology" (Hart, 1987, p. 321). Perhaps this criticism arises from a misapprehension of reversal theory's more limited use of the term *phenomenology*, as referring to the need to make extensive reference to subjective experience and meaning, rather than observable behavior, in order to understand the nature of psychological processes (Apter, 1981c; see also the discussion in chapter 16 in this volume). Nonetheless, the semantic confusion identified by these critics is likely to be pervasive, and it might be useful to consider Sollod's comment: "It is not clear what is added by calling it a structural, phenomenological theory" (Sollod, 1987, p. 323), and to present reversal theory's philosophical underpinnings in a different way.

A further criticism leveled by Sollod (1987) is the "*post hoc, ergo propter hoc* fallacy" (p. 324), or the idea that with new psychotherapeutic approaches there is a tendency for the therapist to attribute positive treatment outcomes to the judicious use of the theory and to then use the treatment success as evidence to prove the validity of the theory. In fairness to reversal theory, this is a criticism that can be applied to any therapeutic approach, and there is a well-known body of literature that indicates that many individuals suffering from psychopathology will show improvement even in the absence of any kind of therapy at all. Consequently, only a very naive therapist (and an arrogant one) would be likely to regard a client's improvement as irrefutable proof of the therapist's theoretical orientation, or even of his or her therapeutic techniques. A related issue that is of particular concern for reversal theory, however, is the lack of carefully conducted outcome research (Sollod, 1987).

CONCLUSION

In considering the broad topic of psychopathology as a whole, it is useful to consider what we regard as constituting mental health. The reversal theory approach suggests that healthy psychological development throughout childhood, and self-actualization in adulthood, requires that people experience regular reversals from one to the other of the telic and paratelic modes (Van der Molen, 1985, 1986b). Consequently, in contrast to conventional theories that equate mental health with "stability," reversal theory asserts that people need a certain element of instability in their lives (Apter, 1989b). This is true not just in relation to the telic and paratelic modes but to all the modes identified in the theory. Impaired mental health can arise when people are unable to reverse fluidly and appropriately between any of the metamotivational modes, or to use appropriate and effective strategies for achieving satisfaction within a particular mode. A reversal theory approach can guide therapists to facilitate in their clients the flexibility and knowledge to achieve optimal satisfaction and effectiveness in all the complexities of their metamotivational experience. To put it at its simplest, they can help clients to be in the right state at the right time in the right way.

15

REVERSAL THEORY IN A
HUMANISTIC PERSPECTIVE

DAVID FONTANA

Humanistic psychology is concerned with the holistic study of man. Maslow (1968), who first proposed the term, believed that two forces, the psychoanalytical and the behavioral, had hitherto dominated psychology. In his view both these (often mutually antagonistic) forces propounded a partial view of man. By their apparent neglect or denial of teleology, of higher order needs, of emotions such as altruism and compassion, of consciousness, of free will, of self-awareness and of a spiritual dimension to human thought and emotion they had, he argued, inevitably hindered the growth of psychology both as a research endeavor and as a practical exercise concerned with the issues of everyday life.

The development of humanistic psychology over the past 30 years, and more recently of transpersonal psychology (which as Maslow predicted has now come to subsume humanistic psychology), has done much to restore the necessary breadth and depth to the subject. In part thanks to its endeavors, consciousness is once more a live issue for many psychologists; self-concepts and other self-related issues have become a focus for serious research endeavor; experience has returned as a legitimate subject for study and debate; and introspection is, within agreed limits, once more a valid mode of enquiry. More controversially, psychology is now seen as legitimately concerned with spiritual needs and beliefs and with the influence these variables have on attitudes, life goals, emotions, personality development, and actual behavior.

The development of this more all-inclusive approach to human psychology highlights the need for a theory of personality and motivation that takes into account the variety and complexity of men and women and the extensive and often self-contradictory nature of individual thought and affect. Such a theory should ideally address personality at all its manifold levels and in all its many contexts, from the routine to the creative, the personal to the social, the casual to the committed, the mundane to the spiritual.

The development of such an all-inclusive theory is clearly a very tall order, but at least we can search for something that gives us comprehensive insights into the fundamental structures of personality and that can accommodate not only the findings of new research but can give pointers to the directions that this research might usefully take. The formidable body of data generated and uncovered by reversal theory since its first appearance in the mid-1970s and the richness and scope of these data suggest that it may well be able to provide us with some of these insights and with some of the necessary pointers.

In a brief overview it is impossible to do justice to the application of reversal theory to humanistic and transpersonal issues. I therefore propose to concentrate on five of the most important of them, namely *self-awareness*, *personal change*, *adult play*, *creativity*, and *spirituality*, to each of which reversal theory has devoted considerable attention. (Other aspects of the relationship between reversal theory and humanistic psychology are explored by Murgatroyd & Apter, 1981a, 1981b, and by Rowan, 1981.)

SELF-AWARENESS

In a state of self-awareness, the individual is conscious of himself or herself as the doer of actions, or as the focus of concern, attention, admiration, and so forth. When in the opposite state of self-forgetting, consciousness is directed outward toward the action itself or toward the behavior or the feelings of others. Fontana (1988) explained that self-awareness and self-forgetting can therefore be thought of as bipolar states and that reversal theory identifies for us the various bipolar metamotivational modes that are associated with, or that prompt reversal into, these respective states. These modes are shown in Table 15.1.

As indicated in the table, in self-awareness the individual is likely, dependent on circumstances, to be in one or more of the telic metamotiva-

Table 15.1.
Metamotivational Modes Experienced in Self-Awareness
and Self-Forgetting

Mode Experienced in Self-Awareness	Mode Experienced in Self-Forgetting
Telic	Paratelic
Negativistic	Conformist
Mastery	Sympathy
Autic	Alloic

tional mode (i.e., monitoring personal performance in goal-directed activity), the negativistic mode (i.e., asserting the self through disagreement or non-conformity with the ideas or behavior of others), in the mastery mode (i.e., experiencing the self as superior to, responsible for, or in a dominating position over others), and the autic mode (i.e., experiencing self and other as distinct). By contrast, in self-forgetting he or she is likely to be in one or more of the paratelic mode (i.e., concentrating on the activity rather than on the self as the doer), the conformity mode (i.e., focusing on group needs and wishes rather than on personal ones), the sympathy mode (i.e., attending to the problems and concerns of others rather than to those of the self), and the alloic mode (i.e., identification with the other).

Fontana (1988) stated that in any given activity the individual may of course reverse several times between these modes and thus between self-remembering and self-forgetting. For example, one moment an individual may be lost in an activity and in the next moment become conscious that self-interest demands the activity meets with a successful outcome. One moment he or she may be concerned with self-assertion and with resisting the wishes of others, the next there may be reversal into a desire to identify with the group rather than risk the isolation to which this self-assertion may lead. One moment there may be the desire to dominate and lead, the next this desire may reverse into sympathy as one recognizes how distressing this masterful behavior may be for others. One moment there may be self-identification, with pleasure or displeasure focused on oneself, the next there may be other-identification with the focus of pleasure or displeasure shifted outward.

Apter (1993) explored what he termed the *structural properties* of these modes and of the reversals between them, arguing that the modes within each pair provide a context for whatever is being experienced at that particular time. To be more specific, each modal pair is characterized by a particular frame of reference that is present in one mode and absent in the opposite. For example, Apter defined *exemption* as the frame of reference in the conformity–negativism pair. When in the conformity mode the individual frames everything in terms of nonexemption—one is not exempt from prevailing rules, norms, and expectations. However, when in the negativistic mode things are framed in terms of exemption, that is, prohibitions, rules, and requirements are there to be ignored or deliberately broken.

Reversal theory argues that the ability to reverse appropriately in the face of realistic appraisals within a given situation (and therefore to frame things appropriately) is an essential feature of psychological health and of social effectiveness (see e.g., Apter, 1991b). To remain rigidly located at one end of a given reversal theory dimension when the occasion requires movement into the opposite end suggests an inflexible or inaccurate world-view and may lower one's chances of success in relating to, and perhaps in handling, other people. Conversely, to reverse too readily may be equally inappropriate and may indicate a different but equally significant error of judgment, or a lack of the self-belief on which consistency typically depends.

Interestingly however, Cowles, Darling, and Skanes (1992) found that when using the Telic Dominance Scale (TDS; Murgatroyd, Rushton, Apter, & Ray, 1978) to explore the difference between participants' perceptions of their worst, ideal, and real selves, the ideal self was seen by both men and women as significantly less telic (and specifically less serious-minded and arousal-avoiding) than either the worst self or the real self. This suggests that in reversal theory terms psychological health may to many people be equated less with the ability to reverse appropriately than with a tendency to remain at the paratelic end of the dimension concerned.

PERSONAL CHANGE

The value of relating reversal theory to self-awareness and self-forgetting is that not only does it provide us with insights into the metamotivational modes concerned, it also provides us with pointers on how to help individuals bring about desired personal and therapeutic change. Once enabled to recognize when and why their position on one or more of the various reversal theory dimensions is inappropriate, individuals can identify reasons for their inflexibility or overflexibility and explore ways in which these problems can be overcome. Such problems may have to do with an inability to appraise a situation with sufficient realism, or it may arise from feelings of insecurity about the self and an exaggerated need to self-defend or self-assert, or it may be due to overloose self-constructs that leave one too easily distracted from purposeful behavior or too vulnerable to the dogmas or wishes of others. Van der Molen (1985) proposed that overrigidity on reversal theory dimensions can serve ultimately to inhibit the development of self-actualization (e.g., Maslow, 1968), and he also proposed that this is primarily because overrigidity mitigates against the exploratory and creative activity essential to the growth of self-actualizing behavior.

The role of reversal theory in counseling and therapy is addressed more fully in chapter 14 of this volume, but it has a particular contribution to make to the creative arts therapies, especially to dramatherapy (Fontana & Valente, 1993a). Dramatherapy has the advantage of giving clients "permission," within a therapeutic and supportive setting, to act out unacknowledged or suppressed aspects of themselves. In reversal theory terms, it can therefore be used to help individuals experience the act of reversing into the opposite end of a relevant dimension or of remaining located at the most appropriate end in face of misguided pressures to reverse (Fontana & Valente, 1993b).

For example, dramatherapy can present a client located rigidly at the mastery end of the mastery–sympathy dimension with a scenario in which he or she is invited to manifest sympathy toward another participant. Initially, there would be no question of a need actually to *experience* feelings of sympathy. The emphasis is simply on acting a sympathetic role. Afterward, the client, the dramatherapist, and the other participants discuss this role and any feelings associated with it. At some point, in this or subsequent sessions, the client typically recognizes that he or she does indeed have the capacity to move into the sympathy mode and to experience it in a genuine way. Hindrances, both conscious and unconscious, to reversal into this mode in appropriate circumstances are uncovered and expressed, and the client is helped to recognize the part these hindrances play in adversely affecting both personal and professional relationships. Such hindrances can then be worked on and, if the therapy goes well, progressively discarded.

Similarly, a client who moves too readily from the mastery into the sympathy mode is encouraged by the dramatherapist to remain dramatically located in the former mode and then to engage in the necessary follow-up discussions and explorations. In the case of personal and professional relationships, the client may present with an inability to express mastery or to remain when necessary in the mastery mode with a spouse, offspring, colleagues, or superiors or subordinates. Thus, he or she may tend to weaken in resolve when faced with bids for sympathy and be too inclined to be people centered when the situation demands the approach be task centered.

These examples indicate how reversal theory coupled with dramatherapy can be of considerable value in a wide range of counseling situations, from family and couples therapy to individuals presenting with problems of low self-acceptance or of social failure. It carries equal relevance to personal and professional growth workshops. In stress management programs, for example, individuals overlocated at the telic end of the telic–paratelic dimension can be helped toward participation in relaxing and nonpurposeful activity and in exploring why such participation has hitherto caused resistance (Fontana & Valente, 1997). In assertiveness training programs, they can be enabled to recognize when mastery is required and how best to reverse appropriately along the mastery–sympathy dimension.

Work of this kind does not necessarily change a client's preferred mode in any given dimension. But it enables the individual to develop a more comprehensive understanding of their psychological life and of their potential for personal–social and professional change and development. As first proposed by Fontana and Valente (1993c), it is even possible to observe preferred styles within whole organizations and institutions. Such preferred styles, dictated either by management preferences or by the nature of the tasks undertaken, may mean that individuals who do not share these preferences may find themselves unsuited to the organization or institution concerned. For example, a preferred paratelic style may be incompatible with a primarily telic institution such as a bank or a firm of accountants, whereas a negativistic style may render one unsuitable for a context in which emphasis is placed on teamwork and corporate action.

ADULT PLAY

The paratelic mode is however of particular importance within the context of play, and for present purposes specifically within that of adult play. Nevertheless, although Apter and Kerr (1991) described *play* as a "deliberately and self-consciously diversionary" activity, they point out that even in play one can enjoy the sense of self-enhancement or self-satisfaction that comes through the achievement of the various goals that may be an integral part of the play concerned (as may happen in games such as golf or chess). Equally, they insist that play can be undertaken in either a mastery or a sympathy mode. Competitive sport, from football to baseball, is in their view the very epitome of mastery play, both for those who take part in it and for those who look on. Gambling may be another good example of mastery play, as may solitary, intellectual games such as crossword puzzles.

When undertaken in the sympathy mode, adult play typically involves self-indulgent (self-sympathetic) activities such as nonserious swimming and walking or other-sympathetic pursuits such as playing with young children or clowning. However, as Apter and Kerr discussed, it is not the activity per se but the metamotivational mode in which it is undertaken that indicates where one is located on any given reversal theory dimension. Thus, although as demonstrated by the above examples, some activities appeal more readily to certain modes than to others, we have to look deeper if we really want to identify the psychological variables involved. (This emphasizes again a crucial tenet of reversal theory—namely that it is often insufficient to draw conclusions solely from behavior if one wishes to understand human functioning.) Apter and Kerr suggested that even gambling, typically undertaken in the mastery mode, can potentially be used when in the sympathy mode—for example, when the gambler's primary aim is to become convinced that he or she is favored by lady luck or by the gods of chance.

Kerr (1991b) has addressed the serious element that can be present in adult play. His research showed that professional sports people, as measured by the TDS, are not only significantly more telic dominant than serious amateurs or recreational amateurs, they also score significantly higher on the Serious-mindedness and Planning Orientation subscales of the TDS. He further reported that the telic metamotivational mode appears to persist, at least in outstanding sportspeople, even after retirement. Even at a mean age of 39.4 years, the scores on the TDS and its subscales of his sample of former national, international, and Olympic swimmers remained significantly higher than those of younger serious and recreational amateurs. Findings of this kind suggest that the metamotivational modes of the individuals concerned appear not to be simply a transitory response to the intensities of the high-powered professional sporting environment, but to manifest enduring characteristics which may predate (as they apparently postdate) this environment.

However, Kerr (1991c) also presented findings that lead us to propose that although dedicated sportspeople appear to be significantly more telic in their approach to play than those of lesser accomplishment, the opposite may be the case if we look at dangerous sports. Skydiving, it appears, is a paratelic experience for veteran divers, and one that permits high arousal to be experienced as playful excitement, whereas for nondivers and beginning divers the activity is viewed as serious and nonplayful and as very definitely goal directed (i.e., as directed toward personal survival) and therefore as unequivocally telic. One would hazard that the same situation prevails for many other hazardous undertakings such as rock climbing and potholing [caving] and even for current recreational crazes like firewalking and recreational drug use.

As Kerr put it, reversal theory thus provides us with the notion that the definition of an act as playful is phenomenological in nature, and is thus dependent on the interpretation of the observer (Kerr, 1991c; see also Apter, 1991b). Elsewhere Kerr (1986, 1988b) indicated that the usefulness of reversal theory in contributing to our interpretation of adult play is further indicated by the correspondence between the view of play that it presents and that propounded by previous influential theorists such as Huizinga (1949) and Caillois (1961). Huizinga stressed that play is essentially a nonserious and spontaneous activity, and he criticized the tendency of modern culture to lose sight of its real nature and convert it into "sport" by burdening it with elaborate rules and by distinguishing between professionals and amateurs (thus converting it from a paratelic into a telic activity). Caillois went further and divided play into four groupings that he saw as characterized respectively by *competition, chance, simulation,* and *vertigo* (perhaps more accurately labeled *sensory*). The first three of these are each restricted by what Caillois referred to as "conventions, techniques, and utensils" and are in Kerr's submission consequently more in keeping with the telic mode, whereas only the last of them forms what he regards as a basic element in the paratelic concept.

Hyers (1991) also drew attention to what he called the irony that play can be turned into work and work turned into play by the frames of mind of those involved. He argued that educators, from the start, consistently placed formal education in the category of work (classwork, labwork, homework, woodwork, etc.), whereas they placed play outside the educational process. He reminded us that this telic orientation is at odds with the origins of education, which, whether in the liberal arts, the fine arts, or in the sciences, is supposed to lie in a zeal for learning. The very origin of the word *study* is the Latin word *stadium*, meaning *zeal*, and the Greek philosophers characterized human beings as laughing animals (*zoion gelastikon*) and saw playfulness (*homo ludens*) and a sense of humor (*homo risens*) as distinctive marks of humanity.

When we overlook the original purpose of education and allow it to be driven by extraneous considerations rather than by an intrinsic zeal for learning, we lay students open to tension, anxiety, depression, tedium, apathy, a sense of meaninglessness, and of course to those twin psychological burdens, success and failure. Although not denying the need for self-discipline and application if learning is consistently to take place, Hyers implied that just as Huizinga considered our culture to be damaged by the atrophy of the play element, so is our education. At its best, education is in his view concerned with the creation and the appreciation and celebration of knowledge, an activity engaged in primarily not for the purpose of attaining goals and grades but for the intrinsic satisfaction that, as an activity, it brings to those who participate in it.

The various arguments of Apter, Kerr, and Hyers all point in the same direction, namely that we ignore the value of the paratelic and of the ability to reverse into it at our psychological peril. Numerous examples, from the poor behavior of sporting superstars and of their supporters to the disaffected youth in our schools can be advanced in support of these arguments. Reversal theory, agreeing as it does with many of the ideas on play of previous authorities, is not telling us anything new here. But its value lies in its ability to codify and categorize, to relate work and play to underlying dimensions of personality, and to draw our attention to the crucial importance for individual and cultural welfare of our ability to reverse between the metamotivational modes necessary for both play and work (Apter, 1991b). By the same token, it draws our attention to the potential damage consequent on undertaking either of these bipolar activities while in the inappropriate mode (Kerr & Apter, 1991).

CREATIVITY

Related at certain levels to play, the creative act is also illuminated to some degree by reversal theory (Broom, 2000). Creativity, partly as a consequence of its varied and controversial nature, remains something of a scientific enigma, and it seems likely that we require a range of explanatory theories when dealing with it rather than any single one. Reversal theory does not explain the inner workings of the creative act any more than the

"Big Five" personality dimensions explain the inner workings of personality, but it enables us to understand something of the phenomenological state that may obtain while creativity is taking place. And it is phenomenological states, composed as they are of mood and intention as well as of cognitive processes, that are central to reversal theory.

Many years ago Ghiselin (1952), in a classic survey of the accounts given by artists and scientists of their own creative processes, identified four typical stages in the creative act, *recognition, incubation, illumination,* and *verification.* Fontana (1985) argued, on the basis of the accounts given by creative men and women in Ghiselin and elsewhere, that these four stages appear to involve reversals between the telic and paratelic modes. The *recognition* stage, in which the scientist recognizes a problem worth exploring and the writer, the painter, or the musician an idea or a theme worth developing, typically involves the telic mode. True, recognition can arrive at unexpected times, but few creative individuals rely on such happy accidents. More often, they actively seek scientific questions worth addressing or starting points for their literary endeavors.

The next two stages, *incubation* and *illumination,* in which some, at least, of the creative endeavor seems to take place at the unconscious level, appears from the accounts available to us to involve at least elements of the paratelic. The scientist or the artist "plays" with ideas, with possible solutions, with possible scenarios, and ways forward. Sometimes such things are deliberately allowed to lie fallow until the moment of inspiration, or illumination, arrives. By contrast, the *verification* stage, the stage of putting scientific theories to the test, or of perspiring over one's writing or painting (genius, we have been reminded, is 90% perspiration) demands a degree of telic involvement, an awareness of what accords with existing scientific knowledge or with good literary or artistic style.

Fontana (1985, 1991b) also suggested that reversal theory provides us with interesting insights into the materials of creativity. For example, artists recognize that when using color in order to convey emotion, the three primary colors, red, yellow, and blue, each have a complementary color that is made up of a combination of the other two (e.g., Govinda, 1977). Thus, the complementary color of red is green (yellow plus blue), that of yellow is violet, and that of blue is orange. Where the primary color is what artists call "active" (i.e., emotionally arousing), as is the case with red and yellow, the complementary color (green and violet) is passive, and where the primary color is passive (blue), the complementary color is active (orange). These various colors are seen by artists as lying along a dimension from the most active to the most passive, that is, red, yellow (the second of the active primary colors), orange (less active because it is not primary), green (the least of the three passive colors as it is complementary to red, the most active), violet, and blue (the most passive). Fontana pointed out that this dimension maps perfectly onto the felt arousal value of colors established by Walters, Apter, and Svebak (1982) in their exploration of the changes in color preferences reported by participants in the course of their various reversals during the working day from paratelic (high arousal) to telic (low arousal) modes.

Fontana also drew attention to the relationship between the telic–paratelic dimension and the order (from most to least moveable) in which the six major three-dimensional forms recognized by artists can be arranged—an order that goes from pyramid through cube, cone, cylinder, and spherical cone to sphere. The pyramid (and the square on which it is based) are the epitome of the extreme telic mode (a point emphasized in our language through the use of *square* as a term for conservation, dependability, serious-ness, and fixity of purpose), whereas the sphere is a symbol of the extreme paratelic mode, typifying as it does fluidity, playfulness, unpredictability, and responsiveness. Thus, in terms of both color and shape we find elements that accord with progression along an important reversal theory dimension. The implications of this for the psychology of creative activity and of aesthetics are many and varied and not hard to seek.

SPIRITUALITY

We now come to spirituality, which is the fourth of the areas to which I suggested at the outset that reversal theory contributes important insights. Spirituality is a difficult concept for the scientist. The existence of a spirit or soul is not demonstrable by known scientific methods, and therefore to many psychologists it does not warrant serious consideration. Yet as Fontana and Slack (1996) pointed out, the majority of human beings across cultures believe in some sort of spiritual reality and many claim to have had experi-ences that they interpret as spiritual. The belief in a spiritual dimension to human nature has historically had a profound effect on human thought, self-concepts, and behavior. In fact, spiritual experiences and beliefs in general have proved across the centuries to be among the most potent influences upon human history. They have affected morality, legality, and the sociocultural order. They have inspired much of the world's greatest music, fine art, sculpture, and architecture. And their misuse has been behind many international conflicts and the religious fundamentalism that prompts intolerance, discrimination, and violence. It is not surprising therefore that Apter (1982a) insisted that "Any serious attempt to develop a psychological theory of human motivation must sooner or later confront the problem proposed by man's religious quest, and any theory which fails to address itself to this problem must be regarded as necessarily incomplete" (p. 276).

Irrespective of the scientist's personal belief systems, spirituality and the religious structures that arise from it are thus an unavoidable area of interest for the psychologist, and it is this area that humanistic psychology, and more particularly transpersonal psychology, set out in part to explore. Apter (1982a, chap. 12; 1985) identified what he called three steps in the development of religious ideas and their accretions. First, there is the human recognition of problems such as evil, suffering, and personal mortality. Second, there is the occurrence of imaginative answers to these problems and the denial of the material world as ultimate reality. Third, there is an institutionalized attempt to take these answers seriously as comprising divine revelations. In his view, the first of these steps primarily involves telic thinking (the serious desire to find solutions), the second paratelic (the imaginative play of ideas leading to such solutions), and the third telic (the hardening of such solutions into dogma). Thus, we have, in the mind of the individuals concerned, a classic case of reversal and counterreversal.

Without quarrelling with this three-step process or with the reversals involved in the first two steps, it is possible to challenge Apter's implication that the revelations of religion are necessarily the product solely of insubstantial imagination. Fontana (1981b, 1991a) pointed out that in Eastern religions and in the Western mystical tradition there is evidence that the paratelic state is a precursor of genuine spiritual experience and is indeed sought by certain specific practices. Zen Buddhism is the most obvious example. Both when meditating on an object or on a koan, the practitioner is instructed to drop linear, logical thinking, or the striving after any particular goal, and to abide in the experience itself. Eventually, after many lesser revelations, the result is what might be described (words are said to be inadequate) as a direct experience of *being*, without conceptualizations or judgments. *Being* is simply what *is*. The mystery of life, if mystery there be, is solved by life itself. The practitioner is the answer to his own question— indeed, he is both question *and* answer and always has been. At this point, as Buddhism tells us, the opposites, the polarities in our thinking and acting, no longer arise. There is no telic and no paratelic and no reversal between them. The practitioner experiences instead the essential unity of his own being. The fragmented, divided self is seen to be unreal, and the practitioner becomes free of it for good (Fontana, 1987, 1999).

Such states of illumination, enlightenment, revelation, or salvation— whatever term one likes to use—are of course very rare. As Hyers (1985) highlighted, it is the continuing emphasis on either the telic or the paratelic mode (and doubtless also on the mastery or the sympathy mode and on the negativistic or the conformist mode) that lies behind much religious diversity. He also drew attention to the self-power as opposed to the other-power dichotomy within religion (in Christian terms the dichotomy between God as imminence and God as transcendence) and to possible reversals between these two states from time to time within the religious life of the individual.

CONCLUSION

In each of the areas touched on, reversal theory can be seen as making important contributions to our understanding. Within the humanistic context it provides us with important ways of identifying the underlying meta-motivational modes, which make sense of what we might call the consistency within diversity apparent when human behavior is investigated as a whole. We can expect many more insights from reversal theory in the years to come.

V

FUTURE DIRECTIONS

16

THE CHALLENGE OF REVERSAL THEORY

MICHAEL J. APTER

What sort of a theory is reversal theory? The definition given at the start of this book was "a structural–phenomenological theory of motivation, emotion, and personality." But now, after 15 chapters, the reader is aware that the theory is rich enough and broad enough to suggest many other possible definitions. Some of these are encompassed within the definition just given, others less so.

Here are some alternative formulations, each bringing out a distinctive general feature of the approach. First, and reflecting the title of this book, reversal theory could be characterized as a theory of motivational styles in everyday life. But it could also be seen primarily as a state theory of personality, in sharp contrast with trait theories and emphasizing the temporal aspects of personality. In a related way it could be described as a systems theory of intra-individual differences. It could also be called a dynamic interactionist theory of personality, in which the term *dynamic* is used to emphasize the way in which the individual is changing, not only in response to situations, but also as a result of independent internal processes. Contrasting with this, reversal theory could be seen as a metamotivational theory of emotion, because one of the central themes is the way in which different emotions can arise from different metamotivational state combinations. But it would also be possible to define it in a more general way as a structural theory of mental states, a kind of experiential morphology. At the center of the theory is a system of binary oppositions generating qualitatively different types of experience of which emotions are only a part. In this respect it could also be seen as a type theory of subjective experience, because the different kinds of experience that it identifies fall into eight distinct types. Because at a certain level it deals with the different ways in which people cope with life, and its stresses and strains, it could be defined as a theory of emotional intelligence (or even, as suggested by Mamali, 1999, motivational intelligence) or perhaps as an experiential theory of lifestyles. And because it is particularly interested in paradoxical behavior and sees this in evolutionary terms, it could be regarded as a biological theory of the irrational side of human nature. These varied definitions highlight different facets of what has become a rich and complex theory. But however complex and multifaceted the theory is, reversal theory has been held together firmly, over the years, by the core structure of motivational oppositions described in Part I of this volume and represented in Figure 1.1.

PARADOXES OF STRUCTURAL–PHENOMENOLOGY

Designating the reversal theory approach as *structural–phenomenological* will seem paradoxical to many. This is because, in the recent history of ideas, structuralism and phenomenology have been generally regarded as opposed to, and even as hostile toward each other, as intellectual traditions.

The conflict between them arises because structuralism tends to disregard subjective life, looking only at its products (such as spoken language, types of text, myth systems, and culinary systems) and understanding these products in terms of their relationships with each other. Phenomenology, however, looks directly at subjective life, understanding phenomena in themselves, through direct intuition rather than in terms of structures of which they might be a part. Reversal theory brings the two approaches together by insisting on looking initially at subjective experience rather than its products and by discerning a universal structure in experience itself. In other words, to put it simply (and as posited in "the structural–phenomenological assumption" in chapter 2 of this volume): Conscious experience has structure.

But the paradoxes go deeper than this, because reversal theory is a structuralism that, it might be said, is not structuralist. Most structuralist thinkers see individual behavior as an expression of larger social structures, like the class structure identified by Marx or the kinship systems of Lévi-Strauss. In their terms, the individual self is seen as being illusory, meaning that personal identity can be disregarded. In strong contrast to this, reversal theory takes the idea of structure and applies it directly to the individual person. The individual now becomes the pivotal locus of analysis, and this turns conventional structuralism upside down: Far from being defunct, the self (although subject to contrasting forms of experience) is alive and thriving in reversal theory. In this way, reversal theory confronts head on the whole postmodernist movement that has emerged from structuralism.

On the phenomenological side, reversal theory constitutes a phenomenology that, as pointed out in the conclusion of chapter 14, is not strictly phenomenological. Phenomenology is suspicious of preconceptions, preferring to look afresh at each phenomenon as it presents itself. Most phenome-nologists take it as a given that one must approach the subject (using the term *subject* in both its senses as a person or as a topic) in a completely open way. But reversal theory has a whole network of interlinking concep-tions that, when brought to bear on a particular experience that someone might have at a particular time, are unavoidably preconceptions. This turns traditional phenomenology on its head. From the reversal theory perspective, science is about the search for universal pattern and structure, and any approach that denies this will ultimately become unproductive—which has tended, regrettably, to be the case with so much of phenomenological psychology over the years.

Despite these problems, the term *structural phenomenology* does capture the starting assumption of the reversal theory approach, which is that subjec-tive experience has structure. Perhaps a preferable term, however, given the objections that can be made, might be something like *systematic experiential-ism* or even Rychlak's (1988) useful term, *rigorous humanism*.

AN EVOLVING THEORY

The patterns discerned by reversal theory, and as described in this volume, constitute a theory that is neither complete nor closed. One should expect changes to be made in the future, in the light of fresh evidence, just as changes have occurred continually in the development of the theory up to the present. In fact, the theory has evolved considerably since its inception in the mid-1970s. Nor is the theory monolithic, despite the formal presenta-tion of the theory as a set of propositions in chapter 2. There are a number of alternative or additional propositions that have been suggested by those working with the theory, and some of these may eventually prevail. For example, Van der Molen (1985) has suggested that reversal to the paratelic will occur not only in response to the three general factors that have been discussed earlier in this volume, but also when the individual experiences an excess of energy. (This derives from Herbert Spencer's classic surplus-energy theory of play, Spencer, 1873.) Fontana and Valente (1997) have argued that reversals between any pair of states can be induced entirely voluntarily. Rea (1993, 1994, 1995, 1997, 2000) has suggested that special superordinate states are possible in which the telic and paratelic states occur simultaneously and are combined. More fundamentally, Frey (1997b) has urged us to consider the possibility that all states in some sense contain their opposites within themselves, such that the ongoing state does not "go overboard" in pursuit of its own value but is restrained to some extent. Lachenicht (1985a) has proposed that another pair of phenomenological states should be included in the theory, which he refers to as "equality" and "inequality" states, and he sees these as "metarelational" rather than "metamotivational."

There are also a number of issues to be resolved. An example would be whether the opposite of parapathic emotions exists. In other words, can good emotions become experienced as bad in the telic state, in the same way that bad emotions can become experienced as good in the paratelic state? (An example might be that of romantic love as a form of anguish in the telic state.) Another issue is whether there is a form of tension that arises when state balance is seriously out of alignment with dominance in a given individual: Does he or she feel a certain kind of malaise when life does not sufficiently allow expression of a dominance?

Looking further into the future, it is certainly conceivable that theories even more distantly related to reversal theory, or even opposed to it in some respects, could emerge that would share the orientation of structural–phenomenology as it has been defined here, without necessarily subscribing to other reversal theory assumptions or interests. Reversal theory would then be one structural–phenomenological theory among others. It would be a welcome development to have company in this theoretical space.

It is also possible for theories that are not necessarily structural–phenomenological to emerge that share with reversal theory some of its key concerns while expressing and developing them in other ways. This does in fact seem to be true of the work of Svetlana Bakhtiarova and her colleagues in Kiev and Moscow. In their version of reversal theory (S. Bakhtiarova, personal communication, 1998), the orientation is not so much toward conscious experience as it is toward personality. That is, their work explores frequent change in certain behavioral characteristics over time. Like reversal theory as presented here, it opposes the static trait conception. But it picks on a set of personality dimensions on which people swing back and forth like a pendulum (rather than switch between discontinuously): Such swings include, for instance, from being authoritarian to being obedient, from being gullible to being tricky, and from underestimating to overestimating oneself. The existence of this formulation implies, perhaps, the need to think in terms of an "extended reversal theory," which would include all those approaches to psychology that emphasize reversible change rather than stability in the individual person over time.

THE CHALLENGE FOR REVERSAL THEORY

The name of this chapter is "The Challenge *of* Reversal Theory." But what are some of the challenges *for* reversal theory? What are some of the problems that reversal theory needs to take on? What are some of the issues that it needs to face? What are some of the research questions that it needs to address? These challenges are of course many and various, and it would be tiresome to catalogue them all in detail. But it is worth noting briefly, under three main headings, some of those that are among the most obvious and immediate.

Empirical Research

Looking at the way in which research has developed on the theory, it is clear that there is a need in the future to move away from the emphasis that has been placed on the telic–paratelic pair of metamotivational states toward a more equal interest in all the pairs of states. The telic and paratelic pair has naturally received the greatest attention so far because it was the first pair to be identified in the theory; but the time has come now for the whole range of states to be reflected more fully in research publications.

A second general point is that, if the spirit of the theory is to prevail, we shall need to concentrate much more on the micro-analysis of the individual over time rather than aggregating across moments of time for a given individual, as occurs in research on dominance. Studies of dominance have their place, of course, but too great an emphasis on this is likely to detract from the main thrust of the theory, which is about the way in which individual people are changing all the time in the course of everyday life. Related to this, some tests of metamotivational aspects of personality that go beyond dominance will also need to be developed, such as tests of lability, and of typical state combinations and state sequences in individuals. This would open up exciting new areas for future research. We shall also need to investigate the type of change that involves change of focality between states rather than looking only at the reversal type of metamotivational change.

When we come to look at particular areas of research, a number of possibilities cry out for attention. Let us consider just a few examples. The development of various new neuroimaging techniques gives rise to the potential for important research on the neural location and dynamics of metamotivational states and reversals. Also, the biochemical and hormonal aspects of all the states are obvious areas for investigation, but especially in respect of the transactional states. In relation to psychopathology, it would be interesting to explore the metamotivational characteristics of the various types of personality disorder, as described in the *Diagnostic and Statistical Manual of Mental Disorders* (American Psychiatric Association, 1994), to see if each type of disorder displays a distinctive pattern. There are many kinds of behavior and experience that have received relatively scant attention from researchers in the past but that play an important part in everyday life and that could be examined systematically in terms of hypotheses derived from reversal theory: forgiveness, teasing, crying, infatuation, devotion, bullying, flirting, procrastination, lying, courage, and so on. Reversal theory researchers have relatively neglected the concept of cognitive synergy, and it would be good to see more work in the future that tested and used this concept. Finally, cross-cultural aspects of metamotivation need to be explored. In the most general terms, we should ask, Can the *mentalities* (to use a useful word from French psychology) of different cultures be systematically elucidated in reversal theory terms?

Applied Research

First, we need to know much more about the basic psychomotor effects of different states—that is, their influence on reaction time, attention span, vigilance, memory, sensitivity to pain, and so forth. Should there be marked differences between opposing states, this would be particularly helpful to know in such areas as sports, school teaching, medicine, and workplace skills. For example, it would be useful to know in medicine if there is a difference in pain sensitivity between the sympathy and mastery states. In teaching, it would be helpful to know if children learn different kinds of things, such as multiplication, French vocabulary, or drawing skills, better in the telic or paratelic states. In coaching sports it would be invaluable to know which particular skills are best performed in which state or state combinations.

Second, and just as important, we need to develop specific techniques that would allow people to come more into control of their own reversal processes. This will be crucial to the successful application of the theory in almost every area in the future. Thus, if it turns out that different sporting skills are better performed in one state than in another, then the athlete will need to learn how to induce the desired state in a reasonably dependable way. Further, if it is the case, as was argued in chapter 14, that some types of psychopathology involve an inability to control the reversal process (either by being stuck in one state or by reversing inappropriately), then clearly the therapist could make enormous use of techniques for helping the client to overcome this inability. A number of techniques have in fact emerged recently, but much more research is needed on them and on their effectiveness.

Theoretical Level

The resolution of some of the issues, and the alternative propositions, mentioned in the previous section of this chapter is clearly a matter of importance for the development of the theory, but this is largely a matter for empirical research in the future. Meanwhile, the theory itself needs to be made more complete in two main respects. First, there is the need for a systematic developmental underpinning for the theory, for an understanding of how the structure of metamotivational pairs emerges during growth and of how these pairs interact with other developmental processes in the infant, child, and adolescent. Second, the theory needs to be able to address psychotic as well as neurotic forms of psychopathology. Work has already started on both of these problems—which turn out to be closely interrelated (Apter, 1999a). There is also a need to develop more rigorous versions of the theory, perhaps stating the theory as a form of dynamic systems theory or putting it in the form of a set of computer models. Work on this is also currently under way (Lee & Branum-Martin, 1999).

THE PROMISE OF REVERSAL THEORY

Let us complete this book in a positive way by outlining eight major benefits that those working with reversal theory believe that it can bring to psychology. In doing so, relevant evidence and arguments are cited from chapters in this book.

Reversal Theory Opens Up a New Level of Psychological Analysis

What reversal theory does is to add a new level of analysis, the metamotivational level, to psychological studies. This level is well recognized in everyday life, where such terms as *serious, challenging,* and *affectionate* are used widely and yet the mental states and orientations to which they refer (such as telic and negativistic) have been generally underemphasized, if not almost entirely overlooked, in late-20th-century psychology. Metamotivational states provide a kind of internal context to behavior. They give a different coloration to things: The same activity can come in different hues depending whether it is undertaken seriously, playfully, and so on. Even a child realizes that the experience of reading something for fun is quite different from reading the same thing for a test. Were this to be recognized by investigative psychologists, it would turn psychology from black and white to glorious Technicolor. The theory adds back value and meaning to psychology by looking at actions in terms of the metamotivational values that they serve.

To put this more technically, reversal theory introduces a set of important moderator variables, the metamotivational states, to psychology. On the basis of the research that has been reported in this book, it can be seen that these moderator variables play a crucial part in determining a range of dependent variables. For example, in chapter 5, Lewis and Svebak showed that the telic and paratelic states have an important effect on a wide range of psychophysiological variables. In chapter 6, Martin and Svebak described evidence to show that whether the telic or paratelic state is operative will determine the way in which stress is experienced. In chapter 7, O'Connell and Cook provided evidence to show that metamotivational state can have an influence on whether people who are trying to give up smoking lapse or not at a given time. There is no need to labor the point by citing more examples: It would be dangerous, in the light of this evidence, to carry out psychological research that did not take metamotivational state into account.

Reversal Theory Broadens the Perspectives of Psychology

Mainstream psychology not only fails to give this level of analysis its due, it also tends implicitly to privilege one state from each pair. As a result, it produces something like "half a psychology."

Thus, traditional psychology privileges the telic state, either not recognizing the paratelic state at all or seeing it as peripheral and special. For example, in animal research on learning, it is assumed that the goal must come first. Thus, it is supposed that the rat in a maze needs the food in the goal box and that it is only because of this (or some related drive) that it attempts to find its way through the maze. First comes the need, then comes the behavior. With no need, there is no behavior. Likewise, in a typical human problem-solving experiment it is assumed that the participant wants to solve the puzzle and as a result tries different strategies in the attempt to do so. First comes the goal, then comes the activity. In other words, where psychologists take motivation into account, they see it as necessarily an instigator of movement toward a future goal rather than a prompt toward current enjoyment. As O'Connell and Cook point out (chapter 7), for example, the strategies recommended by smoking cessation experts assume that the person at all times is aware of the seriousness of continuing to smoke and wishes to plan ahead to achieve its termination. Similarly, Bowers (1985, 1988) and Jones (1981) (cited in chapter 14) point out that those charged with counseling juvenile delinquents seem to assume that these youngsters have the overriding aim of becoming model citizens. Such failures to see the importance of the need to "have fun now" necessarily lead to the failure of intervention programs. None of this is to say that there is no recognition in psychology, and in related applied areas, that the animal or person can enjoy behavior in itself, but this is seen as a special case (e.g., "play," "consummatory behavior," etc.) that needs to be explained, not something that is fundamental.

It is significant that anxiety is the key emotion in emotion research and that more time is spent studying it, by far, than any other form of affect. This is because anxiety is, as we have seen, a telic emotion. And yet, as Gerkovich reminds us (chapter 11) boredom, a paratelic emotion, is an even greater problem in many people's lives, especially when they undertake foolish activities in the attempt to overcome it.

Incidentally, from the reversal theory perspective one can see how Freud created enormous and unnecessary conceptual problems for himself with respect to anxiety. He did this by assuming on the one hand that people spend their lives trying to discharge the unpleasant tension of anxiety and on the other that they spend their lives, however indirectly, seeking erotic pleasure (which implies a need for the pleasure of sexual excitement). It would not be too much to say that this self-created conceptual self-contradiction took him a lifetime of theorization to work out to his own satisfaction.

Traditional psychology also tends to privilege the conformist state over the negativistic. Much of experimental social psychology has been about obedience, the importance of group norms, pressures to comply, authoritarianism, and so on. In other words, as McDermott emphasizes in chapter 9, it has been about the way that people behave when they are in the conformist metamotivational state. It is interesting that comparatively little attention has been paid (in psychology if not in sociology) to dissension, nonconformity, rebellion, confrontation, defiance, and other social manifestations of the negativistic state. This is particularly strange because, for social processes leading to conformity to be needed by society, there must be sources of diversity. Where do these come from? This question is typically left unanswered and even unasked.

With respect to mastery and sympathy, it is the mastery state that has been privileged. From Adler to Bandura, it is power, control, self-efficacy, and other mastery needs that have been assumed to be fundamental. This means that, generally speaking (and with the particular exception of work in family relationships), the mastery state has been central in large tracts of mainstream psychology. The same has also been true in philosophy as it relates to the social sciences from Nietzsche to Foucault. Foucault has even translated sexual relations into essentially matters of power and politics. What ever happened to love? What ever happened to caring? It is as if these human emotions do not exist, or are illusions, or do not matter in the grand scheme of things.

Finally, in much of psychology the assumption seems to be made that everyone is essentially selfish and that people can be understood only in such terms. In other words, the autic state is privileged. Where there appears to be care for others, this is seen as merely a biological trick in which people get pleasant feelings for helping others (e.g., bringing up children). The resulting conclusion is that everything that one does is essentially autic. And yet personal experiences and accounts by people throughout the ages imply that people can be genuinely altruistic and even self-sacrificing. Even more to the point, they can do so even where this provides no personal pleasure at all. Why do people experience compassion? Why do people devote themselves to causes? Why do people ever sacrifice their lives for others? Why, nearer home, do people listen to each other and give each other sympathy? Modern psychology, especially experimental psychology, has precious little to say about such "odd" alloic phenomena.

Reversal Theory Prompts Reexamination of Oversimple Theoretical Assumptions

As argued particularly in chapter 4, reversal theory challenges previous major theories of motivation that make the assumption that motivation is homeostatic. These include drive reduction theory, Freudian theory, the energy theory of Lorenz, and optimal arousal theory. These theories are all, from the perspective of reversal theory, seen as being simplistic in their failure to face up to the complexity and changeability of human desire over time. Motivational systems must be seen as multistable if they are to account for the vicissitudes of human experience.

Furthermore, reversal theory challenges the static notion of a trait, which has been adopted in most of psychometric personality theory and is epitomized currently in the "Big Five" personality traits (see especially chapter 3 in this respect). The concept of trait demands that, along the personality dimensions considered, people have fixed positions that at all times remain more or less the same. And if the trait concept is seen from the reversal theory perspective as being inadequate to deal with the full richness of human life, this is even more the case with personality studies based on the simpler concept of types, such as the many studies using the Myers–Briggs Type Indicator. In all this psychometric research, the temporal aspects of personality are systematically excluded or diminished. As a result, variation is seen as "noise" or measurement error or unreliability. For reversal theory the noise may actually contain the message and accurately portray patterns of change over time.

Reversal theory also challenges currently fashionable cognitive theories of emotion in which, like most previous theories in this area, emotions are assigned fixed places on fixed dimensions. In reversal theory, the dimensions themselves change through the inversions that result from the reversal process. Even more to the point, reversal theory denies that emotions can be reduced to cognition (even if cognitive synergies enter the picture, as described by Coulson in chapter 12). It sees emotion, motivation, and cognition as interacting with and codetermining each other. Cognitions are functions of emotion and (meta) motivation, as well as the other way around. Thus, when a reversal takes place because of satiation, as evidenced, for example, by the work of Lafreniere, Cowles, and Apter (1988) described in chapter 4, the individual will seek cognitions that accord with the new metamotivational state. (This process is discussed in more detail in Apter, 1982a, pp. 69–73.) In this respect, motivation displays primacy over cognition and means that in psychological theory there is a need to allow drive at least some access to the driving seat.

In each of these areas—motivation, personality, and emotion—reversal theory suggests that psychological theorizing could be much more sophisticated than it is. This is a point that Brown makes particularly forcefully in chapter 8. It is an interesting, if puzzling, phenomenon that psychologists are willing to countenance enormous complexity in their methods of statistical analysis but are generally unwilling to do so in their theories.

Reversal Theory Prompts Reexamination of Oversimple Methodological Assumptions

The reversal theory emphasis on the changeability of people over time gives rise to a number of problems for the design of experimental and other studies but also helps to explain why results sometimes do not appear to work out in the way expected (Apter & Svebak, 1992). For one thing, reversal theory would suggest that it is unwise to assume that the score on some trait that someone obtained from a personality test will necessarily correspond with the way that that person is during the actual experiment. Thus, using personality as an independent variable may require some kind of post hoc checking to see whether participants were really oriented at the time of the experiment in the way expected by the experimenter. This means that participants for whom this was not the case can then either be analyzed separately or excluded from the analysis.

Similar problems arise where participants are used as their own controls, with respect to personality, in repeated-measures designs. The same participants may be used at different points in time, but they may in fact have varied in critical ways that are unrelated to the experimental manipulation but that are assumed for control purposes to have remained the same. Again, post hoc testing of metamotivational state would seem to be essential: One cannot simply assume that participants remain with the same states being active throughout the period of the investigation.

There are dimensions of change that have been highlighted in reversal theory that may require the particular attention of researchers. The way that a participant performs in an experiment may be a function of whether he or she is in, say, the telic or the paratelic state at the time. The notorious difficulty in psychology of replicating experimental results may be at least in part due to this kind of problem, especially because the atmosphere and experimenter attitude in different laboratories may differ considerably and induce different metamotivational states. The good news is that it might be possible to make sense of discrepancies between different laboratories, or the same laboratory at different times, by adding in this extra dimension of metamotivation to the analysis. It might also be possible to reduce the variability of results by controlling for those factors that tend to induce reversals.

Reversal Theory Has the Potential to Integrate Different Approaches

On the single thread of metamotivation we can hang all the other levels that have been studied in psychology: behavioral, physiological, unconscious, social. In other words, reversal theory excludes no one; its intended thrust is to integrate approaches and levels. In this sense it is what American politicians call the "Big Tent" and British politicians call the "Broad Church." A good illustration of its potential in this respect is the way in which, as described in chapter 14, the theory provides a "framework for eclectic therapy." In other words, no therapeutic approach is excluded, but the theory provides a general structure for making strategic and tactical decisions. Likewise, in relation to improving performance and satisfaction in the workplace (chapter 13), the theory provides a general approach to which most fashions in management theory can be readily assimilated by showing how they fit into a broader picture.

In general, the objective study of behavior is not excluded by reversal theory, provided it does not itself exclude, as dogmatic behaviorists do, the subjective meaning that the behavior has for the person who performs it. The phenomenological study of subjective meaning is not excluded unless, as in so much phenomenological psychology, behavior in the real world is overlooked. Psychometric testing is not excluded, provided it is appreciated that variance is as interesting as central tendency and that intra-individual differences may underlie inter-individual differences. Psychophysiology is not excluded, provided it is understood that psychophysiological states can only be fully understood in the context of mental states. Cognitive approaches are not excluded provided it is taken into account that these must articulate with affective processes. And constructivist, cultural, and discursive approaches are not excluded, provided it is realized that actions are both prompted and limited within biological structures and constraints and that culture itself derives from biology.

A theory that is able to incorporate, for example, the psychophysiological studies of Svebak and of Cook (chapters 5 and 7), the psychometric work of O'Connell and her colleagues (chapters 3 and 7), the learning theory of Brown (chapter 8), and the humanistic ideas of Fontana (chapter 15) must be broad and integrative, indeed.

Reversal Theory Could Fill the Gap Between Biological and Social Approaches

Psychology has for much of its history had a deep-seated tendency to split between neurology/psychophysiology on the one hand and social/cultural/linguistic psychology on the other. Some have claimed that psychology is really two different and nonoverlapping subjects and that the space between them is empty. But reversal theory, being about individual mental life, fits exactly into this gap. On the one hand, metamotivational states have physiological concomitants. On the other, they enter into different kinds of social discourse.

The study by Svebak and Murgatroyd (1985), described in chapter 5, displays neatly the way in which reversal theory can bring the two sides together. In this study, as we have seen, participants in a psychophysiological experiment were also interviewed about such matters as how they had spent their day. The data from each participant was therefore both physiological and narrative/discursive. Both sets of data were found to fit together nicely in terms of the telic–paratelic dimension (as measured psychometrically). Similarly in Apter and Svebak (1986), also described in chapter 5, rich interview data (this time about the experience of the experiment itself) related to psychophysiological records of the participants during the experiment. In general, as Kerr implies in chapter 10 (see also Kerr, 1999), reversal theory shows how qualitative as well as quantitative methods are needed if research is to be both rigorous and insightful.

The trouble with the neurological/physiological approach is that it omits meaning from the picture. The trouble with the social/discursive approach is that it sees meaning as entirely dissociated from biology. Reversal theory can be interpreted as being about "biological meaning." In this sense the metamotivational states, and the experiential domains to which they relate, provide certain kinds of preprogrammed meanings that can be expressed discursively in a variety of ways. Reversal theory is therefore about what one might term the "collective conscious" (rather than Jung's "collective unconscious"): That is, it is about the universal structures within conscious experience that provide the individual person with certain fundamental and species-wide ways of making sense of the world. In this respect, it spans the gap between the innate and biological on the one hand and the semantic and cultural on the other.

Reversal theory also refuses to set society over against biology in the way that is posited in Freud's classic notion of the id (biology) and the superego (society) as necessarily in conflict with one another. In reversal theory, there is no such essential conflict: Society reflects biology, with different institutions and social processes tending to support the different metamotivational states or at least to provide the occasion for the pursuit of the needs and values that these states represent. Values conflict, of course, but in reversal theory terms these conflicts cut right across the id–superego distinction. It could be argued that the existence of the negativistic state would appear to imply a conflict between people and the social rules that govern them. But in fact, without such rules, and the institutions that apply them, the negativistic state would have nothing to oppose; in reality, rules are needed by the negativistic state as much as they are by the conformist state.

Reversal Theory Encourages Change

Reversal theory regards people as, in the normal way of things, continually changing. Evidence for this assertion was provided particularly in chapter 4, although there is a sense in which all the evidence provided throughout this book has tended directly or indirectly to support this view. In this respect mental health implies, as we have seen in chapters 13 and 14, a kind of instability rather than stability. From this perspective, producing change is not in itself seen as an insurmountable problem. Interventions in people's lives therefore do not involve pushing people into action but rather releasing and guiding inherent change processes in desirable directions. Thus, therapy on the one hand, and workplace counseling on the other, are about encouraging and molding internal propensities for change rather than imposing change on essentially static systems. People may get "stuck," but they have within them what is necessary to get "unstuck." And although they may reverse at inappropriate times, this change process can itself be altered, and the individual can be brought into greater control of the reversal process.

All this puts a much more optimistic and helpful slant on the nature of the problems faced by those in the helping professions, as well as those, like teachers, coaches, priests, managers, and others whose mandate it is to bring out the best in people. As one participant in a reversal theory workshop put it, "All of a sudden, life is full of possibilities." Contrast this, for example, with the psychometric approach that tells people "This is how you are, and we do not expect you to be any different in the future."

Reversal Theory Can Help Psychology Return to Its Origins in Mental Life

Ever since the advent of behaviorism, psychology has lacked confidence in dealing directly with conscious experience. Where it has tried to do so, as in research on perception or attitudes, it has been on the defensive, often attempting to redefine its subject matter in objective terms. (In the process, it has produced such unconvincing formulations as "perceptual behavior".) It is true that cognitive psychology has allowed psychologists once more to speak of mental life. But little recognition has been paid in this newer tradition to feelings, emotions, and desires (unless to assimilate them to cognitions). In any case, references to mental life in these approaches are often inferences drawn from behavior rather than being based directly on individuals' own accounts. It is important, however, not to exaggerate here: Clearly humanistic psychology, discursive psychology, object–relations theory, and other movements have made inroads in recent years. But reversal theory does explicitly, and without apology, take subjective experience—the whole of subjective experience—as its primary domain of discourse. In its own way, therefore, it helps to reconnect psychology to its historical origins as the science of mental life.

CONCLUSION

Is it possible to summarize, in a few words, some of the main things that we have learned from the empirical studies reported in this book? Let us try.

The principal one has to be that there is indeed a meaningful level of analysis—the level that we have called the *level of metamotivation*, or *motivational style*—that plays a crucial part in people's experience and behavior and that has previously been largely ignored in psychology. All the work reported here attests in one way or another to the critical significance of this level.

The second general conclusion that one can draw, both from laboratory studies and observations of people in everyday life, is that change is frequent at the metamotivational level. Normal people change at this level all the time, in the workplace, while playing sports, while interacting with their spouses, while going to parties, and so on. In other words, differences within individuals need to be taken into account as well as differences between individuals.

Third, the phenomenon of reversal—of sudden change between the contrasting ways of experiencing the world, represented by opposite metamotivational states—has been documented in various ways, through interviews, case histories, and laboratory research. It has also been shown that such reversals can be dramatic in their emotional effects, for example, in converting anxiety into excitement and vice versa.

Such reversals can occur not only as a response to changing situations, but spontaneously as well, and this is the fourth main conclusion. Such spontaneity implies that there are internal forces at work as well as external forces and supports the reversal theory idea of satiation of metamotivational states. There is therefore a greater complexity in the relationship between people and their environments than is usually allowed for in other psychological theories. If people change, this is not simply because of their movement through different environments, with different expectations, roles, scripts, and the like, but because of certain innate rhythms.

Fifth, evidence has been presented that there are psychophysiological concomitants of at least one of the pairs of states—the telic and paratelic pair. This means that there is a certain objective reality about these states even though they are identified phenomenologically. It also raises the possibility that the way in which the nervous system is organized may in some way map onto the organization of experience. Furthermore, the psychophsyiological evidence, taken along with the relevant psychometric and clinical evidence, shows that arousal preference is different from arousability—an important distinction that tends not to be made in other theories of motivation and personality.

The sixth point is that people display dominances: They evidence biases toward one state or the other within each pair of states. This has now been abundantly demonstrated through psychometric testing, but at the same time it has been demonstrated in the laboratory and elsewhere that such dominances are not traits in the traditional sense, because people spend periods of time in their nondominant states.

The seventh conclusion also concerns dominances. Case histories provide evidence that people not only change, but need to change, to reverse reasonably frequently, if they are to remain psychologically healthy and to live fulfilled lives. In other words, people need to display *psychodiversity*. This means, among other things, that mental health requires a certain kind of instability and that dominances should not become too extreme.

Finally, we have seen evidence that the same situations can be experienced in very different ways in different states. As a result of this it is perfectly possible for people to enjoy such supposedly unpleasant experiences as those that result from stress, challenge, rule breaking, risk, confrontation, argument, incongruity, and dissonance. In this respect we are now in a better position to understand some of the paradoxes and puzzles cited in the opening paragraph of the introduction to this book.

There are of course many other findings that could have been listed, but these are perhaps the eight that are the most fundamental, and also the most challenging to other approaches in psychology.

In the course of the book, the explanatory range of reversal theory has been demonstrated, along with the complexity of behavior and experience that the theory is able to handle. Sport, humor, crime, addiction, creativity, stress at work, sexual behavior, and a wide variety of pathologies— all these, and many, many other kinds of behavior and experience—have been elucidated in a systematic way. The book has also, as we have just seen, documented the evidence that supports and illuminates these ideas and the way in which they can be applied to real-life problems. And at the core of the theory, underlying all the explanations, experiments, and applications, is always the set of four pairs of opposite motivational styles. Everything stems from and returns to this fundamental series of binary oppositions between seriousness and play, acquiescence and resistance, power and love, self and other. The manner in which these opposites work themselves out in the individual over different developmental stages and in different circumstances, and the way that they are reflected in different cultures and subcultures during different historical periods, may be expected to vary enormously. But if reversal theory is right, the fundamental motivational ground plan will remain the same. For each individual, the basic set of opposite values that underlie action, the basic set of contrasting meanings that underlie experience, and the basic set of conflicting desires that are called on by societal institutions will be the same in all places and at all times. This is the fundamental claim with which reversal theory confronts contemporary mainstream psychology.

REFERENCES

Aero, R., & Weiner, E. (1981). *The Mind Test*. New York: Morrow.

American Psychiatric Association. (1994). *Diagnostic and statistical manual of mental disorders* (4th ed.). Washington, DC: American Psychiatric Association.

Anderson, G., & Brown, R. I. F. (1984). Real and laboratory gambling, sensation seeking and arousal. *British Journal of Psychology, 75,* 401–410.

Anderson, G., & Brown, R. I. F. (1987). Some applications of reversal theory to the explanation of gambling and gambling addictions. *Journal of Gambling Behaviour, 3,* 179–189.

Antonovsky, A. (1987). *Unraveling the mystery of health: How people manage stress and stay well.* San Francisco: Jossey-Bass.

Apter International. (1999a). *The Apter Motivational Style Profile.* Uppingham, England: Author.

Apter International. (1999b). *The Apter Motivational Style Profile Workbook.* Uppingham, England: Author.

Apter International. (1999c). *The Apter Team Contribution System.* Uppingham, England: Author.

Apter International. (1999d). *The Apter Work Impact System.* Uppingham, England: Author.

Apter International. (1999e). *Manual for the Apter Motivational Style Profile.* Uppingham, England: Author.

Apter, M. J. (1966). *Cybernetics and development.* Oxford, England: Pergamon Press.

Apter, M. J. (1971). *The computer simulation of behavior.* New York: Harper. (Original work published 1970 by Hutchinson, London)

Apter, M. J. (1976). Some data inconsistent with the optimal arousal theory of motivation. *Perceptual and Motor Skills, 43,* 1209–1210.

Apter, M. J. (1979). Human action and the theory of psychological reversals. In G. Underwood & R. Stevens (Eds.), *Aspects of consciousness: Vol. 1. Psychological issues* (pp. 45–65). London: Academic Press.

Apter, M. J. (1981a). Experiencing motivation: Twelve propositions from reversal theory. *Self and Society, 9,* 211–220.

Apter, M. J. (1981b). On the concept of bistability. *International Journal of General Systems, 6,* 225–232.

Apter, M. J. (1981c). The possibility of a structural phenomenology: The case of reversal theory. *Journal of Phenomenological Psychology, 12,* 173–187.

Apter, M. J. (1981d). Reversal theory: Making sense of felt arousal. *New Forum, 8,* 27–30.

Apter, M. J. (1982a). *The experience of motivation: The theory of psychological reversals.* London: Academic Press.

Apter, M. J. (1982b). Fawlty Towers: A reversal theory analysis of a popular television comedy series. *Journal of Popular Culture, 16,* 128–138.

Apter, M. J. (1982c). Metaphor as synergy. In D. S. Miall (Ed.), *Metaphor: Problems and perspectives* (pp. 55–70). Atlantic Highlands, NJ: Humanities Press.

Apter, M. J. (1982d). Reversal theory and its relevance to educational psychology. *Education Section Review (British Psychological Society), 6*(1), 33–37.

Apter, M. J. (1983). Negativism and the sense of identity. In G. Breakwell (Ed.), *Threatened identities* (pp. 75–90). London: Wiley.

Apter, M. J. (1984a). Reversal theory and personality: A review. *Journal of Research in Personality, 18,* 265–288.

Apter, M. J. (1984b). Reversal theory, cognitive synergy and the arts. In W. R. Crozier & A. J. Chapman (Eds.), *Cognitive processes in the perception of art* (pp. 411–426). Amsterdam: North Holland.

Apter, M. J. (1985). Religious states of mind: A reversal theory interpretation. In L. B. Brown (Ed.), *Advances in the psychology of religion* (pp. 62–75). Oxford, England: Pergamon.

Apter, M. J. (1987). Reversal theory and human activity. *Voprosi Psykhologii* (USSR) 1, 162–169.

Apter, M. J. (1988a). Beyond the autocentric and the allocentric. In M. J. Apter, J. H. Kerr, & M. P. Cowles (Eds.), *Progress in reversal theory* (pp. 339–348). Amsterdam: Elsevier.

Apter, M. J. (1988b). Reversal theory as a theory of the emotions. In M. J. Apter, J. H. Kerr, & M. P. Cowles (Eds.), *Progress in reversal theory* (pp. 43–62). Amsterdam: Elsevier.

Apter, M. J. (1989a). Reversal theory: A new approach to motivation, emotion, and personality. *Anuario de Psicologia, 42,* 19–29.

Apter, M. J. (1989b). *Reversal theory: Motivation, emotion, and personality.* London: Routledge.

Apter, M. J. (1990a). Reversal theory: Clinical implications. *Anuario de Psicologia*, *44*, 5–17.

Apter, M. J. (1990b). Sport and mental health: A new psychological perspective. In G. P. H. Hermans & W. L. Mosterd (Eds.), *Sports, medicine, and health* (pp. 47–56). Amsterdam: Elsevier.

Apter, M. J. (1991a). Reversal theory and the structure of emotional experience. In C. D. Spielberger, I. G. Sarason, Z. Kulcsar, & G. L. Van Heck (Eds.), *Stress and emotion: Vol. 14. Anxiety, anger, and curiosity* (pp. 17–30). New York: Hemisphere.

Apter, M. J. (1991b). A structural phenomenology of play. In J. H. Kerr & M. J. Apter (Eds.), *Adult play: A reversal theory approach* (pp. 13–30). Amsterdam: Swets & Zeitlinger.

Apter, M. J. (1991c). A structural phenomenology of stress. In C. D. Spielberger, I. G. Sarason, J. Strelau, & J. M. T. Brebner (Eds.), *Stress and anxiety* (Vol. 13, pp. 13–22). New York: Hemisphere.

Apter, M. J. (1991d). Suggestibility: A reversal theory perspective. In J. F. Schumaker (Ed.), *Human suggestibility* (pp. 146–158). New York: Routledge.

Apter, M. J. (1992). *The dangerous edge: The psychology of excitement*. New York: Free Press.

Apter, M. J. (1993). Phenomenological frames and the paradoxes of experience. In J. H. Kerr, S. Murgatroyd, & M. J. Apter (Eds.), *Advances in reversal theory* (pp. 27–40). Amsterdam: Swets & Zeitlinger.

Apter, M. J. (1996). Teoria de la inversion: Motivacion, emotion, y personalidad. [Reversal theory: Motivation, emotion, and personality.] (J. C. Palavecino, Trans.) Barcelona, Spain: EUB.

Apter, M. J. (1997a). Reversal theory, stress, and health. In S. Svebak & M. J. Apter (Eds.), *Stress and health: A reversal theory perspective* (pp. 21–32). Washington, DC: Taylor & Francis.

Apter, M. J. (1997b). Reversal theory: What is it? *The Psychologist, 10,* 217–220.

Apter, M. J. (1998). We can test subpersonalities. *Selection and Development Review, 14*(6), 1.

Apter, M. J. (1999a, June–July). *The developmental origins of the metamotivational states*. Paper presented at the Ninth International Conference on Reversal Theory, Windsor, Ontario, Canada.

Apter, M. J. (1999b). Measurement challenges in reversal theory sport research. In J. H. Kerr (Ed.), *Experiencing sport: Reversal theory* (pp. 19–36). Chichester, England: Wiley.

Apter, M. J., & Apter-Desselles, M. L. (1993). The personality of the patient: Going beyond the trait concept. *Patient Education and Counseling, 22,* 107–114.

Apter, M. J., & Batler, R. (1997). Gratuitous risk: A study of parachuting. In S. Svebak & M. J. Apter (Eds.), *Stress and health: A reversal theory perspective* (pp. 119–129). Washington, DC: Taylor & Francis.

Apter, M. J., & Fontana, D. (1985). Overview and discussion. In M. J. Apter, D. Fontana, & S. Murgatroyd (Eds.), *Reversal theory: Applications and developments* (pp. 179–185). Cardiff, Wales: University College Cardiff Press.

Apter, M. J., Fontana, D., & Murgatroyd, S. (1985). *Reversal theory: Applications and developments*. Cardiff, Wales: University College Cardiff Press.

Apter, M. J., & Kerr, J. H. (1991). The nature, function and value of play. In J. H. Kerr & M. J. Apter (Eds.), *Adult play: A reversal theory approach* (pp. 163–175). Amsterdam: Swets & Zeitlinger.

Apter, M. J., Kerr, J. H., & Cowles, M. P. (1988). *Progress in reversal theory*. Amsterdam: Elsevier.

Apter, M. J., & Larsen, R. (1993). Sixty consecutive days: Telic and paratelic states in everyday life. In J. H. Kerr, S. Murgatroyd, & M. J. Apter (Eds.), *Advances in reversal theory* (pp. 107–122). Amsterdam: Swets & Zeitlinger.

Apter, M. J., Mallows, R., & Williams, S. (1998). The development of the Motivational Style Profile. *Personality and Individual Differences, 24,* 7–18.

Apter, M. J., & Smith, K. C. P. (1976). Negativism in adolescence. *The Counsellor, 23–24,* 25–30.

Apter, M. J., & Smith, K. C. P. (1977). Humour and the theory of psychological reversals. In A. J. Chapman & H. C. Foot (Eds.), *It's a funny thing, humour* (pp. 95–100). Oxford, England: Pergamon.

Apter, M. J., & Smith, K. C. P. (1978). Sexual dysfunction—Depression, anxiety and the reversal theory. *British Journal of Sexual Medicine, 5,* 23–26.

Apter, M. J., & Smith, K. C. P. (1979a). Psychological reversals: Some new perspectives on the family and family communication. *Family Therapy, 6,* 89–100.

Apter, M. J., & Smith, K. C. P. (1979b). Sexual behaviour and the theory of psychological reversals. In M. Cook & G. Wilson (Eds.), *Love and attraction: An international conference* (pp. 405–408). Oxford, England: Pergamon Press.

Apter, M. J., & Smith, K. C. P. (1985). Experiencing personal relationships. In M. J. Apter, D. Fontana, & S. Murgatroyd (Eds.), *Reversal theory: Applications and developments* (pp. 161–178). Cardiff, Wales: University College Cardiff Press.

Apter, M. J., & Smith, K. C. P. (1987). Reversal theory. In B. McGurk, D. Thornton, & M. Williams (Eds.), *Applying psychology to imprisonment: Theory and practice* (pp. 78–95). London: Her Majesty's Stationery Office.

Apter, M. J., & Smith, K. C. P. (1988). The fascination of psychoanalysis. *Changes, 6,* 95–97.

Apter, M. J., & Spirn, N. (1997). Motives for donating blood. In S. Svebak & M. J. Apter (Eds.), *Stress and health: A reversal theory perspective* (pp. 145–156). Washington, DC: Taylor & Francis.

Apter, M. J., & Svebak, S. (1986). The EMG gradient as a reflection of metamotivational state. *Scandinavian Journal of Psychology, 27,* 209–219.

Apter, M. J., & Svebak, S. (1989). Stress from the reversal theory perspective. In C. D. Spielberger & J. Strelau (Eds.), *Stress and anxiety* (Vol. 12, pp. 39–52). New York: Hemisphere.

Apter, M. J., & Svebak, S. (1992). Reversal theory as a biological approach to individual differences. In A. Gale & M. W. Eysenck (Eds.), *Handbook of individual differences: Biological perspectives* (pp. 323–353). New York: Wiley.

Arieti, S. (1976). *Creativity: The magic synthesis*. New York: Basic Books.

Arnheim, R. (1966). *Toward a psychology of art*. Berkeley: University of California Press.

Athabasca University. (1986). *Organizational culture: 400 level course reader*. Athabasca, Alberta, Canada: Author.

Baer, J. S., Kamarck, T., Lichtenstein, E., & Ransom, C. (1989). Prediction of smoking relapse: Analyses of temptations and transgressions after initial cessation. *Journal of Consulting and Clinical Psychology, 57,* 623–627.

Baer, J. S., & Lichtenstein, E. (1988). Classification and prediction of smoking relapse episodes: An exploration of individual differences. *Journal of Consulting and Clinical Psychology, 56,* 104–110.

Baker, J. (1988). Stress appraisals and coping with everyday hassles. In M. J. Apter, J. H. Kerr, & M. P. Cowles (Eds.), *Progress in reversal theory* (pp. 117–128). Amsterdam: Elsevier.

Balswick, J. O., & Macrides, C. (1975). Parental stimulus for adolescent rebellion. *Adolescence, 10,* 253–266.

Barr, S. A., McDermott, M. R., & Evans, P. (1993). Predicting persistence: A study of telic and paratelic frustration. In J. H. Kerr, S. Murgatroyd, & M. J. Apter (Eds.), *Advances in reversal theory* (pp. 123–136). Amsterdam: Swets & Zeitlinger.

Barratt, E. S. (1985). Impulsiveness subtraits: Arousal and information processing. In J. T. Spence & C. E. Izard (Eds.), *Motivation, emotion and personality* (pp. 137–146). New York: Elsevier.

Bateson, G. (1973). *Steps to an ecology of mind*. St. Albans, United Kingdom: Paladin.

Beck, A., Ward, C., Mendelson, M., Mock, J., & Erbaugh, J. (1961). An inventory for measuring depression. *Archives of General Psychology, 4,* 53–63.

Bejerot, N. (1972). *Addiction: An artificially induced drive*. Springfield, IL: Charles C Thomas.

Berlyne, D. E. (1960). *Conflict, arousal, and curiosity*. New York: McGraw-Hill.

Berlyne, D. E. (1961). Conflict and the orientation reaction. *Journal of Experimental Psychology, 62*(5), 476–483.

Berlyne, D. E. (1971). *Aesthetics and psychobiology*. New York: Appleton-Century-Crofts.

Berlyne, D. E. (1978). Curiosity and learning. *Motivation and Emotion, 2*(2), 97–175.

Bishop, M. M. (1994). *An application of reversal theory to the prediction of young adults' safer-sex behaviors*. Unpublished master of arts dissertation, University of Kansas, Lawrence.

Blackburn, R. (1987). Two scales for the assessment of personality disorder in antisocial populations. *Personality and Individual Differences, 8,* 81–93.

Blackmore, M., & Murgatroyd, S. (1980). Anne: The disruptive infant. In S. Murgatroyd (Ed.), *Helping the troubled child: Interprofessional case studies* (pp. 31–42). London: Harper & Row.

Bliss, R. E., Garvey, A. J., Heinold, J. W., & Hitchcock, J. L. (1989). The influence of situation and coping on relapse crises after smoking cessation. *Journal of Consulting and Clinical Psychology, 57,* 443–449.

Boekaerts, M. (1986). Arousal, telic dominance and learning behaviour. In R. Gupta & P. Coxhead (Eds.), *Cultural diversity and learning efficiency: Recent developments in assessment* (pp. 1–26). London: Macmillan.

Boekaerts, M. (1988). Are there two types of arousal avoidance? In M. J. Apter, J. H. Kerr, & M. P. Cowles (Eds.), *Progress in reversal theory* (pp. 275–286). Amsterdam: Elsevier.

Boekaerts, M., Hendriksen, J., & Michels, C. (1988a). The assessment of telic dominance in primary school pupils. In M. J. Apter, J. H. Kerr, & M. P. Cowles (Eds.), *Progress in reversal theory* (pp. 265–274). Amsterdam: Elsevier.

Boekaerts, M., Hendriksen, J., & Michels, C. (1988b). The Nijmegen Telic Dominance Scale. In M. J. Apter, J. H. Kerr, & M. P. Cowles (Eds.), *Progress in reversal theory* (pp. 369–372). Amsterdam: Elsevier.

Bowers, A. J. (1985). Reversals, delinquency and disruption. *British Journal of Clinical Psychology, 25,* 303–304.

Bowers, A. J. (1988). Telic dominance and delinquency in adolescent boys. In M. J. Apter, J. H. Kerr, & M. P. Cowles (Eds.), *Progress in reversal theory* (pp. 231–234). Amsterdam: Elsevier.

Braathen, E. T., & Svebak, S. (1990). Task-induced tonic and phasic EMG response patterns and psychological predictors in elite performers of endurance and explosive sports. *International Journal of Psychophysiology, 9,* 21–30.

Braathen, E. T., & Svebak, S. (1992). Motivational differences among talented teenage athletes: The significance of gender, type of sport and level of excellence. *Scandinavian Journal of Medicine and Science in Sports, 2,* 153–159.

Braman, O. R. (1988). Oppositionalism: Clinical descriptions of six forms of telic self-negativism. In M. J. Apter, J. H. Kerr, & M. P. Cowles (Eds.), *Progress in reversal theory* (pp. 213–222). Amsterdam: Elsevier.

Braman, O. R. (1995). *The oppositional child.* Charlotte, NC: Kidsrights.

Broom, K. (2000). Playing with emergency: A case study of reversal theory in artwork. *American Journal of Art Therapy, 38,* 107–113.

Brown, R. (1986). *Social psychology: The second edition.* New York: Free Press.

Brown, R. I. F. (1987a). Classical and operant paradigms in the management of gambling addictions. *Behavioral Psychotherapy, 15,* 111–122.

Brown, R. I. F. (1987b). Gambling addictions, arousal and an affective decision making explanation of behavioral reversions or relapses. *International Journal of Addictions, 22,* 1053–1067.

Brown, R. I. F. (1988). Reversal theory and subjective experience in the explanation of addiction and relapse. In M. J. Apter, J. H. Kerr, & M. P. Cowles (Eds.), *Progress in reversal theory* (pp. 191–212). Amsterdam: Elsevier.

Brown, R. I. F. (1989). Relapses from a gambling perspective. In M. Gossop (Ed.), *Relapse and addictive behaviour*. London: Croom Helm.

Brown, R. I. F. (1991). Gambling, gaming and other addictive play. In J. H. Kerr & M. J. Apter (Eds.), *Adult play: A reversal theory approach* (pp. 101–118). Amsterdam: Swets & Zeitlinger.

Brown, R. I. F. (1993a). Planning deficiencies in addictions from the perspective of reversal theory. In J. H. Kerr, S. Murgatroyd, & M. J. Apter (Eds.), *Advances in reversal theory* (pp. 205–224). Amsterdam: Swets & Zeitlinger.

Brown, R. I. F. (1993b). Plans and planning—and reversals as jokers in the pack. In J. H. Kerr, S. Murgatroyd, & M. J. Apter (Eds.), *Advances in reversal theory* (pp. 89–106). Amsterdam: Swets & Zeitlinger.

Brown, R. I. F. (1993c). Reversals and switching in multiple personality disorder. In J. H. Kerr, S. Murgatroyd, & M. J. Apter (Eds.), *Advances in reversal theory* (pp. 267–282). Amsterdam: Swets & Zeitlinger.

Brown, R. I. F. (1993d). The roles of arousal, cognitive distortion and sensation seeking in gambling addictions. *Psicologia Conductual, 1*, 375–388.

Brown, R. I. F. (1993e). Some contributions of the study of gambling to the study of other addictions. In W. R. Eadington & J. A. Cornelius (Eds.), *Gambling behavior and problem gambling* (pp. 241–272). Reno: University of Nevada Press.

Brown, R. I. F. (1997). A theoretical model of behavioral addictions—Applied to offending. In J. E. Hodge, M. McMurran, & C. R. Hollin (Eds.), *Addicted to crime?* (pp. 13–65). New York: Wiley.

Brownell, K. D., Marlatt, G. A., Lichtenstein, E., & Wilson, G. T. (1986). Understanding and preventing relapse. *American Psychologist, 41*, 765–782.

Bru, E., Mykletun, R. J., & Svebak, S. (1994). Assessment of musculoskeletal and other health complaints in female hospital staff. *Applied Ergonomics, 25*, 101–105.

Burger, J. M., & Cooper, H. M. (1979). The desirability of control. *Motivation and Emotion, 4*, 391–393.

Caillois, R. (1961). *Man, play and games*. New York: Free Press.

Calhoun, J. E. (1995). Construct validity of the Telic/Paratelic State Instrument: A measure of reversal theory constructs. Unpublished doctoral dissertation, University of Kansas School of Nursing, Lawrence.

Carter, S. (1999). *Renaissance management*. London: Kogan Page.

Cattell, R. B., Eber, H. W., & Tatsuoka, M. M. (1970). Handbook for the Sixteen Personality Factor Questionnaire. Champaign, IL: IPAT.

Cattell, R. B., Horn, J., & Sweney, A. B. (1970). Motivation Analysis Test. Champaign, IL: IPAT.

Chirivella, E. C., & Martinez, L. M. (1994). The sensation of risk and motivational tendencies in sports: An empirical study. *Personality and Individual Differences, 16,* 777–786.

Cogan, N. A., & Brown, R. I. F. (1998). Metamotivational dominance, states and injuries in risk and safe sport. *Personality and Individual Differences, 27,* 503–518.

Cogan, N. A., & Brown, R. I. F. (1999). The experience of risk sport: Dominance, states and injuries. In J. H. Kerr (Ed.), *Experiencing sport: Reversal theory* (pp. 155–174). Chichester, England: Wiley.

Cohen, S., Kamarck, T., & Mermelstein, R. (1983). A global measure of perceived stress. *Journal of Health and Social Behavior, 24,* 385–396.

Cook, M. R., & Gerkovich, M. M. (1993). The development of a Paratelic Dominance Scale. In J. H. Kerr, S. Murgatroyd, & M. J. Apter (Eds.), *Advances in reversal theory* (pp. 177–188). Amsterdam: Swets & Zeitlinger.

Cook, M. R., Gerkovich, M. M., Hoffman, S. J., McClernon, F. J., Cohen, H. D., Oakleaf, K. L., & O'Connell, K. A. (1995). Smoking and EEG power spectra: Effects of differences in arousal seeking. *International Journal of Psychophysiology, 19,* 247–256.

Cook, M. R., Gerkovich, M. M., Hoffman, S. J., McClernon, F. J., & O'Connell, K. A. (1996). Effects of smoking and telic/paratelic dominance on the contingent negative variation (CNV). *International Journal of Psychophysiology, 23,* 101–110.

Cook, M. R., Gerkovich, M. M., & O'Connell, K. A. (1997). Differential EEG effects of smoking in the telic and paratelic states. In S. Svebak & M. J. Apter (Eds.), *Stress and health: A reversal theory perspective* (pp. 103–116). Washington, DC: Taylor & Francis.

Cook, M. R., Gerkovich, M. M., O'Connell, K. A., & Potocky, M. (1995). Reversal theory constructs and cigarette availability predict lapse early in smoking cessation. *Research in Nursing & Health, 18,* 217–224.

Cook, M. R., Gerkovich, M. M., Potocky, M., & O'Connell, K. A. (1993). Instruments for the assessment of reversal theory states. *Patient Education and Counseling, 22,* 99–106.

Cook, M. R., Gerkovich, M. M., Potocky, M., O'Connell, K. A., & Hoffman, S. J. (1991, June). *Progress toward the development of instruments to measure reversal theory constructs.* Paper presented at the Fifth International Conference on Reversal Theory and Health, Kansas City, MO.

Cooper, R. Osselton, J. W., & Shaw, J. C. (1980). *EEG technology* (3rd ed.). London: Butterworth.

Costa, P. T., Jr., & McCrae, R. R. (1985). *The NEO Personality Inventory.* Odessa, FL: Psychological Assessment Resources.

Coulson, A. S. (1991). Cognitive synergy in televised entertainment. In J. H. Kerr & M. J. Apter (Eds.), *Adult play: A reversal theory approach* (pp. 71–86). Amsterdam: Swets & Zeitlinger.

Coulson, A. S. (1995). *The nature of cognitive synergy*. Unpublished doctoral dissertation, University of Wales, Cardiff, United Kingdom.

Cowles, M., Darling, M., & Skanes, A. (1992). Some characteristics of the simulated self. *Personality and Individual Differences, 13,* 501–510.

Cowles, M., & Davis, C. (1985). Strength of the nervous system and reversal theory. In M. J. Apter, D. Fontana, & S. Murgatroyd (Eds.), *Reversal theory: Applications and developments* (pp. 129–143). Cardiff, Wales: University College Cardiff Press.

Cox, T., & Kerr, J. H. (1989). Arousal effects during tournament play in squash. *Perceptual and Motor Skills, 69,* 1275–1280.

Cox, T., & Kerr, J. H. (1990). Self-reported mood in competitive squash. *Personality and Individual Differences, 11,* 199–203.

Cummings, C., Gordon, J. R., & Marlatt, G. A. (1980). Relapse prevention and prediction. In W. R. Miller (Ed.), *The addictive behaviors: Treatment of alcoholism, drug abuse, smoking, and obesity* (pp. 291–321). New York: Pergamon Press.

Deckers, L., & Avery, P. (1994). Altered joke endings and a joke structure schema. *Humor, 7*(4), 313–321.

Deckers, L., & Salais, D. (1983). Humor as a negatively accelerated function of the degree of incongruity. *Motivation and Emotion, 7,* 357–363.

DiClemente, R. J., Forrest, K. A., & Mickler, S. (1990). College students' knowledge and attitudes about AIDS and changes in HIV-preventive behaviors. *AIDS Education and Prevention, 2,* 201–212.

Dixon, M. (1993a, October 27). Not brain-power, but frame of mind. *Financial Times,* p. 29.

Dixon, M. (1993b, October 6). The source of effective innovation. *Financial Times,* p. 14.

Dixon, M. (1994, January 24). The benefits of a switchable personality. *Financial Times,* p. 13.

Dobbin, J. P., & Martin, R. A. (1988). Telic versus paratelic dominance: Personality moderator of biochemical responses to stress. In M. J. Apter, J. H. Kerr, & M. P. Cowles (Eds.), *Progress in reversal theory* (pp. 107–116). Amsterdam: Elsevier.

Dodge, K. A., & Coie, J. D. (1987). Social information processing factors in reactive and proactive aggression in children's peer groups. *Journal of Personality and Social Psychology, 53*(6), 1146–1158.

Doherty, O., & Matthews, G. (1988). Personality characteristics of opiate addicts. *Personality and Individual Differences, 9,* 171–172.

Doherty, S., & McDermott, M. R. (1997, July). *Predicting delinquency.* Poster session presented at the Eighth International Conference on Reversal Theory, Department of Psychology, University of East London, England.

Donovan, E. M., & Chaney, E. F. (1985). Alcoholic relapse and intervention: Models and methods. In G. A. Marlatt & J. R. Gordon (Eds.), *Relapse prevention: Maintenance strategies in the treatment of addictive behaviors* (pp. 351–416). New York: Guilford Press.

Douglas, M. (1966). *Purity and danger: An analysis of the concepts of pollution and taboo*. London: Routledge & Kegan Paul.

Eley, T., Lichenstein, P., & Stevenson, J. (1999). Sex differences in the aetiology of aggressive and nonaggressive antisocial behaviour: Results from two twin studies. *Child Development, 70*(1), 155–168.

Emler, N. (1984). Differential involvement in delinquency: Toward an interpretation in terms of reputation management. *Progress in Experimental Psychology, 13,* 173–239.

Empson, W. (1972). *Seven types of ambiguity*. London: Penguin. (Original work published 1930)

Evans, R. (1994, April–June). A psychological profile of top Australian soccer referees. *Sports Coach,* 17–18.

Eysenck, H. J., & Eysenck, S. B. G. (1969). *Personality structure and measurement*. London: Routledge & Kegan Paul.

Eysenck, H. J., & Eysenck, S. B. G. (1975). *Manual of the Eysenck Personality Inventory*. London: Hodder & Stoughton.

Festinger, L. (1957). *A theory of cognitive dissonance*. Evanston, IL: Row, Peterson, Evanston.

Fiske, D. W., & Maddi, S. R. (1961). A conceptual framework. In D. W. Fiske & S. R. Maddi (Eds.), *Functions of varied experience* (pp. 11–56). Homewood, IL: Dorsey.

Folkman, S., & Lazarus, R. S. (1980). An analysis of coping in a middle-aged community sample. *Journal of Health and Social Behavior, 21,* 219–239.

Fontana, D. (1978). *An investigation of reversal and obsessionality*. Unpublished doctoral dissertation, University of Wales, Cardiff, United Kingdom.

Fontana, D. (1981a). Obsessionality and reversal theory. *British Journal of Clinical Psychology, 20,* 299–300.

Fontana, D. (1981b). Reversal theory, the paratelic state, and Zen. *Self and Society, 9,* 229–236.

Fontana, D. (1983). Individual differences in personality: Trait-based versus state-based approaches. *Educational Psychology, 3,* 189–200.

Fontana, D. (1985). Educating for creativity. In M. J. Apter, D. Fontana, & S. Murgatroyd (Eds.), *Reversal theory: Applications and developments* (pp. 72–88). Cardiff, Wales: University College Cardiff Press.

Fontana, D. (1987). Self-assertion and self-negation in Buddhist psychology. *Journal of Humanistic Psychology* 9(2), 175–195.

Fontana, D. (1988). Self-awareness and self-forgetting: Now I see me, now I don't. In M. J. Apter, J. H. Kerr, & M. P. Cowles (Eds.), *Progress in reversal theory* (pp. 349–357). Amsterdam: Elsevier.

Fontana, D. (1991a). Reversals and the eastern religious mind. In J. H. Kerr & M. J. Apter (Eds.), *Adult play: A reversal theory approach* (pp. 151–162). Amsterdam: Swets & Zeitlinger.

Fontana, D. (1991b). Shape, colour and symbols. In J. H. Kerr & M. J. Apter (Eds.), *Adult play: A reversal theory approach* (pp. 141–150). Amsterdam: Swets & Zeitlinger.

Fontana, D. (1999). Inner transformation and outer behaviour. *Transpersonal Psychology Review: Journal of the Transpersonal Psychology Section of the British Psychological Society, 3*(1), 5–13.

Fontana, D., & Slack, I. (1996). The need for transpersonal psychology. *The Psychologist 9*(6), 267–269.

Fontana, D., & Valente, L. (1993a). Drama therapy and the theory of psychological reversals. *Arts in Psychotherapy, 20,* 133–142.

Fontana, D., & Valente, L. (1993b). A reversal theory approach to the causes and treatment of stress in professional life. *Patient Education and Counseling, 22,* 81–89.

Fontana, D., & Valente, L. (1993c). Reversal theory, dramatherapy and psychological health. In J. H. Kerr, S. Murgatroyd, & M. J. Apter (Eds.), *Advances in reversal theory* (pp. 325–334). Amsterdam: Swets & Zeitlinger.

Fontana, D., & Valente, L. (1997). Stress in the workplace: Causes and treatment. In S. Svebak & M. J. Apter (Eds.), *Stress and health: A reversal theory perspective* (pp. 199–208). Washington, DC: Taylor & Francis.

Foot, D. (1982). *Harold Gimblett: Tortured genius of cricket.* London: Heinemann.

Foot, D. (1996). *Wally Hammond: The reasons why.* London: Robson Books.

Foster, M. L. (1988). Cultural triggering of psychological reversals. In M. J. Apter, J. H. Kerr, & M. P. Cowles (Eds.), *Progress in reversal theory* (pp. 63–76). Amsterdam: Elsevier.

Foster, M. (1993). Reversal theory and the institutionalization of war. In J. H. Kerr, S. Murgatroyd, & M. J. Apter (Eds.), *Advances in reversal theory* (pp. 67–74). Amsterdam: Swets & Zeitlinger.

Frank-Ragan, M. E. (1994). *Reversal theory and the risk-taking sexual behavior of homosexual and bisexual men.* Unpublished doctoral dissertation, University of Kansas, Lawrence.

Frey, K. (1990). *Correlates and distributions of arousal preferences over time.* Unpublished master of science dissertation, Purdue University, West Lafayette, IN.

Frey, K. P. (1991). Sexual behaviour as adult play. In J. H. Kerr & M. J. Apter (Eds.), *Adult play: A reversal theory approach* (pp. 55–70). Amsterdam: Swets & Zeitlinger.

Frey, K. P. (1993). Distance running: A reversal theory analysis. In J. H. Kerr, S. Murgatroyd, & M. J. Apter (Eds.), *Advances in reversal theory* (pp. 157–164). Amsterdam: Swets & Zeitlinger.

Frey, K. P. (1997a). About reversal theory. In S. Svebak & M. J. Apter (Eds.), *Stress and health: A reversal theory perspective* (pp. 3–19). Washington, DC: Taylor & Francis.

Frey, K. P. (1997b, July). *The art of experiencing: Reversal theory perspectives on optimal psychological health.* Paper presented at the Eighth International Reversal Theory Conference, University of East London, England.

Frey, K. P. (1999). Reversal theory: Basic concepts. In J. H. Kerr (Ed.), *Experiencing sport: Reversal theory* (pp. 3–17). Chichester, England: Wiley.

Gallacher, J. E. J., & Beswick, A. D. (1988). Telic state, type A, and blood pressure. In M. J. Apter, J. H. Kerr, & M. P. Cowles (Eds.), *Progress in reversal theory* (pp. 173–178). Amsterdam: Elsevier.

Gallacher, J. E. J., Yarnell, J. W. G., & Phillips, K. M. (1988). Goal orientation, type A behaviour and telic dominance in middle-aged men. *Counselling Psychology Quarterly, 1*, 155–164.

Gamson, W. A., Fireman, B., & Rytina, S. (1982). *Encounters with unjust authority.* Homewood, IL: Dorsey Press.

Gerkovich, M. M. (1997). Understanding sexual risk-taking behavior. In S. Svebak & M. J. Apter (Eds.), *Stress and health: A reversal theory perspective* (pp. 131–142). Washington, DC: Taylor & Francis.

Gerkovich, M. M. (1998). *Modeling sexual risk behavior by heterosexuals.* Unpublished doctoral dissertation, University of Kansas, Lawrence.

Gerkovich, M. M., Cook, M. R., Hoffman, S. J., & O'Connell, K. A. (1998). Individual differences in cardiac and EMG activity after smoking. *Personality and Individual Differences, 25*, 353–364.

Gerkovich, M. M., Cook, M. R., O'Connell, K. A., & Potocky, M. (1993). Reversal theory analysis of relapse crises following smoking cessation. *Patient Education and Counseling, 22*, 91–97.

Gerkovich, M. M., Potocky, M., O'Connell, K. A., & Cook, M. R. (1993). Using the somatic modes of reversal theory to classify relapse crises in ex-smokers. In J. H. Kerr, S. Murgatroyd, & M. J. Apter (Eds.), *Advances in reversal theory* (pp. 235–246). Amsterdam: Swets & Zeitlinger.

Ghiselin, B. (1952). *The creative process.* Berkeley: University of California Press.

Gilbert, D. G. (1995). *Smoking individual differences, psychopathology, and emotion.* Washington, DC: Taylor & Francis.

Gilbert, D. G., Robinson, J. H., Chamberlin, C. L., & Spielberger, C. D. (1989). Effects of smoking/nicotine on anxiety, heartrate and lateralization of EEG during a stressful movie. *Psychophysiology, 26*, 311–320.

Girodo, M. (1985, May). *Telic and paratelic modes in operational undercover and field narcotics agents.* Paper presented at the Second International Conference on Reversal Theory, York University, Toronto, Canada.

Glasser, W. (1976). *Positive addictions.* New York: Harper & Row.

Golding, J., & Mangan, G. L. (1982). Arousing and de-arousing effects of cigarette smoking under conditions of stress and mild sensory isolation. *Psychophysiology, 19*, 449–456.

Gotts, G. H., Kerr, J. H., & Wangeman, J. F. (2000). Towards an international scale of telic-paratelic dominance. *Personality and Individual Differences, 28*, 217–227.

Govinda, A. (1977). Creative meditation and multidimensional consciousness. London: George Allen & Unwin.

Gray, J. (1971). *The psychology of fear and stress.* London: Weidenfeld & Nicolson.

Griffin, M., & McDermott, M. R. (1998). Exploring a tripartite relationship between rebelliousness, openness to experience and creativity. *Social Behaviour and Personality, 26*(4), 347–356.

Grover, J. J. (1999). *The role of reversal theory in moderating occupational stress in British police officers, special constables and civilian support staff.* Unpublished doctoral dissertation, South Thames (Salomon's) Clinical Psychology Training Scheme, Canterbury Christ Church University College, England.

Hall, W. L. (1995, September). Rational people and why they do irrational things: The theory of psychological reversals. *The Health Care Supervisor.*

Hart, J. (1987). Commentary: Why not more phenomenology and less structure? In J. Norcross (Ed.), *Casebook of eclectic psychotherapy* (pp. 320–322). New York: Brunner/Mazel.

Hawes, C. C. J. (1998). *Proactive and reactive rebelliousness as predictors of attitudinal absence and occupational turnover.* Unpublished doctoral dissertation, Department of Psychology, University of East London, London.

Hebb, D. O. (1955). Drives and the C. N. S. (Conceptual Nervous System). *Psychological Review, 62,* 243–254.

Herning, R. I., Jones, R. T., & Bachman, J. (1983). EEG changes during tobacco withdrawal. *Psychophysiology, 20,* 507–512.

Hetherington, R. (1983). Presidential address to the British Psychological Society. *Bulletin of the British Psychological Society, 36,* 277.

Holmes, T. H., & Rahe, R. H. (1967). The social readjustment rating scale. *Journal of Psychosomatic Research, 11,* 213–218.

Howard, R. (1988). Telic dominance, personality, and coping. In M. J. Apter, J. H. Kerr, & M. P. Cowles (Eds.), *Progress in reversal theory* (pp. 129–142). Amsterdam: Elsevier.

Hudson, J. (1998). Stress and arousal in elite youth badminton players: A reversal theory perspective. In A. Lees, I. Maynard, M. Hughes, & T. Reilly (Eds.), *Science and racket sports* (Vol. II, pp. 174–178). London: E. & F. N. Spon.

Hudson, J., & Bates, M. D. (2000). Factors affecting metamotivational reversals during motor task performance. *Perceptual and Motor Skills, 91,* 373–384.

Huizinga, J. (1949). *Homo Ludens: A study of the play element in culture.* London: Routledge & Kegan Paul.

Humphrey, N. K. (1984). *Consciousness regained: Chapters in the development of mind.* Oxford, England: Oxford University Press.

Hyers, C. (1985). Reversal theory as a key to understanding religious diversity. In M. J. Apter, D. Fontana, & S. Murgatroyd (Eds.), *Reversal theory: Applications and developments* (pp. 117–128). Cardiff, Wales: University College Cardiff Press.

Hyers, C. (1991). Education as play. In J. H. Kerr & M. J. Apter (Eds.), *Adult play: A reversal theory approach* (pp. 131–140). Amsterdam: Swets & Zeitlinger.

Hyland, M. E., Sherry, R., & Thacker, C. (1988). Prospectus for an improved measure of telic dominance. In M. J. Apter, J. H. Kerr, & M. P. Cowles (Eds.), *Progress in reversal theory* (pp. 297–312). Amsterdam: Elsevier.

Jenkins, C. D., Rosenman, R. H., & Friedman, M. (1967). Development of an objective psychological test for the determination of the coronary-prone behavior pattern in employed men. *Journal of Chronic Diseases, 20,* 371–379.

Jones, R. (1981). Reversals, delinquency and fun. *Self and Society, 9,* 237–241.

Jones, R. S. P., & Heskin, K. J. (1988). Towards a functional analysis of delinquent behaviour: A pilot study. *Counselling Psychology Quarterly, 1,* 35–42.

Kahn, R. A., & Kureshi, A. (1986). Interacting effect of certain social differences in the relationship between fear of failure and telic dominance. *Journal of Psychological Researches, 30,* 135–139.

Kakolewski, K. E., Goings, K., O'Connell, K. A., Gerkovich, M. M., & Cook, M. R. (1996, August). A laboratory test of the Global Assessment Scale as a measure of telic/paratelic states. *Synergy: The Reversal Theory Newsletter,* 3–4.

Kanner, A. D., Coyne, J. C., Schaefer, C., & Lazarus, R. S. (1981). Comparison of two modes of stress measurement: Daily hassles and uplifts versus major life events. *Journal of Behavioral Medicine, 4,* 1–39.

Keinan, G., Meir, E., & Gome-Nemirovsky, T. (1984). Measurement of risk takers' personality. *Psychological Reports, 55,* 163–167.

Keller, M. L. (1993). Why don't young adults protect themselves against sexual transmission of HIV? Possible answers to a complex questions. *AIDS Education and Prevention, 5,* 220–233.

Kenealy, P. (1981). Drinking and more drinking. *Self and Society, 9,* 241–243.

Kerr, J. H. (1985a). The experience of arousal: A new basis for studying arousal effects in sport. *Journal of Sports Sciences, 3,* 169–179.

Kerr, J. H. (1985b). A new perspective for sports psychology. In M. J. Apter, D. Fontana, & S. Murgatroyd (Eds.), *Reversal theory: Applications and developments* (pp. 89–102). Cardiff, Wales: University College Cardiff Press.

Kerr, J. H. (1986). Play: The reversal theory perspective. In R. van der Kooij & J. Hallendoorn (Eds.), *Play, play therapy, play research* (pp. 67–76). Amsterdam: Lisse, Swets, & Zeitlinger.

Kerr, J. H. (1987a). Cognitive intervention with elite performers: Reversal theory. *British Journal of Sports Medicine, 21,* 29–33.

Kerr, J. H. (1987b). Differences in the motivational characteristics of "professional," "serious amateur" and "recreational" sports performers. *Perceptual and Motor Skills, 64,* 379–382.

Kerr, J. H. (1987c). Structural phenomenology, arousal and performance. *Journal of Human Movement Studies, 13,* 211–229.

Kerr, J. H. (1987d). The theory of psychological reversals: Implications for future work in behavioural medicine. In G. L. Sheppard (Ed.), *Advances in behavioural medicine* (Vol. 4, pp. 61–85). Sydney, Australia: Cumberland College of Health Sciences.

Kerr, J. H. (1988a). *Arousal mechanisms, attention and sports performance.* Unpublished doctoral dissertation, University of Nottingham, Nottingham, United Kingdom.

Kerr, J. H. (1988b). Play, sport and the paratelic state. In M. J. Apter, J. H. Kerr, & M. P. Cowles (Eds.), *Progress in reversal theory* (pp. 77–88). Amsterdam: Elsevier.

Kerr, J. H. (1988c). Soccer hooliganism and the search for excitement. In M. J. Apter, J. H. Kerr, & M. P. Cowles (Eds.), *Progress in reversal theory* (pp. 223–230). Amsterdam: Elsevier.

Kerr, J. H. (1988d). Speed sports: The search for high arousal experiences. *Sportwissenschaft, 18,* 185–190.

Kerr, J. H. (1988e). A study of motivation in rugby. *Journal of Social Psychology, 128,* 269–270.

Kerr, J. H. (1989). Anxiety, arousal, and sport performance: An application of reversal theory. In D. Hackfort & C. D. Spielberger (Eds.), *Anxiety in sports: An international perspective* (pp. 137–151). New York: Hemisphere.

Kerr, J. H. (1990a). Stress and coping in sport: A reversal theory analysis. In G. P. H. Hermans & W. L. Mosterd (Eds.), *Sports, medicine, and health* (pp. 1070–1075). Amsterdam: Elsevier.

Kerr, J. H. (1990b). Stress and sport: Reversal theory. In J. G. Jones & L. Hardy (Eds.), *Stress and performance in sport* (pp. 107–131). Chichester, England: Wiley.

Kerr, J. H. (1991a). Arousal-seeking in risk sports participants. *Personality and Individual Differences, 12,* 613–616.

Kerr, J. H. (1991b). Sport: Work or play? In J. H. Kerr & M. J. Apter (Eds.), *Adult play: A reversal theory approach* (pp. 43–54). Amsterdam: Swets & Zeitlinger.

Kerr, J. H. (1991c). A structural phenomenology of play in context. In J. H. Kerr & M. J. Apter (Eds.), *Adult play: A reversal theory approach* (pp. 31–42). Amsterdam: Swets & Zeitlinger.

Kerr, J. H. (1993a). An eclectic approach to psychological interventions in sport: Reversal theory. *The Sports Psychologist, 7,* 400–418.

Kerr, J. H. (1993b). Employee exercise breaks: Opportunities for reversal. In J. H. Kerr, S. Murgatroyd, & M. J. Apter (Eds.), *Advances in reversal theory* (pp. 247–256). Amsterdam: Swets & Zeitlinger.

Kerr, J. H. (1994). *Understanding soccer hooliganism.* Buckingham, England: Open University Press.

Kerr, J. H. (1997a). *Motivation and emotion in sport: Reversal theory.* Hove, England: Psychology Press.

Kerr, J. H. (1997b). Stress, exercise, and sport. In S. Svebak & M. J. Apter (Eds.), *Stress and health: A reversal theory perspective* (pp. 185–197). Washington, DC: Taylor & Francis.

Kerr, J. H. (Ed.). (1999a). *Experiencing sport: Reversal theory*. Chichester, England: Wiley.

Kerr, J. H. (1999b). Some final considerations. In J. H. Kerr (Ed.), *Experiencing sport: Reversal theory* (pp. 209–228). Chicester, England: Wiley.

Kerr, J. H. (2001). *Counseling Athletes: Applying Reversal Theory*. London: Routledge.

Kerr, J. H., & Apter, M. J. (Eds.). (1991). *Adult play: A reversal theory approach*. Amsterdam: Swets & Zeitlinger.

Kerr, J. H., & Apter, M. J. (1999). The State of Mind Indicator for Athletes. In J. H. Kerr (Ed.), *Experiencing sport: Reversal theory* (pp. 239–244). Chichester, England: Wiley.

Kerr, J. H., & Cox, T. (1988). Effects of telic dominance and metamotivational state on squash task performance. *Perceptual and Motor Skills, 67,* 171–174.

Kerr, J. H., & Cox, T. (1990). Cognition and mood in relation to the performance of squash tasks. *Acta Psychologica, 73,* 103–114.

Kerr, J. H., & Cox, T. (1991). Arousal and individual differences in sport. *Personality and Individual Differences, 12,* 1075–1085.

Kerr, J. H., Frank-Ragan, E., & Brown, R. I. F. (1993). Taking risks with health. *Patient Education and Counseling, 22,* 73–80.

Kerr, J. H., Kawaguchi, C., Oiwa, M., Terayama, Y., & Zukawa, A. (2000). Stress, anxiety and other emotions in Japanese modern dance performance. *Pacific Journal of Psychology, 11* (1), 16–33.

Kerr, J. H., Murgatroyd, S., & Apter, M. J. (Eds.). (1993). *Advances in reversal theory*. Amsterdam: Swets & Zeitlinger.

Kerr, J. H., & Pos, E. H. (1994). Psychological mood in competitive gymnastics: An exploratory field study. *Journal of Human Movement Studies, 26,* 175–185.

Kerr, J. H., & Svebak, S. (1989). Motivational aspects of preferences for, and participation in, "risk" and "safe" sports. *Personality and Individual Differences, 10,* 799–800.

Kerr, J. H., & Svebak, S. (1994). The acute effects of participation in sport on mood: The importance of level of "antagonistic physical interaction." *Personality and Individual Differences, 16,* 159–166.

Kerr, J. H., & Tacon, P. (2000). Environmental events and induction of metamotivational reversals. *Perceptual and Motor Skills, 91,* 337–338.

Kerr, J. H., & Tacon, P. (1999). Psychological responses to different types of locations and activities. *Journal of Environmental Psychology, 19,* 287–294.

Kerr, J. H., & van den Wollenberg, A. E. (1997). High and low intensity exercise and psychological mood states. *Psychology & Health, 12(5),* 603–618.

Kerr, J. H., & van Lienden, H. J. (1987). Telic dominance in masters swimmers. *Scandinavian Journal of Sports Sciences, 9,* 85–88.

Kerr, J. H., & van Schaik, P. (1995). Effects of game venue and outcome on psychological mood states in rugby. *Personality and Individual Differences, 19(3),* 407–409.

Kerr, J. H., & Vlaminkx, J. (1997). Gender differences in the experience of risk. *Personality and Individual Differences, 22,* 293–295.

Kerr, J. H., & Vlaswinkel, E. H. (1993). Self-reported mood and running under natural conditions. *Work and Stress, 7,* 161–177.

Kerr, J. H., & Vlaswinkel, E. H. (1995). Sports participation at work: An aid to stress management? *International Journal of Stress Management, 2,* 87–96.

Khomyk, V. S. (1998). Theoretical and methodological problems of the personality social health study: Phenomenological approach. *Mir Psikhologiyi, 1,* 184–206.

Khomyk, V., & Burmaka, N. (1999, June–July). *Adolescent violence in the Chernobyl area: Self-control, identity, and moral development.* Paper presented at the Ninth International Conference on Reversal Theory, University of Windsor, Ontario, Canada.

Kiernan, K. (1997, July). *Paratelic stress: Reversal theory or differences in optimal arousal levels?* Paper presented at the Eighth International Reversal Theory Conference, University of East London, England.

Kohn, P. M. (1987). Issues in the measurement of arousability. In J. Strelau & H. J. Eysenck (Eds.), *Personality dimensions and arousal* (pp. 233–250). New York: Plenum Press.

Kohn, P. M., Lafreniere, K. D., & Gurevich, M. (1990). The Inventory of College Students' Recent Life Experiences: A decontaminated hassles scale for a special population. *Journal of Behavioral Medicine, 13,* 619–630.

Kourinka, I., Jonsson, B., Kilbom, A., Vinterberg, H., Biering-Sorensen, F., Andersson, G., & Jorgensen, K. (1987). Standardized Nordic questionnaires for the analysis of musculoskeletal symptoms. *Applied Ergonomics, 18,* 233–237.

Kreitler, H., & Kreitler, S. (1972). *Psychology of the arts.* Durham, NC: Duke University Press.

Lachenicht, L. (1985a). A reversal theory of social relations applied to polite language. In M. J. Apter, D. Fontana, & S. Murgatroyd (Eds.), *Reversal theory: Applications and developments* (pp. 144–160). Cardiff, Wales: University College Cardiff Press.

Lachenicht, L. (1985b). Reversal theory: A synthesis of phenomenological and deterministic approaches to psychology. *Theoria to Theory, 64,* 1–27.

Lachenicht, L. (1987). Motivation and emotion. In G. Tyson (Ed.), *Introduction to psychology: A South African perspective* (pp. 227–261). Johannesburg, South Africa: Westro Books.

Lachenicht, L. (1988). A critical introduction to reversal theory. In M. J. Apter, J. H. Kerr, & M. P. Cowles (Eds.), *Progress in reversal theory* (pp. 1–42). Amsterdam: Elsevier.

La Fave, L., Haddad, J., & Maesen, W. A. (1976). Superiority, enhanced self-esteem, and perceived incongruity humour theory. In A. J. Chapman & H. C. Foot (Eds.), *Humor and laughter: Theory, research and applications* (pp. 63–91). London: Wiley.

Lafreniere, K. D. (1993). Reversal theory: An introduction. *Patient Education and Counseling, 22,* 63–71.

Lafreniere, K. D. (1997). Paratelic dominance and the appraisal of stressful events. In S. Svebak & M. J. Apter (Eds.), *Stress and health: A reversal theory perspective* (pp. 35–43). Washington, DC: Taylor & Francis.

Lafreniere, K. D., Cowles, M. P., & Apter, M. J. (1988). The reversal phenomenon: Reflections on a laboratory study. In M. J. Apter, J. H. Kerr, & M. P. Cowles (Eds.), *Progress in reversal theory* (pp. 247–254). Amsterdam: Elsevier.

Lafreniere, K. D., Gillies, L. A., Cowles, M. P., & Toner, B. B. (1993). Arousability and telic dominance. In J. H. Kerr, S. Murgatroyd, & M. J. Apter (Eds.), *Advances in reversal theory* (pp. 257–266). Amsterdam: Swets & Zeitlinger.

Lazarus, R. S. (1993). From psychological stress to the emotions: A history of changing outlooks. In *Annual review of psychology* (pp. 1–21). Palo Alto, CA: Annual Reviews.

Lazarus, R. S., & Folkman, S. (1984). *Stress, appraisal, and coping.* New York: Springer.

Leach, E. R. (1961). *Rethinking anthropology.* University of London: Athlone Press.

Leach, E. R. (1972). Anthropological aspects of language: Animal categories and verbal abuse. In P. Miranda (Ed.), *Mythology* (pp. 39–67). Harmondsworth, United Kingdom: Penguin. (Original work published 1964)

Lee, J., & Branum-Martin, L. (1999, June–July). *Reversal theory as an ecological system.* Paper presented at the Ninth International Conference on Reversal Theory, University of Windsor, Ontario, Canada.

Lee, J., & Pease, D. G. (in press). Development of the Leadership Orientation Inventory. In C. Y. Chiu (Ed.), *Proceedings of the International Conference on the Application of Psychology to the Quality of Education and Teaching* (Vol. 2). New York: Plenum.

Lefcourt, H. M., & Martin, R. A. (1986). *Humor and life stress: Antidote to adversity.* New York: Springer-Verlag.

Lichtenstein, E. (1985, July). *Patterns of relapse and slip episodes.* Paper presented at the National Working Conference on Smoking Relapse, Bethesda, MD.

Lin, Z. Y. (1996). *Research on the relationship between mine workers' risk taking behavior and organizational factors.* Unpublished doctoral dissertation, Institute of Psychology, Chinese Academy of Sciences, Beijing, China.

Lindner, K. J., & Kerr, J. H. (1999). Sport participation and metamotivational orientation. In J. H. Kerr (Ed.), *Experiencing sport: Reversal theory* (pp. 189–208). Chichester, England: Wiley.

Lindner, K. J., & Kerr, J. H. (2000). Motivational orientations in sport participants and non-participants. *Psychology of Sport and Exercise 1,* 7–25.

Lindner, K. J., & Kerr, J. H. (in press). Predictability of sport participation motivation from metamotivational dominances and orientations. *Personality and Individual Differences.*

Loonis, E. (1997). *Notre cerveau est un drogué: Vers une théorie générale des addictions.* Toulouse, France: Presses Universitaire de Mirail.

Loonis E. (1998). Vers une écologie de l'action. *Psychotropes, 4*(1), 33–48.

Loonis E. (1999a). Approche structurale des fantasmes érotiques. *L'Évolution Psychiatrique, 64*(1), 43–60.

Loonis, E. (1999b). Iain Brown: Un modele de gestion hedonique des addictions. *Psychotropes, 5*(3), 59–73.

Loonis, E. (1999c). *Théorie générale de l'addiction: du système d'actions a l'écologie de l'action.* Unpublished doctoral dissertation, University of Toulouse II, Le Mirail, Toulouse, France.

Loonis, E., & Apter, M. J. (2000). Addictions et système d'actions. *L'Encéphale, 26,* 63–69.

Loonis, E., Apter, M. J., & Sztulman, H. (2000). Addiction as a function of action system properties. *Addictive Behaviors, 25,* 477–481.

Loonis, E., Bernoussi, A., Brandibas, G., & Sztulman, H. (2000). Essai de validation de la version française de la Telic Dominance Scale (TDS) Echelle de Dominance Télique. *L'Encéphale.*

Loonis, E., & Sztulman, H. (1998). Le fonctionnement de notre cerveau serait-il de nature addictive? *L'Encéphale, 24,* 26–32.

Lundy, D. (1998). *Godforsaken sea.* Toronto: Knopf.

Mackay, C. J., Cox, T., Burrows, G., & Lazzerini, A. J. (1978). An inventory for the measurement of self-reported stress and arousal. *British Journal of Social and Clinical Psychology, 17,* 283–284.

Maddi, S. R., & Kobasa, S. C. (1984). *The hardy executive: Health under stress.* Pacific Grove, CA: Brooks/Cole.

Males, J. R. (1999). Individual experience in slalom canoeing. In J. H. Kerr (Ed.), *Experiencing sport: Reversal theory* (pp. 101–127). Chichester, England: Wiley.

Males, J. R., & Kerr, J. H. (1996). Stress, emotion and performance in elite slalom canoeists. *The Sport Psychologist, 10,* 17–37.

Males, J. R., Kerr, J. H., & Gerkovich, M. M. (1998). Metamotivational states during canoe slalom competition: A qualitative analysis using reversal theory. *Journal of Applied Sport Psychology, 10,* 185–200.

Mallows, D. (1999, June–July). *Student teachers' motivational style.* Paper presented at the Ninth International Conference on Reversal Theory, University of Windsor, Windsor, Ontario, Canada.

Malmo, R. B. (1965). Physiological gradients and behavior. *Psychological Bulletin, 64,* 225–234.

Mamali, C. (1990). The dynamic of the structural and the infrastructural dimensions of motivation and the telic dominance. *Review of Roumanian Social Science, Psychology Series, 34,* 109–123. (English abstract published in *Synergy, the Newsletter of the Reversal Theory Society,* January 1999, p. 12.)

Mamali, C. (1999). Motivational intelligence and the synergic reversals of the metamotivational states. Unpublished manuscript.

Martin, R. A. (1984, September). *Telic dominance, humour, stress and moods*. Paper given at the International Symposium on Reversal Theory, Gregynog, Wales. (Abstract in *Bulletin of the British Psychological Society, 37*, 1984, Abstract No. 45).

Martin, R. A. (1985). Telic dominance, stress, and moods. In M. J. Apter, D. Fontana, & S. Murgatroyd (Eds.), *Reversal theory: Applications and developments* (pp. 59–71). Cardiff, Wales: University College Cardiff Press.

Martin, R. A., Kuiper, N. A., & Olinger, L. J. (1988). Telic versus paratelic dominance as a moderator of stress. In M. J. Apter, J. H. Kerr, & M. P. Cowles (Eds.), *Progress in reversal theory* (pp. 91–106). Amsterdam: Elsevier.

Martin, R. A., Kuiper, N. A., Olinger, L. J., & Dobbin, J. (1987). Is stress always bad? Telic versus paratelic dominance as a stress moderating variable. *Journal of Personality and Social Psychology, 53*, 970–982.

Martin, R. A., & Lefcourt, H. M. (1983). Sense of humor as a moderator of the relation between stressors and moods. *Journal of Personality and Social Psychology, 45*, 1313–1324.

Martin, R. A., & Svebak, S. (1997). The psychobiology of telic dominance and stress. In S. Svebak & M. J. Apter (Eds.), *Stress and health: A reversal theory perspective* (pp. 69–80). Washington, DC: Taylor & Francis.

Martin-Miller, L. A., & Martin, R. A. (1988). Metamotivational state and emotional response to false heartrate feedback. In M. J. Apter, J. H. Kerr, & M. P. Cowles (Eds.), *Progress in reversal theory* (pp. 255–262). Amsterdam: Elsevier.

Maslow, A. H. (1968). *Towards a psychology of being*. New York: Van Nostrand.

Matthews, G. (1985). Personality and motivational trait correlates of the Telic Dominance Scale. *Personality and Individual Differences, 6*, 39–45.

McDermott, M. R. (1986, December). *Rebelliousness in adolescence and young adulthood: A two-dimensional model*. Paper presented at the Annual London Conference of the British Psychological Society, City University, London, England.

McDermott, M. R. (1987). *Rebelliousness in adolescence and young adulthood*. Unpublished doctoral dissertation, University of Wales, Cardiff, Wales.

McDermott, M. R. (1988a). Measuring rebelliousness: The development of the Negativism Dominance Scale. In M. J. Apter, J. H. Kerr, & M. P. Cowles (Eds.), *Progress in reversal theory* (pp. 297–312). Amsterdam: Elsevier.

McDermott, M. R. (1988b). Recognising rebelliousness: The ecological validity of the Negativism Dominance Scale. In M. J. Apter, J. H. Kerr, & M. P. Cowles (Eds.), *Progress in reversal theory* (pp. 313–325). Amsterdam: Elsevier.

McDermott, M. R. (1989). *Forms of hostility as risk factors for coronary artery disease*. Unpublished master's thesis, University of Manchester, Manchester, England.

McDermott, M. R. (1991). Negativism as play: Proactive rebellion in young adult life. In J. H. Kerr & M. J. Apter (Eds.), *Adult play: A reversal theory approach* (pp. 87–100). Amsterdam: Swets & Zeitlinger.

McDermott, M. R., & Apter, M. J. (1988). The Negativism Dominance Scale. In M. J. Apter, J. H. Kerr, & M. P. Cowles (Eds.), *Progress in reversal theory* (pp. 373–376). Amsterdam: Elsevier.

McLennan, J., & Omodei, M. M. (1995). *Studying dynamic psychological phenomena in real world settings.* Paper presented at the Seventh International Conference on Reversal Theory, Swinburne University, Melbourne, Australia.

McNair, D. M., Lorr, M., & Droppleman, L. F. (1971). *The Profile of Mood States.* San Diego, CA: EDITS.

Miles, M. B., & Huberman, A. M. (1994). *Qualitative data analysis: An expanded source book* (2nd ed.). Thousand Oaks, CA: Sage.

Milgram, S. (1965). Some conditions of obedience and disobedience to authority. *Human Relations, 18,* 56–76.

Milgram, S. (1974). *Obedience to authority.* London: Tavistock.

Miller, J. (1988). Jokes and joking: A serious laughing matter. In J. Durant & J. Miller (Eds.), *Laughing matters: A serious look at humour* (pp. 5–16). Essex, England: Longman Group.

Miller, W. R. (1985). Addictive behavior and the theory of psychological reversals. *Addictive Behaviors, 10,* 177–180.

Moghaddam, F., Bianchi, C., Daniels, K., Apter, M. J., & Harré, R. (1999). Psychology and national development. *Psychology and Developing Societies, 11*(2), 119–141.

Murgatroyd, S. (1981a). Personal crises and reversals. *Self and Society, 9,* 220–228.

Murgatroyd, S. (1981b). Reversal theory: A new perspective on crisis counselling. *British Journal of Guidance and Counselling, 9,* 180–193.

Murgatroyd, S. (1983). *The validity of the Telic Dominance Scale.* Unpublished master's thesis, Open University, Milton Keynes, United Kingdom.

Murgatroyd, S. (1985a). Introduction to reversal theory. In M. J. Apter, D. Fontana, & S. Murgatroyd (Eds.), *Reversal theory: Applications and developments* (pp. 1–19). Cardiff, Wales: University College Cardiff Press.

Murgatroyd, S. (1985b). The nature of telic dominance. In M. J. Apter, D. Fontana, & S. Murgatroyd (Eds.), *Reversal theory: Applications and developments* (pp. 20–41). Cardiff, Wales: University College Cardiff Press.

Murgatroyd, S. (1987a). Combatting truancy: A counselling approach. In K. Reid (Ed.), *Combatting school absenteeism* (pp. 121–130). London: Hodder & Stoughton.

Murgatroyd, S. (1987b). Commentary: Eclecticism or responsiveness? In J. Norcross (Ed.), *Casebook of eclectic psychotherapy* (pp. 272–275). New York: Brunner/Mazel.

Murgatroyd, S. (1987c). Depression and structural–phenomenological eclectic psychotherapy: The case of Gill. In J. Norcross (Ed.), *Casebook of eclectic psychotherapy* (pp. 301–320). New York: Brunner/Mazel.

Murgatroyd, S. (1987d). Humour as a tool in counselling and psychotherapy: A reversal theory perspective. *British Journal of Guidance and Counselling, 15*, 225–236.

Murgatroyd, S. (1988). Reversal theory and psychotherapy: A review. *Counselling Psychology Quarterly, 1*, 57–74.

Murgatroyd, S. (1990). Metamotivational complexity: The case of Justin, obscene phone caller. *Counselling Psychology Quarterly, 3*, 371–381.

Murgatroyd, S. (1991). The nature and social functions of humour. In J. H. Kerr & M. J. Apter (Eds.), *Adult play: A reversal theory approach* (pp. 119–130). Amsterdam: Swets & Zeitlinger.

Murgatroyd, S. (1993a). Metamotivational complexity: The case of Justin, obscene phone caller. In J. H. Kerr, S. Murgatroyd, & M. J. Apter (Eds.), *Advances in reversal theory* (pp. 283–294). Amsterdam: Swets & Zeitlinger.

Murgatroyd, S. (1993b). "Science," physics and psychology: Reversal theory and the nature of psychological science. In J. H. Kerr, S. Murgatroyd, & M. J. Apter (Eds.), *Advances in reversal theory* (pp. 335–362). Amsterdam: Swets & Zeitlinger.

Murgatroyd, S., & Apter, M. J. (1981a). A critique of John Rowan's critique. *Self and Society, 9*, 247–250.

Murgatroyd, S., & Apter, M. J. (1981b). Reversal theory and humanistic psychology. *Self and Society, 9*, 209–210.

Murgatroyd, S., & Apter, M. J. (1984). Eclectic psychotherapy: A structural–phenomenological approach. In W. Dryden (Ed.), *Individual psychotherapy in Britain* (pp. 389–414). London: Harper & Row.

Murgatroyd, S., & Apter, M. J. (1986). A structural–phenomenological approach to eclectic psychotherapy. In J. Norcross (Ed.), *Casebook of eclectic psychotherapy* (pp. 260–280). New York: Brunner/Mazel.

Murgatroyd, S., Rushton, C., Apter, M. J., & Ray, C. (1978). The development of the Telic Dominance Scale. *Journal of Personality Assessment, 42*, 519–528.

Murgatroyd, S., Rushton, C., Apter, M. J., & Ray, C. (1988). The Telic Dominance Scale. In M. J. Apter, J. H. Kerr, & M. P. Cowles (Eds.), *Progress in reversal theory* (pp. 365–368). Amsterdam: Elsevier.

O'Connell, K. A. (1986). A comparison of predictors of early and late relapse. *Health Psychology, 5*(Suppl.), 94–95.

O'Connell, K. A. (1988). Reversal theory and smoking cessation. In M. J. Apter, J. H. Kerr, & M. P. Cowles (Eds.), *Progress in reversal theory* (pp. 181–190). Amsterdam: Elsevier.

O'Connell, K. A. (1991). Why rational people do irrational things: The theory of psychological reversals. *Journal of Psychosocial Nursing, 29*, 11–14.

O'Connell, K. A. (1993a). A lexicon for the mastery/sympathy and autic/alloic states. In J. H. Kerr, S. Murgatroyd, & M. J. Apter (Eds.), *Advances in reversal theory* (pp. 53–66). Amsterdam: Swets & Zeitlinger.

O'Connell, K. A. (1993b). Reversal theory: A new approach to patient education and counseling. *Patient Education and Counseling, 22,* 61.

O'Connell, K. A. (1995, December). The state measure challenge. *Synergy: The Reversal Theory Newsletter,* pp. 1–5.

O'Connell, K. A. (1996). Akrasia, health behavior, relapse, and reversal theory. *Nursing Outlook, 44,* 94–98.

O'Connell, K. A., & Apter, M. J. (1993). Mastery and sympathy: Conceptual elaboration of the transactional states. In J. H. Kerr, S. Murgatroyd, & M. J. Apter (Eds.), *Advances in reversal theory* (pp. 41–52). Amsterdam: Swets & Zeitlinger.

O'Connell, K. A., & Brooks, E. (1997). Resisting urges and adopting new behaviors. In S. Svebak & M. J. Apter (Eds.), *Stress and health: A reversal theory perspective* (pp. 157–171). Washington, DC: Taylor & Francis.

O'Connell, K. A., Cook, M. R., & Gerkovich, M. M. (1997, July). *Development of a smoking cessation program based on reversal theory.* Paper presented at the Eighth International Reversal Theory Conference, London.

O'Connell, K. A., Cook, M. R., Gerkovich, M. M., Potocky, M., & Swan, G. E. (1990). Reversal theory and smoking: A state-based approach to ex-smokers' highly tempting situations. *Journal of Consulting and Clinical Psychology, 58,* 489–494.

O'Connell, K. A., Gerkovich, M. M., Bott, M., Cook, M. R., & Shiffman, S. (2000). Playfulness, arousal-seeking, and rebelliousness during smoking cessation. *Personality and Individual Differences, 29,* 671–683.

O'Connell, K. A., Gerkovich, M. M., & Cook, M. R. (1995). Reversal theory's mastery and sympathy states in smoking cessation. *Image: Journal of Nursing Scholarship, 27,* 311–316.

O'Connell, K. A., Gerkovich, M. M., & Cook, M. R. (1997). Relapse crises during smoking cessation. In S. Svebak & M. J. Apter (Eds.), *Stress and health: A reversal theory perspective* (pp. 95–102). Washington, DC: Taylor & Francis.

O'Connell, K. A., Kakolewski, K. E., Goings, K. L., Gerkovich, M. M., & Cook, M. R. (1997, July). *Development of the Global Assessment of State: Just tell me— Are you telic or paratelic?* Paper presented at the Eighth International Reversal Theory Conference, London.

O'Connell, K. A., & Martin, E. J. (1987). Highly tempting situations associated with abstinence, temporary lapse, and relapse among participants in smoking cessation programs. *Journal of Consulting and Clinical Psychology, 55,* 367–371.

O'Connell, K. A., Potocky, M., Cook, M. R., & Gerkovich, M. M. (1991). *Metamotivational state interview and coding schedule instruction manual.* Kansas City, MO: Midwest Research Institute.

O'Connell, K. A., Potocky, M., Gerkovich, M. M., & Cook, M. R. (1993). A reversal theory approach for categorizing strategies used to cope with temptations to smoke. In J. H. Kerr, S. Murgatroyd, & M. J. Apter (Eds.), *Advances in reversal theory* (pp. 225–234). Amsterdam: Swets & Zeitlinger.

O'Connor, K. (1982). Individual differences in the effect of smoking on frontal-central distribution of the CNV: Observations on smokers' control of attentional behavior. *Personality and Individual Differences, 3*, 271–285.

O'Connor, P. R. (1992). *Reversal theory and mother–child compatibility.* Unpublished doctoral dissertation, University of Tasmania, Hobart, Australia.

Olds, J., & Milner, P. (1954). Positive reinforcement produced by electrical stimulation of spetal areas and other regions of rat brain. *Journal of Comparative and Physiological Psychology, 47*, 419–427.

Oppliger, P. A., & Zillmann, D. (1997). Disgust in humor: Its appeal to adolescents. *Humor, 10*, 421–437.

Orr, E., & Westman, M. (1990). Does hardiness moderate stress, and how? A review. In M. Rosenbaum (Ed.), *Learned resourcefulness: On coping skills, self-control, and adaptive behavior* (pp. 64–94). New York: Springer.

O'Shaughnessy, N. J., & Guido, G. (1996). La Reversal Theory: Implicazioni per la pubblicita ed il marketing aziendale. *Rivista Italiana di Ragioneria ed Economia Aziendale*, May-June, 238–248.

Palmer, J. (1994). *Taking humour seriously.* London: Routledge.

Perkins, K. A. (1996). Sex differences in nicotine versus nonnicotine reinforcement as determinants of tobacco smoking. *Experimental and Clinical Psychopharmacology, 4*, 166–177.

Pilon, P. (1998). *Reactions to arousal and ambiguity: An application of reversal theory.* Unpublished doctoral dissertation, University of Windsor, Windsor, Ontario, Canada.

Pomerleau, O. F., & Pomerleau, C. S. (1984). Neuroregulators and the reinforcement of smoking: Towards a biobehavioral explanation. *Neuroscientific Biobehavioral Review, 8*, 503–513.

Popkess-Vawter, S. (1998). Reversal theory and overeating: A new paradigm to study weight control. *Western Journal of Nursing Research, 20*(1), 67–83.

Potocky, M., Cook, M. R., & O'Connell, K. A. (1993). The use of an interview and structured coding system to assess metamotivational state. In J. H. Kerr, S. Murgatroyd, & M. J. Apter (Eds.), *Advances in reversal theory* (pp. 137–150). Amsterdam: Swets & Zeitlinger.

Potocky, M., Gerkovich, M. M., O'Connell, K. A., & Cook, M. R. (1991). State-outcome consistency in smoking relapse crises: A reversal theory approach. *Journal of Consulting and Clinical Psychology, 59*, 351–353.

Potocky, M., & Murgatroyd, S. (1993). What is reversal theory? In J. H. Kerr, S. Murgatroyd, & M. J. Apter (Eds.), *Advances in reversal theory* (pp. 13–26). Amsterdam: Swets & Zeitlinger.

Pribram, K., & McGuiness, D. (1975). Arousal, activation, and effort in the control of attention. *Psychological Review, 82*, 116–149.

Puntoni, S. (1999). *Brand and consumer personality in the analysis of purchase intention: An extension of the theory of planned behavior.* Unpublished doctoral dissertation, Faculty of Statistics, University of Padua, Padua, Italy.

Purcell, I. P. (1999a). *Expertise, decisions and emotions in the performance of male golfers*. Unpublished doctoral dissertation, Curtin University of Technology, Perth, Australia.

Purcell, I. P. (1999b). Verbal protocols and structured interviews for motives, plans and decisions in golf. In J. H. Kerr (Ed.), *Experiencing sport: Reversal theory* (pp. 69–100). Chichester, England: Wiley.

Purcell, I. P., Kerr, J. H., & Pollock, C. M. (1996). Plans, decisions and emotions in golf. In *Coaches report of the Applied Sports Research Program*. Canberra: Australian Sports Commission.

Purcell, I. P., Kerr, J. H., & Pollock, C. M. (2000). *Metamotivation, stress and emotion of high and low skill golfers*. Manuscript submitted for publication.

Rabkin, J. G., & Struening, E. L. (1976). Life events, stress, and illness. *Science, 194*, 1013–1020.

Ratcliffe, M. A., Dawson, A. A., & Walker, L. G. (1995). Eysenck personality inventory L-scores in patients with Hodgkin's disease and non-Hodgkin's lymphoma. *Psycho-oncology, 4*, 39–45.

Rea, D. W. (1993). Reversal theory explanations of optimal experience. In J. H. Kerr, S. Murgatroyd, & M. J. Apter (Eds.), *Advances in reversal theory* (pp. 75–88). Amsterdam: Swets & Zeitlinger.

Rea, D. (1994). Motivating at-risk students with reversal theory. In J. Miller (Ed.), *Addressing the problems of youth at risk: Approaches that work* (pp. 139–148). Statesboro: Georgia Southern University.

Rea, D. (1995). Motivating at-risk students with serious fun. In D. Rea & R. Warkentin (Eds.), *Youth at risk: Reaching for success* (pp. 22–36). Dubuque, IA: Brown & Benchmark.

Rea, D. (1997). Achievement motivation as a dynamical system: Dancing on the "edge of chaos" with "serious fun." (ERIC Document Reproduction Service No. ED415287)

Rea, D. (2000). Optimal motivation for talent development. *Journal for the Education of the Gifted, 23*(2), 187–216.

Reinecke, J., Schmidt, P., & Ajzen, I. (1996). Application of the theory of planned behavior to adolescents' condom use: A panel study. *Journal of Applied Social Psychology, 26*, 749–772.

Rhys, S. (1988). Mastery and sympathy in nursing. In M. J. Apter, J. H. Kerr, & M. P. Cowles (Eds.), *Progress in reversal theory* (pp. 329–338). Amsterdam: Elsevier.

Rimehaug, T., & Svebak, S. (1987). Psychogenic muscle tension: The significance of motivation and negative affect in perceptual-cognitive task performance. *International Journal of Psychophysiology, 5*, 97–106.

Robinson, P. (1976). Q Ach Need for Achievement Scale. In L. Cohen (Ed.), *Educational research in classrooms and schools: A manual of methods and materials*. London: Harper & Row.

Robinson, T. O., Weaver, J. B., & Zillmann, D. (1996). Exploring the relation between personality and the appreciation of rock music. *Psychological Reports, 78*, 259–269.

Rosenbaum, M. (Ed.). (1990). *Learned resourcefulness: On coping skills, self-control, and adaptive behavior.* New York: Springer.

Rosenstock, I. M., & Kirscht, J. P. (1974). The Health Belief Model and personal health behavior. *Health Education Monographs, 2*, 470–473.

Rothenberg, A. (1979). *The emerging goddess: The creative process in art, science, and other fields.* Chicago: University of Chicago Press.

Rotter, J. B. (1975). Some problems and misconceptions related to the construct of internal versus external control of reinforcement. *Journal of Consulting and Clinical Psychology, 43*, 56–67.

Rotter, J. B. (1982). *The development and application of social learning theory: Selected papers.* New York: Praeger.

Rowan, J. (1981). Reversal theory: Critique. *Self and Society, 9*, 244–246.

Ruch, W. (1994). Temperament, Eysenck's PEN system, and humor-related traits. *Humor, 7*, 209–244.

Rychlak, J. F. (1988). *The psychology of rigorous humanism* (2nd ed.). New York: New York University Press.

Sandler, I. N., & Lakey, E. (1982). Locus of control as a stress moderator: The role of control perceptions and social support. *American Journal of Community Psychology, 10*, 65–80.

Scheier, M. F., & Carver, C. S. (1987). Dispositional optimism and physical well-being: The influence of generalized outcome expectancies on health. *Journal of Personality, 55*, 169–210.

Scott, C. S. (1985). The theory of psychological reversals: A review and critique. *British Journal of Guidance and Counselling, 13*, 139–146.

Scott, C. S. (1986). Susan—a study in reversal theory. *Counselling, 57*, 12–15.

Seldon, H. (1980). Patricia: A problem of adjustment. In S. Murgatroyd (Ed.), *Helping the troubled child: Interprofessional case studies* (pp. 56–70). London: Harper & Row.

Sell, L. (1991). *Motivational characteristics of elite triathletes.* Unpublished master's thesis, West Chester University, West Chester, PA.

Shakespeare, W. (1623). *Hamlet, Prince of Denmark.* In The First Folio, Mr. William Shakespeare's comedies, histories & tragedies (pp. 152–280). London: Jaggard & Blount.

Shelley, D., & Cohen, D. (1986). *Testing psychological tests.* London: Croom Helm.

Shelley, E. (1999). *Reversal theory and teacher stress.* Unpublished master's dissertation, Psychology, University of Tasmania, Hobart, Australia.

Shiffman, S. (1984). Coping with temptations to smoke. *Journal of Consulting and Clinical Psychology, 52*, 261–267.

Slattery, P., & Apter, M. J. (1996). Finding a stake in the future. *The Secretary*, 56, 16–18.

Smith, B. D., & Principato, F. (1982). Effects of stress and conflict difficulty on arousal and conflict resolution. *British Journal of Psychology*, 73, 85–94.

Smith, B. D., & Principato, F. (1983). Effects of conflict and field structure on arousal and motor responses. *British Journal of Psychology*, 74, 213–222.

Smith, K. C. P., & Apter, M. J. (1975). *A theory of psychological reversals*. Chippenham, Wiltshire, United Kingdom: Picton.

Smith, K. C. P., & Apter, M. J. (1977). Collecting antiques: A psychological interpretation. *Antique Collector*, 48(7), 64–66.

Snyder, C. R., Harris, C., Anderson, J. R., Holleran, S. A., Irving, L. M., Sigmon, S. T., Yoshinobu, L., Gibb, J., Langelle, C., & Harney, P. (1991). The will and the ways: Development and validation of an individual difference measure of hope. *Journal of Personality and Social Psychology*, 60, 570–585.

Sollod, R. N. (1987). Commentary: Is there truth in psychotherapeutic packaging? In J. Norcross (Ed.), *Casebook of eclectic psychotherapy* (pp. 322–324). New York: Brunner/Mazel.

Spencer, H. (1873). *The principles of psychology*. New York: Appleton.

Spicer, J., & Lyons, A. C. (1997). Cardiovascular reactivity and mode-dominance misfit. In S. Svebak & M. J. Apter (Eds.), *Stress and health: A reversal theory perspective* (pp. 81–92). Washington, DC: Taylor & Francis.

Srull, T. K. (1987). Pulling in the reins of reversal theory. *Contemporary Psychology*, 32(5), 442–443.

Stenner, P., & Marshall, H. (1995). A Q methodological study of rebelliousness. *European Journal of Social Psychology*, 25, 621–636.

Stewart, E., Summers, J. J., & Thorne, G. (1995, July). *The affect of telic dominance and telic state measures in baseball and karate*. Paper presented at the Seventh International Reversal Theory Conference, Swinburne University, Melbourne, Australia.

Stone, A., & Neale, J. (1984). New measure of daily coping: Development and preliminary results. *Journal of Personality and Social Psychology*, 46, 892–906.

Stone, A. A., & Shiffman, S. (1994). Ecological momentary assessment in behavioral medicine. *Annals of Behavioral Medicine*, 16, 199–202.

Storr, A. (1976). *The dynamics of creation*. Harmondsworth, United Kingdom: Penguin.

Storr, A. (1993). *Music and the mind*. London: HarperCollins.

Summers, J., & Stewart, E. (1993). The arousal performance relationship: Examining different conceptions. In S. Serpa, J. Alves, V. Ferriera, & A. Paulo-Brito (Eds.), *Proceedings of the VIII World Congress of Sport Psychology* (pp. 229–232). Lisbon, Portugal: International Society of Sport Psychology.

Svebak, S. (1982). *The significance of motivation for task-induced tonic physiological changes*. Unpublished doctoral dissertation, University of Bergen, Bergen, Norway.

Svebak, S. (1983). The effect of information load, emotional load and motivational state upon tonic physiological activation. In H. Ursin & R. Murison (Eds.), *Biological and psychological basis of psychosomatic disease: Advances in the biosciences* (Vol. 42, pp. 61–73). Oxford, England: Pergamon Press.

Svebak, S. (1984). Active and passive forearm flexor tension patterns in the continuous perceptual–motor task paradigm: The significance of motivation. *International Journal of Psychophysiology, 2*, 167–176.

Svebak, S. (1985a). Psychophysiology and the paradoxes of felt arousal. In M. J. Apter, D. Fontana, & S. Murgatroyd (Eds.), *Reversal theory: Applications and developments* (pp. 42–58). Cardiff, Wales: University College Cardiff Press.

Svebak, S. (1985b). Serious-mindedness and the effect of self-induced respiratory changes upon parietal EEG. *Biofeedback and Self-Regulation, 10*, 49–62.

Svebak, S. (1986a). Cardiac and somatic activation in the continuous perceptual–motor task: The significance of threat and serious-mindedness. *International Journal of Psychophysiology, 3*, 155–162.

Svebak, S. (1986b). Patterns of cardiovascular–somatic–respiratory interaction in the continuous perceptual-motor task paradigm. In P. Grossman, K. Janssen, & D. Vaitl (Eds.), *Cardiorespiratory and cardiosomatic psychophysiology* (pp. 219–230). New York: Plenum.

Svebak, S. (1988a). Personality, stress and cardiovascular risk. In M. J. Apter, J. H. Kerr, & M. P. Cowles (Eds.), *Progress in reversal theory* (pp. 163–172). Amsterdam: Elsevier.

Svebak, S. (1988b). Psychogenic muscle tension. In M. J. Apter, J. H. Kerr, & M. P. Cowles (Eds.), *Progress in reversal theory* (pp. 143–162). Amsterdam: Elsevier.

Svebak, S. (1988c). A state-based approach to the role of effort in experience of emotions. In V. Hamilton, G. H. Bower, & N. Frijda (Eds.), *Cognitive science perspectives on emotion, motivation and cognition* (pp. 145–171). Dordrecht, The Netherlands: Martinus Nijhoff.

Svebak, S. (1990). Personality and sports participation. In G. P. H. Hermans & W. L. Mosterd (Eds.), *Sports, medicine, and health* (pp. 87–96). Amsterdam: Elsevier.

Svebak, S. (1991a). One state's agony, the other's delight: Perspectives on coping and musculoskeletal complaints. In C. D. Spielberger, I. G. Sarason, J. Strelau, & J. M. T. Brebner (Eds.), *Stress and anxiety* (Vol. 13, pp. 215–229). New York: Hemisphere.

Svebak, S. (1991b). The role of effort in stress and emotion. In Z. Kulcsar, G. L. Van Heck, & C. Spielberger (Eds.), *Stress and emotion: Anger, anxiety, and curiosity* (Vol. 14, pp. 121–133). New York: Hemisphere.

Svebak, S. (1993). The development of the Tension and Effort Stress Inventory (TESI). In J. H. Kerr, S. Murgatroyd, & M. J. Apter (Eds.), *Advances in reversal theory* (pp. 189–204). Amsterdam: Swets & Zeitlinger.

Svebak, S. (1997). Tension- and effort-stress as predictors of academic performance. In S. Svebak & M. J. Apter (Eds.), *Stress and health: A reversal theory perspective* (pp. 45–56). Washington, DC: Taylor & Francis.

Svebak, S. (1999). Links between motivational and biological factors in sport: A review. In J. H. Kerr (Ed.), *Experiencing sport: Reversal theory* (pp. 129–151). Chichester, England: Wiley.

Svebak, S., & Apter, M. J. (1984). Type A behaviour and its relation to seriousmindedness (telic dominance). *Scandinavian Journal of Psychology, 25,* 161–167.

Svebak, S., & Apter, M. J. (1987). Laughter: An empirical test of some reversal theory hypotheses. *Scandinavian Journal of Psychology, 28,* 189–198.

Svebak, S. & Apter, M. J. (Eds.). (1997). *Stress and health: A reversal theory perspective.* Washington, DC: Taylor & Francis.

Svebak, S., Braathen, E. T., Sejersted, O. M., Bowim, B., Fauske, S., & Laberg, J. C. (1993). Electromyographic activation and proportion of fast twitch versus low twitch muscle fibers: A genetic disposition for psychogenic muscle tension. *International Journal of Psychophysiology, 15,* 43–49.

Svebak, S., Braathen, E. T., Sejersted, O. M., Bowim, B., Fauske, S., & Laberg, J. C. (1990). Biopsy assessment of fast and slow twitch muscle fibers: Prediction of tonic EMG activation in perceptual-motor task performance. *Psychophysiology, 27* (Suppl.), 568.

Svebak, S., & Grossman, P. (1985). The experience of psychosomatic symptoms in the hyperventilation provocation test and in non-hyperventilation tasks. *Scandinavian Journal of Psychology, 26,* 327–335.

Svebak, S., Howard, R., & Rimehaug, T. (1987). P300 and quality of performance in a forewarned "Go–NoGo" reaction time task: The significance of goal-directed lifestyle and impulsivity. *Personality and Individual Differences, 8,* 313–319.

Svebak, S., & Kerr, J. (1989). The role of impulsivity in preference for sports. *Personality and Individual Differences, 10,* 51–58.

Svebak, S., & Martin, R. A. (1997). Humor as a form of coping. In S. Svebak & M. J. Apter (Eds.), *Stress and health: A reversal theory perspective* (pp. 173–184). Washington, DC: Taylor & Francis.

Svebak, S., & Murgatroyd, S. (1985). Metamotivational dominance: A multimethod validation of reversal theory constructs. *Journal of Personality and Social Psychology, 48,* 107–116.

Svebak, S., Mykletun, R., & Bru, E. (1997). Back pain and work stress. In S. Svebak & M. J. Apter (Eds.), *Stress and health: A reversal theory perspective* (pp. 57–67). Washington, DC: Taylor & Francis.

Svebak, S., Nordby, H., & Ohman, A. (1987). The personality of the cardiac responder: Interaction of seriousmindedness and Type A behavior. *Biological Psychology, 24,* 1–9.

Svebak, S., Storfjell, O., & Dalen, K. (1982). The effect of a threatening context upon motivation and task-induced physiological changes. *British Journal of Psychology, 73,* 505–512.

Svebak, S., & Stoyva, J. (1980). High arousal can be pleasant and exciting: The theory of psychological reversals. *Biofeedback and Self-Regulation, 5,* 439–444.

Svebak, S., Ursin, H., Endresen, I., Hjelmen, A. M., & Apter, M. J. (1991). Back pain and the experience of stress, efforts and moods. *Psychology and Health, 5*, 307–314.

Tacon, P., & Abner, B. (1993). Normative and other data for the Telic Dominance and Negativism Dominance Scales. In J. H. Kerr, S. Murgatroyd, & M. J. Apter (Eds.), *Advances in reversal theory* (pp. 165–176). Amsterdam: Swets & Zeitlinger.

Tacon, P., & Kerr, J. H. (1999). Metamotivational states in sport locations and activities. In J. H. Kerr (Ed.), *Experiencing sport: Reversal theory* (pp. 175–187). Chichester, England: Wiley.

Thomas-Peter, B. A. (1988). Psychopathy and telic dominance. In M. J. Apter, J. H. Kerr, & M. P. Cowles (Eds.), *Progress in reversal theory* (pp. 235–244). Amsterdam: Elsevier.

Thomas-Peter, B. A. (1993a). Negativism and the classification of psychopathy. In J. H. Kerr, S. Murgatroyd, & M. J. Apter (Eds.), *Advances in reversal theory* (pp. 313–324). Amsterdam: Swets & Zeitlinger.

Thomas-Peter, B. A. (1993b). Sadistic fantasy and its treatment: Theoretical formulation and illustrative case study. In J. H. Kerr, S. Murgatroyd, & M. J. Apter (Eds.), *Advances in reversal theory* (pp. 295–312). Amsterdam: Swets & Zeitlinger.

Thomas-Peter, B. (1996). The structure of emotion in personality disordered aggressors: A motivational analysis. *Journal of Forensic Psychiatry, 7*, 26–40.

Thomas-Peter, B., & McDonagh, J. D. (1988). Motivational dominance in psychopaths. *British Journal of Clinical Psychology, 27*, 153–158.

Tippett, M. (1987). *The mask of time: Preface to the libretto.* Audiocassettes and compact disks. London: EMI Records.

Torild Hellandsig, E. T. (1998). Motivational predictors of high performance and discontinuation in different types of sports among talented teenage athletes. *International Journal of Sports Psychology, 29*, 27–44.

Trimpop, R. M., Kerr, J. H., & Kirkcaldy, B. (1999). Comparing personality constructs of risk-taking behavior. *Personality and Individual Differences, 26*, 237–254.

Tucker, D. M., & Williamson, P. A. (1984). Asymmetric neural control systems in human self-regulation. *Psychological Review, 91*, 185–215.

Turner, S., & Heskin, K. (1998). Metamotivational dominance and use of tobacco and alcohol among adolescents. *Psychological Reports, 83*, 307–315.

Van der Molen, P. P. (1984). Bi-stability of emotions and motivations: An evolutionary consequence of the open-ended capacity for learning. *Acta Biotheretica, 33*, 227–251.

Van der Molen, P. P. (1985). Learning, self-actualisation and psychotherapy. In M. J. Apter, D. Fontana, & S. Murgatroyd (Eds.), *Reversal theory: Applications and developments* (pp. 103–116). Cardiff, Wales: University College Cardiff Press.

Van der Molen, P. P. (1986a). The evolutionary stability of a bi-stable system of emotions and motivations in species with an open-ended capacity for learning. In J. Wind & V. Reynolds (Eds.), *Essays in human sociobiology* (Study Series No. 26, Vol. 2, pp. 189–211). Brussels, Belgium: V. U.B.

Van der Molen, P. P. (1986b). Reversal theory, learning and psychotherapy. *British Journal of Guidance and Counselling, 14,* 125–139.

van Gennep, A. (1960). *The rites of passage.* London: Routledge & Kegan Paul.

Vlaswinkel, E. H., & Kerr, J. H. (1990). Negativism dominance in risk and team sports. *Perceptual and Motor Skills, 70,* 289–290.

Walters, J., Apter, M. J., & Svebak, S. (1982). Colour preference, arousal and the theory of psychological reversals. *Motivation and Emotion, 6,* 193–215.

Weinberg, G. (1998). *Motivation in ultra distance runners: A reversal theory approach to optimal experience.* Unpublished doctoral dissertation, Fielding Institute, Santa Barbara, CA.

Wendel, S. (1999). *Reversal theory: Motivations for overeating in obese dieting individuals.* Unpublished doctoral dissertation, School of Nursing, University of Kansas Lawrence.

Wicker, F. W., Hamman, D., Hagen, A. S., Reed, J. L., & Wiehe, J. A. (1995). Studies of loss aversion and perceived necessity. *Journal of Psychology, 129*(1), 75–89.

Wicker, F. W., Thorelli, I. M., Barron, W. L., III, & Willis, A. C. (1981). Studies of mood and humor appreciation. *Motivation and Emotion, 5,* 47–59.

Wilson, B. A. (1993). Metamotivational states of tennis players in a competitive situation: An exploratory study. In J. H. Kerr, S. Murgatroyd, & M. J. Apter (Eds.), *Advances in reversal theory* (pp. 151–156). Amsterdam: Swets & Zeitlinger.

Wilson, B., & Wilson, L. L. (1996). Multiple selves operating within relationships. *Journal of Family Psychotherapy, 7*(2), 41–51.

Wilson, B., & Wilson, L. L. (1997). The multiple selves of the therapist. *Journal of Family Psychotherapy, 8*(2), 73–82.

Wilson, B. A., & Wilson, L. L. (1998). The desire to control others. *Journal of Family Psychotherapy, 9*(2), 15–26.

Wilson, B. A., & Wilson, L. L. (1999). Offense mechanisms in couples. *Journal of Family Psychotherapy, 10*(2), 31–48.

Wilson, C. P. (1979). *Jokes: Form, content, use and function.* London: Academic Press.

Wilson, G. V. (1999). Success and failure and emotional experience in sport. In J. H. Kerr (Ed.), *Experiencing sport: Reversal theory* (pp. 39–68). Chichester, England: Wiley.

Wilson, G. V., & Kerr. J. H. (1999). Affective responses to success and failure: A study of winning and losing in competitive rugby. *Personality and Individual Differences, 27,* 85–99.

Wilson, G. V., & Phillips, M. (1995, July). *A reversal theory explanation of emotions in competitive sport*. Paper presented at the Seventh International Conference on Reversal Theory, Melbourne, Australia.

Wyer, R. S., Jr., & Collins, J. E. (1992). A theory of humor elicitation. *Psychological Review, 99,* 663–688.

Young, J. A. (1998). *Professional tennis players in flow: Flow theory and reversal theory perspectives*. Unpublished doctoral dissertation, Faculty of Science, Monash University, Melbourne, Australia.

Zajonc, R. B. (1966). Balance, congruity and dissonance. In M. Jahoda & N. Warren (Eds.), *Attitudes: Selected readings* (pp. 261–278). Harmondsworth, United Kingdom: Penguin. (Original work published 1960)

Zuckerman, M. (1974). The sensation seeking motive. In B. Maher (Ed.), *Progress in experimental personality research* (Vol. 7). New York: Academic Press.

Zuckerman, M. (1979). *Sensation seeking: Beyond the optimal level of arousal*. Hillsdale, NJ: Erlbaum.

Zuckerman, M. (1994). *Behavioral expressions and biosocial bases of sensation seeking*. Cambridge, England: Cambridge University Press.

AUTHOR INDEX

SUBJECT INDEX

metamotivational states of
    appropriate expression of, 258
    for completeness, 256, 257
    matching and flexibility of,
        257–258
Environment
    in enhancement of humor, 244
    of gambling
        paratelic arousal and, 156
        reversal and, 27–28
Event state balance, 49, 72
Exhaustiveness, 39
Experience sampling, 71

Family
    inappropriate strategies in, 278
    interpersonal problems in, 277–278
Feelings, in metamotivational states, 13t,
    14, 41, 42f
Felt arousal. See Arousal
Felt identification, defined, 14–15, 41
Felt negativism, defined, 14, 41
Felt significance, defined, 14, 41
Felt toughness, defined, 14, 41
Felt transactional outcome
    defined, 42, 197, 200
    and emotion, 43
    measurement of
        with mood checklist, 201
        performance-induced changes in,
            201
    of winners and losers, 201–202
Flow experiences, 90
Focality, 39, 305
Freud, S., 23, 165, 309, 313
Frustration, in reversal, 46, 85–87
Functional fictions, 48
Functionally inappropriate strategies, 50
    chronic anxiety from, 269
    depression from, 270–271
    description of, 266–267
    in obsessionality, 274
    in oppositional child, 267

Gambler, temporally inappropriate strate-
    gies of, 267
Gambling
    bet size and, 158
    in arousal regulation, 227

environment of
    paratelic arousal and, 156
    normal, 156
    paratelic—telic reversals in,
        156–157
    positive hedonic tone and, 156
    risk, arousal, paratelic state in, 227
    subjective experience in, 156–157
    telic state ending of, 157
Gambling addiction
    early focus on, 155–158
    reversal theory analysis of, 156–158
        extension of, 158–160
Gender, and risk behavior, 226–227
Gimblett, H., 4
Goals-and-means. See Means-and-ends

Hammond, W., 4
Health habits, negativism and, 177–178
Heart rate
    manipulation by threat, 106–107,
        113
    smoking effect on, 148
Hebb, D. O., optimal arousal theory of,
    18–20, 19f, 92–93
Hedonic management
    addiction in, 160–161
    arousal in, 159–160
    as crisis management
        in addiction, 162
    as model of addiction, 164–165
    uncertainty principle and, 160
Homeostasis, 19, 26–27, 92–95
Humanistic perspective
    adult play in, 292–294
    creativity in, 294–296
    personal change in, 290–292
    self-awareness in, 288–290
    spirituality in, 296–298
Humanistic psychology, 287–288
Humor. See also Comic synergy
    and boost in felt arousal, 244
    as coping mechanism, 245
    criteria for, 242
    in eclectic psychotherapy, 279–280
    enhancement of
        factors in, 244–245
    as paratelic cognitive synergy, 239,
        241–242
    and paratelic mode

Negativism Dominance Scale, *continued*
    validity of, 172–173
Negativism State Measure (NSM), 57
Negativistic–conformist pair
    in smoking cessation, 144
Negativistic state, 6f, 9
    characteristics of, 12
    defined, 40, 167
    functions of, 168
    as response to requirement
        of external agent, 167
        of self, 168
    and risk behavior, 216–217
Nijmegen Telic Dominance Scale
    (N—TDS), 68
Nursing, 82–83, 252

Observation, in assessment and diagnosis,
    281–282
Obsessionality
    description of, 274
    from inappropriate reversal, 275
    obsessive personality *versus* obses-
        sional neurotic, 275
Offense mechanisms, 23
Oppositional children, 168–169, 267
Oppositional defiant disorder, paratelic,
    playful negativism in, 181
Optimal arousal theory
    Hebb, 18–20, 19f
    reversal theory response to, 20–22
Organizations
    brand image in, 254–255
    corporate culture in, 255
    diagnostic and profiling instruments.
        See Apter Motivational Style Pro-
        file (AMSP); Apter Team Contri-
        bution System (ATCS); Apter
        Work Impact System (APWIS)
    leadership style in, 253–254
    paratelic state in
        for employee work fulfillment, 257
        for innovation and team spirit,
        256
    reversal theory research in, 251–252
Overexcitement depression, in paratelic
    mode, 271

Parachuting, 83, 92, 225–226

Paradoxical behavior, defined, 5–6
Parapathic emotion, 23, 48, 304
Paratelic Dominance Scale (PDS), 67–
    68, 70
    arounsal and hedonic tone and, 93
    in electromyography gradient study,
        90
    psychometric properties of, 67–68
    in risk-taking, 92
    in sexual risk-taking, 223
Paratelic state, 6f, 8
    addiction reinforcement in, 157
    characteristics of, 12
    cognitive synergy experience in, 236
    core motivational value of, 13t, 14
    gambling in, 156
    in organizations, 256–257
    physiological features of, 114t
    protective frames and, 219
    and spirituality, 297
Personality disorder, 305
Phenomenology
    in reversal theory. *See also* Structural
        phenomenology
        conceptual preconceptions in,
        302–303
        versus theoretical concept of,
        283–284
Phobia, inappropriate reversal in, 270
Play
    divisions of, 293
    in mastery mode, 292
    paratelic state and, 8, 308
    play—work reversal and, 292–294
    professional athletes
        telic dominance in, 188–192,
        292–293
    in sympathy mode, 292
Playfulness—spontaneity, and risk behav-
    ior, 216
Pro-autic state, 11, 48
Profane time, 136–137
Profile of Mood States (POMS), 131
Propositions
    for reversals, 45–46
    for reversal theory, 37–51
        behavioral indeterminacy, 39
        bistability, 39
        completeness, 40
        dominance, 39
        exhaustiveness, 39

focality, 39
hedonic tone, 39
motivational experience, 38
motivational oppositionality,
  38–39
salience, 39–40
for stress, 48
Protective frames, 47, 218–219
changes in, 219–220
description of, 217
individual differences in, 219
phenomenological zones of experience and, 217–218
in preservation of paratelic state,
  219
reversals in, 220
subjective determination of, 219, 220
types of, 47–48
Protofunctions, 17–18
Psychodiversity, 26, 256, 316
Psychological health, appropriate reversal
  for, 289–290
Psychopathology
chronic anxiety, 269–270
delinquency, 272–273
depression, 270–272
diagnostic taxonomy for, 264–268
eclectic psychotherapy in, 279–284
inappropriate strategies
  functionally inappropriate, 50,
    266–267
  socially inappropriate, 50, 268
  temporally inappropriate, 50, 267
interpersonal problems, 277–279
obsessionality, 274–275
phobia, 270
psychopathy, 273–274
sexual dysfunction, 275–276
sexual perversion, 276–277
structural disturbances in
  inappropriate reversal, 265–266
  inhibited reversal, 264–265
Psychopathy
description of, 273
dominant modes in, 274
hedonic tone—felt arousal—felt
  transactional outcome relationship in, 274
negativistic mode in, 274, 275
Psychophysiology—metamotivation experiments

cardiovascular functioning, 92, 105–
  107, 108f, 109
continuous perceptual motor-task
  paradigm in, 99
cortical activity, 109–111
electromyographic measurement of
  physiological change
in task performance, 100
manipulation in
  by threat and reward, 99, 100–
    101, 102–103
metamotivation measurement instruments in, 99–100
methodology and design of, 98–100
psychophysiology and lifestyle,
  111–113
respiratory functioning, 105, 107f
skeletal muscle tension, 100–104
Psychosis, 18, 306
Psychotherapy
eclectic
  reversal theory framework for,
    279, 312
  facilitation of mode change in, 279
  information gathering strategies in,
    281–282
reversal theory approach to
  as complementary, 283
  criticisms of, 283–284
teaching appropriate reversals in,
  258, 281, 314
therapeutic decision making in
  choice of approaches in, 280
  implications of, 280–283
  metamotivational modes in,
    280–281
  telic-paratelic reversals and, 281

Questionnaires. *See also* Self-report questionnaires
in assessment and diagnosis, 282
self-report, 56–59

Rebelliousness, 9
in cigarette and alcohol use, adolescent, 176–177
in delinquency, 181–182
description of, 167
disgust—sensitivity and, 176

Rebelliousness, *continued*
music preference and, 175–176
proactive, 168, 170
as paratelic negativism, 171
prosocial outcome of
and creativity, 184
reactive, 170
in delinquency, 181–182
as sympathy negativism, 171
Rebellious state, defined, 167
Relationships
alloic state and, 6f, 10
autic state and, 6f, 10
in counseling, 277–278
in experience, 7, 41
Religion, 297–298
Religious states of mind, 297
Respiratory functioning
under threat and nonthreat conditions, 105, 107f
Reversal
causes of, 27–29
environmental situations, 27–28,
45–46, 84
frustration, 28, 46
involuntary, 29, 303
satiation, 28–29, 46
defined, 39
induction research
in contingency, 83–85
in frustration, 85–87
in satiation, 87–89
over time, 78–83, 87–89
propositions for, 45–46
in sport, 29, 196–197
Reversal synergy
ambiguous, two-way, 232–233
defined, 231–232
as one-way change, 232
Reversal theory, 4
applications to behavior and experience, 4–5
applied research in
in psychomotor effects of states,
306
in techniques for control of reversal processes, 306
basic assumptions in, 38
benefits of
as bridge between biological and social approaches, 313–314

broadens perspectives of psychology, 308–310
encourages change, 314
integrates different approaches
and levels, 312
metamotivational level of analysis, 307–308
re-examination of theoretical assumptions, 310–311
return to subjective experience,
314–315
bistability, mutistability in, 26–27
challenges for, 304–305
in applied research, 306
in empirical research, 305
at theoretical level, 306–307
characteristics of
general, 5–6
concepts and definitions in, 38–50
hypotheses derived from, 50
concepts in
clinical problems and, 49–50
cognitive synergy, 49
dominance and state balance, 49
emotions, 47–48
self and other, 48–49
stress, 48
conceptual framework of, 50–51
content areas of, 4
core structure of, 40–47
concepts associated with, 47–50
definition of, 3
alternative formulations of, 301
dominance measures of, 63–70
empirical research in
micro-analysis of individual over
time, 305
whole range of states and, 305
evolution in
additional propositions and, 303
additional states in, 303–304
issues for resolution in, 304
with orientation toward personality, 304
flow diagram of concepts in, 30–32,
31f
illustration of, 32–33
hypotheses derived from, 50
measures in, 55–76, 76t
metamotivational state in
identification problems in, 61–63

Sexual perversion, *continued*
    socially inappropriate strategies in, 276–277
Sexual risk behavior
    conscious decision in, 222–223
    implications of, 222
    individual differences in, 223–224
    in negativistic- *versus* conformist-dominance, 224
    paratelic dominance and, 223
    in paratelic- *versus* telic-dominance, 224
    reversal theory research in, 222–224
    safety-zone frame in, 221
    structural model of, 224
Shimmering, 46
Signifier/signified synergy, in art work, 239
Simulation, in assessment and diagnosis, 282–283
Single identity synergy, 234
Situational state balance, 49, 71
Situation analysis, in assessment and diagnosis, 282
Skeletal muscle tension
    decreased with smoking, 148
    electromygraphic measurement of change
        in task performance, 100
        under telic and paratelic extremes, 101, 102f
        under threat of electric shock, 100–101
Smoking cessation
    interventions in
        breathing maneuvers, 148–149
        challenges to, 149–151
        negative affect and, 150–151
        separation of arousal-avoidance and telic components, 149–150
        urges—states relationship and, 150
    irrational behavior in, 139
    lapses in
        states and reasons in, 141
    psychophysiological studies of, 145–148
        contingent negative variation in, 147–148
        gender differences in, 146
        heart rate in, 148

skeletal muscle responses, 148
spectral analysis of electroencephalograph, 146–147
telic *versus* paratelic dominance in, 147, 150
relapse in
    negativism state and, 177
research on tempting situations in, 140–141, 142f, 143–145
    Ecological Momentary Assessment studies, 141, 143–144
    mastery–sympathy pair in, 144–145
    negativistic–conformist pair in, 144
    retrospective reports in, 141, 142f
    telic—paratelic pair in, 141, 143
reversal theory of
    communication to participants and colleagues, 151–152
    complexity of, 151–152
    tempting situation outcome in negativistic-conformist pair in, 177
Soccer hooliganism
    safety-zone frame in, 221–222
    socially inappropriate strategies in, 268
Soccer spectating, negativism in, 180
Social effectiveness, appropriate reversal for, 289–290
Socially inappropriate strategies, 50
    case of Justin: obscene telephone calls, 268
    in children, 268
    delinquency as, 272
    description of, 268
    in sexual perversion, 276–277
    soccer hooliganism as, 268
Somatic emotions, 24, 204
Somatic pairs, defined, 24, 42–43
Somatic State Questionnaire (SSQ), 56, 58, 134
    for dominance, 91
    in health habits, 178
    in negativism, 170
    in real life situation, 63
    in sport, 197
    in stress, 68, 134
Spirituality, 288, 296–298
    paratelic state and, 297

Transactional pairs, 24, 42
Transactions, 9–10
    in experiencing, 7, 40–41
    mastery state and, 6f, 10
    sympathy state and, 6f, 10
Transition humor, 242
Transpersonal psychology, 287, 288
Trauma zone of experience, 217, 218f
Type A behavior, telic dominance and,
    136

Values, propositions for, 45–46
Ven dee Globe race, 5

Verbal protocol reports, in sports and
    exercise studies, 213
Verbal self-descriptions
    interviews, 58–59
    and coding, 59–60
    think-aloud monologues, 60,
        211–212
Vicariance, 75, 164
Vulnerability, in addiction, 161, 162

Ways of Coping Scale, 128

Zen Buddhism, 297

ABOUT THE EDITOR

Michael J. Apter, PhD, is a research psychologist who has spent most of his career developing the theory—reversal theory—that is the subject of this book. He has published numerous papers and is the author or editor of 13 other books, which among them have been translated into eight languages. He has a doctorate from Bristol University in the United Kingdom and has taught at the University of Wales in Cardiff for 20 years. Subsequently, he has been a visiting professor at Purdue University, Northwestern University, and Yale University. He has traveled widely and held visiting positions in Canada, Spain, Norway, Belgium, and France. He is currently a visiting researcher at Georgetown University in Washington, DC. Dr. Apter is founder and director of Apter International, which is a management consultancy company serving clients worldwide. He is a Fellow of the British Psychological Society and a Life Fellow of the Netherlands Institute of Advanced Studies.